FEMINIST INTERPRETATIONS OF ARISTOTLE

RE-READING THE CANON

NANCY TUANA, GENERAL EDITOR

This series consists of edited collections of essays, some original and some previously published, offering feminist re-interpretations of the writings of major figures in the Western philosophical tradition. Devoted to the work of a single philosopher, each volume contains essays covering the full range of the philosopher's thought and representing the diversity of approaches now being used by feminist critics.

Already published:

Nancy Tuana, ed., *Feminist Interpretations of Plato* (1994)

Margaret A. Simons, ed., *Feminist Interpretations of Simone de Beauvoir* (1995)

Bonnie Honig, ed., *Feminist Interpretations of Hannah Arendt* (1995)

Patricia Jagentowicz Mills, ed., *Feminist Interpretations of G. W. F. Hegel* (1996)

Maria J. Falco, ed., *Feminist Interpretations of Mary Wollstonecraft* (1996)

Susan Hekman, ed., *Feminist Interpretations of Michel Foucault* (1996)

Nancy J. Holland, ed., *Feminist Interpretations of Jacques Derrida* (1997)

Céline Léon and Sylvia Walsh, ed., *Feminist Interpretations of Søren Kierkegaard* (1997)

FEMINIST INTERPRETATIONS OF ARISTOTLE

EDITED BY CYNTHIA A. FREELAND

THE PENNSYLVANIA STATE UNIVERSITY PRESS
UNIVERSITY PARK, PENNSYLVANIA

Luce Irigaray, "Place, Interval: A Reading of Aristotle, *Physics IV*," is reprinted by permission of the publishers, The Athlone Press and Cornell University Press, from Luce Irigaray, *An Ethics of Sexual Difference*. Translated by Carolyn Burke and Gillian Gill. Copyright © 1993 by Cornell University.

Linda R. Hirshman, "The Book of 'A,'" is used by permission of the author and the publisher. Published originally in 70 *Texas Law Review* 971 (1992). Copyright © 1992 by the Texas Law Review Association.

Martha C. Nussbaum, "Aristotle, Feminism, and Needs for Functioning," is used by permission of the author and the publisher. Published originally in 70 *Texas Law Review* 971 (1992). Copyright © by the Texas Law Review Association.

Library of Congress Cataloging-in-Publication Data

Feminist Interpretations of Aristotle / edited by Cynthia A. Freeland.
    p. cm. — (Re-reading the canon)
    Includes bibliographical references and index.
    ISBN 0-271-01729-5 (cloth : alk. paper)
    ISBN 0-271-01730-9 (pbk. : alk. paper)
    1. Aristotle. 2. Feminist theory. I. Freeland, Cynthia A. II. Series.
  B485.F46 1998
  185—dc21   97-19442
                                                 CIP

It is the policy of The Pennsylvania State University Press to use acid-free paper for the first printing of all clothbound books. Publications on uncoated stock satisfy the minimum requirements of American National Standard for Information Sciences—Permanence of Paper for Printed Library Materials, ANSI Z39.48-1992.

To my parents

Contents

Preface   ix
Nancy Tuana

Acknowledgments   xiii

Introduction   1
Cynthia A. Freeland

Part One: Theoretical Knowledge

1 Feminist Readings of Aristotelian Logic   19
   Marjorie Hass

2 Place, Interval: A Reading of Aristotle, *Physics* IV   -   41
   Luce Irigaray

3 On Irigaray on Aristotle   59
   Cynthia A. Freeland

4 Aristotle's Theory of Knowledge and Feminist Epistemology   93
   Deborah K. W. Modrak

5 Form, Normativity, and Gender in Aristotle: A Feminist
   Perspective   118
   Charlotte Witt

6 Sex and Essence in Aristotle's *Metaphysics* and Biology   138
   Marguerite Deslauriers

Part Two: Practical and Productive Knowledge

7   The Virtue of Care: Aristotelian Ethics and Contemporary
      Ethics of Care   171
      Ruth Groenhout

8   The Book of "A"   201
      Linda Redlick Hirshman

9   Aristotle, Feminism, and Needs for Functioning   248
      Martha C. Nussbaum

10 Tragedy, Citizens, and Strangers: The Configuration of
      Aristotelian Political Emotion   260
      Barbara Koziak

11 Feminism and the Narrative Structures of the *Poetics*   289
      Angela Curran

12 (Re)positioning Pedagogy: A Feminist Historiography of
      Aristotle's *Rhetorica*   327
      Carol Poster

    Selected Bibliography   351

    Contributors   357

    Index   359

Preface

Take into your hands any history of philosophy text. You will find compiled therein the "classics" of modern philosophy. Since these texts are often designed for use in undergraduate classes, the editor is likely to offer an introduction in which the reader is informed that these selections represent the perennial question of philosophy. The student is to assume that she or he is about to explore the timeless wisdom of the greatest minds of Western philosophy. No one calls attention to the fact that the philosophers are all men.

Though women are omitted from the canons of philosophy, these texts inscribe the nature of woman. Sometimes the philosopher speaks directly about woman, delineating her proper role, her abilities and inabilities, her desires. Other times the message is indirect—a passing remark hinting at woman's emotionality, irrationality, unreliability.

This process of definition occurs in far more subtle ways when the central concepts of philosophy—reason and justice, those characteristics that are taken to define us as human—are associated with traits historically identified with masculinity. If the "man" of reason must learn to control or overcome traits identified as feminine—the body, the emotions, the passions—then the realm of rationality will be one reserved primarily for men,[1] with grudging entrance to those few women who are capable of transcending their femininity.

Feminist philosophers have begun to look critically at the canonized texts of philosophy and have concluded that the discourses of philosophy are not gender-neutral. Philosophical narratives do not offer a universal perspective, but rather privilege some experiences and beliefs over others. These experiences and beliefs permeate all philosophical theories whether they be aesthetic or epistemological, moral or metaphysical. Yet this fact has often been neglected by those studying the traditions of philosophy. Given the history of canon formation in Western philosophy, the perspective most likely to be privileged is that of upper-class, white males. Thus, to be fully aware of the impact of gender biases, it is imperative that we re-read the canon with attention to the ways in which philosopher's assumptions concerning gender are embedded within their theories.

This series, *Re-Reading the Canon*, is designed to foster this process of reevaluation. Each volume will offer feminist analyses of the theories of a selected philosopher. Since feminist philosophy is not monolithic in method or content, the essays are also selected to illustrate the variety of perspectives within feminist criticism and highlight some of the controversies within feminist scholarship.

In this series, feminist lenses will be focused on the canonical texts of Western philosophy, both those authors who have been part of the traditional canon, as well as those philosophers whose writings have more recently gained attention within the philosophical community. A glance at the list of volumes in the series will reveal an immediate gender bias of the canon: Arendt, Aristotle, de Beauvoir, Derrida, Descartes, Foucault, Hegel, Hume, Kant, Locke, Marx, Mill, Nietzsche, Plato, Rousseau, Wittgenstein, Wollstonecraft. There are all too few women included, and those few who do appear have been added only recently. In creating this series, it is not my intention to reify the current canon of philosophical thought. What is and is not included within the canon during a particular historical period is a result of many factors. Although no canonization of texts will include all philosophers, no canonization of texts that exclude all but a few women can offer an accurate representation of the history of the discipline as women have been philosophers since the ancient period.[2]

I share with many feminist philosophers and other philosophers writing from the margins of philosophy the concern that the current canonization of philosophy be transformed. Although I do not accept the position that the current canon has been formed exclusively by power relations, I do believe that this canon represents only a selective history of the tradition. I share the view of Michael Bérubé that "canons are at once the location, the index, and the record of the struggle for cultural representation; like any other hegemonic formation, they must be continually reproduced anew and are continually contested."[3]

The process of canon transformation will require the recovery of "lost" texts and a careful examination of the reasons such voices have been silenced. Along with the process of uncovering women's philosophical history, we must also begin to analyze the impact of gender ideologies upon the process of canonization. This process of recovery and examination must occur in conjunction with careful attention to the concept of a canon of authorized texts. Are we to dispense with the notion of a tradition of excellence embodied in a canon of authorized tests? Or, rather than abandon the whole idea of a canon, do we instead encourage a reconstruction of a canon of those texts that inform a common culture?

This series is designed to contribute to this process of canon transformation by offering a re-reading of the current philosophical canon. Such a re-reading shifts our attention to the ways in which woman and the role of the feminine is constructed within the texts of philosophy. A question we must keep in front of us during this process of re-reading is whether a philosopher's socially inherited prejudices concerning woman's nature and role are independent of her or his larger philosophical framework. In asking this question attention must be paid to the ways in which the definitions of central philosophical concepts implicitly include or exclude gendered traits.

This type of reading strategy is not limited to the canon, but can be applied to all texts. It is my desire that this series reveal the importance of this type of critical reading. Paying attention to the workings of gender within the texts of philosophy will make visible the complexities of the inscription of gender ideologies.

Notes

1. More properly, it is a realm reserved for a group of privileged males, since the texts also inscribe race and class biases that thereby omit certain males from participation.

2. Mary Ellen Waithe's multivolume series, A History of Woman Philosophers (Boston: M. Nijhoff, 1987), attests to the presence of women.

3. Michael Bérube, Marginal Forces/Cultural Centers: Tolson, Pynchon, and the Politics of the Canon (Ithaca: Cornell University Press, 1992), 4–5.

Acknowledgments

This book is a collaborative project in a real sense, and I thank the authors for their many suggestions as well as for their commitment and hard work in producing and revising their papers. Many of them, especially Charlotte Witt and Angela Curran, served as sounding-boards at all stages of this project, and I am very grateful to them. I also thank Martha Nussbaum for her suggestion of including the *Texas Law Review* articles reprinted here, and of course Nancy Tuana and Sandy Thatcher for their general interest and support.

Work on this project was done both at my academic home, the University of Houston, and while I was on leave as a visiting fellow at the Australian National University. I am grateful to both institutions for their support, and to my friends in philosophy and women's studies at both universities, and especially Penelope Deutscher, Paul Thom, and Natalie Stoljar in Canberra, and Sheridan Hough and Anne Jaap Jacobson in Houston.

My husband Krist Bender took his sharp editorial pencil to everything I wrote here and exercised unusual computer wizardry in scanning printed materials to compile the bibliography. Lynn Gillespie also cheerfully transcribed my messy scribbles into neat text for the bibliography.

This volume is dedicated to my parents, Betty June and C. Alan Freeland. Aristotle says children are as inferior to parents as humans are to gods, "for they have conferred the greatest benefits, since they are the causes of their being and of their nourishment, and of their education from their birth; and this kind of friendship possesses pleasantness and utility also, more than that of strangers, inasmuch as their life is lived more in common" (*Nicomachean Ethics* VIII, 12). Though we can never repay what we owe, I do indeed thank and honor my parents for their many years of support, love, and understanding, for their continuing interest in my philosophical work, and for our real friendship as adults.

Finally, Aristotle also tells us of the immense debt we owe our philosophy teachers: "their worth cannot be measured against money, and they get no honour which will balance their services, but still it is perhaps enough, as it is with the gods and with one's parents, to give them what one can." (NE IX, 1) Again, to do a small part to repay this debt, I take this opportunity to express my thanks to the teachers of the history of philosophy from whom I learned so much as an undergraduate at Michigan State University: Albert Cafagna, Herbert Garelick, Rhoda Kotzin, Craig Staudenbaur, and especially Harold Walsh, who introduced me to the complex challenges and pleasures of Aristotle.

Introduction

Cynthia A. Freeland

The essays in this volume follow upon a well-developed phase of critical feminist studies of Aristotle, lasting about fifteen years.[1] This literature has been mainly negative, as feminists have found much to disparage and little to salvage in Aristotle. Typically he fares much worse than Plato in feminist reevaluations of the Western canon—at times to the point where they seem figured as the evil and good twins of ancient Greek philosophy. Although Plato denigrates the feminine in his characterization of the cosmic *hystera* of the *Timaeus*, he also exhibits laudable feminist leanings in the *Republic* when he acknowledges the possibility of female excellence and proposes educating women into philosophy-queenhood.[2] By contrast, with the possible exception of some aspects of Aristotle's ethics (its emphasis on the particular, friendship and connection, and the value of emotions), the horizons of the Peripatetic's thought have seemed to loom dark indeed, and feminists have roundly attacked Aristotle's logic, epistemology, science, and most of all, biology and politics. It is hard, after all, to forget such notorious assertions as the claim that a man's virtue is to command, a woman's to obey; that women have fewer teeth than men; or that we contribute nothing but matter to our offspring.

Perhaps understandably provoked by this misogyny, feminist essays on Aristotle have tended to take on a polemical, often angry, tone. Donna Haraway, for example, faults Aristotle as the originator of a particular approach toward knowledge: "[T]he analytic tradition, deeply indebted to Aristotle and to the transformative history of "White Capitalist Patriarchy" . . . turns everything into a resource for appropriation, in which an object of knowledge is finally itself only matter for the seminal power, the act, of the knower. Here, the object both guarantees and refreshes the power of the knower, but any status as agent in the productions of knowledge must be denied the object. It—the world—must, in short, be objectified as a thing, not as an agent."[3]

To take another example, in "Woman is Not a Rational Animal," Lynda Lange wrote, "Aristotle's facts, it seems clear, come dressed in the full regalia of Greek philosophy and social practices. Thus he explains all, but challenges nothing, and all heaven and earth is marshalled in interlocking hierarchies patterned after the structure of Greek society."[4] Lange denies that her purpose is to "malign" Aristotle the individual. I suggest, however, that a certain degree of intense criticism like hers or Haraway's may have been necessary, representing an initial stage of feminist grappling with our philosophical ancestors and heritage, a stage marked by critical rebellion and the need to clear away the ground to make ourselves a new space.

Although certainly this book was not undertaken with the aim of rehabilitating Aristotle, I think that it nevertheless shows feminist scholarship progressing into more subtle dimensions of inquiry about this canonical Greek forefather. Feminists now are looking more deeply into Aristotle's influence and questioning the possibility or advisability of an escape from "The Philosopher," as Aquinas denominated him. If we ourselves philosophize within the tradition he and Plato helped found, then we too may owe him a debt: in our abstract thinking, our search for principles, our meditations on virtue, or even our reflections on nature, essence, and sexual difference.

Feminism is historically a product of liberal modernism, with its emphasis on individual autonomy, rationality, and rights. As modernism and liberalism come under scrutiny, feminists may well seek significant alternatives in an earlier, classical era that did not share the same modernist framework and its grounding view of the individual. From the essays in this volume, then, written with a late twentieth-century vantage point on feminism, we may learn not only about Aristotle but about feminist methodology in reencountering the history of philosophy.

These essays have been selected and organized so as to extend across and follow the structure of works and topics in the Aristotelian corpus as traditionally given. Part One begins with an essay about Aristotle's logic by Marjorie Hass. It moves on to an initial consideration of a fundamental Aristotelian natural science, physics, in essays by Luce Irigaray and myself. There follows an examination of Aristotle's epistemology by Deborah Modrak. From this the subject changes to the abstract science of metaphysics, which is the main focus of Charlotte Witt's article. A final essay by Marguerite Deslauriers considers Aristotle's views on gender and essence in both his metaphysics and his biological works. From these abstract and theoretical sciences, Part Two moves on to consider the practical fields of ethics and politics in essays by Ruth Groenhout, Linda Hirshman, Martha Nussbaum, and Barbara Koziak. Part Two concludes with articles by Angela Curran and Carol Poster that examine the "productive" sciences of poetics and rhetoric.

As the editor watching and coaxing articles along their way, I began to discern four primary types of approach in this volume. Of course, more than one of these will often be used in any one individual essay; but to highlight the variations in approach, I shall somewhat artificially introduce these essays by placing each into just one category.

Aristotle on Women and the Feminine

One kind of feminist exploration in this book involves the examination of what Aristotle has to say on women and the feminine. In these studies, an author looks mainly at particular texts and examines their doctrines so as to assess their significance, internal consistency, and ultimate implications. This is perhaps the most traditional approach to critical feminist history of philosophy, and it is also typical of many other essays on Aristotle written by feminists. The essays herein most exemplary of this method are those by Luce Irigaray, Marguerite Deslauriers, and Deborah

Modrak, focusing on Aristotle's physics, biology, and theory of knowledge, respectively.

Luce Irigaray's essay "Place, Interval: A Reading of Aristotle, *Physics* IV" meditates upon the repression of the feminine in Aristotle's treatment of place. Irigaray seeks to consider whether Aristotle's physics, or at least his definition of place in *Physics* IV, is "male" and what it might mean to assert this. Irigaray's style and method of historical exegesis are far from traditional. As in other writings,[5] her theme here concerns how the Western tradition of philosophy has been constituted as a male discourse exemplifying certain biases or bound by certain preconceptions—even in a quite abstract sphere such as theorizing about the definition of place.

Irigaray, following Heidegger, regards place as a mode of human subjectivity, not simply as something external that can be "objectively" studied and described. Heidegger saw that we move *through* space, but Irigaray focuses in her meditations inspired by Aristotle on place in our *own* bodies. She suggests that Aristotelian place is that of hard, objective bodies viewed from the outside, rather than of soft, open bodies experienced from within, as having gaps, fissures, and as issuing the flows of sexual secretions. Feminists more familiar with some of Irigaray's earlier essays, such as "This Sex Which Is Not One,"[6] will perhaps be surprised to find she departs in this essay from her earlier account of a more restricted female sphere of two lips, autoerotically self-touching. Here instead we find Irigaray exploring the broader sphere of communion and interactions between differently sexed bodies.

Marguerite Deslauriers, in "Sex and Essence in Aristotle's *Metaphysics* and Biology," is interested in exploring how a scientific conception can be related to, or can ground, broader social and political viewpoints and systems. She asks at the start of her essay, "Are women perceived to be different from men because women are economically, socially, and politically subordinate to men, or are women subordinate to men in these ways because they exhibit certain anatomical and physiological (or psychological) differences from men?" Obviously, questions about nature versus nurture continue to haunt us today, as feminists remain very concerned about how to answer questions about the relations between sexual difference and an alleged human essence.

Deslauriers's essay explores the tensions in Aristotle's accounts of sex and essence in both his biology and *Metaphysics*. She shows that there is a contradiction between Aristotle's *metaphysical* analysis of sex in relation to essence and his *political* claims about women's inferiority. That is, in metaphysics, men and women (or males and females generally) cannot be said to differ in essence. And yet Aristotle assumes in his biology and politics that females are inferior. Deslauriers points out that this is just an assumption, not a claim he argues for. According to Deslauriers, the only way out of this problem is for Aristotle to invoke matter to account for this difference between the sexes; males and females differ in matter but not in essence. Claims about the feminine's link to matter are not easily removable from Aristotle's overall metaphysical approach. Thus Aristotle's *Metaphysics* may get things "right," so to speak, about the fact that women are fully human, but his biological works, like his ethical and political works, seek to deny this through an implicit assumption of certain normative links between maleness and form, and femaleness and (inferior) matter.

Deborah Modrak, in "Aristotle's Theory of Knowledge and Feminist Epistemology," applies insights from feminist epistemology to the analysis of Aristotle's general scientific method, as set out in his *Posterior Analytics* and exemplified in various theoretical sciences. Modrak looks at general themes in Aristotle's theory of knowledge, focusing on the paradigm of scientific knowledge. She aims to consider how well his epistemological framework stands up to some of the key criticisms made in recent feminist epistemology. Such criticisms are typically aimed at a post-Cartesian conception of scientific knowledge, and so it is interesting to see whether they are equally applicable to an ancient empiricist method like Aristotle's.

More specifically, referring to the feminist epistemology of Lorraine Code, Modrak explores whether "Aristotle's conception of demonstrative science embodies the same ideals of objectivity, impartiality, and universality that Code finds problematic in recent epistemology." In addition to this initial question, Modrak also asks whether in Aristotle's system the knower or community of knowers is gendered so as to exclude women. And third, she considers the claim (made by Mary Daly, Luce Irigaray, and Simone de Beauvoir) that male-authored texts in the traditional canon deprive women of knowledge by erasing the feminine. Modrak considers possible defenses of Aristotle against these three lines of feminist criticism, but ultimately she leaves them standing.

Aristotle in the Tradition

The second approach taken by some of the essays in this volume moves away from the study of specific texts and their implications for our understanding of women and the feminine. Instead, these essays assume a broader perspective that considers Aristotle in his foundational role for subsequent developments in the Western tradition. So the focus shifts from single texts in the Aristotelian corpus onto the ways in which his works influenced much of the rest of Western European philosophy. Although in principle this sort of work could be done for almost any part of Aristotle's theory, here the essays on his logic and aesthetic theory by Marjorie Hass and Angela Curran are most illustrative of this kind of approach.

Marjorie Hass situates her article, "Feminist Readings of Aristotelian Logic," within current controversies over the value of feminist attacks on the alleged "maleness" of logic. These attacks run the risk of perpetuating sexist stereotypes about "irrational" and intuitive women. More specifically, Hass examines chapters devoted to Aristotle in a recent, prominent, and controversial feminist critique of logic, Andrea Nye's *Words of Power: A Feminist Reading of the History of Logic.*[7] Hass shows that Nye's criticisms of logic in general and of Aristotle in particular are misplaced. What is crucial in Nye's attack are alleged problems caused by overzealous "abstraction." But Hass argues that abstraction is *not* problematic; instead, it is crucial (and empowering) for feminist political theory. It is relevant to consider these issues in relation to Aristotle because he was the inventor of logic as a formal system of evaluating arguments in the abstract by studying their form.

Although she rejects Nye's form of feminist logic critique, Hass finds more that is worthwhile in the criticisms of logic advanced by Luce Irigaray and Val Plumwood. These thinkers call for feminist alternatives to what has come to be standard deductive logic—and interestingly enough, their call is echoed in other contemporary criticisms from within the field of logic itself, for example, from intuitionist or entailment logics. The logical schemes envisaged by Irigaray and Plumwood would encompass more situated and fluid ways of using formal systems to describe and analyze reality and diverse experiences. Hass argues that, in Aristotle's case, we can glimpse something of such an alternative by looking to his account of negation, which is richer and more complex than that allowed by most contemporary formal systems.

Also focused more broadly upon Aristotle's foundational role in relation to canonical standards and values is Angela Curran's "Feminism and the Narrative Structures of the *Poetics.*" Curran argues that there are deep and radical problems with traditional aesthetic theory grounded in Aristotle's *Poetics*. Not only is there an initial difficulty in understanding how Aristotle's own account of tragedy might apply to many of the most famous Greek tragic heroines—Iphigenia, Hecuba, Antigone—there is a much deeper problem concerning his fundamental analysis of tragic response and catharsis. Curran argues that Aristotle's justification of tragic art rests upon an unsatisfactory conception of art's social role. On Aristotle's moralistic view of tragedy, an audience cannot be prompted to respond to tragedy with an intellectual, political critique—even if the tragedy itself suggests that the prevailing order is hierarchical, racist, sexist, and generally oppressive.

Because Aristotle's aesthetic theory does not permit a critical relationship between the viewer and tragedy, Curran argues that feminists must articulate an alternative that makes plain why Greek tragedy should matter to viewers. Developing a Brechtian feminist aesthetics, Curran shows how specific tragedies about women can challenge elements in the ideology of patriarchy, and also how Brechtian performance techniques could aid in the construction of these readings. What remains, interestingly, is a key legacy of Aristotle's aesthetic theory that Brecht misunderstood, namely, the important role that emotions may play in our identifications, empathy, and critical thinking about characters (especially women) depicted in art.

Feminists Recover Aristotle

So far I have described feminist approaches that focus on "The Philosopher's" views of women and the feminine, or his importance for a subsequent tradition. A third sort of feminist approach in this volume involves using an essay on Aristotle as the occasion to bring into focus some aspects of feminism itself. Here, the author's aim may be less to see how feminists can challenge Aristotle than to see whether a critical reading of Aristotle can offer any resources for feminism. This represents a newer approach within feminist critical studies of the history of philosophy. The essays here by Charlotte Witt, Ruth Groenhout, Linda Hirshman, Martha Nussbaum, and Barbara Koziak each find that certain of Aristotle's views offer alternatives to some standardly accepted contemporary feminist views: about the relation of the scientist to nature, about the ethics of care, or about the links between traditional liberal politics or welfare state theory and feminism.

Charlotte Witt's "Form, Normativity, and Gender in Aristotle: A Feminist Perspective," problematizes objectivity in feminist theories of science and metaphysics. She reexamines the ways in which gender enters into Aristotle's theory, offering a new interpretation that focuses on his hylomorphism in metaphysics. Witt reviews the details of Aristotle's views about the primacy of form and about the presence of teleology within nature and reality, highlighting the associations between form and maleness and matter and femaleness. She finds that Aristotle attached the norms of his culture to his hylomorphism, but she does not think it is clear that his assumption of cultural norms preceded or somehow caused his views about metaphysical norms. In Aristotle's view, nature itself includes values and goal-directedness, which a theorizer must discover and respect.

Witt next notes that many feminist analyses of scientific method criticize the alleged, but dubious, objectivity of an inquirer who is in fact culturally situated and enmeshed in cultural assumptions of value. But these criticisms often share an assumption typical of modernist science more generally, about the value-neutrality of nature. Witt writes, "Perhaps the value-neutrality of the objective scientist and his disinterested relationship to inert quantitative nature are all of a piece, and part of the task for feminists is to reconceive a richer image of the objects of theory to go along with the richer description of the theorizer and their relationship." This means that an "objective" account might *precisely* be a value-laden account. Such an approach would begin from new views about the relationship of the observer or practicing scientist to an organic, holistic nature.

Witt reexamines Aristotle's metaphysics with the thought that it may offer intriguing grounds for a richer conception of objectivity, one that reveals assumptions of contemporary feminist science critiques. Ruth Groenhout, in "The Virtue of Care: Aristotelian Ethics and Contemporary Ethics of Care," reflects on how Aristotelian ethics could suggest ways to improve upon some increasingly standard approaches within feminist ethics—those known collectively as the "ethics of care" approach. Groenhout begins by noting, as Witt does, the hierarchies implicit in Aristotle's metaphysics and their connection with his ethics and politics. This assemblage of views would seem to leave little room for feminists to find a foothold. However, she argues that a synthesis of Aristotelian-based virtue ethics with the feminist ethics of care can be preferable to either account on its own.

Groenhout faults Aristotle's ethics for its concentration on the production of an intellectual life, and she faults the ethics of care for lacking a thorough political basis. The inclusion of features drawn from Aristotle's sort of virtue ethics can help the ethics of care position meet two standard types of criticism: that it glorifies traits that have traditionally led to women's subservience, and that it is unable to produce concern for those outside the "circle of care." This synthetic approach can add to the ethics of care a greater concern for personal excellence and political participation, while balancing Aristotelian ethics so as to make it less hierarchical and oppressive.

In the symposium reprinted here from the *Texas Law Review*, Linda Hirshman and Martha Nussbaum debate the value of Aristotle's politics for reformulation of feminism on a new, or rather perhaps old, classical base of political theory. They consider whether Aristotle's framework for ethics and politics offers a viable alternative to much contemporary feminist politics and legal theory, which emerged from a liberal framework emphasizing liberation and tolerance.

Hirshman's "The Book of 'A' " argues that Aristotle's ethics and politics offer a significant resource for contemporary feminist jurisprudence, and for addressing such vexed issues as surrogacy and selective service. She highlights three areas in which feminists can draw upon Aristotle. First, his ethical theory has elements in common with feminist moral epistemologies. For example, feminists who emphasize consciousness-raising "are using two very traditional Aristotelian methods: canvassing the appearances and conversing about justice with people who speak the same language about justice as the questioner does." Second, Aristotle views the human condition as inherently political; and third, feminists may usefully draw upon Aristotle's conception of the ideal life for citizens. Aristotle offers substantive answers about the political community in a way that visions of liberal equality do not.

Nussbaum, in "Aristotle, Feminism, and Needs for Functioning," agrees in principle with Hirshman's conviction that Aristotle offers resources for feminist political practice, though she disagrees about the details. As Nussbaum sees it, Aristotle's chief strength is his insistence on scrutinizing needs for functioning and distributions of basic goods. She argues that to place the emphasis here would correct some deficiencies of modern bourgeois feminism, which fails to recognize that many of the most pressing problems facing the world's women are matters of basic needs—for food, shelter, medical care, and protection from violence. Nussbaum also argues that Aristotle's moral methodology is not so conservative as some claim, "for the allegedly conservative method actually prompts a sweeping and highly critical scrutiny of all existing regimes and their schemes of distribution, as well as of the preferences that result from and support these distributions."

Barbara Koziak's "Tragedy, Citizens, and Strangers: The Configuration of Aristotelian Political Emotion," also argues that an Aristotelian political theory offers a basis for feminist critiques of modern liberal views. Modern political theory has adopted a narrow conception of rationality, splitting off the allegedly rational public sphere from a private domain where emotions have free play. This dichotomy has unfortunate gender overtones: not only does it confine women to the role of unpaid caregivers, but it rules emotions out of court in the public realm. Koziak explores Aristotle's alternative view of rationality and especially his conception of *thumos*, or emotion, in *Politics* VII and the *Poetics*. Based on an extended reading of Euripides' *Iphigenia in Tauris*, she argues that, for Aristotle, the focus of tragic and political "recognition" is on "good" political emotions that ground our kinship and behavior toward both fellow citizens and strangers. Koziak comments, "Feminist political theorists should ask, How do we generate public institutions that encourage public benevolence and public recognition of essential similarity?" Such institutions are essential if we are to resolve pressing current issues, such as welfare or immigration, that do in fact stir our emotions concerning "strangers" in our midst.

Feminists Rewrite Western Philosophy

The fourth and final approach to feminist analysis in the essays in this volume moves from feminist reflections upon Aristotle into broader reflections about what feminism amounts to in, or tell us about doing, the history of philosophy. This more methodological issue is at the heart of Irigaray's essay and of her general strategy of "going back into the philosopher's house." Other authors (Hass, Modrak) touch on this Irigarayan strategy, and it becomes the focus in my own essay, which is prompted by Irigaray's unusual style of revisiting the historical figures in the canon. It is also central in Carol Poster's reflections about the construction of canons in rhetoric.

My essay, "On Irigaray on Aristotle," began as an attempt to lay out some of Irigaray's key points about Aristotle in a more straightforward fashion, clarifying her often difficult style so as to permit an assessment of her critique—such as her claim that he has omitted any reference to the permeable spatial identities of pregnant bodies. But to evaluate Irigaray, it became necessary also to provide a study of her provocative method in her essay on Aristotle on place. I contrast her idiosyncratic feminist re-reading of canonical figures to those in more traditional history of philosophy.

Traditional history of philosophy follows certain broad principles of interpretation, such as charity and contextualization. It seeks to recapture or reconstruct an author's intentions, construed in the most favorable way for maximum coherence, before evaluating their force, consistency, and impact on subsequent theorists. By contrast, Irigaray contextualizes philosophical works in an entirely different way, considering, for example, not how well Aristotle's theory of place anticipates Einsteinian space, but how it illustrates a pervasive male philosophical attitude toward the "emptiness" of the female body. From this point of view, which holds that the Western philosophical tradition has been oppressive and has omitted the feminine, we have little reason to be charitable in our interpretations. Instead, Irigaray advocates a kind of subjective, critical, and ironic reading of texts. I argue, however, that there is a contradiction in her feminist methodology between her idiosyncratic, subjective, personal "readings" of texts and her general view that feminists must understand "the" meaning that historical texts have had for the tradition.

Carol Poster's "(Re)positioning Pedagogy: A Feminist Historiography of Aristotle's *Rhetorica*" broadens the perspective to consider how a text like Aristotle's *Rhetoric* becomes canonical within a discipline. Briefly reviewing the history of rhetoric, she argues that feminists should reject the recent elevation of Aristotle's *Rhetoric* to the canon in this field, as it exemplifies a bias against pedagogy that in turn is antiwoman.

Poster argues that Aristotle's *Rhetoric* was never a significant text in the history of rhetoric, which was dominated instead by "manuals" that emphasized methods of teaching. Only in recent times, when a need was felt for seminal, canonical works of theory, has this text been elevated so as to lend authority to a discipline of study that lacks status. This status problem arises in part precisely because of the pedagogical focus that continues in rhetoric and its associated field of composition studies. These fields all lack status, Poster argues, because of the prevalence of women within them. Thus she concludes not only that we must reconsider the construction of the canon, but we must also reconsider the status hierarchies of the academy itself. She considers, and rejects, Richard Rorty's evaluation of four diverse methods of doing the history of philosophy.[8] Whereas Rorty denigrates "doxography" (the "who said what when" approach), Poster argues that this approach may not only be an essential corrective, but that it is appropriate, and in fact dominant, within introductory courses at most institutions in the contemporary world—institutions that are lower than the elite realm occupied by Rorty himself, but where the majority of professors and students live, study, and teach today.

Conclusion

As should be evident from these brief characterizations, the essays in this volume share no single perspective about Aristotle; nor do they share a single perspective about feminism. They stem from a variety of disciplines; they are liberal, antiliberal, or Marxist in spirit; analytic or "Continental" in method; theoretical or practical in focus; critical, revisionist, or ameliorative in tone. Not only do we find a more complex Aristotle here who is a more intriguing figure for feminism; we find a more intriguing feminism itself.

Some common themes emerge in this volume. Because Aristotle can justly be called the founder of "essentialism," it is no surprise that one of these themes concerns women's "essence" in relation to metaphysics, biology, and politics. The simple view is that Aristotle said women have a biologically based essence that is distinct and inferior to that of men, and hence, that women deserve their subordinate status. Such essentialism is now rejected as an illegitimate kind of naturalism that ignores differences among women or the diverse facts of women's experience.

But various authors here disagree both about what Aristotle has to say on an alleged female essence and about feminism's current skepticism about women's essence. Whereas Modrak thinks that it is clear that Aristotle's abstract notion of essence is gendered, Deslauriers argues that Aristotelian species essences are not gendered. A still different interpretation is offered by Witt, who finds that the alleged formal deficiency of women does not amount to anything essential about our nature. Supplementing Witt's view of the normative nature of form in Aristotle is Hirshman's allusion to the problematic hierarchies Aristotle seemed to want to borrow from biology and relocate to politics.

Not all feminists are opposed to the claim that women have some sort of essence, whether biological or not. Groenhout and Hirshman think feminists should not be so suspicious of claims about essence and biological difference. Referring to specific concrete social issues such as selective service and surrogacy, Hirshman emphasizes that some biological differences between males and females are real and significant for moral or legal discussion. Groenhout suggests that a modern virtue ethics, combining strengths of Aristotelian and feminist care approaches, may *need* to be essentialist, at least in propounding an account of human flourishing that involves caring.

Another theme of many of these essays—on both Aristotle's theoretical and practical works—is the nature and value of objectivity and its role as a criterion of knowledge. Modrak and Hass discuss whether Aristotle's views are vulnerable to feminist criticisms of logic or of mainstream epistemology, but they lean toward different answers. While Hass does find that some critiques of the abstraction of logic bear on Aristotle, she holds it is false to say (as Andrea Nye does) that his logic emerges in a context of domination, or that abstraction is always politically problematic; she also finds in Aristotle's complex account of negation potential resources for a critique of standard deductive logics. On the other hand, Modrak endorses feminist critics of Aristotle's epistemology. Similarly, my essay, following Irigaray's, brings feminist science critiques to bear on Aristotle's fundamental procedures in physics. Modrak also directs us to feminist philosophers of science who question whether objectivity is ever really possible, and who favor a more "situated" approach to knowledge. This has echoes in Witt's recommendations that feminists might look to Aristotle's metaphysics as an example of how to make a theory more objective by describing a reality that itself includes values.

The consensus is somewhat negative on Aristotle's views in epistemology and theoretical reasoning, but Groenhout, Hirshman, Nussbaum, Poster, and Koziak agree in finding many useful features for feminism in Aristotle's moral and political theory. Groenhout notes that, as in modern feminist views, Aristotelian moral reasoning emphasizes the individual context of actions, rather than attempting to apply abstract, universal, impersonal principles. Hirshman similarly sees Aristotle as offering an alternative to the liberal (Kantian/utilitarian) emphasis on rules and universality. Nussbaum goes so far as to detail five strengths of the Aristotelian approach to moral reasoning, including a balance of the particular and general, of public and private, and "a subtle defense and justification of many emotions." Poster similarly notes that rhetoric, as described by Aristotle, recognizes both public and private employments, including options for women's reasoning that are broader than what he allows in his formal theory of dialectic.

Feminists like Nussbaum regard Aristotle's account of the emotions and their role in moral and political reasoning as much preferable to Plato's account; Aristotle describes a cognitive role for emotions so that he does not simply valorize reason over the emotions. Along these lines, Koziak argues that Aristotle valued (and can teach us to value) emotions like pity and sympathy, as prompted in tragedy, as these help foster political recognition and community. While admitting some of these points, Curran still argues that Brecht was right to criticize Aristotle for emphasizing emotional responses to tragedy, at the cost of stunting our intellectual and critical responses to the social conflicts in tragic narratives.

Several authors here do voice some criticisms of Aristotle's views on moral value. (The exception is Hirshman, who seems to endorse and recuperate his views enthusiastically as a corrective to liberal feminism.) Nussbaum thinks he needs at least one major corrective from liberalism concerning the limits of government authority and interference, and protection of personal liberties. Similarly, though Groenhout sees Aristotelian-based virtue ethics as containing resources to be used to correct deficiencies in the feminist ethics of care, she notes that latter-day Aristotelian communitarians like Sandel and MacIntyre are notorious for their sexism.

One of the most difficult questions that many of these essays raise concerns how we read someone like Aristotle, who occupies a position very remote from our own in time, place, and sensibility. Hirshman asks whether Aristotle is "the original bad actor . . . setting in motion twenty-four-hundred years of philosophical misogyny." Some authors, such as Witt, withhold judgment about how his cultural values affected his metaphysics. Most, however—Modrak, Deslauriers, Irigaray, myself, and Curran—are very direct in implicating Aristotle within the sexism of his time and culture. Recall the dichotomy I cited at the start between Aristotle and Plato: a key reason for holding Aristotle responsible for not rethinking his cultural presuppositions is that many think Plato *was* able to escape the blinders of his culture.

A deep question remains about what it means to read Aristotle as a feminist. Perhaps what all the authors collected here agree upon, despite other differences in topic or approach, is that it is no longer acceptable to read Aristotle's works while ignoring issues of gender, as most major works on his metaphysics, science, ethics, and so forth, have done. We are not satisfied to read important books on any aspect of Aristotelian philosophy that simply ignore gender or treat it as irrelevant to his views—whether on politics or physics, poetics or proofs. Many of these writers, accordingly, might second Irigaray's remark that the philosophical order must not only be questioned, but *disturbed.*[9] We cannot create disturbance from some place outside the Western tradition, however, since we too are parts of it. In this book, then, the authors invite readers to join us as we "go back inside the philosopher's house."

Notes

1. Begun, notably, in *Discovering Reality: Feminist Perspectives on Epistemology, Metaphysics, and Philosophy of Science*, ed. Sandra Harding and Merrill B. Hintikka (London: D. Reidel, 1983). For further sources, see the Selected Bibliography.

2. For some background on Plato's views of women, see Gregory Vlastos, "Was Plato a Feminist?" *Times Literary Supplement*, 17–23 March 1989; Julia Annas, "Plato's *Republic* and Feminism," *Philosophy* 51 (1976): 307–21; and Annas, *An Introduction to Plato's Republic* (Oxford: Clarendon Press, 1981), 181–85. See also Nancy Tuana, ed., *Feminist Interpretations of Plato* (University Park: Pennsylvania State University Press, 1995).

3. Donna Haraway, "Situated Knowledges: The Science Question in Feminism and the Privilege of Partial Perspective." *Feminist Studies* 14, no. 3 (Fall 1988): 592.

4. "Woman is Not a Rational Animal," in *Discovering Reality*, 14.

5. Luce Irigaray, *Speculum of the Other Woman* (Ithaca: Cornell University Press, 1985).

6. Luce Irigaray, "This Sex Which Is Not One," in *This Sex Which Is Not One* (Ithaca: Cornell University Press, 1985).

7. Andrea Nye, *Words of Power: A Feminist Reading of the History of Logic* (New York: Routledge, 1990).

8. Richard Rorty, "The Historiography of Philosophy: Four Genres," in *Philosophy in History*, ed. Myles Burnyeat, Richard Rorty, and Jerome Schneewind (Cambridge: Cambridge University Press, 1984), 49–75.

9. Luce Irigaray, "Questions," in *This Sex Which Is Not One*, 159.

Part One

Theoretical Knowledge

1

Feminist Readings of Aristotelian Logic[1]

Marjorie Hass

Feminist transformations of the Western philosophical tradition have reached far beyond what Louise M. Antony and Charlotte Witt describe as the "document-and-deplore strategy of laying bare the explicit, but arguably excisable, sexism in this or that mainstream work."[2] Feminists have begun to interrogate the very concepts that constitute the tradition itself: reason, objectivity, abstraction, and validity. However, feminist critics of these concepts have themselves been attacked by those who see in them a return to sexist stereotypes describing women as irrational and incapable of abstract logical thought. The complexity of this debate, and the fury with which it is waged, have a particular urgency for any feminist evaluation of Aristotle—a founder of the tradition and the inventor of logic and abstract science.

In this essay I look at three feminist critics of formal logic. I begin with Andrea Nye's discussion of Aristotelian logic in her book, *Words of Power: A Feminist Reading of the History of Logic*, I argue that her criticism is ultimately founded on the claim that logic is in several important ways too *abstract*, representing a retreat from the lived world in ways inimical to the aims of feminism. I argue that Nye's rejection of Aristotelian logic is ultimately untenable and that formal logic ought not be rejected by feminists on the grounds that it is too abstract a representation of reasoned discourse. I turn then to an alternative feminist strategy for evaluating logic. This way of proceeding, found in the work of both Luce Irigaray and Val Plumwood, explores the abstract categories and operations of logic more specifically in order to determine ways that they embody patriarchal assumptions. This second strategy is, I suggest, more compelling. Rather than calling for the total rejection of formal logic and its related disciplines, Irigaray and Plumwood challenge us to find richer and less biased representations of logical relations.

It might seem odd to begin a discussion of feminist criticisms of logic by focusing on Aristotelian logic. But though Aristotelian logic cannot be seen to rival mathematical logic in either its power or utility, there are several reasons why Aristotle's logical writings provide an excellent starting place for a discussion of feminist critiques of logic. As I suggested above, feminist critiques of logic tend to problematize the very idea of a formal logic rather than specific technical or theoretical developments. With Aristotle we see the origins of formal logic. If there are problems with the very idea of abstract representations of the "form" of an argument they ought be found in the original beginnings of logic.

Aristotle's logical writings include *Categories* and *On Interpretation*, which present his underlying theory of terms and propositions; *Prior Analytics*, which develops his formal theory of the syllogism; *Posterior Analytics*, which gives an account of proof or demonstration; and *Topics*, which concerns arguments that establish what is probable or plausible but not scientifically certain. Although there is controversy about the order in which Aristotle composed these works, particularly the order of *Prior Analytics* and *Posterior Analytics*, it is likely that *Posterior Analytics* (even if written earlier) represents the ultimate goal of his logical investigations in showing how the theory of the syllogism can be applied to yield scientific understanding. Logic was not, for Aristotle, a science in its own right, but an underlying technique for establishing scientific knowledge. As Robin Smith tells us, "Aristotle made proofs themselves an object of study in order to answer questions about the possible structures of the demonstrative sciences. This is what led him to develop the theory of deductions in the *Prior Analytics*, rather in the same way that Hilbert's desire to resolve certain mathematical questions led to his concept of proof theory."[3] It is Aristotle's recognition that the validity of an argument lies in its *structure* and that syllogistic structures can be enumerated and rigorously evaluated that makes formal logic possible. Each of the feminist critics discussed here is in some way responding to this originary insight.

Logic, Power, and Silence

Andrea Nye presents a reading of Aristotle's logic as part of her larger study of logic, *Words of Power: A Feminist Reading of the History of Logic*.[4] In this pathbreading, controversial work, Nye argues that a theory of logic is impossible for "there is no one Logic for which such a theory can account, but only men and logics" (*WP* 5). Most of the published commentary on Nye's book has focused on her critique of modern symbolic logic; less attention has been paid to her specific reading of Aristotelian logic.[5] Nye subtitles her chapter on Aristotle, "Mechanisms of Deceit," emphasizing her principal criticism. Aristotle's logic, she argues, does not achieve his stated goal of generating systematic and certain knowledge. Nor does it provide a tool for demonstrating new truths. Instead, claims Nye, logic provides a mechanism for elevating clever argumentation at the expense of the truth. Aristotle allows syllogistic consequence to usurp truth as the standard for acceptable belief. As a result, discussion of "real-life" problems such as slavery and sexism can be suppressed in favor of abstract logical "games." Logical proficiency becomes a "badge of office" for elite men; a way of solidifying power (*WP* 48).

For Nye, Aristotle's logic achieves these dubious powers chiefly through its myopic concern for valid reasoning. To illustrate, she gives us an example of logic in action from Aeschylus's trilogy *The Orestea*. Here, Orestes, the murderer of his mother is able to escape the natural consequences of his crime through clever uses of syllogistic reasoning. He successfully argues that the Erinyes must persecute him no longer. For they are bound to persecute only those who have committed the worst of crimes: the murder of one's own blood relation. By showing that a mother

and son are not, strictly speaking, blood relations (since she merely carries the paternal seed), Orestes is able to conclude that he has not committed the crime of murdering his blood relation. Nye uses this example
to illustrate the danger of relying on a syllogism to establish conclusions.
When syllogistic argumentation became the standard, she argues, "success depended not on guilt or innocence, but on cleverness and dexterity
in argument" (WP 45). The truth is abused by Orestes' "logic," yet he
wins the day. More generally, since logical skill rests in the hands of a
few elite men, truth will continue to be skewed for their advantage. The
powerless will continue to be powerless, having no *logical* response in the
face of syllogistic reasoning.

Nye's analysis of logic's dangers is made clearer by her diagnosis of the
causes of Orestes' victory. In interpreting Orestes' triumph, Nye blames
the fact that "there is no discussion of what happened, of the circumstances of [Clytemnestra's] crime, of Clytemnestra's reasons for killing
her husband Agamemnon of the senseless slaughter at which he had
officiated at Troy, of his brutal murder of their daughter. There is no
discussion of Orestes's crime, of the fact that he entered by stealth and
as a guest, thus also transgressing the duty of guest and host" (WP 45).

Thus, for Nye, it is the erasure of the concrete, particular circumstances surrounding the murder that ultimately allows for Orestes' absolu-
tion. Orestes' guilt, she argues, is *obscured* by his abstract discussion of
murder, made possible by his use of syllogistic reasoning. Syllogistic reasoning pays attention only to the logical structure of Orestes' argument
rather than to its content. Aristotle's syllogistic allows us to determine
the validity of an argument by looking only at the argument's structure
of form. So, for Nye, it is by abstracting the logical form of an argument
from its content and context that logic achieves its problematic ends: "by
isolating syllogistic forms of an argument . . . Aristotle's theory of the
syllogism made possible [the] bracketing of the truth (WP 47). The abstract form of an argument supersedes its concrete content and logic becomes a "mechanism of deceit."

It follows, for Nye, that Aristotle's logic is needed only by Athenian
elites. It is, she argues, only "a professional disputant, working his way
through a complex series of predications removed from any substantial
reality, [that] might indeed make the mistake of not seeing in inference
(WP 42). The typical farmer, Nye assures us, concerned with the concrete reality of foals and mules will have no need of Aristotelian logic.
The division she makes here between the farmer's substantive reality and

the logician's abstract discourse that cuts [him] off from that reality is, I think, the heart of her criticism of Aristotelian logic. Apparently for Nye, reality is substantive, concrete, and immediate. A logical system is needed only by those far enough removed from concrete concerns to warrant a tool for avoiding the development of false judgments. Logic is dangerous, on this view, in large part because it makes sense only in a context in which the logician is already removed from the real concerns of women and other oppressed people.

Nye's rejection of logic goes beyond its appearance in Orestes' case. For Aristotle might agree with Nye that syllogistic logic should not be used to determine Orestes' moral culpability. In his view, ethical behavior requires a virtuous psychic constitution rather than attention to the abstract dictates of scientific methodology. Nye, however, condemns the use of abstract logic even in the scientific project itself. When Aristotle produces false scientific "knowledge," Nye holds the syllogism at fault (even while acknowledging that he begins with false premises). Formal logic, she argues, allows the false, sexist beliefs of men to be fixed and "elaborated into necessary truths (*WP* 59).

From the logician's perspective Nye had simply misdiagnosed the problem. Orestes' innocence is not falsely established by an abstract logic that fails to attend to the particulars of the case. It is not established by the logic at all. The Aristotelian logician would not approve of Orestes' argument and could use resources from within Aristotelian logic to dispute it. Nye presents two different versions of Orestes' argument. In the first one, she recounts it as follows: "[Orestes] tries to prove that from [the Erinyes'] own premise that murder of a parent is unforgivable, it follows that Orestes's crime is not unforgivable because a mother is not a parent (*WP* 45). Although Nye implies that Aristotelian logic endorses this argument, it is not in fact valid. Orestes' argument has the logical form traditionally called "AE in the first figure."[6] In *Prior Analytics* Aristotle argues that the premises in such a form can never yield a valid conclusion:

> For it is possible for the first extreme to belong to all as well as to none of the last. Consequently, neither a particular nor a universal conclusion becomes necessary; and, since nothing is necessary because of these, there will not be a deduction. Terms for belonging to every are animal, man, horse; for belonging to none, animal, man, stone.[7]

Aristotle's strategy is to demonstrate invalidity by producing a counter-model showing that the proposed conclusion need not be true when the proposed premises are true.[8] By this method, Aristotle gives us the means to demonstrate that Orestes' argument is invalid.

Nye's other presentation of Orestes' argument calls for a different response from the Aristotelian logician. Nye has Orestes arguing that "Mother and child have not the same blood, so a matricide is not guilty of killing a parent; Orestes killed his mother, therefore he is not guilty of killing a parent" (WP 45). This argument also in the first figure, has EA premises. It is an instance of the valid form that came to be known as "Celarent" by medieval scholars. Although the syllogism is valid, Aristotle does provide the resources for rejecting the conclusion. Nye's diagnosis is to blame the fact that "there is no discussion of what happened, of the circumstances of the crime" (WP 45). But surely the real problem with this argument is that it begins with a false premise; i.e., that a matricide is not guilty of killing a parent. And it is clear from Aristotle's presentation of logic in both Prior Analytics and Posterior Analytics that a conclusion is demonstrated only when a valid syllogism begins with true premises.[9] So again, Aristotle's logic gives us the means to reject Orestes' claim to have absolved himself.

It might seem then that the logician has had the final word. In drawing on Aristotle's logic to avoid accepting Orestes' conclusion, the logician leaves Nye without a problem to diagnose. Logic's flaws are not in need of explanation since the major flaw Nye identifies—the establishing by logic of false claims—does not exist. Although the logician's response to Nye is accurate, I think it is not far-reaching enough. Within Nye's discussion of Aristotelian logic, lie the seeds of a rejoinder. For have I not, in presenting a logical refutation of Orestes' argument simply repeated the deeper error? In framing a response in the language of Aristotelian logic, the logician again retreats to an abstract representation of concrete events. Once again, it could be claimed, the larger truth is distorted. While the logician's response does show that Orestes has failed to establish his innocence, Nye could claim it does not contribute to a larger understanding of his actions and their context. It does not account for, or encourage discussion of, the horror of a murderer set free, or the limited, patriarchal perspective that makes the father the sole parent. Nothing in the logician's story of invalidity and false premises answers Nye's charge that the abstract concepts of logic are a retreat from what is central and important for women's lives. Unless the critique of logical form is examined and rejected, the logician's response cannot get off the ground.

We have seen in Nye's argument an underlying assumption that logic's abstract formalism dangerously distorts reality by giving primacy to form and structure at the expense of attention to content and context. This distortion has two interrelated components: (1) logic emerges only in a context of oppression and domination, and (2) logic elevates the formal elements of language and hence demotes and erases the contexts from which concrete utterances derive its meaning. Attention to situation and to embodied knowledge are, in the words of Teresa De Lauretis, "the stuff of feminist theory."[10] What I explore in the next section of this essay is whether the feminist recognition of the importance of contextualized thinking precludes abstract discourses, such as formal logic. In evaluating the two components of Nye's criticism, I shall show that Aristotle has a less bifurcated understanding of the relation between form and content than is apparent in Nye's reading of his logical writings.

Responding to Nye

Nye is certainly correct that a distinction between form and content is essential to Aristotle's syllogistic. Aristotle's stated task in *Prior Analytics* is to "say through what premises, when, and, how every deduction comes about."[11] Aristotle can undertake this project only because deductions are differentiated simply in virtue of their logical forms. Were Aristotle to identify a deduction with its particular content, or its individual context of utterance, he would need to consider infinitely many deductions and the promise of *Prior Analytics* would remain unfulfilled. The concept of logical form is abstract then in the sense that it achieves generality— allowing (potentially) infinitely many deductions to be discussed in a finite amount of time—by emphasizing similarities among arguments that differ in other ways. For Aristotle, syllogisms with differing contents can nonetheless share a common structure; i.e., a similar pattern of relationships between the individual terms that make up the syllogism. This sort of structural abstraction is at the heart of all deductive sciences, meaning that much is at stake in the rejection of formal logic. As Val Plumwood reminds us in her commentary on Nye's rejection of logic:

The area of intellectual activity potentially destroyed by such a program to eliminate abstraction and anything which departs from 'normal' language begins to look alarmingly large—not only mathematics (which can be derived from logic and involves a similar level of abstraction) and large areas of science, but 'computer programming, statistics, economic models . . .' and no doubt a great deal more we might not want to lose.[12]

And is it not just these technological arenas that are touched by Nye's program? Abstract representations of structure are familiar to us in such formats as an ordinary calendar, which represents the "same" order of days and months in differing years or a dressmaker's pattern, which allows the "same" dress to be made from a variety of different materials. While the abstract concepts of logic may be unfamiliar, they are no more inherently abstract than the everyday structural concepts of days and months, or patterns and blueprints. As I have argued, this element of Nye's argument does not turn on anything specific to logic but on the possibility for structural abstraction in general.

Does logic emerge only in a context of domination? Although Nye is, of course, correct to point out that Aristotelian logic was developed by a member of an elite class for use by other men of his class, there is nothing in either the practice of abstract thought or in its very conception that makes it solely the property of an elite men. Identifying abstract representations of structure with oppressor consciousness ignores and devalues the thought and speech that emerges from a variety of locations within our cultural and social hierarchies. Indeed, abstract representations of structural relations are found among cultural "outsiders" as well as among "insiders." Sociologist Carol B. Stack, has found, for example, that the complex logic of kinship relations among members of a low-income African-American community she calls "The Flats" require a highly developed and abstract representational mechanism.[13] A variety of terms have been developed by members of the community to represent subtle distinctions and relations between kin. Community members use these abstract representations to reason about both specific interpersonal relations and about general features of relatedness and kinship. Far from being imposed by the dominant culture, the abstract structural discourse of kinship found in "The Flats" emerges independently and often in direct contrast to dominant culture representations of kinship.

Although mathematics has received more attention than logic in the rich literature describing deductive sciences in non-Western cultures, we have no shortage of evidence that formal mathematical and logical systems have emerged in a variety of cultural contexts. Systems such as classical Indian logic or Arabic geometry are certainly no less abstract than the ones we have inherited from Aristotle and his contemporaries.[14] In addition, people in many cultures engage in abstract logic "games" often as part of larger religious or social practices.[15]

These examples show that abstract representations of logical relations develop in a variety of social and historical contexts; they need not be imposed from above on a dominated group. Although Nye stresses the ways that logical proficiency can be used to dominate others, such skill can also be used for liberatory ends. Development of abstract representations of the experience of domination, and the structural forces that create the domination, is often a crucial step in ending that domination. Far from signifying a retreat from women's lived experiences, the very kind of abstracting process that leads Aristotle to a conception of logical form often leads to the emergence of a feminist consciousness. The ability to name logical fallacies and identify the mistakes in reasoning used to "prove" one's inferiority is often exhilarating.[16] To ignore these examples, or perhaps worse, to interpret them as a form of "bad faith"—a mirroring of the oppressor's thought rather than an authentic expression of lived experience—does not do justice to the multifaceted nature of logical proficiency.

The second element of Nye's critique is the claim that formal logic emphasizes the abstract structure of an inference at the expense of its concrete content. This criticism confuses an uninterpreted calculus with a fully interpreted, applied logic. While the formal properties of a logical calculus can be investigated for their own sake, once we apply the logic to a situation (say, by using it to evaluate the validity of an actual inference) we are working with both form and content. Taking an argument made in a natural language and applying the principles of a formal logic to it requires a balance between form and content. Were Orestes to claim, for example, that his argument is valid, he would need to show that his argument could be translated into the language of the formal system in such a way that it instantiates a valid form. This would require paying attention to the meanings of the particular words used in the argument. Since logical variables are univocal, Orestes would need to justify his translation by showing that he is not equivocating on, for example, the meaning of the term "murder." One of the virtues often claimed for the application of formal logic to informal discourse is that this translation process, far from erasing the importance of the discourse, serves to expli-cate it more fully. When logic is considered as more than an uninterpre-ted formal calculus, the claim cannot be made that it erases the concrete in favor of the purely formal.

That form and content are *intertwined* in applied logic is particularly evident in Aristotle's logic. Aristotle is ultimately concerned with ap-plied logic, what we would now call an "intended interpretation" of the formal structure, and his presentation reflects this interest. We see it, for example, in Aristotle's tendency to offer both a syntactic and a semantic definition of key terms, such as "contradiction," or the syllogistic "places" (major, middle, and minor). In *On Interpretation*, Aristotle tells us that two sentences are contradictory when they have the same subject and the same predicate but one is positive and the other is negative.[17] Since the distinction between negative and positive propositions is itself purely syn-tactic, indicated by the presence or absence of the (Greek equivalent of) the string 'not', contradiction is defined as a purely syntactic relation.[18] In *Categories*, however, we are told that contradictories are distinguished from other forms of opposition because "in this case and in this case only, it is necessary for one opposite to be true and the other to be false."[19] Here the distinguishing mark of the relation is semantic, not syntactic. Further, the definitions conflict in the case of both quantified and modal propositions.[20] Consider the pair 'Every dog is brown / Every dog is not brown'. On the syntactic definition they ought to count as contradicto-ries: they share a subject and predicate and differ only in the addition or exclusion of the negative marker. On the semantic definition, however, they fail to be contradictories because it is not necessary that one must be true. In response to this conflict, it is clear that Aristotle prefers the semantic definitions of contradiction, a choice he again makes in the case of conflicting definition of the major term. In giving precedence to the semantic definition of these key terms, Aristotle demonstrates the way that form and content are equally the concern of applied logic: the logician must understand the speaker's meaning before she can reliably apply the formal apparatus to the speaker's utterances.

In addition to the introduction of semantic definitions, Aristotle al-ways provides a concrete, natural language example of any given formal relation. His introduction of concrete terms in his logic in this way has led some commentators to rebuke him for introducing too many nonfor-mal elements into his logic.[21] But again, it is because Aristotle is interested in applied logic that a purely formal logic will not suffice. In using concrete examples and counterexamples as part of his proof method, Aristotle makes the applicability of his logic to concrete situations the ultimate test of its adequacy.[22]

Finally, Aristotle is careful to spell out another important relationship between the formal elements of logic and its application to concrete situations. Formal logic, on his view, cannot provide knowledge by itself. Observation, the collection of information, is essential to Aristotle's conception of the production of knowledge. Logic can help us draw out consequences of our observations, but for Aristotle there can be no purely formal knowledge of the world. Syllogisms proceed from premises and these initial premises are derived from dialectical reflection on the best-informed common opinion. It is unlikely that women were participants in this dialectical process of articulating the common opinions that ground scientific results. The biases in Aristotle's science can be explained in large part by the exclusionary process that determines the initial premises rather than by the logical process that derives conclusions from these premises.[23]

My evaluation of Nye's argument has consequences for Nye's positive program. She claims that abstaining from abstract thought or talk will result in a greater recognition of lived differences and a less distorted understanding of reality. Nye advises abandoning logic in favor of a cognitive process she calls "reading." This, for her, is a way of thinking about a claim that pays attention only to the particular circumstances of its utterance, the social and historical conditions of the utterer, and the immediate content of the given claim (WP 183). In treating each situation individually rather than as "of a type," Nye believes we shall understand situations more clearly and without the distortion that emerges when we use the abstract rules of logic to analyze and evaluate situations (WP 153).

But we have good reason to think that "reading" in Nye's sense is impossible without a prior commitment to a language containing abstract categories, concepts, and terms. As John Ellis argues, a language without abstract categories is impossible precisely because of the incredible variation within experience:

> No two situations are exactly alike. The notion of a different label for each different situation is an impossible one. First the label would be meaningless to speaker B unless he had been present at

and had witnessed all of the situations himself . . . second, the number of labels would soon become so large that neither [speaker] A nor [speaker] B could possibly remember their reference. But third . . . this language would have no real uses. It would be limited to the mere recall of past situations.[24]

Ellis argues here that abstraction cannot be erased from language, leaving a purified concrete discourse behind.[25] Language itself requires the development of a system of categorization that allows for the grouping together of things *different* from one another. Antirealists can argue that the groupings are, in an important sense, arbitrary and could be accomplished in a variety of ways. But some such grouping is required if we are to have language that allows for communication and full human thought. The challenge for feminists is not to abandon generality in either language or logic, but to offer an account of it that respects both similarity and difference.[26]

I have argued that while Aristotelian logic is certainly abstract in its dependence on structural concepts such as "logical form," this kind of abstraction is not necessarily oppressive or inimical to concern for concrete contents and contexts. In arguing that logic is not particularly problematic simply on the grounds of its being an abstract discourse, I have by no means foreclosed the possibility of feminist analysis and criticism of logic. Cynthia Freeland has argued that a feminist evaluation of Aristotelian logic must begin with *Categories* and "[consider] Aristotle's rationale for articulating reality in just the way he did, asking if and how his categories reflect aspects of patriarchy."[27] Such a project would involve a close examination of the *specific* formal concepts that logic introduces. In the final section of this essay, I investigate two projects that share in this spirit: Luce Irigaray's and Val Plumwood's indictment of logical negation.

Irigaray, Plumwood, and Logical Negation

Luce Irigaray offers a criticism of formal logic that rests, not on the simple fact of logic's abstractness, but on the way that logic provides an abstract representation of relations among statements. For Irigaray, logic encodes an abstract representation of the world as it appears from the perspective of patriarchy. Unlike Nye, Irigaray does not directly reject logic per se, but rather indicates the need for alternative representational schemes that can lead us to a richer understanding of logical relations.

For Irigaray, Western culture is dominated by a symbolic structure that makes possible the representation and enactment of cultural fears, desires, and "unconscious" cultural meanings. This cultural "Imaginary" is, she argues, rooted in the repression of sexual difference. The languages, institutions, and practices of Western culture permit only a male subject. Within these representational mechanisms of Western culture, women are representable only as "the other of the same"; i.e., as partial subjects, ultimately derivative upon male subjectivity.[28] Irigaray's writing urges us to think our way out of this situation and create the possibility for acknowledging and representing full female subjectivity and radical sexual difference, "the other of the other." Because the source of female subordination is so deeply connected to the constitutive structures of Western culture, the intervention Irigaray proposes is in many ways analogous to psychoanalysis.[29] As if it were an analysand, Western culture must be listened to, its unconscious thoughts must be made conscious, its resistances analyzed. By this means, the present destructive Imaginary can be transformed into an Imaginary that represents sexual difference and allows for productive and satisfying relations between male and female subjects. It is in this therapeutic way, then, that Irigaray approaches the culture's dominant practices.

In her essay "Is the Subject of Science Sexed?" Irigaray argues that the practice of science is not gender-neutral. She points out the ways that the features of scientific practice (e.g., erasing intuition, privileging the visible, projecting an idealized and universal model onto the world) "reveal and isomorphism in man's sexual imaginary which must remain rigorously masked."[30] Further, she argues, scientific discoveries must always be expressed in the language of formal logic. In this language she says:

There is then no sign:

- of *difference* other than the quantitative
- of *reciprocity* (other than within a common property or a common whole)
- of *exchange*
- of *permeability*
- of *fluidity*.

Syntax is governed by:

- *identity with,* expressed by property and quantity
- *noncontradiction* with ambiguity, ambivalence, polyvalence minimized
- *binary opposition*; nature/reason, subject/object, matter/energy, inertia/movement.[31]

Irigaray criticizes here the negation operator, not of Aristotelian logic, but of classical logic.[32] Classically, the negation operator represents a relation of quantitative and exclusive difference. Negation is governed by the law of noncontradiction and the law of the excluded middle meaning that a proposition and its negation cannot both be true, but at least one must be true.[33] Irigaray points to what is absent, what is resisted, in the classical conception of negation: both a conception of difference as genuine otherness and a conception of difference as fluid and ambiguous. The negation of classical logic is not genuine otherness since it makes the proposition and its negation commensurable. They are always open to comparison on a single scale and one can always be reduced to the other (by adding or removing the negation symbol). One is always better (truer) than the other. We cannot simply let them exist equally in their difference; one must always be rejected. Neither, however, can they fully interact. This is to say that the classical negation operator is not fluid. There can be no shades of negation, no nuanced slippage from a proposition to its negation. The gap between a proposition and its negation is clearly and unambiguously demarcated.

For Irigaray, the first of these resisted conceptions of negation—negation as otherness—is precisely the one that does justice to a full recognition of sexual difference. The experience of sexual difference is an experience of *wonder*, she says, for "man and woman, woman and man are always meeting as though for the first time because they cannot be substituted for each other. I will never be in a man's place, never will a man be in mine. Whatever identifications are possible, one will never exactly occupy the place of the other—they are irreducible one to each other."[34] Sexual difference, unlike the difference of classical negation, is a total and irreducible difference in which the poles of difference coexist equally and fully.

Nonetheless, says Irigaray, we are now prevented from experiencing the wonder of sexual difference in part because of the second resistance. In also resisting a conception of negation as fluid and ambiguous, classical logic resists what Irigaray takes to be difference as it appears within the female Imaginary. Whereas, for Irigaray, classical negation is isomorphic to our symbolic representation of masculinity as definite and rigidly distinct, fluid negation is isomorphic to a representation of women as merged, undifferentiated, and connected. The primacy of classical logic, with its masculine representation of negation, exemplifies Irigaray's charge that the Imaginary of Western culture is a male imaginary. Rethinking logical negation as both otherness and fluid difference, then, becomes part of a project of transformation that will ultimately allow for women's equality and the emergence of a reciprocal relation between women and men.

Although some commentators have taken Irigaray as arguing for a complete rejection of logic, I suggest that she is not critiquing logic, per se, but the primacy of a particular type of logic; i.e., the classical logic described above, which Irigaray identifies as "the semantics of incomplete beings (Frege)."[35] Just as she calls for a new way of speaking (*langage*) rather than a total new language (*langue*), I believe it is consistent with her criticism of the language of logic to see her as calling for new, other, ways of speaking logic that might perhaps uncover those "trivalent or polyvalent theories that still appear to be marginal."[36]

How might attention to these marginalized logics encourage a broader understanding of difference? One possibility is suggested by Val Plumwood.[37] Plumwood, too, argues that classical negation represents a dualistic and hierarchical form of difference, inimical to feminist understandings of otherness: "The negation of classical logic has features of radical exclusion of the alien other . . . as well as exhibiting other features which are characteristic of dualism."[38] Classically, a proposition and its negation are maximally distinct. Conjoining them produces a contradiction and causes the logic to collapse. The negated proposition has no independent specificity but is interpreted as the absence or lack of the positive proposition. For Plumwood, these features of classical negation are implicated in the "logic of domination" that underlies oppressive social structures such as patriarchy and colonization. Under patriarchy, women and men are understood as maximally distinct, different in kind not merely degree. Men and masculinity are taken as the norm, women are defined in terms of what they lack in comparison to men.

In pointing out the relationship between classical negation and the patriarchal conception of otherness Plumwood insists that logic per se need not be rejected. Instead she calls for a "reworking" of classical logic, believing that "none of the features of dualistic otherness or classical negation is an inevitable feature of logic, negation, otherness, or reasoning."[39] She points to relevance logic as an available alternative in which negation "can be interpreted as expressing a notion of otherness as non-hierarchical difference . . . it is neither a cancellation of, nor a lack or absence of a specific condition, but another and further condition—a difference—yielding the concept of an other which is not just specified negatively but is independently characterized and with an independent role on its own behalf."[40] This is similar to Irigaray's conception of sexual difference but not to the second, fluid conception of difference of the female Imaginary. In different ways, both Irigaray and Plumwood provide a ground for a feminist critique of classical logic by showing the limited and biased representation of negation it contains and both challenge us to investigate more acceptable feminist alternatives. In the next section I describe how that negation functions in Aristotelian logic and consider the extent to which Aristotelian negation is implicated in this critique.

Negation in Aristotelian Logic

Negation functions differently in Aristotelian logic than in the classical logic described above. Whereas classical logic contains a single (contradiction-inducing) negation operator, Aristotle identifies four different types of opposition:

1. correlation (e.g., 'double' and 'half')
2. contrariety (e.g., 'bad' and 'good')
3. privation (e.g., 'blindness' and 'sight')
4. contradiction (e.g., 'he sits' and 'he does not sit')

His syllogistic allows for the formal representation of two of these forms of opposition, contrariety and contradiction. Contradictory negation functions analogously to the negation operator of classical logic. It is governed by the law of noncontradiction and the law of the excluded middle; i.e., for any pair of contradictory sentences, they cannot both be true but one must be true.[41] Contrariety, however, is governed only by the law of noncontradiction; although two contrary sentences cannot both be true, both may be false.

Aristotle's richer catalogue of oppositional categories has been taken as evidence for the superiority of his logic by several contemporary logicians for reasons having nothing to do with feminist understandings of difference.[42] Bucking the prevailing wisdom that "propositional logic is prior to the logic of terms," modern-day defenders of (contemporary versions of) Aristotelian term logic, point frequently to the richer representation of negation made possible in such a logic. But, as I shall argue, even Aristotle's conception of contrariety is not equal to the task of fully representing "nonhierarchical otherness."

Contrariety does have several features that make it a less hierarchical form of negation than contradiction. In the first place, contrariety need not be dualistic. A single term can have a variety of contraries. Color terms, for example, are nondualistic contraries in that 'This is (all) red' precludes 'This is (all) blue', and also 'This is (all) yellow', 'This is (all) green, and so forth. Second, the contrary of a given sentence is structurally parallel to the original sentence. In *On Interpretation*, Aristotle gives the following example: The contradictory of 'Every man is just' is 'Not every man is just', its contrary is 'Every man is not-just'.[43] As can be seen in this example, contradictory negation is structurally compound; i.e., the denial that a predicate applies to a subject is syntactically derivative upon the initial affirmative statement. Contrariety, however, is structurally affirmative. Here one affirms that the contrary of the original predicate applies to the subject. Unlike contradiction, contrary negation produces two affirmative statements.

Finally, contrary terms need not be specified in terms of lack or absence or some specified property. As I indicated above, Aristotle distinguishes contrary terms from both correlates and privatives. Correlates are commensurable in that their specifications are interdependent (X is half Y, just in case Y is double X). Privatives indicate the presence or absence of an already specified property (A sighted person possesses sight; a blind person lacks it). Contraries on the other hand indicate properties that are specified independently.

What are the results of taking 'Pat is a woman' and 'Pat is a man' as contraries rather than contradictories? For one thing, both of these sentences could be false (although they could not both be true). For another, 'woman,' and 'man' must be specified independently, without defining one in terms of the other or defining one as lacking some specified property. This understanding of difference approaches the nonhierarchical difference called for by Plumwood and Irigaray.

There are, however, caveats. Plumwood, in particular, argues for a notion of negation in which the opposing statements are not maximally
distinct; i.e., in which both can be asserted without collapsing the system.
This does not occur in the case of contrariety. Also, there is nothing in
Aristotle's logic that mirrors the fluid form of negation that Irigaray
points to as absent in the classical understanding.

A further complication is that Aristotle himself took 'male' and 'female' as contraries and yet was able to advocate a sexist hierarchical
politics. The apparent tension between understanding 'male' and 'female'
as contrary terms and advocating a politics in which the men are the
natural rulers of women, points to an important feature of the specification of contrary terms. Aristotle's definition and presentations of contrariety often presume that the contrary terms can be syntactically
specifiable; i.e., the contrary of a term is formed by adding a negative
marker to the initial term.[44] This means that the contrary of 'blue' in
Aristotle's logic is not really the pluralistic set 'red, green, yellow, and so
forth'. In Aristotle's logic, the contrary of 'blue' is 'nonblue' which erases
the different ways that something can not be blue. Further, the syntactic
specification of the contrary of 'blue' requires taking 'blue' as the central
color and demoting other colors to merely 'nonblue' status. The results
of the syntactic specification of contrariety can be seen even more clearly
in the case of gender. If this relationship requires the specification of a
syntactic difference between 'woman' and 'man', 'woman' will need to be
interpreted as 'nonman' and hierarchy will be reinstated.[45]

Earlier I argued that Aristotle often prefers semantic definitions when
they conflict with syntactic ones but this is not clearly true in his discussions of the logic of gender. Aristotle's writings reveal a tension between
the semantic and syntactic specifications of contrariety in the case of
gender. Although his formal definitions of contrariety require purely syntactic differences between contraries, his examples are often semantically
contrary only. For example, Aristotle claims that 'male' and 'female' are
contraries but unlike many other contrary pairs do not designate different
species.[46] To explain why, he posits that difference in sex is a difference
of matter, not a difference of essence: the terms are more like 'pale/dark'
than 'man/horse'. The terms, he says, name modifications in the human
species but they are material not essential modifications. But his claim
elsewhere that men are the natural rulers of women implies that 'woman'
is not being interpreted as specifying a property of its own, independent
of, yet contrary to, 'man'.[47] Instead the contrariety of the pair man/

woman results from 'woman' being understood as 'nonman' and naturally ruled by 'man'. The syntactic specification of contraries allows for a slip-page away from the understanding of contrariety indicated by Aristotle's other examples.

Ultimately then, Aristotle's logic is neither simply a tool for domination, mere "words of power," nor a tool to be used unreflectively by feminists. His syllogistic offers resources for conceptualizing nonhierarchical forms of difference although it cannot fully represent all of theses forms. Recognizing the biases and limits of a particular logical representation does not mean that logic itself must be rejected. Close examination of logics currently marginalized—multivalent logics, relevance logic, and Aristotelian logic, for example—can provide resources for feminist reflection on the nature of difference.

Notes

1. I am especially grateful to Cynthia Freeland for her encouragement and helpful responses to earlier versions of this paper. A Summer Research Grant from Muhlenberg College made work on this paper possible.

2. Louise M. Antony and Charlotte Witt, A Mind of One's Own: Feminist Essays on Reason and Objectivity (Boulder: Westview, 1993), xiii.

3. Robin Smith, "Introduction," in Prior Analytics, trans. Robin Smith (Indianapolis: Hackett, 1989), xiv.

4. Andrea Nye, Words of Power: A Feminist Reading of the History of Logic (New York: Routledge, 1990); hereafter cited as WP.

5. See, for example, Joan Weiner's review of Words of Power, in Journal of Symbolic Logic 59, no. 2 (June 1994), and Carol Guen Hart, "Power in the Service of Love: John Dewey's Logic and the Dream of a Common Language," Hypatia 8, no. 2 (Spring 1993).

6. This means that the major term (the predicate in the conclusion) appears as the predicate of the first premise while the minor term (the subject of the conclusion) appears as the subject of the second premise. A third term, the "middle" term, serves as both the subject of the first premise and the predicate of the second. In this case, the major term is "unforgivable acts," the minor term is "Orestes's crime," and the middle term is "acts of murder of a parent." The first premise is universally affirmative (A), while the second is universally negative (E). The premises would thus say:

>   All acts of murder of a parent are unforgivable acts.
>   No crime of Orestes is an act of murder of a parent.

The purported conclusion is:

>   No crime of Orestes is an unforgivable act.

7. Prior Analytics, 26a5–10.

8. Aristotle's strategy here is actually a bit more complex; he is trying to show that (what

is now called) an AE syllogism in the first figure produces *no* conclusion whatsoever. He gives two countermodels: the first having a universal affirmative conclusion and thus ruling out any negative conclusions; the second having a universal negative conclusion and thus ruling out affirmative conclusions.

9. *Prior Analytics*, 24b10.

10. Teresa De Lauretis "The Essence of the Triangle or, Taking the Risk of Essentialism Seriously: Feminist Theory in Italy, the U.S., and Britain," in *The Essential Difference*, ed. Naomi Schor and Elizabeth Weed (Bloomington: Indiana University Press, 1994), 11.

11. *Prior Analytics*, 25b30.

12. Val Plumwood, "The Politics of Reason: Towards a Feminist Logic," in *Australasian Journal of Philosophy* 71, no. 4 (December 1993).

13. Carol B. Stack, *All Our Kin: Strategies for Survival in a Black Community* (New York: Harper and Row, 1974).

14. For a discussion of the complexities of Indian logic, see Chapter 1.3, *A Natural History of Negation*, by Laurence R. Horn (Chicago: University of Chicago Press, 1989). A good introduction to non-Western mathematics is *Multicultural Mathematics*, by David Nelson, George Ghevergheses Joseph, and Julian Williams (Oxford: Oxford University Press, 1993).

15. Marcia Ascher describes several such "games" in her book *Ethnomathematics: A Multicultural View of Mathematical Ideas* (Pacific Grove, Calif.: Brooks Cole, 1991). For example, the game of Dish, a game of chance requiring complex probability assignments is played by the Northeastern Iroquois peoples at community ceremonial festivals. It is played to bring honor to the clan and, sometimes, health to a sick person.

16. The women students in my logic classes often provide examples of this. They often return from holiday visits home with reports of "turning the tables" on a sibling's or parent's use of apparently logical reasoning.

17. *On Interpretation*, trans. E. M. Edghill, in *The Basic Works of Aristotle*, ed. Richard McKeon, (New York: Random House, 1941), 17a25–34.

18. Ibid., 19b24–27.

19. Ibid., 13b2–4.

20. I do not discuss Aristotle's modal logic in this paper. For a helpful discussion of this topic, see Cynthia Freeland's paper, "Aristotle on Possibilities and Capacities" in *Ancient Philosophy* 6 (1987).

21. For a discussion of this controversy see Jonathan Lear, *Aristotle and Logical Theory* (Cambridge: Cambridge University Press, 1980), especially 54–61 and 70–75.

22. Another way that Aristotle mediates between form and content is through his elucidation of informal fallacies, such as circularity. While a circular argument is legitimately valid from a purely formal standpoint, it does not serve the purpose of generating new knowledge.

23. See for example, Nancy Tuana, "The Weaker Seed: The Sexist Bias of Reproductive Theory," in *Feminism and Science*, ed. Nancy Tuana (Bloomington: Indiana University Press, 1989). In this volume, see Cynthia Freeland, "On Irigaray on Aristotle" and Deborah Modrak, "Aristotle's Theory of Knowledge and Feminist Epistemology."

24. John M. Ellis, *Language, Thought, and Logic* (Evanston: Northwestern University Press, 1994), 28.

25. Aristotle himself makes a similar point: "It makes no difference even if one were to say a word has several meanings. . . . If however they [meanings] were not limited but one were to say that the word has an infinite number of meanings, obviously reasoning would be impossible; for not to have one meaning is to have no meaning, and if words have no meaning our reasoning with one another, and indeed with ourselves, has been annihilated." In *Metaphysics*, trans. W. D. Ross, in *The Basic Works of Aristotle*, ed. McKeon 1006b. Aristotle is not ruling out multiple meanings for the same expression as long as there are only finitely many such interpretations.

26. Many feminist philosophers are actively engaged in this project. Diana Fuss argues that the Lockean notion of nominal essences provides a nonessentialist theory of generality that may be useful for feminist theorizing. See "Reading Like a Feminist," in *The Essential Difference*, ed. Schor and Weed. Natalie Stoljar argues that general terms can be interpreted as Wittgensteinian "cluster concepts" ("Essence, Identity and the Concept of Woman," *Philosophical Topics* [Fall 1995]). Rachel Joffe Falmagne provides an interesting nonessentialist account of "concrete universals" that allows for generality ("The Abstract and the Concrete," in *Cultural Psychology and Activity Theory: Essays in Honor of Sylvia Scribner*, ed. L. Martin, K. Nelson, and E. Tobach (Cambridge: Cambridge University Press, 1994).

27. "Nourishing Speculation: A Feminist Reading of Aristotelian Science," in *Engendering Origins: Critical Readings in Plato and Aristotle*, ed. Bat Ami Bar-On (Albany: State University of New York Press, 1994), 185.

28. Women are represented, for example, as a man's mother, his sister, his wife, his assistant, or as a receptacle for his penis or sperm.

29. This interpretation is suggested by Margaret Whitford. She discusses the complex relationship between Irigaray's methodology and her critical readings of Freud, Lacan, and psychoanalytic practice in *Luce Irigaray: Philosophy in the Feminine* (New York: Routledge, 1991); see especially 33–38.

30. "Is the Subject of Science Sexed?" trans. Carol Mastrangelo Bové, in *Feminism and Science*, ed. Nancy Tuana (Bloomington: Indiana University Press, 1989), 61.

31. Ibid., 62.

32. This logic, also called symbolic logic or Fregean logic, is the one that derives from Gottlob Frege's *Begriffsschrift*. In its contemporary form, it is currently the standard logic taught in schools. Alternative logical systems are usually described in terms of the ways they deviate from this logic. Nye uses the term "classical logic" to refer to ancient logic, including Aristotelian logic.

33. Nye occasionally confuses these two laws. She says, for example, "Aristotle was not willing to give up the law of the excluded middle. Knowledge cannot be one of those ambiguous bodily individuals who so often both are and are not what we desire of them" (*WP* 51). The second statement might be taken to violate the law of noncontradiction but it cannot be read as a violation of the law of the excluded middle. Further, as we shall see below, Aristotle's logic includes a form of negation that is not governed by the law of the excluded middle.

34. Luce Irigaray, "Sexual Difference," in *An Ethics of Sexual Difference*, trans. Carolyn Burke and Gillian C. Gill (Ithaca: Cornell University Press), 13.

35. Irigaray, "Is the Subject of Science Sexed?" 62.

36. Ibid., 63.

37. See Val Plumwood, "The Politics of Reason: Towards A Feminist Logic," in *Australasian Journal of Philosophy* (1993), and *Feminism and the Mastery of Nature* (New York: Routledge, 1993).

38. "The Politics of Reason," 455.

39. Ibid., 458.

40. *Feminism and the Mastery of Nature*, 58.

41. For Aristotle's presentation and discussion of the four forms of opposition see *Categories*, trans., E. M. Edghill in *The Basic Works of Aristotle*, ed. McKeon, 11b15–14a25.

42. See George Englebretsen, *Three Logicians: Aristotle, Leibniz, and Sommers and the Syllogistic* (The Netherlands: Van Gorcum, 1981) and Lawrence Horn, *A Natural History of Negation*.

43. *On Interpretation*, 19b30–35.

44. In the original Greek, the difference between contrariety and contradiction is indicated also by word order.

45. From the perspective of the logic, either term could be taken as the central term.

46. *Metaphysics*, 1058b15–25. For further discussion of this aspect of Aristotle's work, see Marguerite Deslauriers, "Sex and Essence in Aristotle's *Metaphysics* and Biology" in this volume.

47. *Politics*, trans. Benjamin Jowett, in *The Basic Writings of Aristotle*, ed. McKeon, 1260a10.

2

Place, Interval

A Reading of Aristotle, *Physics* IV

Luce Irigaray

"Further, too, if it is itself an existent, it will be somewhere. Zeno's difficulty demands an explanation: for if everything that exists has a place, place too will have a place, and so on ad infinitum*"* (Aristotle, *Physics* IV, 209a, fifth difficulty; p. 355).[1]

If the matrix is extendable, it can figure as *the place of place*. It is the first place that can ever be situated in a progression to infinity. So, does this explain the nostalgia? The entry into an indefinite number of places? The quest for the unique in the downshift of places? The belief in a certain God so as to stop falling or expanding immediately to infinity through the suppression of all platforms of duration, of space-time.

I go on a quest through an indefinite number of bodies, through nature, through God, for the body that once served as place for me, where I (male/female) was able to stay contained, enveloped.[2] Given that, as far as man is concerned, the issue is to separate the first and the last place. Which can lead to a double downshift: both of the relation to the unique mother and of the relation to the unique God. Can these two downshifts come together? Can the quest to infinity for the mother in women result in a quest for infinity in God? Or do the two quests intersect ceaselessly? With place indefinitely switching from the one to the other? Modifying itself moment by moment. Or even transmuting itself from one envelope to the other? I become for God the container, the envelope, the vessel, the place for which I quest? Nonetheless the split between first and last place has still to be resolved.

As for woman, she is place. Does she have to locate herself in bigger and bigger places? But also to find, situate, in herself, the place that she is. If she is unable to constitute, within herself, the place that she is, she passes ceaselessly through the child in order to return to herself. She turns around an object in order to return to herself. And this captures the other in her interiority. For this not to occur, she has to assume the passage between *the infinitely large and the infinitely small.* Given that, ultimately, those two places cannot really be delineated. Except perhaps as *a grain of sand* in the reasoning of man? Or as *nest in her for her?* Passage from one place to another, for her, remains the problem of place as such, always within the context of the mobility of her constitution. She is able to move within place as place. Within the availability of place. Given that her issue is how to trace the limits of place herself so as to be able to situate herself therein and welcome the other there. If she is to be able to contain, to envelop, she must have her own envelope. Not only her clothing and ornaments of seduction, but her skin. And her skin must contain a receptacle. She must lack

—neither body,
—nor extension within,
—nor extension without,

or she will plummet down and take the other with her.

And this fall continues to infinity, since there is nothing to stop it:

—given that returning to the mother is impracticable, or impossible,
—given the world here below, life and death itself in relation to God,
—given that sexual difference is irreducible.

"Again, just as every body is in place, so, too, every place has a body in it. What then shall we say about growing things? It follows from these premisses that their place must grow with them, if their place is neither less nor greater than they are" (209a, 6th difficulty, p. 355).

Another difficulty reinforces those of

—life in the womb,
—sexual relation,

or indeed the difficulties posed by nature and by place and body in their as yet uncovered principial relations, both physical and metaphysical.

At issue is the extension of place, of places, and of the relation of that extension to the development of the body and bodies. An issue either forgotten or ignored in the junction of physics and metaphysics, since these two dimensions have been set aside or dislocated, but an issue still alive today (resurrected from its place of repression, psychoanalysts might say).

In this journeying from one place to another, one must distinguish *"place which is common and in which all bodies are"* from that *"which is the proper and primary location of each body"* (209a, 2; p. 356).

The universe contains all bodies. The sky, the air, the earth are containers that are not specific to each of us (male or female). But each of us (male or female) has a place—this place that envelops only his or her body, the first envelope of our bodies, the corporeal identity, the boundary, that which delineates us from other bodies. Form and configuration also determine one's size and all that makes one body unsubstitutable by another. Could this be called a corporeal *surveying*? As well as a virtual one. For this place is the form of each thing but also its extendable matter or the interval of size. It is—according to Plato, with whom Aristotle agrees on this issue—both *container* and *extension*. Which means that it must also be growth between the different forms. And that growth is not alien to it. That growth is in some way given within and with place itself. Yet, since place participates in the determinations of matter and form, it is hard to penetrate. Separated one from the other, matter and form are similarly difficult to penetrate.

Place would in some way be the "nature" of matter and form, the habitat in which both wed without ceasing, and in their extension. To infinity.

This would be so for both masculine and feminine if the split between them (in the division of both work and nature) were bridged. But it can be bridged only by passing back through the definition of place and of the singular situation of the sexes in relation to place.

"But it is at any rate not difficult to see that place cannot be either of them. The form and the matter are not separate from the thing, whereas the place can be separated. As we pointed out, where air was, water in turn comes to be, the one replacing the other; and similarly with other bodies. Hence the place of a thing is neither a part nor a state of it, but separable from it. For place is supposed to be something like a vessel—the vessel being a transportable place. But the vessel is no part of the thing. In so far, then, as it is separable from the thing, it is not the form: qua *containing, it is different from the matter"* (209b, first reason; p. 356).

Place cannot be simply matter *or* form, on one side or the other side of growth and becoming. Thus, matter *and* form cannot be separated from the thing; place can. In fact place reveals itself as a result of that separability. Without being reduced to either a part or a state of either matter or form, it appears like a *vessel* (which may possibly be a variant of place because it is subject to *locomotion?*)

This means:

—it is not to be reduced to form in that it is separable from the thing,
—it is not to be reduced to matter in that it is a container or envelope.

Is it defined here as a mold that embraces the thing? Or else receives it? A transportable mold. Neither coextensive with nature nor adhering to it, since it can be moved.

"Also it is held that what is anywhere is both itself something and that there is a different thing outside it" (209b, second reason; p. 257).

That this bond is neither matter nor form is also evident from the fact that anything that is situated somewhere is per se some thing; given that only through its situation is this thing in a "thing" other than itself. Place is thus not the thing but that which permits the thing to be insofar as the thing can exist in and outside place.

"(Plato, of course, if we may digress, ought to tell us why the form[3] and the numbers are not in place, if 'what participates' is place—whether what partici-

*pates is the Great and the Small or the matter, as he has written in the Ti-
maeus)*" (209b, third reason; p. 357).

What is the nature of ideas and numbers if they are not part of place
even though place has its role to play in the great and the small? This
question, which Aristotle treats as a digression, is in fact essential. Where
are ideas and numbers situated if they are not in place? Even though they
must borrow "matter" from place if they are to exist? Do ideas and numbers bring place down on the side of residual matter? Or the empirical?
Does their nonsituation in place consecrate a split between sensible and
ideal? Leaving undecided the issue of where ideas and numbers come
from? As well, perhaps, as the issue of their inscription in the world? Is
this duality of place, on the one hand, and ideas and numbers, on the
other, one of the symptoms of the divorce between masculine and feminine? In order to overcome the attraction for the first and unique place,
does man, at his best, practice with ideas and numbers as independent
from place? This "ascension," which is not inscribed in place, makes a
return to place possible only in the form of a downfall, a plunging into
the abyss, and so on.

*"Further, how could a body be carried to its own place, if place was the matter
or the form? It is impossible that what has no reference to motion or the distinction of up and down can be place. So place must be looked for among those
things which have these characteristics."* (210a, fourth reason: p. 357).

The independence of place in relation to matter and form may be
understood by this to mean that place itself is that toward which there is
locomotion. When separated from place, the thing feels an attraction to
place as a condition of existence. If I may return to the parallel I have
been drawing between the issue of place and the issue of sexual difference,
I shall affirm that the masculine is attracted to the maternal-feminine as
place. But what place does the masculine offer to attract the feminine?
His soul? His relation to the divine? Can the feminine be inscribed or
situated there? Is this not the only place where he can live, contrary to
what has always been assumed? For the masculine has to constitute itself
as a *vessel* to receive and welcome. And the masculine's morphology,
existence, and essence do not really fit it for such an architecture of
place. Except through a reversal in place of the maternal-feminine or by
welcoming the divine in spirit or mind? What is, in the masculine, the
relation between these two vessels? Is he able to receive woman in the
reverse of herself? In the mourning for herself? Can he beckon to her and

welcome her into himself once he has separated himself from her? Since he must separate himself from her in order to be able to be her place. Just as she must move toward him. If any meeting is to be possible between man and woman, each must be a place, as appropriate to and for the other, and toward which he or she may move. According to Aristotle, such a place would have to be characterized, among other things, by the dimensions of up and down, which are in fact consistently associated with the physical laws of gravitation, as well as with the economy of desire. Place would be directed up or down rather than into expansion-contraction, according to the theory elaborated about it. And to the conception of place which is still and forever Aristotle's.

"If the place is in the thing (it must be if it is either shape or matter) place will have a place: for both the form and the indeterminate undergo change and motion along with the thing, and are not always in the same place, but are where the thing is. Hence the place will have a place" (210a, fifth reason; p. 357).

If place is in the thing—which is necessarily so—place is in the place. There is a *place of place*. In effect form and the indeterminate are transformed and are moved with the thing; they do not stay in the same place but stay where the thing is.

The place is in the thing, and the thing is in the place. *Place is within and without and accompanies movement*; it is its cause and accompanies it. In an extension to infinity. With each place containing the one before it. It remains to establish where the *highest point* and *the threshold* are which allow extension to take place. Is extension possible without overturning and turning over at each phase? Unless the thing is made to explode endlessly? Unless each of us returns to his or her place to find his or her cause again and then returns toward the other place, the place of the other. Which would mean that, at each phase, there were two places interdetermining each other, fitted one in the other. Two motors of place? Two causes of place? And their coming together. Two pulses and their transformations. Of the one, of the other, and their interdeterminations. At least two. To infinity then?

Do these two pulses always fit into each other the same way? That is, with one always inside and the other out? Or sometimes in, sometimes out? Given that place is at the same time the inside and the outside, it may be imagined that the same cause does not always act within, or the same without. That, conceivably, there would be a reversal of envelopes? Which assumes that teleology is not always a forward tropism but permits reversing, turning over, crossing over. The interlacing, the embrace, of goals also as well as of the impulsion of things. Of things and of their situations? Of vessels? If so, place would mold itself from the one to the other, from the inside to the outside, from the outside to the inside. Place would twist and turn on itself. By passing through the other? Between past and future, endlessly?

If woman could be inside herself, she would have at least two things in her: herself and that for which she is a container—man and at times the child. It seems that she can be a container only for one thing, if that is her function. She is supposed only to be a container for the child, according to one moral position. She may be a container for the man. But not for herself.

Obviously, she cannot contain the child and the man in the same way. She is not the same "vessel." But, here again, the definition of vessel is not complex enough. There is a competition among:

—the container for the child,
—the container for the man,
—the container for herself.

In that competition, the first place is virtually the only place. The second is merely a sort of perforation aiming toward the first: a passage, not really a place. The third is something forbidden or impossible—set up by the excision from the *hylē* perhaps? It is necessary, Freud writes, for woman to turn away from her mother in order to enter into desire of and for man. If she remains in empathy with her mother, she remains in her place. So her mother remains a mold for her? Back into herself she turns her mother (and) herself. She interiorizes her container-mother in herself-as-container. Between the two, she exists. And is this possible only through an idealization of the container? *Of place?* Not only of a being or of a thing but of place. Now place in this context always constitutes an inside. How is an inside to be sublimated, remembered?

There is also the question of becoming a thing for the self and for the other. Man and woman would, presumably, not become things at the same time. Perhaps woman would become a thing before *marriage*, man after? Woman would become from within, man from without?

"Further, when water is produced from air, the place has been destroyed, for the resulting body is not in the same place. What sort of destruction, then, is that?

"This concludes my statement of the reasons why space must be something, and again of the difficulties that may be raised about its essential nature" (210a; p. 357).

In this regard the question arises:

—of detumescence,
—of ejaculation,
—of the procreation of a child

in relation to the sexual act. There occurs, in fact, a destruction of place through the passage to another place. How can we work out a problematic of place that would involve not cutting or annihilation but a rhythmic becoming in relation to place? Return to the self so as to move again toward the other? Self-absorption in order to regain the tensing toward, the expansion . . .

In fact place exists, but does it modify itself? Its essence is difficult to define. Essence, apparently, is to be reserved for generation, for engendering and for its matrix, but not for place and its modifications of place?

"Since the vessel is no part of what is in it (what contains something primarily is different from what is contained), place could not be either the matter or the form of the thing contained; but must be different—for the latter, both the matter and the shape, are parts of what is contained" (210b; p. 358).

Thus matter and form are not place. If I take up the analogy with the relation between the sexes (unless thought is what is analogous to that relation? According to Freud, everything is sexuality, and thought can be nothing but a sublimation of sexuality or an anticipation of that sublimation), the womb is a container for the child (who takes form there perhaps?), the woman's sex (organ) is a container for man's sex (organ), which takes, keeps, or metamorphoses its form therein.

The female sex (organ) is neither matter nor form but *vessel*. This vessel may have its form altered, and by woman as well. Therefore she is also matter and form insofar as she is woman. With regard to the child this is less certain. It is the child that gives extension to the womb. The sexual relation is still often imagined as the relation of child to womb, stretching a fabric in order to take up residence there (but anxious about having either not enough or too much space).

In the male realm, there would be seducing, caressing, assuming a shape, spending, and then collapse into formlessness or regression to the fetal position. Do we take it that in love he is both *him* and the *plus one* of the child?

In the female realm there would be the sexual act. She gives form to the male sex (organ) and sculpts it from within. She becomes the container and the active *place* of the sexual act. Maternity is an extra. Linked to the fusion of the two: beyond form? And beyond genetics? An act more passive than passivity? Eternally confused with the sexuation of the female body. Which, for its part, would not have to be especially passive. It seems that in the imaginary there is an inversion between the female sexual act and the maternal sexual act—modes substituted for each other. Or else the conception and the pregnancy are forgotten. The mother is considered to be "active" because she has been imagined after the birth of the child, during maternity. Hasn't woman been imagined as passive only because man would fear to lose mastery in that particular act? Which accounts for his occasional violence? So the functions of mother and wife would be inverted from the point of view of place as well as from the point of view of the man-woman functions.

"*Place is what contains*[4] *that of which it is the place*.

"*Place is no part of the thing*.

"*The primary place of a thing is neither lesser nor greater than the thing*.

"*Place can be left behind by the thing and is separable*." (210b–211a; p. 359).

It is hard not to think of the membranes enveloping the fetus. Since the envelope doesn't fit the thing exactly during gestation, she, and indeed he, the fetus, and the female they and the male they, are in quantitative relations that change constantly between the greater and the smaller.

We may be reminded of the skin too. But the skin is constitutive of the thing, and we cannot separate ourselves from it.

And how can we avoid remembering the sexual act as well and notably the female sex (organ) as a place? In the confusion it potentially sets up with man's first "home" but also with his *skin*. The woman's sex (organ) is supposed in some way to serve as skin to the man's sex organ, to man himself. Without access to that other dimension: the *mucous*. Dimension of the sexual act? Of its approach, its economy, its communion beyond skins.

Up and down are properties of all places. Astonishingly there is no suggestion here of a *spherical* place where no clear-cut distinction between up and down would obtain. Notwithstanding, sexuality partakes in the up and the down, in rising and falling. Bodies in this context are sometimes lighter, sometimes heavier, sometimes warmer, sometimes colder, and so on. But bodies also face the issue of fitting one inside the other, without thereby altering the other dimensions. Can this be understood as the constitution, together, of a spherical or almost spherical form?

Research about place is always governed by movement according to place. If, in regard to "heaven," more thought is given to the fact that it is "in place" than to anything else, this is because "it is in constant movement." Movement can either be "locomotion" or "increase and diminution." These both in fact mean a change of place. While remaining within the womb, the child changes place. While remaining within the woman, the man changes place. Both are smaller or greater in relation to the envelope which keeps them inside. Which is also them, in fact, as well as the relation between the two.

"We say that a thing is in the world [dans le ciel] in the sense of in place, because it is in the air, and the air is in the world; and when we say it is in the air, we do not mean it is in every part of the air, but that it is in the air because of the surface of the air which surrounds it; for if all the air were its place, the place of a thing would not be equal to the thing—which it is supposed to be, and which the primary place in which the thing is actually is" (211a; p. 359).

If it is the whole of the air that is place, each thing will not be equal to its place. Yet this equality would be the immediate place of the thing.

"When what surrounds [l'enveloppe], then, is not separate from the thing, but is in continuity with it, the thing is said to be in what surrounds it, not in the sense of in place, but as a part in a whole" (211a; p. 359).

Can this be understood of the *body* and in its relation to the *skin*? In a different way from the *fetus* in its relation with the first enveloping membranes and the umbilical cord. Even though the fetus is a continuum with the body it is in, even though it passes from a certain kind of continuity to another through the mediation of fluids: blood, milk. . . . The fetus has a peculiar status which can mean that the child fantasizes itself as a part of that whole that is the mother's body. And it is true that he be- longs to that body and is fed by that body until he comes into the world. That part of the whole, of a whole, that the fetus partially is will affect the fantasy of the penis also. Whence the fantasies of castration, perhaps? If the penis did not present itself in fantasy as forming a part of another whole, it would not be imagined as separate from the whole to which it "belongs." Obviously, the movement of the penis is partially linked to another whole. Is it double? For the self and for the other. But why is the temporary end of a certain movement, or its suspension, called castration or separation of a body unless man desires to become once more part of a matrical body? Which is impossible. On the other hand, there are times when that relation of places in the sexual act gives rise to a transgression of the envelope, to a porousness, a perception of the other, a fluidity. And so it becomes possible to imagine that generation of a certain kind might occur by crossing membranes and sharing humors with the other.

"But when the thing is separate and in contact, it is primarily in the inner surface of the surrounding body, and this surface is neither a part of what is in it nor yet greater than its extension, but equal to it; for the extremities of things which touch are coincident.

"Further, if one body is in continuity with another, it is not moved in that but with that. On the other hand it is moved in that if it is separate. It makes no difference whether what contains is moved or not" (211a; p. 359).

When the envelope in separate and simply in contact, the body is immediately inside the outermost surface of the envelope, which neither forms a part of its contents nor is bigger than the interval of extension of the body, but equal to it; for the extremities of the things in contact are joined.

Once again, the whole issue of the fetus's relation to place (or of the point to the boundary limiting its growth?) and of the male sex (organ) to the female sex (organ) is bound up with this problematic of how the body fits the envelope. Fitting and separate—is this the horizon for the meeting of the sexes in its different dimensions? With reversals of enve- lopes and envelopings almost to infinity?

Or else:

—Is it possible here to think of the genetic (?) capital received and of the skin, of the skins joined to this genetic capital. "My" skin, in theory, corresponds to my growth.

—In gestation, there will always be a gap, an interval between the body that is in the envelope and the envelope itself which will more or less fit that body, and the amniotic fluid which separates the two.

—The envelope as here defined can also be related to some "ideal" sexual act. Since the elasticity of the tissues allows an approach to that ideal. (But there are transmutations, sublimations, and transfers in the physiology of the envelopes with endless growing and unfolding . . .).

What is place? Shape? Matter? Interval between the two? Extremities? *"There are just four things of which place must be one"* (211b; pp. 359–60). Two of these it obviously cannot be:

—*Place is not form.* By the property it has of surrounding, of being an envelope, form appears to be place: the boundaries of what surrounds and what is surrounded are the same. In actual fact, these are two boundaries but not of the same being. Form is the boundary of the thing; the place, the boundary of the surrounding body.

—*Place is not the interval* (*"some sort of extension between the extremities"*). Whereas the container remains, that which is contained changes. The interval which is intermediary *between the boundaries* appears to be something insofar as it is independent of the displaced body. This is not so, but it happens *in the place of one body or other*, provided it be one of those bodies who can move and whose nature it is to enter into contact.

The change of the body and the modification of the interval represent an important issue in the economy of desire. The *locomotion toward* and *reduction in interval* are the movements of desire (even by expansion-retraction). The greater the desire, the greater the tendency to overcome the interval while at the same time retaining it. An interval that might perhaps be occupied by the transformed body? Overcoming the interval is the aim of desire, the cause of locomotion. The interval approaches zero when skins come into contact. It goes beyond zero when a passage occurs to the mucous. Or a transgression of touch through the skin. Given that the problem of desire is to suppress the interval without suppressing the other. Since desire can eat up place, either by regressing into the other on the intrauterine model or annihilating the existence of the other in one way or another. If desire is to subsist, a double place is necessary, a double envelope. Or else God as subtending the interval, pushing the interval toward and into infinity. The irreducible. Opening up the universe and all beyond it. In this sense, the interval would produce place.

"*The extension between the extremities is thought to be something, because what is contained and separate may often be changed while the container [l'enveloppe] remains the same (as water may be poured from a vessel)—the assumption being that the extension [l'intervalle] is something over and above the body displaced. But there is no such extension. One of the bodies which change places and are naturally capable of being in contact with the container falls in—whichever it may chance to be*"(211b; p. 360).

Does sexuality encounter that aporia or that question in which it competes with the question of God?

Certainly, apart from the fact that, in the eroticism of the different senses or thresholds of the body, the interval remains in play as place, or the possibility of place, it is particularly insistent with regard to the *lips* (and perhaps the eyelids?). And to everything in the female sex which figures the abyss. Oscillations between the infinitely small and the infinitely large?

The womb, for its part, would figure rather as place. Though of course what unfolds in the womb unfolds in function of an interval, a cord, that is never done away with. Whence perhaps the infinite nostalgia for that first home? The interval cannot be done away with.[5]

"*. . . all the portions of the two together will play the same part in the whole which was previously played by all the water in the vessel; at the same time the place too will be undergoing change; so that there will be another place which is the place of the place, and many places will be coincident. There is not a different place of the part, in which it is moved, when the whole vessel changes its place: it is always the same: for it is in the place where they are that the air and the water (or the parts of the water) succeed each other, not in that place* *in which they come to be, which is part of the place which is the place of the whole world [du ciel entier]"* (211b; p. 360).

The elements fill the universe. They can potentially be transformed one into another, but they always fill the whole up equally. The universe is conceived as a closed vessel, the receptacle for all the elements.

"The matter, too, might seem to be place, at least if we consider it in what is at rest and is thus separate but in continuity. For just as in change of quality there is something which was formerly black and is now white, or formerly soft and now hard—this is just why we say that the matter exists—so place, because it presents a similar phenomenon, is thought to exist—only in the one case we say so because what was air is now water, in the other because where air formerly was there is now water" (211b; p. 360).

The proof of place is thus seen to lie in the transformation of elements in place.

Place necessarily is *"the boundary of the containing body [corps enveloppant] at which it is in contact with the contained body [corps enveloppé]. (By the contained body is meant what can be moved by way of locomotion)"* (212a; p. 361).

The boundary of the "containing body" can be understood of the womb. If it has no outside, desire can go on to infinity. Is this the way with the desire for God that does not know the outside of the universe?

But sexual desire that goes toward the womb and no longer returns to it also goes toward infinity since it never touches the boundary of the "containing body." Instead of perceiving the body that contains it *hic et nunc,* it goes toward another container. Instead of moving across the actual container in the direction of the other through porosity, it remains nostalgic for another home.

So there is never any idea that the boundary of the containing body might be the skin, while passing through the mucous membranes and through the body and the flesh. The boundary of the containing body might be the bodily identity of woman, reborn and touched anew by inner communion, and not destroyed by nostalgia for a regression in utero. The dissociation of love and desire would, in this case, have little meaning, nor would the sexual have an amoral, or nonethical, character. On the contrary, the sexual *act* would turn into the act whereby the other gives new form, birth, incarnation to the self. Instead of implying the downfall of the body, it takes part in the body's renaissance. And there is no other equivalent act, in this sense. Most divine of acts. Whereby man makes woman feel her body as place. Not only her vagina and her womb but her body. He places her within her body and within a macrocosm, releasing her from her potential adherence to the cosmic through her participation in a microsociety.

As man re-creates woman from outside, from inside-outside, he re-places himself outside, as an actor outside, a creator outside. By actively putting himself outside, he re-sculpts a body for himself. By using a tool? He reconstructs his own body as a result of engendering the body of the other. By using his hand, his penis—which is not merely a tool of pleasure, but a truly useful tool of alliance, incarnation, creation.

Woman, insofar as she is a container, is never a closed one. Place is never closed. The boundaries touch against one another while still remaining open. And can they do so without necessarily touching the boundaries of the body contained? There are two touches between boundaries; and these are not the same: the touch of one's body at the threshold; the touch of the contained other. There is also the internal touch of the body of the child, with mother and child being separated by one envelope or several. Within this container the child moves. Is it possible to speak of locomotion? It seems not. Where would the child move to? Toward the place that nourishes him, toward the exit that leads from one place to another place? And again toward that movement of growth within the place?

"Hence the place of a thing is the innermost motionless boundary of what contains it" (212a; p. 361).

❧

"If then a body has another body outside it and containing it [qui l'enveloppe], it is in place, and if not, not" (212a, 5; p. 361).

It seems that a fetus would be in a place. And man's penis for as long as it is inside the woman. Woman is in the house, but this is not the same type of place as a living bodily site. On the other hand, place, in her, is in place, not only as organs but as vessel or receptacle. It is place twice over: as mother and as woman.

"That is why, even if there were to be water which had not a container, the parts of it will be moved" (212a, 5; p. 361).

A certain representation of feminine jouissance corresponds to this water flowing without a container. A doubling, sought after by man, of a female *placelessness*. She is assigned to be place without occupying a place. Through her, place would be set up for man's use but not hers. Her jouissance is meant to "resemble" the flow of whatever is in the place that she is when she contains, contains herself. "Wine," perhaps, that man might spill out in the sexual act? Elixir of ambrosia, and of place itself.

Is there some jouissance other than that of place? Is this not the jouissance which goes from the most elementary to the most subtle? From in utero to heaven, from earth to heaven, from hell to heaven, and so on. And isn't food a matter of introducing something into a place, and of being able to keep it in, or not? The body and foods play roles that escape the "subject." For the most part.

Reduction to fluidity would seem, then, to be the nonprocreative aspect of female jouissance. Separation of place from that which it contained? Of place. Separation of the container from its contents so that it/he/she is left empty? For the other. As well as for that other "solid": the child. Division of woman into two: on the one hand, she is habitually devalued in relation to the fluid; on the other hand, she is valued in relation to the solid. But this valuation process is ambiguous as far as she is concerned since it deprives her of the subtlest part of herself: place as such, the place she contains, invisibly. And which, in most cases, is diffused without being noticed? Or is diffused profanely. Even unconsciously and involuntarily.

This place, the production of intimacy, is in some manner a transmutation of earth into heaven, here and now. Providing she remembers? An alchemist of the sexual and one who tries to keep the sexual away from repetition, degradation. Attempts to keep it and sublimate it. *Between.* In the interval of time, of times. Weaving the veil of time, the fabric of time, time with space, time in space. Between past and future, future and past, place in place. Invisible. Its vessel? Its container? The soul of the soul?

A second container, imperceptible and yet there, offered up to man in the sexual relation. How fitting if the container were offered back to her in a sort of irradiation outside of her "grace" from within. She would be re-contained with place in place. Thanks to her partner. A kind of permanent assumption, perhaps? Or else the place she has woven in her womb would return to her as place of her conception? She would be re-contained by that weaving of space-time that she has secretly conceived.

Nothing more spiritual, in this regard, than female sexuality. Always working to produce a place of transcendence for the sensible, which can become a destructive net, or else find itself, remain, in endless becoming. Accompanying cosmic time. Between man's time and the time of the universe. Still faithful to the one and seeking to find a rhythm in the other, perhaps?

Unfortunately, the two are often cut apart. Those two rhythms are not only no longer harmonious but are cut off from one another. Does this produce false gods and false hells? To avoid this, an alchemy of female desire is needed.

"The parts of it will be moved (for one part is contained in another) while the whole will be moved in one sense, but not in another" (212a, 5; p. 361).

Do the parts of the whole envelop one another mutually? Is there no part that destroys another? Do the parts of the body contain one another mutually? Is there no part that destroys another? In love, it would be fitting if the parts of the whole—the union of man and woman— enveloped one another *mutually* and did not destroy one another's envelopes. How fitting if the two-way journeys from the one to the other became places for enveloping. If the portions of place traversed in order to move away and then back were to become space-times that mutually recovered and were not eliminated, annihilated, used up to provide fuel for other kinds of locomotion, or transformed into voids, separations, rather than bridges. Between the one and the other, there should be mutual enveloping in movement. For the one and the other move around within a whole. And often the one and the other destroy the place of the other, believing in this way to have the whole; but they possess or con- struct only an illusory whole and destroy the meeting and the interval (of attraction) between the two. The world is destroyed in its essential symbol: the copula of the sex act. It is opened up to the abyss and not to welcome generation, the search for creation.

"For as a whole it does not simultaneously change its place, though it will be moved in a circle: for this place is the place of its parts. And some things are moved, not up and down, but in a circle; others up and down, such things namely as admit of condensation and rarefaction" (212b, 5; p. 361).

The whole, in fact, does not change place but moves in a circle. The universe turns round and round? Moves around? And the love between man and woman likewise, had it not been brutally cut into two (see Plato, *Symposium*). According to that story, man and woman were once joined together in such a way that they rolled around, locked in embrace. Then they were split apart, but endlessly each seeks to find the lost half and embrace once more. Unless the one or the other claims to be the whole? And constructs his world into a closed circle. Total? Closed to the other. And convinced that there is no access to outside except by opening up a wound. Having no part in the construction of love, or of beauty, or the world.

Could it be that anything that moves in a circle moves in relation to another? In two directions? With a place of attraction. A place of place. Where bodies embrace? Both in and not in the same place: with the one being in the other that contains. But, by wishing to give, he or she constitutes the other as receptacle? Unless he refuses. (Cf. Nietzsche, "On the Great Longing," in *Thus Spoke Zarathustra:* "I gave you all," but "which of us has to be thankful? Should not the giver be thankful that the receiver received," formed himself into a *place.* "Oh my soul, I gave you all; I thank you for having received," for having become place.)[6]

Does man become place in order to receive and because he has received female jouissance? How? Does woman become place because she has received male jouissance? How? How does one make the transition here from physics to metaphysics? From the physical receptacle for the penis to the enveloping of a receptacle that is less tangible or visible, but which makes place?

Notes

1. Page references following the quotations from Aristotle, *Physics* IV, 1–5, are to *The Complete Works of Aristotle: The Revised Oxford Translation*, ed. Jonathan Barnes, trans. R. P. Hardie and R. K. Gaye (Oxford: Oxford University press, 1987), 1:354–62.

2. (The French translations of Aristotle cited by Irigaray use different forms of the world "envelope," whereas the English translations refer to "container." Since "envelope" has been an important word in Irigaray's vocabulary since *Speculum of the Other Woman*, this translation frequently doubles "container" and "envelope" in order to link the text with the cited passages from Aristotle and with Irigaray's earlier writings.—Trans.)

3. (In the French Budé edition used by Irigaray, this phrase is rendered as "les idées et les nombres."—Trans.)

4. (In the French Budé edition used by Irigaray, this phrase is rendered as "l'enveloppe première."—Trans.)

5. See Luce Irigaray, *La Croyance même* (Paris: Galilée, 1983). (Irigaray also includes this essay in *Sexes and Genealogies*, trans. Gillian C. Gill [New York: Columbia University Press, 1993]—Trans.)

6. Friedrich Nietzsche, *Thus Spoke Zarathustra*, trans. Walter Kaufmann in *The Portable Nietzsche* (New York: Viking, 1964), 333. (Irigaray's text combines exact citation with paraphrase.—Trans.)

3

On Irigaray on Aristotle[1]

Cynthia A. Freeland

By now, of course, feminists have done a lot of mining in the field of Aristotle studies, turning up real gems of sexism.[2] Aristotle is right up there with certain other figures like Nietzsche and Schopenhauer as bad patriarchs of philosophy. Feminists have rightly criticized certain of his views in biology and political theory. However, they have not pushed this project as deeply as possible so as to explore theories of gender in his metaphysics and science. Many traditional approaches in feminist history of philosophy are piecemeal and ameliorative. The writings of French feminist philosopher Luce Irigaray are interesting to me because she addresses many canonical figures in the history of philosophy with an approach that is more comprehensive, radical, and constructive. In her essay, "Place, Interval: A Reading of Aristotle, *Physics* IV," from her book

An Ethics of Sexual Difference, she analyzes a section of Aristotelian philosophy, his *Physics*, that does not seem on the face of it to have much to
do with gender or sexism. She also makes the deep and intriguing claim
that we need to study the history of philosophy seriously in order to
launch ourselves on the path toward real alternatives, introducing a new
and liberatory ethics and politics.

Irigaray's essay will be astonishing to the Aristotle scholar who reads it
unaware of Irigaray's earlier writings.[3] Amid passages that quote from
Aristotle's abstract discussion of place, the reader is plunged into a vortex
of sublimation, sexuality, wombs, female sex organs, fetal positions, and
love. Skins commune, and porous bodies share humours. It may seem
unclear whether one is reading Aristotle scholarship, a primitive biology
text, or an erotic novel. I offer a quotation from Irigaray's essay to convey
the flavor of her writing:

> In love, it would be fitting if the parts of the whole—the union of
> man and woman—enveloped one another *mutually* and did not
> destroy one another's envelopes. How fitting if the two-way jour-
> neys from the one to the other became places for enveloping If
> the portions of place traversed in order to move away and then
> back were to become space-times that mutually recovered and
> were not eliminated, annihilated, used up to provide fuel for other
> kinds of locomotion, or transformed into voids, separations, rather
> than bridges. (57)

Irigaray is a poetic, metaphorical, lyrical writer who represents a radical
feminist approach to re-reading the canonical texts of the mostly male
tradition of western philosophy. She clearly has scholarly tools: trained
as a philosopher, linguist, and psychoanalyst, she reads Greek, refers in
her works to other philosophers and texts, and quotes at length from the
relevant chapters of *Physics* IV. Yet Irigaray works against these scholarly
tools in her poetic method.[4] Reading her then is far different from reading
the usual commentators on the *Physics*. Clearly, style is paramount to
Irigaray's method of reading. An *Ethics of Sexual Difference* also offers well-
informed but very idiosyncratic readings of five other figures from the past
to the present of philosophy: Plato, Descartes, Spinoza, Merleau-Ponty,
and Levinas. Similarly, her earlier *Speculum of the Other Woman* also focused an unusual lens on the Western canon, on philosophers from Plato
to Kant and Hegel.[5] Though Irigaray is both knowledgeable about and

eager to explore the history of philosophy, her project is not a typical project of scholarly interpretation. Nor is she doing with Aristotle what feminists usually do.

Irigaray makes her broad ethico-political aim clear in writing on Aristotle's theory of place near the beginning of *An Ethics of Sexual Difference*:

> We must, therefore, reconsider the whole question of our conception of place, both in order to move on to another age of difference (each age of thought corresponds to a particular time of meditation on difference), and in order to construct an ethics of the passions. We need to change the relations between form, matter, interval, and limit, an issue that has never been considered in a way that allows for a relationship between two loving subjects of different sexes. (11–12).

A number of questions come to mind in reading this passage. What is an age of difference? Why do we need to reconsider place, form, matter, interval, and limit to construct an ethics of the passions? And what is meant by an ethics of the passions? The phrase sounds antique, reminiscent of Descartes or Spinoza. Isn't it odd to see Irigaray claiming that our goal is to allow for the relationship between two loving subjects of different sexes—given that in her notorious "This Sex Which Is Not One," she articulated the view that heterosexual sex can only be a kind of violation and disruption of a woman's bodily integrity, understood in terms of "lips" that are self-touching?[6]

These questions lead to other larger questions about the merits of Irigaray's feminist philosophical project. She is a very controversial figure who has provoked serious and sometimes harsh critique for her alleged elitism, essentialism, utopianism, biological reductionism, scientism, and/or lingering modernism.[7] Can her readings of the history of philosophy escape these criticisms, and can they prove useful for feminism as we move into the twenty-first century?

To answer these questions, my plan is as follows. First, I shall provide an overview of *Physics* IV, 1–5, as seen by more traditional scholars, and contrast Irigaray's approach. Second, I describe Irigaray's methodology. I argue that she moves between a negative, somewhat moderate project that says that Aristotle's text on place is problematic because it utilizes *gendered concepts*, and a positive, and more radical, project of uncovering the feminine—which she says is missing in the history of Western thought—and restoring it. In the third section, which focuses on the details of Irigaray's reading of Aristotle, I describe two weak or mistaken points she makes and three strong claims. She really is saying something that sounds odd: that Aristotle's physics, with all its importance in Western thought, is gendered male. It is exciting and controversial to assert something like this, and I shall explore what such a claim means. Irigaray's goals include feminist science critique, but they go beyond this and involve the desire to ground an alternative feminist ethics and politics. I want to consider these broader aims and assess Irigaray's view that a radical approach to philosophical texts like Aristotle's can promote a liberatory politics, and so my concluding comments will focus on her contributions to feminist science critique, ethics, and the history of philosophy.

Aristotle's Text: An Overview

In the revised Oxford translation, the first five chapters of *Physics* Delta are short, less than nine pages long. Irigaray's essay is also fairly short. She follows the order of Aristotle's exposition in her own essay and quotes from numerous passages, adding her own commentary and reflections.

Chapters 1–5 of Aristotle's *Physics IV* are not easy ones in themselves. They address abstract issues about how to define place in relation to bodies, as well as Zeno's notorious puzzles that involve infinite regresses—about whether, say, place must have a place. The discussion is complex and may occur in terms that are alien to us, but we need at least some overview of it in order to understand Irigaray's critique.

Aristotle lays out four possible options for defining place: form or shape (*morphē*); matter (*hulē*); extension or interval between extremes (*diastema ti to metaxu ton eschaton*); or the extremes or limits (*ta eschata*). He argues against the first three and concludes that place must be defined in terms of the fourth, the limits or extremes. So he defines place (at 212a5–6) as "the limit of the surrounding body, at which it is in contact with that which is surrounded." A second definition is proposed at 212a20–21; place is "the first unchangeable limit of that which surrounds."

To picture Aristotle's options, I shall give an example.[8] Imagine a snowglobe that I saw on holiday in Sydney, Australia, containing a miniature version of the Sydney Opera House. Now, what is the *place* of the opera house in the snowglobe? It is not the *form* of the opera house—that distinctive, complex, yet recognizable winged-sail shape. The form of a thing is what surrounds the thing, so it seems like place, but Aristotle maintains that place must be separable from a body, and its form is not. That is, the form is more intrinsic and inseparable from the opera house than is its place, since it can change its place but not its form. For similar reasons, place cannot be the *matter* of the opera house; matter also is not separable from a thing, as place should be.

Third, he denies that place is the *extension* of the opera house; i.e., the space between its intervals. By this Aristotle has in mind a kind of vacant spatial bubble in the middle of the snowglobe, just waiting to be filled by the opera house. This will not do because he does not think any such extension-like entity can be defined apart from a body or in terms of its occupation by some merely potential body or series of bodies. What remains, then, is the fourth candidate: place is the "limits" of the opera house, in the sense of the *innermost edge of whatever it is that contains the opera house*. We have to understand this as the borders ("limits") at which the watery stuff of the snowglobe meets all the curves and shapes of the opera house within it.

Aristotle's inquiry here is one of foundational philosophical analysis. G. E. L. Owen has argued that these chapters from the *Physics* should not really be considered "science" but rather philosophy.[9] I think this is a point Irigaray might agree with. That is, this is *not* an instance of the empirical *scientific* method, but instead a *conceptual* or philosophical inquiry utilizing the *dialectical* method. Many questions raised about this text in other scholarly discussions are historical.[10] How is Aristotle indebted to his predecessors? Does he describe their views adequately and accurately? Does he overcome their problems? Other questions are more philosophical. What are Aristotle's main candidates for answering the question, What is place? How does his answer here compare to his analysis of place in the *Categories*?[11] What exactly is the "real" definition of place? What are Aristotle's data, and how does his theoretical explanation account for these data? How good a theory of place does Aristotle provide, in terms of either his own context, or of subsequent philosophical and scientific thinking? Henry Mendell argues Aristotle failed to develop a scientific or modern conception of space, and Edward Hussey thinks that even Plato's receptacle theory is more modern and Einsteinian than Aristotelian place.[12]

In sum, in the history of philosophy we are trained to ask and answer only certain questions. We read Aristotle for historical information, and assess his completeness, coherence, consistency, scientific, and philosophical value. Usually we also look at a sample text like this one as part of a larger treatise, with connections to the rest of that treatise, to topics like the void and time, and also across the corpus (e.g., to the analysis of natural places in *De Caelo* or of natural movements in *Generation and Corruption*).

Instead of those questions, here are the kinds of questions Irigaray asks: What can Aristotle say about amorphous fluid entities like blood, semen, mucous, and milk? As Tina Chanter puts it, "Why does the protective membrane so vital to the process of birth, or the blood and milk that are essential to the fetus and the infant, have no place in a consideration of bodily places and transitions?"[13] What is the place of the penis—in the vagina-sheath? What is the place of the fetus? What place does the masculine offer to attract the feminine? What is the woman's own place, if she is only the place for the child or the man? Can we provide an account of place to ground loving relationships between differently sexed subjects?

By the standards of analytic history of philosophy, Irigaray breaks the rules and is a terrible scholar. She does quote extensively from Aristotle, and she treats parts of the text in order, but her quoting is idiosyncratic and selective, and she takes passages out of context. But of course, she is not trying to meet these standards or rules. Irigaray reads Aristotle's account for its impact on a pervasive and continuing, grounding conception of gendered, sexually distinct subjects. Or, as Chanter (*Ethics of Eros*) explains, "She is asking what it has meant, philosophically, to ground certain phenomena on others, who has been responsible for the hierarchies that are promulgated in such a process, and who has been excluded by such systematic thinking" (150); and she "sees in Aristotle's text the obliteration of sexual difference" (151).

Overview of Irigaray

Why should a feminist choose to address in particular Aristotle's *Physics*, with all its seemingly abstract discussions of such gender-free notions as place, time, motion, causation, the Prime Mover, and so forth? Does Irigaray really want to say that physics is "male"? This sounds radical and will immediately provoke suspicion. In feminist philosophy of science, there have been well-based criticisms of male bias in the formulation of some sciences, mainly human and biological sciences. But physics seems impregnable, as do other "pure" philosophical concepts that Irigaray criticizes: language, truth, knowledge. What can be meant by saying that any of these universal, objective things is male, or omits the feminine?[14]

A start on this can be made by turning to some other recent feminist critiques of the history of science or philosophy that focus on a search for hidden gendered concepts. The notion of a "gendered concept" has been advanced by feminists writing about the maleness of ethics and aesthetics. Carolyn Korsmeyer explains as follows: "[Gendered concepts are] concepts that, lacking any obvious reference to males or females, or to masculinity and femininity, nevertheless are formulated in such a way that their neutral quality and universal applicability are questionable."[15] For example, in aesthetics, the notion of the sublime is a gendered concept because of its association with things that are hard, rough, jagged, and awe-inspiring, including not just mountain peaks but military heroes.[16]

Now, feminists can with some plausibility point out that there are important gendered concepts in Aristotle. A pair of gendered concepts lie at the heart of his metaphysics, namely, form and matter.[17] Though these concepts seem like abstract components of a neutral reality, they bear strong gender associations. Form is active, superior, and intelligible; in humans it is associated with rationality. Matter is passive, chaotic, inferior, muddied, and unintelligible. Plato directly associates matter with the womb or uterus. And in the *Physics* Aristotle says that matter yearns for form, as the female for the male and the ugly for the beautiful (I,9,192a20–23). Irigaray took this remark of his as an epigraph in an earlier essay on Aristotle ("How to Conceive (of) a Girl").[18]

Irigaray's feminist approach involves an effort to show that many more philosophical concepts are in fact gendered than one might normally assume. She says:

> [I]t is indeed precisely philosophical discourse that we have to challenge, and disrupt, inasmuch as this discourse sets forth the law for all others, inasmuch as it constitutes the discourse on discourse. . . . Thus we have had to go back to it in order to try to find out what accounts for the power of its systematicity, the force of its cohesion, the resourcefulness of its strategies, the general

applicability of its law and its value. That is, its position of mastery and of potential reappropriation of the various productions
of history.[19]

Irigaray wants to go beyond the negative aim of demonstrating that
philosophy has omitted the feminine; she also has the positive aim of
creating new concepts and a language that will begin to create the feminine or an intellectual space for it. She refers to this as grounding a new
conception of sexual difference. But to do this creating, she somehow
needs to speak the feminine. She has to use a language or set of tools to
demonstrate those very tools' inadequacy. Irigaray's aim sounds paradoxical. However, to use language to show language's inadequacy is actually
a common philosophical strategy shared by such other diverse thinkers
in the Western tradition as Heraclitus, Nietzsche, the early Wittgenstein,
Heidegger, and Derrida.

Where she is different is focusing specifically on gender. Irigaray feels
that the feminine has been omitted in all Western discourse except for
mystical writings like Saint Teresa's. Referring to mystical discourse, she
writes, "This is the only place in the history of the West in which woman
speaks and acts so publicly."[20] Irigaray seeks to learn not only from these
mystics but also from the schizophrenics whose distorted language production she studied as a linguist.[21] Her experiments with language evoke
parallels with Derrida, though she denies that she is using deconstruction.
Even so, Irigaray's method does, like Derrida's, involve a sort of blueprint
or guide to the interrogation of philosophical texts. She advocates many
strategies aimed at showing the marginalization of the feminine.[22] These
include excess, laughter, mimicry, and the psychoanalytic reading of si-
lences and repressions.[23] She also attempts to create a nonlinear style of
reading and writing and to disrupt dichotomies. Despite Irigaray's training as a psychoanalyst, her readings are not reductively psychoanalytic in
nature. She has written very critically on both Freud and Lacan, and I
think that her use of psychoanalytic concepts, such as castration or desire, should often be read as quotational or ironic.[24]

Irigaray is a "difference feminist" who thinks that the feminine must
be granted its own "specificity" in relation to language (153) so that we
can "secure a place for the feminine within sexual difference" (159).[25]
This is not a question of elaborating another "concept": "There is no
question of another *concept* of femininity. To claim that the feminine can
be expressed in the form of a concept is to allow oneself to be caught up

again in a system of 'masculine' representations, in which women are trapped in a system of meaning which serves the auto-affection of the (masculine) subject."[26]

When a questioner complains about not knowing what "masculine discourse" means, she replies "Of course not, since there is no other" (140). Philosophical mastery can't be approached head-on (150), although women are tempted to do so, to demonstrate that we too can belong, or "go back inside the philosopher's house." However, "it [i]s necessary to deploy other languages" (151), and to "destroy with nuptial tools, have a fling with the philosophers" (150). This language of violence reappears in other guises: she speaks of a disruptive excess, and also of "jamming the machinery": "In other words, the issue is not one of elaborating a new theory of which woman would be the subject or the object, but of jamming the theoretical machinery itself, of suspending its pretension to the production of a truth and of a meaning that are excessively univocal. Which presupposes that women do not aspire simply to be men's equals in knowledge."[27]

Irigaray illustrated her recommended textual approach with examples of readings in her earlier *Speculum of the Other Woman*. Much of the book turns its critical lens on Freud and Lacan, but roughly half is devoted to historical figures of philosophy. And more than a fourth of it, entitled "Plato's Hystera," develops a complex deconstructive reading of Plato's analogy of the Cave in the *Republic*, which she also links to his analysis of the receptacle in the *Timaeus*.[28] Certain themes begin to emerge, such as Plato's use of negative metaphors to describe female sexuality and bodily functioning, and his assignment to the male of a kind of completeness and independence in generating philosophical subjects.

> It is God-the-Father who created the heaven, and the stars, and these convert you to his idea. To his image. This world is "true" only insofar as it is engendered by Him alone, and related to Him alone. This is fairly evidently the case for everything that dominates and stands above the earth, treading her under foot, under its erection. . . . Engendering the real is the father's task, engendering the fictive is the task of the mother—that "receptacle" for turning out more or less good copies of reality.[29]

Speculum includes much less on Aristotle than on Plato, just the short article "How to Conceive (of) a Girl," in which she focuses on the *Gen-*

eration of Animals and associates its problems in addressing female contributions to reproduction with his problems in conceptualizing prime matter.[30] She points out that according to Aristotle, woman's whole existence is an accident of reproduction, a kind of genetic montrosity (167). So she asks, "What is woman's form—mere privation?" (165). If seen as all gaps and fissures, woman will not be recognized as having any being. She is "neither one nor the other. . . . Thus, this 'lack of qualities' that-makes the female truly female ensures that the male can achieve his qualifications. In order to take full possession of himself, man will need to take over not only the potentiality and potency, but also the place, and all the little chinks (re)produced in his ceaseless drive to transform anything different and still self-defining into his own likeness" (165–6). Other essays in *Speculum* also offer hints of what is to come in *An Ethics of Sexual Difference*. Among these is "Volume—Fluidity," which describes men as seeking firm foundations and solid ground, and women as never closing up into a volume.[31]

Tina Chanter explains that Irigaray's re-reading of Aristotle on place is a deliberate echoing and revision of Heidegger's re-reading of Aristotle on time in *Being and Time* and later works; and it is also indebted to Derrida's commentary on Aristotle on time, "*Ousia* and *Grammē*."[32] Setting Derrida aside, I shall just briefly review what Chanter says is relevant about Heidegger. Heidegger interrogated the fundamental concepts of time (in *Being and Time* and *Basic problems of Phenomenology*) as part of his search for the "meaning of being." He studied time as a basic philosophical category that structures a subject's experience of the world. Heidegger also showed considerable interest in his later works in the subject's relations to space and location, or spatiality. For example, in "Building Dwelling Thinking" he wrote," space is not something that faces man. It is neither an external object nor an inner experience. It is not that there are men, and over and above them space."[33] Without going into details of Heidegger exegesis, I note that his work does set a precedent for what might otherwise appear quite strange in Irigaray's essay: that she should study Aristotle's views on place or physical space in order to get at certain key points about the construction of subjects.[34] Just how gender, or *sexually distinct* subjects, will come into play remains to be seen. As a prelude, we can note that whereas Irigaray is interested in the *interiority* of bodily experience of our own spaces, Heidegger, despite what he says (just quoted), still seems to situate humans in an *external* space or in an imaginative occupation of such space: "Spaces, and with them space as such—

'space'—are always provided for already within the stay of mortals. Spaces open up by the fact that they are let into the dwelling of man. To say that mortals *are* is to say that *in dwelling* they persist through spaces by virtue of their stay among things and locations."[35]

Key Points in Irigaray

Irigaray's discussion is dense and difficult. I am going to try to represent (= re-present) what she is doing by breaking it down, as best I can, into five distinct points or themes. Two of these seem mistaken, and I shall say why at the start. However, the other three seem very intriguing. Before beginning, I reiterate the importance of Irigaray's style. I am trying to translate things out of her style into more straightforward language. But, as with any philosopher who chooses a distinctive style, from Plato and Heraclitus up to Wittgenstein and Derrida, this may involve a misrepresentation—something she herself seems to warn the reader about:

> Gestures made in accordance with a style do not constitute a formal model. Even if fashion does try to take it over, even if imitation does caricature it or use part of its content, a style remains irreducible. It cannot be reduced to a grid that can be transposed or imposed elsewhere. A style resists coding, summarizing, encrypting, pigeon-holing in differently programmed machines.[36]

Irigary's style in this essay encompasses the general strategies I mentioned earlier: laughter, mimicry, excess, teasing or flirting, questioning, and finally, criticizing. Excess shows up in her exaggerated satire and also in her erotic, even occasionally lubricious, writing about skins, sculpting, penis-tools, mucous, and intercourse. To translate her style into specific concrete points may also be problematic because in many cases she is questioning or suggesting rather than arguing or stating something. Much of what I represent as criticism really takes the form of satire or ridicule, or gentle poking of fun.[37] Finally, Irigaray's style involves another strategy very common in philosophy: to scrutinize something under a philosophical lens in a way that defamiliarizes it to us. Here she is doing this to our ordinary notions of sexual intercourse and maternity. (Scrutinizing with another lens is part of what is implied in the selection of the title of

Speculum for her earlier book, as in her frequent discussions of mirrors.) This is a project continuous with other philosophers' similar aims—such as Socrates' attempts to defamiliarize the Athenian accepted notions of virtue, Augustine's puzzlement about time, Descartes's meditations on wax, Marx's treatment of the mysteries of the table-become-commodity, and so forth.

Irigaray has acknowledged and written about the difficulty of her own style, and what she says about this is interesting and can serve us as an admonition:

> Hence the resistance. What is it all about? What exactly is she saying? What is its, already given, meaning? The answers to these questions are not forthcoming, especially out of context, which sometimes leads to the objection that the thought is esoteric. But any text is esoteric, not because it conceals a secret, but because it constitutes the secret, the not-yet-revealed or the never-exhaustively-revealable. The only reply that can be given to the question of the meaning of the text is: read, perceive, feel. . . . *Who are you?* would be a more pertinent question, provided that it does not collapse into a demand for an identity card and an autobiographical anecdote. The answer would be: *and who are you? Can we meet? Talk? Love? Create something together? Thanks to which milieu?*[38]

I turn now to Irigaray's text and my recounting of its themes. First, here are the two points she makes that I consider weak.

1. Aristotle's conception of place and the cosmic order is limited because it is up-down and not spherical. Aristotle's assumption that every body has "above" and "below" is an external and objective, rather than internal and subjective, conception of place. She suggests that an alternative view of place or space would focus instead on "in and out" or "expansion/contraction." Pregnancy and sexual intercourse offer paradigms that problematize the notion of a body as an inviolate space located in a place that is "outside," and raise interesting questions about whether indeed two bodies can be in one place at the same time. She writes,

> Up and down are properties of all places. Astonishingly there is no suggestion of a *spherical* place where no clear-cut distinction between up and down would obtain. Notwithstanding, sexuality

partakes in the up and down, in rising and falling. Bodies in this context are sometimes lighter, sometimes heavier, sometimes warmer, sometimes colder, and so on. But bodies also face the issue of fitting one inside the other, without thereby altering the other dimensions. Can this be understood as the constitution, together, of a spherical or almost spherical form? (50)

The allusion to Aristophanes' fabled spherical beings is deliberate here, since she quotes from his story in Plato's *Symposium* later in her text, and concludes with some allusions to Aristotle's own generalization of his account of place to the cosmic order (quoting from 212a34–b3). Again this calls up for her images of the sphericality of the world order, of a universe turning round and round, reminiscent of Aristophanes' tale of the initial man and woman locked together in their embrace. Irigaray sees a split as occurring when one half of the initial totality (the male half) claimed to be the whole, "and constructs his world into a closed circle" (58).

The problem with this critique is that Aristotle does actually hold a picture of spherical place or space in the cosmos.[39] In a spherical cosmos there is, to be sure, an absolute up and down, conceived of as, respectively, outside and center.[40] But this kind of relative up and down seems similar to what Irigaray is after, and is not clearly objective rather than subjective. Aristotle is willing to relativize up and down to subjects at least in the sense that what is down for plants, their roots, corresponds to what is up for persons, our mouths.[41] These views are stated in other texts and not in the *Physics*, but nevertheless they mitigate her criticisms.

2. Next, Irigary criticizes Aristotle because he does not sufficiently conceptualize the place of growing things, most notably, of the fetus growing within the maternal body. His axioms about place assert, for example, that place is what contains the thing, and that it is neither greater nor less than the thing. She remarks "It is hard not to think of the membranes enveloping the fetus" (49). She is suggesting that place considered as container or envelope must in some cases be constantly shifting.

Again, the problem with this criticism is that Aristotle does recognize that growth is a very complex and difficult intellectual problem, which he addresses at fairly great length in I, 5 of the *Generation and Corruption*. He also focuses a good deal of attention on the subject of fetal or embryonic growth and development in his biological works.[42] There he is concerned precisely with how to define food and how to understand the transformation of food from, say, grass into cow's flesh or from apples into human flesh and blood. As part of this inquiry he also discusses the nature of fetal growth and of maternal nourishment for the fetus. Now, it is true that there may be flaws in these other texts that Irigaray, or other feminists, might wish to attack (and that she did attack in *Speculum*). For example in his *Generation and Corruption* treatment of growth Aristotle is concerned to deny that two bodies can be at one place at the same time, even in somewhat anomalous-seeming situations of growth; and there are well-known and oft-discussed problems with his account of how the fetus acquires form from its father and matter only from its mother. Nevertheless, on Aristotle's behalf it must be said that he did not ignore these problems. Besides, his account has the virtue of generality. Whereas Irigaray would seem to have us concentrate on implications of human pregnancy for human subjects, Aristotle treats pregnancy as a biological phenomenon, thus linking us as humans not only to other animals but even to insects or plants, which also exhibit the phenomena of growth and reproduction.

I next turn to the three more interesting points Irigaray is making in this essay, points where her criticisms are more deep and intriguing. These points are all connected, and I review them as they build up in order of importance.

1. Irigaray criticizes Aristotle because he works with a basic map of data and of conceptual possibilities that are limited by gender preconceptions about both metaphysics and physics. His data are problematic because he overlooks certain unusual, interstitial kinds of things, including mucous, skins, and various fluids. Mucous is interesting because it is like place, in that it covers a skin-container, but it also is hard to locate because it "oozes" from within a body. It violates his categorical distinction between form and matter. In numerous passages Irigaray seems to celebrate mucous as the lubricant bridging both the literal and conceptual gap between bodies, including male and female bodies. Mucous brings a dimension to the sexual act that she describes as a "communion beyond skins" (50). She even compares mucous to angels as agents of a communion between spirit and flesh.[43] I shall have more to say about this comparison below.

Semen also seems to come into the same category, and is particularly linked to the uncategorizableness of the penis, as something that grows and then has detumescence. She seems to be suggesting that Aristotle ignores the problematics of the place (plus shape, matter, and form) of this most unusual and useful organ in favor of a typically Greek obsession with the hard, perfectly isolated phallus.[44] Such an object may be suited for exhibition and display, but it does not represent the biological reality of the metamorphosing penis, let alone its activity in intercourse.[45]

Even when Aristotle does treat a fluid, like water, he seems to turn it into a kind of analogue of a hard body and worries about what place that water is in. Irigaray implies that water and fluidity in general are like jouissance, an excess Aristotle cannot categorize. So she remarks upon his discussion of a replacement problem concerning water at 212a33:

> A certain representation of feminine jouissance corresponds to this water flowing without a container. A doubling, sought after by man, of a female *placelessness*. She is assigned to be place without occupying a place. Through her, place would be set up for man's use but not hers. Her jouissance is meant to "resemble" the flow of whatever is in the place that she is in when she contains, contains herself. "Wine," perhaps, that man might spill out in the sexual act? Elixir of ambrosia, and of place itself. (55–56).

This leads her in turn to a discussion of food, and she remarks upon the apparent oddity of introducing food into a subject as introducing something into a place. "The body and food play roles that escape the 'subject.' For the most part" (56).

So also does Aristotle's argument exclude another possibility that he does not consider conceptualizable: the interval. Remember that this is like the empty vacant spatial bubble in the snowglobe example. Aristotle regards this as problematic, but Irigaray notes that he does not give good reasons; rather, he just seems unable to conceive of the interval as a merely potential place. Irigaray spends a good deal of time criticizing his exclusion of the *third* of his four candidates, place as the interval or space between extremities. She is intrigued by Aristotle's inability to conceive of such a merely potential space and asks, How does the philosopher manage to conceive the empty space here? The answer is: he fills it. Hence she says, "overcoming the interval is the aim of desire" and "desire can eat up place" (52–53).

2. Irigaray's fourth criticism is complex. Aristotle wrestles with puzzles about place in relation to his fundamental concepts of matter and form. Since Aristotle's account of matter and form themselves carry strong gen-

der associations, it is no surprise that place turns out to have gender associations as well. But these associations are problematic in some ways that even Aristotle ought to have recognized. We must force the problems into recognition so as to begin to reconceive the relations between the sexes, or to ground it as a loving relation between them (to use her words).

As I said earlier, Aristotle associates form with the masculine and matter with the feminine. Place seems rather like both of these. It is like form because it seems to resemble the container that gives a thing its definition or shape. But place is like matter because it also is the exact amount of space that the matter of a thing takes up. It grows and shifts along with the thing's matter. In fact, place in Aristotle is quite a peculiar concept that Irigaray pokes fun at, saying it amounts to a "transportable mold" (44). She plays on this peculiarity so as to disturb or disrupt Aristotle's neat divisions between form and matter and between the masculine and the feminine. Much of her critique speaks quite specifically and explicitly about the form and matter of the male or female genitals. We should recall that elsewhere she has attacked broad cultural conceptions of the female genitals as an empty gap, a space, a nothing—or to put it in this context, as an empty place.[46]

Irigaray seems to be asking, What is the matter and/or the form of either the female or the male (realm, sexual organ)? Although woman as container seems associated with place, she says this *container* is very like the allegedly masculine *form*, because a container is what gives something its distinctness and shape (43). Even in seemingly passive and subordinate roles, women are resistant, in the sense that the container is never really fixed, determinate, and in particular never closed. So she writes "Place is never closed" (55).

And doesn't sex alter the very form of these sex organs? The female is neither matter nor form but vessel. What about the male?

> In the male realm, there would be seducing, caressing, assuming a shape, spending, and then collapse into formlessness or regression to the fetal position. . . . In the female realm there would be the sexual act. She gives form to the male sex (organ) and sculpts it from within. She becomes the container and the active *place* of the sexual act. Maternity is an extra. . . . An act more passive than passivity? (49).

In other words, sex should make us reconceive our own special, secret, inner places.

Further, she imagines the place of coming together in intercourse as the place where form and matter wed, interact, and mingle. Literal intercourse becomes the metaphor for a new kind of interactive relation between the sexes, conceived as complementary wholes of form and matter, rather than complementary halves (with the masculine half the more significant and dominant of the two). She writes about a kind of wholeness in intercourse that should serve to banish male fears of castration: "On the other hand, there are times when that relation of places in the sexual act gives rise to a transgression of the envelope, to a porousness, a perception of the other, a fluidity. And so it becomes possible to imagine that generation of a certain kind might occur by crossing membranes and sharing humours with the other" (51).

3. Finally, Irigaray wants to discuss fundamental values in Aristotle's system. To understand her points here we need to remember that place in Aristotle is crucially linked to his teleology through his theory of the goal-directedness of nature in general and of human lives in particular. This is so because in his theory cosmic place and physical motion throughout the universe depend upon God, the Unmoved Mover. Irigaray regards Aristotle's teleology as gendered and problematic. Just as the cosmic teleology of nature ultimately goes back to God, so also is He/It the object of human desires to be ethical—in particular of our goal of becoming intellectuals or philosophers, as described in Book X of his *Ethics*.[47] Irigaray wants to launch a very basic critique of both Aristotle's cosmic teleology and his human ethics, which are both flawed because of Aristotle's gender biases. That is, his own final definition of place is part and parcel of an overall systematic outlook that prohibits an acceptable ethics of the passions; so it must be rejected and its very grounds must be reconceived. Irigaray begins to do this by tracing the influence of his gender biases from physics quite far afield into theology and ethics, explaining how such a basic natural concept in physics as place plays a role in these broader spheres.

With this somewhat therapeutic aim in mind, Irigaray's essay begins by diagnosing an apparent alternative Aristotle sees between two kinds of place, our initial place and our ultimate place. The initial place or starting point seems to be the maternal womb, which gets associated with the material feminine, and the ultimate place or final end is God the father figure, who in his pure actuality is associated with both form and masculinity. The way Irigaray puts this point is by considering how Aristotle gets trapped by Zeno's puzzle about whether place will have a place. For men, she says, this abstract puzzle about the place of place is absorbing because it is linked to pursuit of a true place beyond all regresses: either the place of pure matter (mother) or of pure form that has no place (God the father).

Again in the therapeutic mode, Irigaray suggests that this pursuit is not really healthy for men, as it requires either a fantasy of return to origins or another fantasy of escape from all material reality into the realm of pure thought in the Platonic heaven.[48] For women the situation is no better, but it is different. To see why, we must recall another aspect of the links between place and teleology in Aristotle, his view that there are natural places to which the elements return because of their "desire" to be in their proper place.[49] Thus fire goes up and earth goes down, each naturally to its appropriate place in the cosmos. Irigaray, assuming Aristotle makes this link between natural place and goals, notes that women who serve as places for men (in the sense of literal containers during maternity and intercourse) must thereby be goals of a sort for men. Of course, this is not really enough for *women*, particularly because of the problem of conceptualizing how the male partner in intercourse offers a "place" or goal for the woman.

Pursuing this line in some detail, Irigaray asks whether, if woman is a place, women has a place or is her own place. This is a question about what women's goals can be in the context of Aristotle's gendered teleology. Her readings proceed on the general hypothesis that woman is a place; i.e., a sort of vessel or receptacle. Sometimes she seems to mean this literally, as when she speaks of the woman as the place of the penis or of the fetus. Sometimes she means it more figuratively, as in speaking of the woman as an empty place with no subjectivity, the contrast term to the male subject. In either case she means to allude to standard male philosophical and psychological conceptions of the female body or of female sex organs as an empty place (receptacle) rather than as *something*.[50] (This is the thesis of her notorious "This Sex which Is Not One.") She also speaks about woman as an envelope, as a vessel: What does she contain, the man, child, herself? (47).

In her discussion of Aristotle's chapter 2, a dialectical chapter in which Aristotle is arguing against Plato, Irigaray plays with these associations between form and maleness, and matter and femaleness. If on a sexualized reading, the female body is the natural place attracting the male, why should the masculine attract the feminine? Can the masculine body be a *place* or vessel for the feminine? Does the male offer the female a place, does he receive and welcome her? Can there be a reversal of envelopes (47)? "Can he beckon to her and welcome her into himself once he has separated himself from her? Since he must separate himself from her in order to be able to be her place. Just as she must move toward him. If any meeting is to be possible between man and woman, each must be a place, as appropriate to and for the other, and toward which he or she may move" (45–46).

This line of thought builds up to a climax in which Irigaray sketches an alternative picture of intercourse that could ground a new ethics. Perhaps to highlight it, this vision is bracketed in between two passages that quote Aristotle's own final definition of place. Thus she does not so much comment directly on his definitions as comment on them indirectly by contrast to what she is asking the reader to imagine:

> The boundary of the containing body might be the bodily identity of woman, reborn and touched anew by inner communion, and not destroyed by nostalgia for a regression in utero. The dissociation of love and desire would, in this case, have little meaning, nor would the sexual have an amoral, or nonethical, character. On the contrary, the sexual *act* would turn into the act whereby the other gives new form, birth, incarnation to the self. Instead of implying the downfall of the body, it takes part in the body's renaissance. And there is no other equivalent act, in this sense. Most divine of acts. Whereby man makes woman feel her body as place. Not only her vagina and her womb but her body. He places her within her body and within a macrocosm, releasing her from her potential adherence to the cosmic through her participation in a microsociety.
>
> As man re-creates woman from outside, from inside-outside, he replaces himself outside, as an actor outside, a creator outside. By actively putting himself outside, he re-sculpts a body for himself. By using a tool? He reconstructs his own body as a result of engendering the body of the other. By using his hand, his penis—which is not merely a tool of pleasure, but a truly useful tool of alliance, incarnation, creation. (54–55)

In sum, Irigaray is interrogating the concept of natural place from Aristotle's *Physics* because she thinks, and she is right to think, that this is closely tied also to his metaphysics (the hylomorphic theory of being) as well as to his theology and ethics. So when she asks near the end, "How does one make the transition here from physics to metaphysics?" (58), she seems to be asking what there is, ontologically, that grounds the very existence of place. It is helpful in understanding this to keep in mind Chanter's point about Heidegger as relevant background, since Irigaray is also asking about how a metaphysical picture of the subject would incorporate place as a sort of physicality or spatiality, constitutive of subjective experiences.

Conclusions/Assessment

I shall now try to assess Irigaray's discussion, dividing my remarks into three broad areas or ways of reading her essay: as feminist science critique; as prologue to a liberatory ethics and politics; and as history of philosophy. The first of these is perhaps the most visible area of her concern, but it is closely connected to her deeper ethical aims; and both of these in turn are grounded in her strategy of textual interpretation.

On the first issue, feminist science critique, I conclude that despite its initial strangeness, Irigaray's essay has much in common with other versions of this enterprise within feminist philosophy, for example those of Sandra Harding;[51] in fact Irigaray has written more standard feminist science critique on other topics.[52]

In this essay she poses five basic questions about Aristotle's treatment of place in the *Physics* that add up to an attack on his scientific method, especially upon his assumptions or what she terms "intuitions." I argued that two of her criticisms seemed misplaced but that the other three were more plausible, particularly in raising questions about his methodology. Aristotle always starts off a science by citing *endoxa*, the opinions of sources who are the many, the wise, or the most reputable.[53] These expert opinions frame his entire inquiry in several ways. They supply him with some of the data that his own theory must explain, and they also identify the kinds of issues and questions about a subject, such as place, that it will be important for his own theory or definition to explain. The *endoxa* cited are always from experts who are males. (In fact, I can't recall a single case of a woman expert being cited in any Aristotelian survey of *endoxa*. A female sort of principle about place is only indirectly mentioned in the *Physics* if you can count a quote from Hesiod about "broad-bosomed earth" as a kind of primeval generative place.)

Irigaray's methodological correction to Aristotle, then, can be seen as supplying *endoxa* from a different set of reputable experts, women.[54] (In the essay "A Chance for Life" her advice to women is "Never give up subjective experience as an element of knowledge.")[55] For example, we should recognize that place in sexual intercourse is sometimes a container that seems to contain several bodies, or that the pregnant woman's body is both herself, and yet also a container of sorts. Irigaray would suggest that it is strange and remarkable that not one example of the eight ways of "being in" concerns a fetus being in a woman. When Aristotle mulls over problems generated by a body's growth, such as whether place can grow with a body, he does not take into account this kind of basic example. Similarly, Irigaray suggests ways to query the treatment of even abstract issues such as Zeno's puzzle about whether place can be in a place. Aristotle's and the experts' accounts of what is appropriate to consider in discussing place and bodies recognize only definite fixed bodies and containers. There is no room anywhere within the approved scientific approach for inquiring about fluids, bodies containing or merging with other bodies, the skin's relation to the body, interior sexual spaces of either male or female bodies, changing shapes and interiorities of pregnant bodies, and so on. In short, physics leaves out much that is important about ourselves as physical subjects, and this has implications even now for familiar ways in which we see ourselves, or fail to see women, as human subjects. I submit Irigaray's account of these experiences, in the reputable report of her text, as a new *endoxon* for the revised Aristotelian science of physics to consider.

Since Irigaray also attacks Aristotle's assumptions and conclusions because of the values that are implicit in them, her critique recalls other feminist science critiques that note the inextricable links between scientific practices and their applications, or between the scientist and broader values of his or her society. Interestedness compromises science's purported purity and objectivity. Another way to put this point is to say that she questions the impact of science's repression of sexual difference. Thus, even in an abstract concept such as place, or in the mechanics of solids, Irigaray sees embedded the particular value positions of patriarchy, and she diagnoses these as unfortunate and neurotic. Such critiques are not restricted to Aristotle or to ancient science; she has made similar points about contemporary practices in physics or other sciences as being linked to exploitative values.[56] As Whitford explains, especially since Chernobyl, Irigaray has emphasized an ecofeminist position expressing concern for the scientific domination and destruction of nature.[57] So Irigaray complains that "we are faced with men who are prisoners of their own civilization."[58]

For Irigaray, science critique necessarily leads to a liberatory ethics and politics; so I turn next to consider the feminist implications of Irigaray's essay in these fields. Her critique of the discourse and categories of the Western tradition is meant to stimulate us to envision an alternative. In psychoanalytic terms, only when the repressions are lifted can the neurotic patient (the Western tradition) begin to become healthy in its thoughts and choices. As she puts it, her challenges to Western conceptions of reality, science, ethics, and politics—beginning with the ancient Greeks—should enable us to begin to construct a new ethics of the passions. Recall her aim, which I quoted at the start of my paper. By an "ethics of the passions" Irigaray does not have in mind something broad and general like Spinoza did in his approach to rationalizing the passions. Quite the contrary: she has in mind creating a new cosmic sense of the physicality and spatiality of a human body, so as specifically to construct a conceptual basis for a loving, desiring, but nondominative and nonexploitative relation between two differently sexed subjects.

Irigaray's approach in reading Aristotle on place involves a number of assumptions. She assumes first that there is now a certain problem: the lack of a satisfactory account of gendered subjects and how they may enter into such a loving relation. Second, philosophy created this problem, which is in part a conceptual one. In particular, a philosophical theory of physical place created and sustains it. Third, philosophy can solve it: a revised theory of place or space can help to open up new approaches within ethics. Obviously all these assumptions are subject to critical examination. I shall grant Irigaray only the first point, that there is a problem. But how does she think philosophy created the problem? And how can philosophy solve it?

Again it is helpful to see her position here as that of the psychoanalyst who diagnoses the neuroses of our society and cultural outlook (violence against women and nature, all modes of inequality between the sexes) and seeks their source in some fundamental, originary repression—of the feminine. Philosophy created the problem because it helped formulate the basic conceptual scheme in which we still think about bodies and about ourselves as sexed bodies. But why look at Aristotle's *Physics* to see this rather than at his ethics and politics? Is the claim that his account in the *Physics* grounds those accounts? I think it is something more deep and metaphorical; this is also why she does not particularly attend to Aristotle's accounts of growth in *Generation and Corruption* or to his specific accounts of the growth processes in reproduction in *Generation of Animals*. Aristotle's discussion, like others in the Western tradition, represses the feminine. Women's bodies have an emptiness or interior place that is at times the container for a segment of men's bodies and at times the container for a baby. This "container" view of women is neurotic and harmful: it derogates our status as subjects, during either intercourse or pregnancy, and enforces a passive view of women's active participation in either kind of process. To go further, it thereby helps to legitimize pictures of women as property or as rapeable bodies rather than subjects, or as baby-producers who have no basic right to autonomy, to abortion and in general to choices about sexuality and pregnancy.

But Irigaray also assumes that since philosophy is part of the problem, it must be part of the solution. To change things, and to produce "health," the repressions must be lifted by an act of *interpretation* of the symptoms. It may seem unclear why changing metaphors, concepts, or discourse should change women's material realities. Because of this emphasis both on the importance of ideas in philosophy and the reformist aspects of the enterprise, Irigaray has frequently been criticized as idealist, modernist, and utopian, with views unrealistically based upon the belief that ideas can affect and alter material reality.[59] These objections are linked to other charges that Irigaray is problematic politically because of her elitism, essentialism, and biological reductionism. I believe that none of these charges really stick and that others have plausibly defended her on these points.[60] I cannot add a great deal to these other excellent discussions, but do want to note the relevance for this debate of certain points from her article on Aristotle. The charges of essentialism and biological reductionism in particular seem refuted by the essays in *An Ethics of Sexual Difference*, even if (as I doubt) they may have been true for earlier essays like "This Sex Which Is Not One."[61]

I have tried to show that in the Aristotle essay Irigaray lampoons Aristotle's understanding of place to undermine a traditional approach that fixes male and female essences. Her challenge to the Aristotelian is to admit that matter and form both characterize both sexes. In the passage

I described above as the "climax" of her critique, she envisages a new experience of intercourse between two bodies with fluid, not fixed, borders and identities. Conceiving the male "envelope" is one such metaphorical, not literal, physical, or reductionist way of advancing such a fluid conception in which bodies are remade and even reconfigured. The body is important, since we are all inescapably embodied. But I do not believe that this foregrounds biology or any alleged physical essence. There is no evidence that she regards all bodies as significantly alike, or as having some predetermined nature—not all bodies of men, or all those of women. She suggests plurality or difference when she writes that "in order for an ethics of sexual difference to come into being, we must constitute a possible place for each sex, body, and flesh to inhabit."[62]

Even more important, Irigaray's emphasis on mucous reflects the undecidability of the body and its boundaries. This view is reinforced by her initially strange link between mucous and angels. Like mucous, she says, angels are crucially indeterminate or undecideable creatures which bridge gaps: "The angel is that which unceasingly passes through the envelope(s) or container(s), goes from one side to the other, reworking every deadline, changing every decision, thwarting all repetition."[63]

To speak of angels is to speak of bodies transcended, of carnal desire that is also psychological or as she puts it "spiritual," and linked to wonder. Her description of wonder emphasizes our inability to fix, reduce, or pin down either the female or the male: "Sometimes a space for wonder is left to works of art. But it is never found to reside in this locus: between man and woman. Into this place came attraction, greed, possession, consummation, disgust, and so on. But not that wonder which beholds what it sees always as if for the first time, never taking hold of the other as its object. It does not try to seize, possess, or reduce this object, but leaves it subjective, still free."[64]

Angels play a number of vital roles in Irigaray's opening essay, which is also the title essay, in An Ethics of Sexual Difference. One of their key functions is to serve as go-betweens crossing the gap between "God" and the human realm. Irigaray interprets this as holding out the hope that there may indeed be some kind of mediation between the spirit and the flesh, the transcendent and the immediate. But they are also temporal mediators who were said traditionally to appear to foretell future events, "mediators of that which has not yet happened."[65] And as we all know, their prophesies often concern births or marriages (hence Irigaray's wry comment "They are not unrelated to sex") (15). Thus angels, as she discusses them, foretell a new period in which human men and women change and improve their relations. To say this is to say also that angels play a third role, making desire spiritual, or making the carnal also ethical. This is hinted at in the passage on wonder just quoted. And finally, Irigaray toys with that classic, stereotypical problem about angels on the head of a pin: "One of the questions which arises about them is whether they can be together in the same place" (16). Shifting the focus of this question to her own concerns, Irigaray muses about the dawn of a new sexual ethics in which man and woman would "sometimes inhabit the same place" (17).

This discussion of angels and of spiritual desire obviously sounds a religious note, and I think that Irigaray's vision of a new alternative must be seen to have a visionary, even messianic aspect—moreso than commentators have recognized. Irigaray's is a radical, rather than liberal, feminist approach, and at the center of her vision is a significant personal transformation comparable to a religious conversion.[66] This is so despite her skepticism and distrust of traditional religions that have upheld male notions of a paternal "God": "The most extreme progression and regression goes under the name of God" (17). She insists that no important reframing of gender relations can be achieved until the fundamental concepts and metaphors underlying Western thought are revisited and revised:[67]

> When women want to escape from exploitation, they do not merely destroy a few "prejudices," they disrupt the entire order of dominant values, economic, social, moral, and sexual. They call into question all existing theory, all thought, all language, inasmuch as these are monopolized by men and men alone. They challenge *the very foundation of our social and cultural order*, whose organization has been prescribed by the patriarchal system. (165).

No concrete transformations can take place in, say, the economic realm without "transforming culture and its operative agency, language. Without such an interpretation of a general grammar of culture, the feminine will never take place in history, except as a reservoir of matter and of speculation" (155).

Irigaray is calling for a politics of personal transformation that, like the psychoanalytic cure that occurs through recognizing and lifting repressions, must include a renewal of consciousness and awareness that is genuinely reformatory, like a religious vision. Thus perhaps instead of describing her position as utopian, elitist, or idealist, I would describe it as "spiritual": what is at stake is a new religious outlook that can even be described as an approach that makes us gods or "God" (given of course that we remain fully armed with a skeptical awareness of past exploitative and dominative uses of this concept/Being). Thus she writes,

> And if the divine is present as the mystery that animates the copular, the is and the being in sexual difference, can the force of desire overcome the avatars of genealogical destiny? How does it manage this? With what power does it reckon, while remaining nevertheless incarnate? Between the idealistic fluidity of an unborn body that is untrue to its birth and genetic determinism, how do we take the measure of a love that changes our condition from mortal to immortal? Certain figures of gods become men, of God become man, and of twice-born beings indicate the path of love.[68]

In this new era a new sexual ethics may become possible. She says, "For this, "God" is necessary, or a love so attentive that it is divine" (19). And she emphasizes the continuum between private and public transformation that might emerge from this more-than-psychological state or capacity: "A genesis of love between the sexes has yet to come about in all dimensions, from the smallest to the greatest, from the most intimate to the most political" (17).

At the heart of Irigaray's therapeutic/spiritual project is a fundamental task of interpretation, the interpretation of crucial historical texts that, like infantile primal scenes, still haunt our memories and outlooks. Thus the third and final area in which I must assess Irigaray's contributions is the history of philosophy, and in particular the theory of textual interpretation.[69] While one could read Irigaray to learn about *Aristotle* it is probably more accurate to say of my essay that I am reading Irigaray on Aristotle to learn about *her*—and beyond this, to explore alternative ways of engaging with the historical tradition in philosophy. I do think that it is a deep and worthwhile philosophical question to ask what we are doing when we do the history of philosophy, and that Irigaray has an original and stimulating way of answering this question. She challenges some of our most cherished presumptions about how to proceed in the history of philosophy.

One such presumption is the principle of charity. Interpretation aims to re-create the author's intended text with maximal coherence and plausibility. Some may hold, with reason, that Irigaray is unnecessarily uncharitable to Aristotle. Irigaray certainly does not relate chapters 1 through 5 of *Physics* V to any of the rest of this book, nor does she draw links to Aristotle's other scientific treatises—something I faulted her for above. Had she looked to his biological works, for example, she might have uncovered some practices or principles that other feminist philosophers of science endorse, such as his holism or identification of scientific intelligence with purposes in nature.[70] And since the problems Irigaray diagnoses seems to arise in or have ramifications for the field of ethics or possibly psychology, one might say that to resolve them we ought to look to the foundations of these fields, including the works of Aristotle. But she does not discuss those works (at least, not here). Other feminists do find resources in Aristotle's ethics and politics despite his repugnant views about women and slaves. After all, Aristotle's *Ethics* is a kind of ethics of the passions, and he emphasizes the integration of rationality with emotions, as well as the importance of community and of friendship and love. This is not an atomistic ethics of utilitarian pleasure-seekers.[71]

Irigaray's lack of charity is connected to her violation of another standard principle, of treating texts in context—of larger works, of an individual's oeuvre, or of an era. But why after all should she follow the principle of charity, or of context? Rather than treating Aristotle as a philosopher with potential contributions to the history of physics and metaphysics, she sees him as "neurotic," his text a symptom of a collective repression. You don't interpret neurotic texts sympathetically if what you are after is a cure. Indeed, Irigaray does adhere in her own unique way to a principle of context, insofar as she reads the subject of place not only as it is treated in Aristotle but both backward and forward through the history of philosophy. Thus the book *An Ethics of Sexual Difference* also includes discussion of Plato on place (which she also treated at length in *Speculum*), as well as of Descartes and Spinoza on space, place, and envelopes, and continues on up until the contemporary world. It is the value and implications of this tradition that she wants to question.

Perhaps the most sacred principle of standard history of philosophy that Irigaray violates is the principle of "objectivity" of interpretation. That is, texts have a meaning and we seek to discern the author's meaning in interpretation, even if only as a necessary prelude to our evaluation and ultimate disagreement or dismissal. But it is part of Irigaray's approach to insist in the spirit of the psychoanalyst on the subjectivity of interpretation. She even invites such interpretations of her own work; recall the passage I cited above in which she responded to resistance about her style, claiming that texts are always "esoteric" and "never-exhaustively revealable." Not only are her interpretations subjective, they are also personal, unique, and idiosyncratic. They seem to leap from subject to subject, to speak endlessly on minor points while ignoring major ones, and to look at familiar issues through an odd lens.

Paradoxically, however, this subjectivity only seems to extend so far. In the end I confess to finding a disturbing self-contradiction in Irigaray's historical and interpretive methodology. Despite her insistence on the esoteric, subjective, and personal, there is after all in an important sense "a" meaning of the text for her (and for us, by implication). This is the meaning it has had for the tradition. Irigaray's picture of the Western tradition as suffering from a particular neurosis or repression requires that the "cure" be based on a true or correct diagnosis. Feminists who want to change things have to struggle at great length (many would say, too great) with these abstract and aging philosophical texts precisely because these constitute philosophical discourse as the discourse of mastery that lays down the law for other discourses. So there is in some sense "a" meaning of philosophical texts for the ongoing tradition. Hence Irigaray can write without batting an eye about "the conception of place which is still and forever Aristotle's" (46), as if there is indeed something out there and fixed—as if the tradition is a massive fortress or prison.

Now it is altogether true that this prison is a fortress made of faulty fallible thoughts. Often Irigaray uses the metaphor of the mirror as she charges the tradition with reflecting only itself. This is why we need her alternative lens, her curved specular mirror, to picture what has been absent. Because someone like Irigaray can read the gaps and repressions in the texts of the tradition, we can see that this fortress has chinks. But it is still highly resistant, and it still imprisons us. For a reform, or an escape, we must understand precisely this prison, which stems from precisely these texts, which seem to assert precisely these things. Just imagine trying to escape from a tradition composed of texts if we cannot do anything to fix the meaning of those texts! That would be a hall of mirrors that requires a unique speculum indeed as an aid to our escape.

Appendix: A Brief Overview of Aristotle's *Physics* IV, 1–5

Another way to consider the possibility that there are gendered concepts in Aristotle's discussion of place in the *Physics* is to consider that they may be potentially involved in one of three ways: in the formulation of the questions about place; in the specification of an answer; and in citing supporting arguments for this answer. Perhaps the occurrence of gender as a consideration would have a different meaning or impact at each level; I would find this interesting, and maybe suggestive concerning points of Aristotle's scientific method. This division reflects my own interest in methodological questions about Aristotle's procedure in offering scientific explanations.[72]

To indicate how this search would go, I suggest a track through Aristotle's text, dividing it into the three sections I have laid out just above (formulation of questions, proposal of definition, defense of definition). I summarize how Aristotle proceeds, and in very rough outline what he says.

Formulation of questions about place

The first section addressing the formulation of basic questions and concerns about place occupies chapters 1, 2, and 3 in Aristotle.

First, in chapter 1, Aristotle asserts that place exists. This accords with his scientific view that we cannot define what does not exist. He offers several defenses of this claim: things must be somewhere; there is change of place; and place seems to exist, as demonstrated a certain power (*tina dunamis*) it exerts to effect natural motions. He even quotes from Hesiod's *Theogony*, about how "broad-bosomed earth" emerged from Chaos as the original place of all things. The next stage in chapter 1 is the list of a number of difficulties (*aporiai*) about place. In generating this list, Aristotle refers often to claims or opinions of experts, mostly Plato and Zeno. So Owen is right in pointing out the important role of *ta endoxa*, in this case opinions of wise men or experts, in this discussion.

Chapter 2 is a more specific consideration of the genus of place, beginning with the view of another expert, Plato, and considering whether place could be either form or matter. Again, based on this expert opinion, more difficulties or *aporiai* are generated; Aristotle says these suggest place is neither form nor matter, but he nevertheless will return to consider these options below as significant candidates (in chapter 4) when he offers his own definition.

Chapter 3 provides a complex analysis of the notion of "being in" by listing eight possible ways of being in, such as a finger being in a hand, "man" in "animal," health in hot and cold things, and so forth. From these he identifies one as primary: being in in the sense of being in a vessel. He again returns to certain *aporiai* such as Zeno's problem about place being in place, an infinite regress problem, and asks whether a thing can be in itself, or whether two things can be in one place.

Formulation of possible answers, and a definition

I now turn to the second part of the text, and I shall consider Aristotle's actual answer to the question, What is place? In chapter 4, Aristotle does quite a lot before supplying his own definition of place. He first generates a list of six axioms stating evident facts or *phainomena* about place. These are are things "thought truly to belong to it." They include such points as that place is the first thing surrounding a body, that it may be left behind an object and is separable from it, and so forth. This list is taken as methodologically interesting by commentators like Owen, because he calls these kinds of conceptual observations the data that his theory must explain or account for in order to be successful. In more Aristotelian terms, these are the attributes that belong *kath'hauto* to the subject place, and we are seeking a satisfactory definition that will work as a middle term demonstrating how and that these attributes indeed do belong in this way to place. Furthermore, Aristotle says that the correct account of place must explain why the puzzles arise that he has already noted.

Aristotle proceeds by surveying four possible options for answering the question, What is place? They are form or shape (*morphē*); matter (*hulē*); extension or interval between extremes (*diastēma ti to metaxu ton eschaton*); or the extremes or limits (*ta eschata*). He argues against the first three and concludes that place must be defined in terms of the fourth, the limits or extremes. He reaches the definition, at 212a5–6, that place is "the limit of the surrounding body, at which it is in contact with that which is surrounded." A second definition is proposed at 212a20–21, where place is described as "the first unchangeable limit of that which surrounds." Commentators, such as Ross and Hussey, have argued that these two definitions are inconsistent (Ross remarks Aristotle seemed unaware of the inconsistency; Hussey thinks the second proposal is an interpolation).

Defense of the answer

Finally I turn to the third part of my mapping of the text. This concerns the arguments on behalf of the proposed definition of place. In chapter 5, Aristotle follows a typical procedure of arguing for his definition. First he argues that his proposed definition solves the *aporiai* about place from chapter 1. This discussion is difficult because he does not treat them in order and his discussion is repetitious. Commentators do not find it very clear just how various of the *aporiai* are solved by his account. Both Ross and Hussey trace through his different responses and point out that he never even mentions two out of his initial list of six (numbers 3 and 4).

Next he argues that it is a virtue of his definition that it fits well with certain other issues concerning place. Not only does his definition solve the difficulties, it grounds his theory of natural place. It can explain the place of the world system as a whole (see Hussey, *Aristotle's Physics*, 119). Allegedly it explains not only why bodies are carried to their own place when out of it, but why they remain within it. This section of chapter 5 too is very quick, and even Aristotle admits it is an obscure account that will be made clear later (presumably referring to *Generation and Corruption*).

Notes

1. Work on this paper was supported by a Faculty Development Leave from the University of Houston and a Visiting Fellowship at the Australian National University. I thank both institutions for their support, and Paul Thom for inviting me to the ANU. I am also grateful to audiences at both institutions for helpful questions and comments on earlier versions read to (respectively) the Women's Studies Program and the Australasian Aristotelian Society. For other comments I thank Marguerite Deslauriers, Penelope Deutscher, Sheridan Hough, Deborah Modrak, Patricia Yongue, and Krist Bender. Charlotte Witt and Angela Curran generously read and commented on multiple drafts, and I am much indebted to them.

2. See the Introduction to this volume, and also Cynthia Freeland, "Nourishing Speculation: A Feminist Reading of Aristotelian Science," in *Engendering Origins*, ed. Bat-Ami Bar On (Albany: State University of New York Press, 1994), 145–87.

3. Luce Irigaray, "Place, Interval: A Reading of Aristotle, *Physics* IV," in *An Ethics of Sexual Difference*, trans. Carolyn Burke and Gillian C. Gill (Ithaca: Cornell University Press, 1993), 34–55; reprinted, this volume, Chapter 2. Subsequent page references to Irigaray are to this essay, unless otherwise indicated, with pagination referring to the reprinted version in Chapter 2.

4. For discussion of Irigaray's distinctive approach, see Margaret Whitford, *Luce Irigaray: Philosophy in the Feminine* (London: Routledge, 1991).

5. *Speculum of the Other Woman*, trans. Gillian C. Gill (Ithaca: Cornell University Press, 1985).

6. See Irigaray, "This Sex Which Is Not One," in *This Sex Which Is Not One*, trans. Catherine Porter (Ithaca: Cornell University Press, 1985; orig. publ. France, 1977), 23–33.

7. Discussion of these issue in relation to Irigaray's feminism are extensive. For examples, see Maggie Berg, "Luce Irigaray's 'Contradictions': Poststructuralism and Feminism," *Signs* 17 (1991): 50–70; Naomi Schor, "This Essentialism Which Is Not One: Coming to Grips with Irigaray," in *The Essential Difference*, ed. Naomi Schor and Elizabeth Weed (Bloomington: Indiana University Press, 1994), 40–62; Judith Butler, *Gender Trouble: Feminism and the Subversion of Identity* (New York: Routledge, 1990); and Diana Fuss, " 'Essentially Speaking': Luce Irigaray's Language of Essence," in *Revaluing French Feminism*, ed. Nancy Fraser and Sandra Lee Bartky (Bloomington: Indiana University Press, 1992), 94–112. For an overview of these and other criticisms that includes a defense against them, see Margaret Whitford, *The Irigaray Reader* (Oxford: Blackwell, 1991), 1–15, and *Philosophy in the Feminine*.

8. I owe the idea of my example to Henry Mendell's article "*Topoi* on *topos*: The Development of Aristotle's Concept of Place," *Phronesis* 32 (1987): 206–31.

9. G. E. L. Owen, "*Tithenai ta Phainomena*," in *Articles on Aristotle*, vol. 1, *Science*, ed. Jonathan Barnes, Malcolm Schofield, and Richard Sorabji (London Duckworth, 1975), 113–26, esp. 116. For discussion, see also Robert Bolton's articles, "The Epistemological Basis of Aristotelian Dialectic," in *Biologie, Logique, et Metaphysique*, ed. Pierre Pellegrin and Daniel T. Devereux (Paris: C.N.R.S. 1990), 185–236; and also "Aristotle's Method in Natural Science: *Physics* I," in *Aristotle's Physics: A Collection of Essays*, ed. Lindsay Judson (Oxford: Clarendon Press, 1991), 1–29.

10. For examples of the traditional approach see Mendell, cited above; and also Simplicius, *Commentary on Book 4.1–5 and 10–14 of the Physics of Aristotle*, trans. J. O. Urmson (London: Duckworth, 1992); Edward Hussey, *Aristotle's Physics, Books III and IV*, translated with notes (Oxford: Clarendon Press, 1983); and W. D. Ross, *Aristotle's Physics: A Revised Text with Introduction and Commentary* (Oxford: 1936).

11. Henry Mendell "*Topoi*," argues there is an out-and-out inconsistency, and that the *Physics* rejects the earlier, *Categories* account of place.

90   Theoretical Knowledge

12. Mendell, "*Topoi*," 231, Hussey, *Aristotle's Physics*, xxxi.

13. Tina Chanter, *Ethics of Eros: Irigaray's Rewriting of the Philosophers* (New York: Routledge, 1995), p. 157.

14. For discussion of this issue in Aristotle, see Charlotte Witt's essay, Chapter 5, this volume. On feminist science critiques, a good overview is Sandra Harding's *The Science Question in Feminism* (Ithaca: Cornell University Press, 1986). For a more general discussion of the "maleness" of physics, see Sharon Traweek, *Beamtimes and Lifetimes: The World of High Energy Physicists* (Cambridge: Harvard University Press, 1988).

15. Carolyn Korsmeyer, "Gendered Concepts and Hume's Standard of Taste," in *Feminism and Tradition in Aesthetics*, ed. Peggy Zeglin Brand and Carolyn Korsmeyer (University Park: The Pennsylvania State University Press, 1995), 49–65. See also Jean Grimshaw, *Philosophy and Feminist Thinking* (Minneapolis: University of Minnesota Press, 1986).

16. See Paul Mattick Jr., "Beautiful and Sublime: 'Gender Totemism' in the Constitution of Art," in *Feminism and Tradition in Aesthetics*, ed. Brand and Korsmeyer, 27–48.

17. See Charlotte Witt's essay, Chapter 5 this volume.

18. In *Speculum*, 160–67.

19. "The Power of Discourse and the Subordination of the Feminine," in *This Sex Which Is Not One*, 74.

20. "La Mystérique," in *Speculum*, 191.

21. See Margaret Whitford, ed., *The Irigaray Reader*, 3.

22. See Irigaray, *This Sex Which is Not One*, particularly the two essays "Questions" (119–69) and "The Power of Discourse and the Subordination of the Feminine" (68–85).

23. For an excellent discussion of Irigaray's style, focusing on the role of mimicry, see Ping Xu, "Irigaray's Mimicry and the Problem of Essentialism," *Hypatia* 10 (1995): 76–89.

24. For an overview of Irigaray in relation to the other "French Feminists," particularly Kristeva and Cixous, see Kelly Oliver, *Reading Kristeva: Unraveling the Double-Bind* (Bloomington: Indiana University Press, 1993), chap. 6; Toril Moi, *Sexual/Textual Politics: Feminist Literary Theory* (London: Methuen, 1985), and Elizabeth Grosz, *Sexual Subversions* (Boston: Allen and Unwin, 1989).

25. On difference feminism, see Natalie Stoljar, "Essentialism in Feminist Philosophy," *Philosophical Topics* 23 (1995): 261–93.

26. "Questions," in *This Sex*, 122–23; subsequent references in this paragraph are to this same essay.

27. "The Power of Discourse," in *This Sex*, 78.

28. Irigaray, "Plato's Hystera," in *Speculum*, 243–364.

29. "Plato's Hystera," in *Speculum*, 300.

30. "How to Conceive (of) a Girl," in *Speculum* 160–68; subsequent references in this paragraph are to this essay.

31. "Volume—Fluidity," in *Speculum*, 227–40.

32. Chanter, *Ethics of Eros*, 147–49.

33. Martin Heidegger, "Building Dwelling Thinking," in *Poetry, Language and Thought*, trans. Albert Hofstadter (New York: Harper & Row, 1971), p. 156. (I am grateful to Sheridan Hough for providing these quotations from Heidegger and discussing his views with me.)

34. Irigaray also compares the roles of space and time in the constitution of subjectivity in Kant, in the introductory essay of *An Ethics of Sexual Difference*, "Sexual Difference," 7.

35. Heidegger, "Building Dwelling Thinking," 157 (Heidegger's emphasis).

36. "The Three Genres," in *The Irigaray Reader*, ed. Whitford, 148.

37. See Ping Xu, "Irigaray's Mimicry," on the role of laughter in Irigaray, pp. 83–84.

38. "The Three Genres," in *The Irigaray Reader*, ed. Whitford, 148–49.

39. This objection was raised by Rick Benitez.

40. See *De Caelo* IV, 1, especially 308a8–33.

41. See *De Anima* II, 4, 416a2–6.

42. See *Generation of Animals* II, 1–4, especially the discussion of embryonic nourishment at 740a24–b2.

43. "An Ethics of Sexual Difference," 16–17.

44. Kelly Oliver notes, "Irigaray suggests that this phallocratic economy of desire is operated by a mechanics of solids. . . . Irigaray attempts to recover the repressed mechanics of fluids that lies behind the mechanics of solids in the traditional psychoanalytic account of desire. She enlists the penis in order to show that it is operated by a mechanics of fluids, sperm (and blood)" (*Reading Kristeva*, 171).

45. I owe this point to Deborah Modrak.

46. Irigaray, "This Sex Which Is Not One."

47. On Aristotle's teleology, see Charles Kahn, "The Place of the Prime Mover in Aristotle's Teleology," in *Aristotle on Nature and Living Things: Philosophical and Historical Studies Presented to David M. Balme on His Seventieth Birthday*, ed. Allan Gotthelf (Pittsburgh: University of Pittsburgh Press, 1985), 183–205.

48. Irigaray criticized this conception at length in *Speculum*; see the illustrative quotes on Plato cited above.

49. See *De Caelo* IV, 3 and 4.

50. As Ping Xu explains, "By elaborating the seemingly essentialist 'facts' of female sexual specificity covered up by phallogocentric discourse in order to maintain its selfsame system, Irigaray is in fact mimicking the discourse that has always been fabricating essentialist and 'sexed' 'facts' and 'truth' about female (as well as male) sexuality" ("Irigaray's Mimicry," 77–78).

51. See Harding, *The Science Question in Feminism* (Ithaca: Cornell University Press, 1986); *Whose Science? Whose Knowledge? Thinking from Women's Lives* (Ithaca: Cornell University Press, 1991); and *The "Racial" Economy of Science: Toward a Democratic Future* (Bloomington: Indiana University Press, 1993).

52. Irigaray discusses the sexed nature of science, including what she calls "scientific intuitions," in the essay "An Ethics of Sexual Difference," 117–18. See also her essay, "Is the Subject of Science Sexed?" trans. Carol Mastrangelo Bové, in *Feminism and Science*, ed. Nancy Tuana (Bloomington: Indiana University Press, 1989), 58–68; and "A Chance for Life," in *Sexes and Genealogies*, trans. Gillian C. Gill (New York: Columbia University Press, 1993), 185–206.

53. See the articles by Owen and Bolton mentioned above.

54. Not that it would necessarily make a difference, as Dirk Baltzly pointed out to me, to have someone like Theano participating as a mathematical expert. What is important is for the woman to speak *as* a woman. This interestingly resembles Sandra Harding's conception of "strong objectivity" based upon a democratic inclusiveness in the participation in science; see Harding, *"Racial" Economy*, 17–19.

55. Irigaray, "A Chance for Life," in *Sexes and Genealogies*, 203.

56. See Irigaray, "A Chance for Life."

57. Whitford, *The Irigaray Reader*, 11.

58. See "A Chance for Life," 202.

59. For a valuable discussion of the charge of utopianism and a defense against it, see Margaret Whitford, *Luce Irigaray: Philosophy in the Feminine*, chap. 1, 9–25.

60. Particularly those of Xu and Whitford, already mentioned.

61. Thus it is worth noting that a critical essay like Fuss's does not refer to Irigaray's more recent works nor to any essays in *An Ethics of Sexual Difference*.

62. "An Ethics of Sexual Difference," 18–19.

63. Ibid., 15.
64. Ibid., 13.
65. Ibid., 15; subsequent references in this paragraph and the next two are to this essay.
66. Irigaray does recommend intermediate modes of political change and action, and she has participated increasingly in political movements, particularly in Italy. She does insist (in "Questions," in *This Sex Which Is Not One*) that activism is appropriate in the intermediate realm:

> In concrete terms, that means that women must of course continue to struggle for equal wages and social rights, against discrimination in employment and education, and so forth. But that is not enough: women merely "equal" to men would be "like" them, therefore not women. Once more, the difference between the sexes would be in that way canceled out, ignored, papered over. So it is essential for women among themselves to invent new modes of organization, new forms of struggle, new challenges. (165–66)

> I think the most important thing to do is to expose the exploitation common to all women and to find the struggles that are appropriate for each woman, right where she is, depending upon her nationality, her job, her social class, her sexual experience, that is, upon the form of oppression that is for her the most immediately unbearable. (166–67)

For more on Irigaray's politics, see also Whitford, *The Irigaray Reader*, 10–11.

67. So she says things (in *This Sex Which Is Not One*) like "Contemporary political practice . . . is masculine, through and through (127); "No 'women's politics' exists, not yet, at least not in the broad sense" (p. 165); "Women have made gains, but these can easily be lost" (128); women's issues are "co-opted" by political parties (165).

68. "An Ethics of Sexual Difference," 19. Subsequent references in this paragraph are also to this essay.

69. I have found Richard Rorty's essay "The Historiography of Philosophy: Four Genres" very stimulating as I approached this topic in relation to Irigaray. See Rorty, in *Philosophy in History*, ed. Richard Rorty, J. B. Schneewind, and Quentin Skinner (Cambridge: Cambridge University Press, 1984), 49–75.

70. See my "Nourishing Speculation."

71. See Ruth Groenhout's essay, Chapter 7, this volume.

72. See my discussion of Aristotle's methodology in "Scientific Explanation and Empirical Data in Aristotle's *Meteorology*" in *Biologie, Logique et Metaphysique Chez Aristote* (Paris: C.N.R.S., 1990), 287–320.

4

Aristotle's Theory of Knowledge and Feminist Epistemology

Deborah K. W. Modrak

Feminist epistemologists have raised a number of troubling questions about the way philosophers have characterized knowledge.[1] In order to distinguish knowledge from mere belief, philosophers have set out various conditions on knowing. Sometimes these requirements have been very stringent and traits such as certainty and infallibility have been emphasized. Sometimes these requirements are weaker, allowing for knowledge of probabilities and even best guesses. Despite these differences among modern epistemological theories, feminist epistemologists have argued that the modern conception of rationality and of the epistemological enterprise itself are gendered and engender theories that replicate or are conducive to the replication of gender hierarchies.[2] Most of this criticism has been directed at contemporary theories, and historically based critiques of traditional epistemologies have, for the most part, concentrated on modern authors, starting with Descartes in the seventeenth century.[3] I plan to use feminist epistemologies as a tool for examining Aristotle's conception of knowledge.

Lorraine Code in a recent influential book on feminist epistemology concludes that "as long as 'epistemology' bears the stamp of the postpositivist, empiricist project of determining necessary and sufficient conditions for knowledge and devising strategies to refute skepticism, there can be no feminist epistemology. I have shown that the conceptions of knowledge and subjective agency that inform this project are inimical to feminist concerns on many levels: ontological, epistemological, moral, political. Ideals central to the project—ideals of objectivity, impartiality, and universality—are androcentrically derived."[4]

Code's view as encapsulated here will provide an instructive foil to Aristotle's epistemology, which is certainly empiricist while not postpositivist and which may prove at the end of the day to embody androcentric ideals. The appropriate starting for any investigation of Aristotle's epistemology is his discussion of knowledge in the *Posterior Analytics*. This is the only extended treatment of epistemology in the Aristotelian corpus and despite detractors it has been and continues to be accepted as canonical.[5] The first question I plan to address is whether Aristotle's conception of demonstrative science embodies the same ideals of objectivity, impartiality, and universality that Code finds in recent epistemology. The *Posterior Analytics* sets out the requirements for a demonstrative science, and these requirements provide the framework for understanding Aristotle's remarks about method in many of his later writings.[6] These texts will be the focus of the first part of my investigation.

My second question is prompted by Code's discussion of the autonomy of reason. "Beliefs that knowers can and should be self-sufficient, and that objects of knowledge are independent and separate from them, yield a composite picture of knowledge in which autonomy is a privileged value. A dominant feature of this picture is the assumption that knowledge is a product of inquiry that stands alone in the sense that details of the processes of its production are irrelevant to its structure, content, and/or evaluation."[7] Here the question for me is whether Aristotle's conception of the knower and/or his conception of a community of knowers is such that either conception is gendered. This question will be investigated primarily in light of Aristotle's description of the acquisition of the first principles of science in the final chapter of the *Posterior Analytics* and the first two books of the *Metaphysics*.

My third question is prompted by Simone de Beauvoir's critique of essentialist thinking about women. De Beauvoir writes:[8] "Just as for the ancients there was an absolute vertical with reference to which the oblique was defined so there is an absolute human type, the masculine. Woman has ovaries, a uterus; these peculiarities imprison her in her subjectivity, circumscribe her within the limits of her own nature. . . . Thus humanity is male and man defines woman not in herself but as relative to him: she is not regarded as an autonomous being" (xxvii–xxviii).

De Beauvoir's insight that human essence has been conceived by Western thinkers in a way that obfuscates the historical existence of women and proffers instead an objectified feminine essence has been developed by, among others, Luce Irigaray and Mary Daly.[9] Daly has argued that male-authored texts in all fields have systematically deprived women of knowledge of ourselves by erasing (excluding) or grossly distorting the characteristics, the bodies, and the lived experience of woman and depriving women of even a vocabulary in which to describe our natures and oppression. My question is whether Aristotle's essentialism is vulnerable to some or all of these criticisms. Does he in effect erase women from his texts unless he is specifically addressing gender differences? The texts to be discussed here are ones that speak to the issue of a human essence, and these are found in a number of works from the *Metaphysics* to the biological treatises.

I shall attempt to save Aristotle from the most serious feminist charges against him. This defense will prove only of limited assistance, as it will leave some of the feminist objections to Aristotle's epistemological views and practices standing.

Demonstrative Knowledge

We suppose ourselves to possess unqualified scientific knowledge . . . when we know the cause on which the fact depends, as the cause of that fact and of no other, and further that the fact could not be other than it is. (*Post. Anal.* 71b9–12; Mure trans.)

These lines give expression to the conception of knowledge that guides Aristotle's detailed account of knowledge in the *Posterior Analytics*. The stance taken here seems to make good philosophical sense. It is a view that Aristotle's audience would most likely grant him as would many, more recent philosophers. His words have a remarkably up-to-date ring to them. Yet it is this ideal that spawns a conception of epistemic require-ments in the *Posterior Analytics* that in its modern versions is often under attack by feminists. Code, as we have seen, charges that the ideals of objectivity, impartiality, and universality are androcentrically derived. Since the central ideals in Aristotle's account of demonstrative knowl-edge are universality and necessity, the question becomes whether these Aristotelian ideals are the same as or have as consequences the postposi-tivist ideals criticized by Code. Feminists including Code have called at-tention to the many historical circumstances in which the sex of the knower has shaped and distorted the operative notion of universality, and so I shall examine whether Aristotle's gendered concept of the human essence is a consequence of the epistemic ideals he accepts.[10]

To have unqualified knowledge one must have, Aristotle goes on to argue, certain knowledge of universal propositions expressing necessary predications. The epistemic ideal is satisfied, Aristotle believes, when that fact that we claim to know is deduced from its cause, construed as a set of necessary and sufficient conditions for the fact to obtain. This condition is met when we have a syllogism in the first figure, first mood, the conclusion of which is the fact that is known and the middle term is the cause of the fact. That is, the premises Aab (every a is b) and Abc (every b is c), not only entail the conclusion Aac (every a is c), but also establish that the predication of c of a is necessary, because the conclu-sion is derived through a middle term that is the cause of Aac. In short, the object of knowledge could be no other than it is.

On this picture, the particular and time-bound are eliminated from consideration except insofar as they are subsumable under universals ex-pressing timeless truths. If I eat one of the two pears in front of me, only one will remain. This bit of perceptual "knowledge" can be deduced from the universal proposition that the subtraction of one from two yields one. The universal proposition provides the weak epistemic warrant that the claim about the particular pears has.[11] For Aristotle, strictly speaking, I cannot know in the strict sense that any claim about the particular pears, for instance, that there are two pears on the table, is true, because the particulars are apprehended only for so long as I observe them. I have a true belief about them but not knowledge. Knowledge consists in generalizations about the natures of pears and numerical relations. The difficulty here from a feminist perspective is that human beings, both as knowers and as objects of knowledge, exist in particular circumstances; historical differences in gender, class, race, social or political milieu will, like the peculiar features and existence of our two pears, disappear as proper objects of knowledge to be replaced by abstractions that eliminate individual differences. All too often in the history of science, this process of abstraction has engendered generalizations that were distorted by the historical circumstances, gender, and social class of the scientist.[12]

The universality of the premises and conclusion in a demonstrative syllogism are formal constraints that partially secure the epistemic objective of certainty. "An attribute belongs universally to a subject when it can be shown to belong to any random instance of that subject (*Post. Anal.* 73b32–33). Universal claims by their very nature make abstraction central to scientific method. The scientist may attend to individual cases but does so with an eye to the general characteristics of the observable particulars. The physicist, Aristotle points out, abstracts the notion of physical bodies in motion from the other features of actual bodies (1077b23–31). The modern ideal of disinterested objectivity that is marked by detachment from particular circumstances is arguably a direct outcome of the ancient emphasis on universality.[13] Postmodern feminists have argued that the ideal of detachment is derived from male sexuality.[14] Other feminists have criticized the ideal of impartiality (detachment from particular circumstances) on the grounds that it has had pernicious consequences in the history of science. Code is especially critical of the limitations of ethical theories, both Kantian and utilitarian, that embody this ideal.[15] While Aristotle's ethical theory is more sensitive to particular circumstances than modern ethical theories, the ideal of universality as embodied in his model of demonstrative science is implicated insofar as the Aristotelian concept of universality has detachment from particular circumstances as a consequence.

Since for Aristotle, logical rigor and syntactically universal premises are not sufficient to warrant an unqualified claim to know, the question becomes to what extent do the further requirements of necessity and proof through a causal middle term increase the emphasis on detachment from the concreteness of actual observations and experiments? Aristotle defines necessity by appeal to the notion of per se (essential) predication. He gives four different accounts of per se predication in *Posterior Analytics* I.4, two of which are central to his account of demonstrative knowledge.

> Per se attributes are (1) such as belong to their subject as elements in its essential nature (e.g. line thus belongs to triangle, point to line) . . . (2) such that while they belong to certain subjects the subjects to which they belong are contained in the attribute's own defining formula. Thus straight and curved belong to line. (*Post. Anal.* 73a34–39; Mure trans.)

Aristotle's clear intent is to make the connection between subject and predicate in a sentence, where the predicate is said of the subject essentially, a matter of definition.[16] This conception of per se predication is all of a piece with Aristotle's oft-repeated claim that the definiens of a concept is one, even though the verbalization of the definiens typically consists of several terms. Aristotle pictures the practice of scientific definition as the act of unpacking a single concept and in the course of this predicating one term of another. At the end of the chapter, when Aristotle sums up his position at 73b17–20, it is in the language of the first two definitions:

> So far then as concerns the sphere of connexions scientifically known in the unqualified sense, all attributes which are essential either in the sense that their subjects are contained in them, or in the sense that they are contained in their subjects, are necessary as well as consequentially connected with their subjects. (*Post. Anal.* 73b16–18; follows Mure trans.)

In short, a necessary premise expresses a relation between an attribute and its subject that is secured by a definitional nexus. This is Aristotle's preferred definition of necessity. A universal relation between the two items expressed in a proposition is necessary just in case the definition of the subject or predicate includes the other. The definition of a triangle contains the concept of a line and hence the geometrical definition of triangle and other propositions derived from the definition express necessary truths. Here a comparison of Euclid's formulation of the definition may prove instructive: "Rectilineal are those which are contained by straight lines, trilateral figures being those contained by three" (Euclid, *Elements*, Def. 19, T. Heath trans.).

The rigorous notion of necessary espoused in the *Posterior Analytics* obviously rules out any sort of flexibility that would allow a model science to take account of different contexts or distinctive individual characteristics. To be a human being is to have certain characteristics essentially, on this model, and only these common characteristics will be mentioned in scientific statements about human beings. The definition of per se predication in the *Posterior Analytics* seems especially well suited to formal sciences such as geometry, from which Aristotle draws his examples, and perhaps least suited to sciences dealing with biological individuals, where variability seems the rule.[17]

Aristotle's conception of per se predication introduces a stronger constraint on universality than the modern ideal of universality. If as Code and other feminists have charged the ideal of universality is problematic, then the ideal of necessary connections espoused by Aristotle would be even more problematic because it privileges essences over historically existing objects and individuals. Part of the appeal of per se predicates for Aristotle is that necessary statements will *ex hypothesi* be universal in form. The belief that science is about the universal, not the particular, is not a peculiarly Aristotelian ideal—as is evident from the debates about the status of statistical laws in twentieth-century philosophy of science. This ideal, however, drives a more abstract conception of the objects of inquiry than would be the case, were the particulars recognized as objects in their own right. This tendency is enhanced by Aristotle's offering per se predication as the way to guarantee the universality of demonstrative premises. The object of inquiry is not simply to discover universal generalizations, which hold true of particular cases, but to discover essences that are distinctive of the kinds under which particulars fall. Discovering that a universal generalization seems to hold of a sample of the natural kind is a first step toward understanding the essential characteristics of the kind. The latter is the object of the inquiry.

A universal generalization acknowledges in a weak sense the existence of particulars; in contrast, an essence focuses attention exclusively upon universal and necessary characteristics.[18] As Aristotle points out, the actual size of the triangle that the geometer imagines plays no role in her reasoning (*De Mem.* 450a1–8). The geometer may imagine or draw a small triangle in order to solve a problem that posits a large triangle. One can assign any magnitude one wishes to these token triangles as long as

the assignments are consistent with the essential characteristics of triangles. When concrete individuals are viewed as exemplars of essential
characteristics, many of their actual concrete characteristics become irrelevant and others open to reinterpretation. The combination of abstraction from particular circumstances and selection of certain
characteristics as typical of the kind in question provides an opening for
ideologically driven norms to shape the universal that results. That Aristotle would believe that the biologist should discover the set of characteristics that are essential to human beings is not surprising, for this belief
follows from the application of his norm of universality to the study of
biological individuals. That the theory that results in *Generation of Animals* assimilates being female to being maimed is surprising at least to the
modern reader.[19]

Sexual dimorphism is, as Aristotle recognizes, a universal characteristic
of many species. He also believes that biological individuals of both sexes
belong to the same species and that the species is the level at which
determinations of essence should be made. Because the species is the
primary object of study, the individual is of interest only insofar as she or
he exhibits the essential characteristics of the species. Aristotle is forced
by his conception of science to choose one sex or the other as more
typical of the species and to treat the other sex as deviant. Not surprisingly, he chooses the male.[20] "That is why wherever possible and so far
as possible the male is separate from the female, since it is something
better and more divine in that it is the principle of movement for generated things, while the female serves as their matter" (*Gen. An.* 732a6–10).
This example lays bare the crux of the issue for many feminists. When
faced with a choice between specimens of different sexes, both with equal
claim to be exemplars of the species, Aristotle decides in favor of the
male. This is but one case among many, where the abstract ideal of a
model representative of a natural kind has been used in a way that has
lessened the claim by particular subgroups within it to full membership in
the kind. In the case of sciences dealing with human beings the abstract
conception of the species has been interpreted repeatedly in the history
of science and philosophy in a way that furthers the interests of the dominant racial, economic, or gender classes.[21]

Even so, a proponent of idealized models might argue that it is not the
abstraction of distinctive species characteristics that is at fault in such
cases. Rather, it is the failure to distance himself sufficiently from the
particulars that prevents Aristotle from viewing sexual differences as a

disjunctive pair of characteristics that belongs to the species. In biological writings other than the *Generation of Animals*, Aristotle adheres to this more abstract, and arguably less objectionable, universal conception of human being. The difficulty with this defense is that in many contexts sexual difference cannot be ignored; the *Generation of Animals* is just such a context. It is not possible to describe animal reproduction without acknowledging different sex roles in reproduction. Aristotle attempts to explain these anatomical differences in terms of a model where he is limited to the species essence or form and its realization in matter; thus female bodies and reproductive functions are analyzed in terms of the failure of the species form to replicate itself fully. The sad truth is that the simpler and more comprehensive an explanatory paradigm is, the more limitations it will impose on the explanation of any sort of intra-species differences, even ones that are as widespread as reproductive differences.[22]

Knowers

Because human beings are not only objects of knowledge but knowing subjects, applying the epistemic ideal developed in the *Posterior Analytics* to the epistemological task of characterizing knowers will lead to a similarly generic and abstract conception of the knower. This conception of the knower also has a counterpart in contemporary epistemology. Lorraine Code says of Anglo-American mainstream epistemology today:

> The question 'Who is S?' <in 'S knows that p'> is regarded neither as legitimate nor as relevant. . . . If it matters who S is, then it must follow that something peculiar to S's character or nature could bear on the validity of the knowledge she or he claims: that S's *identity* might count among the conditions that make that knowledge claim possible. For many philosophers, such a suggestion would undermine the cherished assumption that knowledge can—and should—be evaluated on its own merits. (2)[23]

Code has argued, as have other feminist epistemologists, that this conception of an ideal knower masks the way in which mainstream epistemology is embedded in a specific set of interests, those of a privileged group of white men (x). If indeed an abstract conception of the knower serves particular gender and class interests, Aristotle's conception of knowledge in the *Posterior Analytics* may be even more problematic than its modern counterpart. At least on the modern schema, "S knows that p", the knower is acknowledged and must be taken into account in the conditions laid down as necessary and sufficient for the satisfaction of the schema; for instance, S knows that p if and only if S believes that p and p is true.[24] Aristotle emphasizes the characteristics of 'p' and ignores the knower almost entirely. The object of knowledge is realized in a human mind but only its characteristics, universality, necessity, and so forth are relevant to the question of its being an object of knowledge. In a striking illustration of this approach in the *Metaphysics*, Aristotle asserts that the formal cause of the statue is the art of sculpting (1032a32–14). The object of knowledge, in this instance, the rules of sculpting, determine the application of the rules and the knower serves only as the efficient cause of the statue. The extent to which the knower as a person has given way to a knowing mind in Aristotle's epistemology should be clear from *Posterior Analytics* II.19. The knowing mind is eclipsed in turn by an explanation that emphasizes the realization of the universal as a cognitive object. Considering the matter of grasping first principles, the most comprehensive universals, Aristotle describes the process of acquiring universals four different times in *Posterior Analytics* II.19; he describes the process twice in terms of the cognitive capacities involved—perception, experience, art and science—and twice in terms of the emergence of the universal from perceptions of concrete individuals. Here is his final description:

> What we have just said but not said clearly, let us say again: when one of the undifferentiated things makes a stand, there is a primitive universal in the mind [ψυχή] (for though one perceives the particular, perception is of the universal, e.g. of man but not of Callias the man); again a stand is made in these, until what has no parts and is universal stands, e.g., such and such an animal <stands>, until animal does, and in this <a stand is made> in the same way. (*Post. Anal.* 100a15–b3, Barnes trans.)

The process begins with the perception of objects in the world. These objects present themselves as concrete individuals and, simultaneously, as exemplifications of universals. The characteristics of an individual (e.g., Callias) are determined by the kind of thing the individual is. Callias cannot have four legs; if he is not maimed, he must have hands rather than paws. Such human characteristics differentiate him from all nonhuman objects including other animals, and they are much more important and immediately present to sense than the features of his hands that differentiate him from other humans. Thus Aristotle claims that the perception is not properly speaking of Callias the man but of man; i.e., it is of (an exemplification of) the universal human being. This universal is a natural kind. To apprehend it is to grasp a feature of the world. The object not only exemplifies a particular species; it also exemplifies the other universals that the species falls under; Callias is not only a human but also an animal and also a living being.

Aristotle portrays the mind's apprehension of the broader universals, such-and-such animal and animal, not as the immediate consequence of the perception of the individual but rather as a consequence of the recognition that the individual exemplifies a lower-level universal. Just as the characteristics of the natural kind, human being, are largely determined by its falling under the broader universal, such and such animal (e.g., tame pedestrian), and that in turn by falling under animal. In Aristotle's description of the acquisition of the universals, human and animal, the universal, human, is stripped of the peculiar features of the perceptible particular; similarly, the more comprehensive universal, animal, contains fewer individuating features than the narrower one.

It is also noteworthy that this description, like its three predecessors in II.19, is centered on a series of cognitions and cognitive processes. The few references to the mind (soul) in this context emphasize its passivity, its role as the seat of the cognitive processes. This is deliberate, no doubt, for Aristotle insists upon the agency of external object of perception in the *De Anima*.[25] In II.19, we are told that the soul is capable of undergoing (πάσχειν) a process that issues in knowledge of universals. In the *Metaphysics*, when describing rudimentary generalizations, Aristotle talks about many memories producing the faculty (δύναμις) of experience (980b29). By sketching the details of the cognitive process in a way that makes the apprehension of a universal the result of successive manifestations of an external object as an object of cognition, Aristotle hopes to eliminate any peculiarly mental characteristics of the objects of knowledge that would suggest the need to posit an ideal reality of the sort espoused by Plato. In the process, however, Aristotle has embraced the Platonic conception of a knowing mind abstracted from any of the concrete particularities of an actual person. By analyzing the process of apprehending the universal in terms of a series of cognitive states, Aristotle has in effect reduced the knower to general, abstract cognitive powers. The fact that the knower is a particular human being having personal, interpersonal, gender and class interests is completely obscured.

The knower is the transparent agent through which the world makes itself known. Not only is the knower without individual characteristics or interests, the knower is more recipient than agent in the act of knowing. Questions about the sex of the knower would seem to be entirely inappropriate in this context. This is problematic, Code believes, because it reinforces the myth of the idealized, disinterested knower that has historically masked the way in which the interests of knowers have been reflected in their scientific and philosophical theories.[26] That said, Aristotle's reductive analysis arguably does not yield a gendered concept of the knower; the analysis yields a series of cognitive acts, construed as the unfolding of a cognitive capacity that develops out of perception. The cognitive capacity in question is a capacity possessed by all humans and not other animals, and there is no mention of gender in Aristotle's description. Even if Aristotle's conception of the knowing mind is accepted on these grounds, a feminist critic might point out that having a human mind is only a necessary condition for belonging to the community of knowers, as Aristotle envisages it.

The subject of knowledge in *Posterior Analytics* II.19 is simply the human subject identified with its characteristic cognitive capacities for perception and intellection. In the first chapter of the *Metaphysics*, the same subject is revisited and knowledge is viewed as a historical artifact, acquired over time and through the efforts of many thinkers. Just as the individual moves from the particulars of sense perception to the universals of art and science, collectively humans have moved from the immediate concerns of survival, initially met through ad hoc solutions based on perception and experience, to the arts based on generalization that enabled effective problem solving and ultimately generated leisure time. With leisure, people were able to achieve the abstract level of understanding characteristic of mathematics, the other theoretical sciences and philosophy (981b17–25). Appealing to a historical process might have prompted Aristotle to explore the conception of knowledge as a social construction, that he tacitly recognizes, but it does not. It serves only to buttress his optimism about human cognitive capacities: "The investigation of the truth is in one way hard, in another easy. An indication of this is found in the fact that no one is able to attain the truth adequately, while, on the other hand, we do not collectively fail, but every one says something true about the nature of things and while individually we contribute little or nothing to the truth, by the union of all a considerable amount is amassed" (*Met.* II.1.993a30–b4; Ross trans.).

Optimism about the collective cognitive powers of humans is unexceptionable from a feminist perspective but the notion of a community of knowers is more problematic. Few philosophers, Aristotle included, have wanted to make membership in the actual community of knowers universal. The determination of whose beliefs should be taken seriously is often discussed at the outset of an Aristotelian treatise. In *Nicomachean Ethics* I.3, for instance, Aristotle limits the study of political science, which includes ethics, to older men of experience and mature character (1095a2–11). In *Metaphysics* I.1, Aristotle treats leisure as an absolute requirement for the person engaged in theoretical reasoning. In concrete social terms, however, a class that has leisure, such as Aristotle's Egyptian priests, is materially supported by the classes that do not have leisure.

Another striking feature of the *Metaphysics* account is that Aristotle places much greater emphasis on the role of experience as the cognitive faculty through which the mind moves from perceptible particulars to abstract universals than he did in the *Posterior Analytics*. The role of experience in the apprehension of objects of knowledge limits access to the community of knowers to a much smaller and more homogeneous group than the group made up of all humans having normal rational capacities. To see why this is true, let us turn to Aristotle's description of the role of experience in the acquisition of knowledge.

> Now art arises when from many notions gained by experience one universal judgment about a class of object is produced. For to have a judgment that when Callias was ill of this disease this did him good, and similarly in the case of Socrates and in many individual cases, is a matter of experience; but to judge that it has done good to all persons of a certain constitution, marked off in one class, when they were ill of this disease, e.g. to phlegmatic or bilious people when burning with fever—this is a matter of art.

One sees or hears that Socrates is ill and observes that a particular medication improves his condition, similarly with Callias. Insofar as these observations concern the present state of individual persons, the observer is operating at the level of perception; insofar as the observer employs past observations in the present, memory is operative. Experience as defined in this passage comes into play when past and present observations are grouped together and common features are recognized and generalizations based on these features are made. Aristotle remarks that experience can be as useful in a particular instance as art (981a13–b9); whether Socrates is given the appropriate medicine on the basis of experience or on the basis of the art of medicine will make no difference to his recovery.[27]

By grouping together appropriate memories, the experienced person is able to make use of generalizations and to bring past observations to bear on the present situation. Insofar as this person employs generalizations, experience can be said to produce homespun universals, and Aristotle's description of experience in the *Posterior Analytics* suggests as much.[28] What experience does not yield are universals in the technical sense of the *Posterior Analytics*' definition of universal (73b27–29), and Aristotle marks the divide between experience and art by employing the contrast between particular and universal in the strict sense.[29] The scope of the universals of art and science should be such that the universal is predicable of all and only those objects which exemplify the universal characteristic at issue.

According to *Metaphysics* I, unlike experience, art and science provide an understanding of causes. Through experience, a person recognizes that such and such is so but not why it is so.[30] In this respect too, experience is more akin to perception than science (cf. 981b10–11). Knowledge that something is the case precedes knowledge of its cause (89b29–31). Aristotle envisages a progressive development where there are not quantum jumps between cognitive stages but rather smooth transitions from one stage to another as understanding deepens. First, we see that a particular medication benefits an ill Socrates; in time we grasp that this type of medication alleviates the suffering of other individuals having similar symptoms; subsequently we understand why the medication is beneficial when we recognize the regularity governing its effectiveness.

A moment's reflection on this example reveals that having cognitive access to the relevant medical universal will be limited to those persons whose life experiences involve the treatment of illness and who have the means to acquire the medication involved. This is the sort of limitation that falls outside the scope of the epistemological theory and yet has important consequences for actual knowers that has prompted feminists to charge that traditional epistemology has served to maintain the dominance of particular racial and gender groups.[31] One might grant that this holds of the person who discovers the relevant universal without agreeing that anyone who possesses the universal must have had appropriate experiences. Aristotle, however, points out the severe limitations of abstract knowledge of the universal: "For the physician does not cure man, except in an incidental way, but Callias or Socrates or some other called by some such individual name, who happens to be a man" (*Met*. 981a18–20, Ross trans.). The art of medicine consists in knowledge of the universal regularities governing human health. These universals are culled from the experience of treating ill human beings. But unless the medical practitioner is able to apply the appropriate universal to an actual case of illness in an individual, the practitioner will fail to exercise the art. Even though the theoretical sciences do not bring universals to bear on particulars in the way that the arts must, the continuity of the process from experience to art to science ensures that putative knowledge here, too, would be evaluated in terms of how well the universal fit observation.

While any human being may be capable of having the experience required to grasp the universals of a particular art or science, only certain humans will have had it. Moreover, even having the folk "knowledge" that leads one to give the medicine the first time is itself a function of prior experience. Experience is inescapably shaped by one's historical situation—as Aristotle clearly acknowledges in *Metaphysics* I. The community of knowers in a field will be limited to those persons whose past experiences equip them with the cognitive materials required for the grasp of the relevant universals; in the case of the arts, experience will also be required in order to exercise the art. As a result, knowers will primarily be members of the dominant social and gender classes, because there is a much greater likelihood that the members of these classes will have had the necessary experiences. In light of the abysmally restricted access that even upper-class Athenian women had to education and participation in public life, an Athenian woman was not likely to become a member of any actual community of knowers; nor is she represented in any paradigmatic community of knowers described by Aristotle. To have experience of the sort relevant to either the theoretical or practical sciences is to have lived in a fashion that is not accessible to women or lower-class men.[32]

The community of knowers is also de facto gendered through Aristotle's appeal to *endoxa* (the opinions of the many, or the learned) as the starting points of inquiry.[33] The *endoxa* that Aristotle actually appeals to are without exception the opinions of sophists, other philosophers or mature men of experience (in the case of ethics). The *endoxa* typically provide Aristotle's starting point in an inquiry and so his selection of experts affects the outcome. It is not idle then to ask whose opinions will be included among the *endoxa*. Aristotle subjects the *endoxa* to critical scrutiny, and this does lead to the outright rejection of some *endoxa* and the modification of others; nevertheless, the outcome of his investigation is shaped by his original choices. Which *endoxa* are included and which are ignored at the outset of an inquiry will have an enormous impact on the outcome of the inquiry. Gender bias becomes all but inescapable, because only the opinions of males are included by Aristotle.[34]

Aristotelian Essences and Sexual Difference

It has become clear that by restricting demonstrative science to universal and necessary principles, Aristotle forces a level of abstraction upon science that lends itself to distorted conceptions of women such as we find in Aristotle's *Generation of Animals*. In this section, the notion of essence as developed by Aristotle in *Metaphysics* VII will be examined in light of de Beauvoir's charge that essentialist thinking about humanity has led to the conception of women as beings lacking autonomy and thus as something less than fully human. This criticism is echoed in Irigaray's charge that the feminine and sexual difference has been obliterated from Western thought.[35] In a similar vein, Mary Daly uses the term "erasure" for the myriad ways in which scholars have ignored the actual situation of women and have obfuscated the ways in which societies have silenced, maimed, or killed their female members. From male-identified literature, history, and social science, Daly argues, women have been erased.[36] The question then becomes whether Aristotle's conception of essence and form in the central books of the *Metaphysics* results in the omission or erasure of women from philosophical discussions of the human essence.[37]

Aristotle's account of essence is motivated by a conceptual difficulty that he faces, namely, the need to find objects that are unchanging to serve as the objects of definition and knowledge—since only such objects will satisfy the epistemic requirements set out in the *Posterior Analytics*. Aristotle wants to meet this requirement without positing Ideal objects. The analysis of concrete particulars into form and matter and the identification of form with species essence is Aristotle's solution to the problem he inherits from Plato: "Plato . . . assumed that there can be no general definition of sensible things which are always changing. These entities he called 'Ideas' and held that all sensible things are named after them and in virtue of their relation to them; for the plurality of things which bear the same name as the Forms exist by participation in them" (*Met.* 987b4–11).

While rejecting Platonic Ideas, Aristotle accepts many of the epistemic requirements defended by Plato; namely, that objects of knowledge must be unchanging universals, substances and essences, and that definitions expressing the essences of basic objects secure the foundations of knowledge. Natural languages also depend upon the existence of objects having many of the characteristics of Platonic Ideas. Notwithstanding, Aristotle believes that Plato's ideal objects are an ontological complication that can be avoided by a proper analysis of the ontological underpinnings of science and language.

When Aristotle first approaches the topic of essence in *Metaphysics* VII 4, he describes his remarks as linguistic (λογικῶς) and then immediately justifies this approach by pointing out that the essence of each thing just is what the thing is said to be in itself (*kath' hauto*). Aristotle goes on to argue that the essence of a thing excludes all extraneous (nonessential) characteristics and that the statement of the essence is a synonymous paraphrase that captures the nature of the definiendum without circularity or redundancy. If 'surface' is mentioned in the definiens of surface, then the definition is unsatisfactory. But synonymy is not enough according to Aristotle: "Therefore there is an essence only of those things whose formula (λόγος) is a definition (ὁρισμός). For we have a definition not where we have a word and a formula identical in meaning . . . but where there is a formula of something primary; and primary things are those which do not imply the predication of one element in them of another element" (1030a6–11; Ross trans.).

This conception of essence leads Aristotle to conclude that only substances have essences and definitions chiefly, primarily and simply (1031a13).[38] This very narrow notion of essences excludes many of the features of concrete objects. The expression 'pale man' that designates a compound object has no definition, strictly speaking. A single term, snubness, for instance, whose referent is compound (concavity in a nose) is similarly indefinable, according to Aristotle. Accidental unities (pale man, for instance) coincide with concrete substances (Socrates, for example) and thus Aristotle concludes that essence is one with the substance only in the case of indivisible species (1032a4–6, 1037b2–7).

Does the role that species essences play in Aristotle's epistemology lead to the erasure of women? At first glance, the reverse would seem to be true, the single human essence would (or should) be gender-neutral since it is the essence of both males and females. The essence is, however, identified with the form of the species and the form as substance type is realized in different materials to constitute different individuals. As noted above, according to the *Generation of Animals* the form when realized in a male animal is a more perfect exemplar of the species form than a female animal. A feminist critique of Aristotelian essences might press the case against Aristotle further by arguing that the very analysis of substance in terms of form and matter, which is fundamental to Aristotle's ontology in the central books of the *Metaphysics*, is androcentric. On this view, the identification of the male animal with form and the female with matter in the biological writings would not be the result of ideology creeping into Aristotle's biology and possibly distorting a gender-neutral ontology; the ontology is gendered and thus engenders the outcome in the biology. While other authors in this volume discuss these issues in detail, in the present context, a brief overview of the difficulty will be given in order to see why feminists have criticized Aristotelian ontology.[39]

According to Aristotle, form is actuality whereas matter is potentiality; form is unitary and specific whereas matter is amorphous; form is active whereas matter is passive.[40] A natural, living being is the expression of a species form, the source of its essential characteristics, in a particular body. The weak claim would be that Aristotle's characterization of form and matter when applied to biological, gendered individuals lend themselves to the identification of form with the male and matter with the female. De Beauvoir points out that a unitary conception of the human being fosters the acceptance of the male as the paradigm with the result that the female is viewed as inessential, as passive rather than as an autonomous agent.[41] The stronger claim to be found in one version or another in a number of recent writers, including Luce Irigaray and Mary Daly, is that these notions are themselves gendered.[42] Gendered concepts distort the reality of the lived experience of women and they deprive women of a vocabulary for characterizing our experiences; thus if Aristotle's abstract conception of essence and form is gendered, it should be rejected by feminists. Moreover, as Irigaray has argued, the very logic of identity and singularity is derived from the sexuality of the male; female sexuality has no single organ and thus no single locus for self-identification.[43] This multiplicity means that all attempts at finding a single female essence are doomed to failure; in addition, there can be no satisfactory characterization of sexual difference that accords with the logic of identity.

There is no question that for Aristotle, unity and self-identity are marks of substances having essences: "Each thing itself, then, and its essence are one and the same in no merely accidental way, as is evident both from the preceding arguments and because to know each thing, at least, is just to know its essence, so that even by the exhibition of instances it becomes clear that both must be one" (*Met.* 1031b18–22; Ross trans.). If Irigaray is right and the notion of sameness and identity are expressions of phallic sexuality, then Aristotle's abstract notion of essence is gendered. Even if she is not, his notion of species-specific, unitary essences is inadequate, because it does not allow for an egalitarian account of sexual difference.

Aristotle's Defense

We have seen that many of the epistemic requirements embraced by Aristotle as well as his analysis of the acquisition of knowledge and the nature of essence are vulnerable to critiques of the sort found in feminist epistemologies. At the same time, it is at least arguable that Aristotle has a way to avoid many of these criticisms. What can be (or should be) said on Aristotle's behalf?

The requirements of demonstrative science, namely, universality and necessary premises, seemed to eliminate all more particular claims from consideration, to obscure differences among individuals, and to leave little or no room for the recognition of the complexities of human subjects. Aristotle seems to acknowledge this difficulty in the *Nicomachean Ethics*—at least to the extent of recognizing that different sciences have different methods.[44]

> Now fine and just actions, which political science investigates, admit of much variety and fluctuation of opinion so that they may be thought to exist only by convention, and not by nature. And goods also give rise to a similar fluctuation because they bring

harm to many people; . . . we must be content, then in speaking
of such subjects and with such premisses to indicate the truth
roughly and in outline, and in speaking about things which are
only for the most part true and with premisses of the same kind
to reach conclusions that are no better. (*N.E.* 1094b14–23; Ross
trans.)

This is but one instance in many where Aristotle shows a willingness to
modify the requirements of demonstrative science in order to adapt them
to the subject matter at hand. Nowhere is this so striking, perhaps, as in
his modification of the concept of necessity in different scientific contexts.

In *Posterior Analytics* I.4, the favored definition of necessary predication
makes necessity a consequence of definition. Demonstrative premises
would be necessarily true, because true by analysis; their truth could be
determined solely by appeal to the meanings of their constituent parts.[45]
However, even in *Posterior Analytics* I.4, a nonanalytic sense of necessity
is introduced with the mention of a causally determined necessity. In
other works, moreover, the weakening of the condition on belonging
necessarily to belonging in every instance allows the laws of empirical
cosmology to be viewed as just as necessary as the axioms of geometry.[46]
What is, perhaps, most striking, is the extension of necessity in the biological treatises to include attributes of a species that are not essential.[47]
Having abandoned the requirement that the attribute belong essentially
to the subject, Aristotle substitutes a weaker relation between the subject
and its hypothetically necessary attributes, such that hypothetical necessity is mediated through a strong teleological principle of natural development. The flexibility that Aristotle displays in adapting his epistemic
principles to fit disciplines dealing with living creatures from biology to
political science suggests there is more common ground between Aristotle and contemporary feminist critics of science than might at first appear.

That said, it must be admitted that Aristotle's willingness to modify
epistemic requirements to allow for individual variation is not so great as
to allow for the abandonment of the goals of universality and necessary
causal relations in the theoretical sciences nor to abandon completely
the goal of universality in the practical sciences.[48] Admitting exceptions
to universal principles is not the renunciation of universal principles.
Moreover, Aristotle would be even more unwilling to relinquish the ideal

of a separate object of knowledge that makes itself known to the knowing mind, since this ideal is embedded not only in his epistemology but also in his conception of human cognition. Yet feminist critics of science and traditional epistemologies have often emphasized the actual conditions under which theories are produced and this emphasis has resulted in their rejection of the idealized notion of the known stripped bare of the social conditions under which the theory is constructed.[49]

The knower is not male on Aristotle's account because in an important sense the knower is not embodied but rather the actualization of a cognitive capacity possessed by any adult human being. Nevertheless, his conception of the knower is arguably gendered. If the notion of the autonomy of reason is androcentric as feminists have argued, then Aristotle's conception is gendered. In addition, as we have seen, Aristotle appeals to the community of experts in a field to provide the norms for that field. He assumes that this community will prove to be self-correcting—at least over time. This assumption may seem unwarranted when we consider the history of science and philosophy where it is very evident that communities of experts often fail to correct the dominant theoretical paradigm even in the face of enormous amounts of evidence against the theory. All too often, such resistance has also preserved the class interests of the experts. Aristotle might say in defense that as egregious as some of these failures have been, they have been corrected by later theorists; i.e., that the method is self-correcting. Unquestionably, had the community of experts in a particular area included women, Aristotle would have accepted the judgment of the community. In principle, his appeal to a community of experts is not androcentric.

While some feminist epistemologists have voiced a commitment to a science that is free from gendered values, and such a goal is arguably consistent with Aristotle's epistemology, if not his practice, Longino (among others) has argued that this commitment is wrong-headed.

> But if scientific methods generated by constitutive values cannot guarantee independence from contextual values, then that approach to sexist science won't work. We cannot restrict ourselves simply to the elimination of bias, but must expand our scope to include the detection of limiting and interpretive frameworks and the finding or construction of more appropriate frameworks. . . . Instead of remaining passive with respect to the data and what the data suggest, we can acknowledge our ability to affect the

course of knowledge and fashion or favor research programs that are consistent with the values and commitments we express in the rest of our lives. From this perspective, the idea of a value-free science is not just empty, but pernicious.[50]

Finally, there is the question of whether Aristotle's conception of invariant essences as the proper object of knowledge is vulnerable to a feminist critique. While it is beyond dispute that the way in which Aristotle conceives the human essence is androcentric, there remains the question of whether the method is in principle defensible. Had Aristotle conceived human nature in a gender-neutral way, would the strategy have produced an androgynous conception of human nature and excellence? The obstacle to using essences as a way to neutralize gender, racial, or economic class biases in science is that of finding truly universal characteristics of human beings that will prove useful in social science or even medicine. In light of the well-documented, historical tendency of scientists and philosophers to identify desirable traits with the characteristics of the dominant social and gender class and undesirable ones with those of subordinate groups, separating Aristotle's insistence on essences as fundamental to knowledge from the results it produced in his theorizing is itself suspect from a feminist standpoint.[51] The historical correlation between Aristotelian ways of conceptualizing human essence and sexual difference and the role these conceptualizations have played in advancing the dominant gender and class interests may lend some support to the feminist critics who charge that his ontological commitments are an expression of his phallic sexuality.

In the preceding section, I attempted to save Aristotle's position from feminist criticisms. In conclusion, it must be admitted that this effort was only partially successful. Aristotle is most vulnerable at the points where his idealized conception of knowledge and its objects is challenged by the socially sensitive contexts in which theorizing by actual human beings takes place. It is at these junctures where epistemic ideals are applied to human differences that Aristotle's own efforts as a biologist and political scientist display gender and economic class biases, and these contexts call into question the ability of the ideals of universality, objectivity, and autonomy to ensure that actual theories are free from bias.

Notes

1. To talk about "feminist epistemology" and "mainstream epistemology" as monolithic wholes is misleading, since a variety of positions fall under each label. Still for the sake of brevity, I shall on occasion make just such generalizations. For a helpful discussion of different types of feminist epistemologies, see Sandra Harding, "Feminist Justificatory Strategies," in *Women, Knowledge, and Reality: Explorations in Feminist Philosophy*, ed. Ann Garry and Marilyn Pearsall (Boston, Unwin Hyman, 1989), 189–201.

2. See, for instance, Sandra Harding, *The Science Question in Feminism* (Ithaca: Cornell University Press, 1986); Donna Haraway, "Situated Knowledges: The Science Question in Feminism and the Privilege of Partial Perspective," *Feminist Studies* 14 (1988): 575–9 Evelyn Fox Keller, *Reflections on Gender and Science* (New Haven: Yale University Press, 1985); Genevieve Lloyd, *The Man of Reason: "Male" and "Female" in Western Philosophy* (Minneapolis: University of Minnesota Press, 1984); Naomi Scheman, "Though This Be Method, Yet There is Madness in It," in *A Mind of One's Own: Feminist Essays on Reason and Objectivity*, ed. Louise M. Antony and Charlotte Witt (Boulder, Colo.: Westview, 1993). For a discussion of Aristotle's philosophy of science in relation to the issues raised by several of these authors, see Cynthia Freeland, "Nourishing Speculation" in *Engendering Origins: Critical Feminist Readings in Plato and Aristotle*, ed. Bat-Ami Bar On (Albany: State University of New York Press, 1994).

3. See, for instance, Susan Bordo, *The Flight to Objectivity: Essays in Cartesianism and Culture* (Albany: State University of New York Press, 1987); Genevieve Lloyd, *Man of Reason*. For a feminist critique of feminist readings of seventeenth-century epistemology, see Margaret Atherton, "Cartesian Reason and Gendered Reason" in *A Mind of One's Own*: ed. Antony and Witt.

4. Lorraine Code, *What Can She Know? Feminist Theory and the Construction of Knowledge*, (Ithaca: Cornell University Press, 1991), 314.

5. For a detailed defense of the claim that Aristotle employs the epistemic criteria developed in the *Posterior Analytics* throughout his career, see D. K. W. Modrak, "Aristotle's Epistemology: One or Many Theories? in *Aristotle's Philosophical Development: Problems and Prospects*, ed. W. Wians (Lanham, Md: Rowman & Littlefield, 1995). Terence Irwin is a particularly articulate spokesman for the view that Aristotle's conception of knowledge changes over time (*Aristotle's First Principles*) [Oxford: Clarendon Press 1988).

6. See Modrak, "Aristotle's Epistemology."

7. *What Can She Know?* 110.

8. Simone de Beauvoir, *The Second Sex*, trans. H. M. Parshley, (New York: Random House, 1989), introduction.

9. Luce Irigaray, *This Sex Which is Not One* (Ithaca: Cornell University Press, 1985); Mary Daly, *Gyn/Ecology: The Metaethics of Radical Feminism* (Boston: Beacon, 1990). See also Monique Wittig, "One is Not Born a Woman," *Feminist Issues* 1 (1981): 47–54; 2 (1982): 63–68. Irigaray's positions are discussed at some length in Cynthia Freeland, Chapter 3, this volume.

10. In Chapter 5 of this volume, "Form, Normativity, and Gender in Aristotle: A Feminist Perspective," Charlotte Witt discusses many of the same issues in her first section; we arrive at somewhat different conclusions.

11. For a detailed account of this phenomenon, see Deborah Modrak, *Aristotle: The Power of Perception*, chap. 7 (Chicago: University of Chicago Press, 1987).

12. See note 2 for citations of feminist epistemologists who argue for this claim.

13. Feminists are not of one mind about whether the ideal of disinterested objectivity is in principle problematic. For an articulate presentation of feminist arguments in favor and against this ideal, see articles by Naomi Scheman and Louise Antony in *Metaphilosophy*, July 1995.

14. Cf. Cynthia Freeland, Chapter 3, this volume.

15. Code, *What Can She Know?* 71–79.

16. To summarize a chapter that has been the subject of a recent book and has been discussed at length in numerous other contexts may prove to be rash. See Michael Ferejohn, *The Origins of Aristotelian Science* (New Haven: Yale University Press, 1991) for a detailed study of this chapter; also see Richard McKirahan, *Principles and Proofs: Aristotle's Theory of Demonstrative Science* (Princeton; Princeton University Press, 1992) and J. Barnes, trans. and commentary, *Aristotle's Posterior Analytics* (Oxford: Clarendon Aristotle Series, 1975).

17. Aristotle weakens this requirement in the biological treatises and modifies it substantially in the ethical and political treatises. Whether this practice gives him a way to meet the objections of feminists will be considered below.

18. I shall consider below whether Aristotelian essences or forms are gendered.

19. *Generation of Animals* 737a25–30, 775a9–17. Genevieve Lloyd claims on the basis of the former passage that Aristotle attributes defective capacity to reason to women ("The Man of Reason," in *Women, Knowledge and Reality: Explorations in Feminist Philosophy*, ed. Ann Garry and Marilyn Pearsall [Boston: Unwin Hyman, 1989], 112); I do not believe this passage supports any particular theory of rationality; rationality itself is not mentioned.

20. See also Charlotte Witt, Chapter 5, this volume; Marguerite Deslauriers, Chapter 6, this volume, "Sex and Essence in Aristotle's *Metaphysics* and Biology;" and Cynthia Freeland, "Nourishing Speculation" in *Engendering Origins*, ed. Bat-Ami Bar On.

21. Cf. Louise Antony, who argues that the fact that traditional epistemic ideals have been misused for ideological and social ends does not show that the ideals themselves should be jettisoned; see her "Quine as Feminist: The Radical Import of Naturalized Epistemology" in *A Mind of One's Own*, ed. Antony and Witt.

22. In the practical sciences Aristotle loosens his strictures on universality. Whether this practice provides a way out of the difficulties discussed in this section will be taken up below. Cf. Ruth Groenhout, Chapter 7, this volume, "The Virtue of Care: Aristotelian Ethics and Contemporary Ethics of Care."

23. Code, *What Can She Know?* 1991.

24. For the sake of illustration, I give a minimal set of conditions; most post-Gettier problem attempts to state necessary and sufficient conditions for knowledge add further conditions.

25. See Deborah Modrak, *Aristotle: The Power of Perception*, Part One (Chicago: University of Chicago Press, 1987).

26. Code, *What Can She Know?* See also S. Harding, Jane Flax, "Postmodernism and Gender Relations in Feminist Theory," *Signs* 12 (1987): 621–43; Alison Jaggar, *Feminist Politics and Human Nature* (Totowa, N.J.: Rowman and Allenheld, 1983).

27. Cf. *Nicomachean Ethics* VI.7 1141b16–21: This is why some who do not know, and especially those who have experience, are more practical than others who know; for if a person knew that light meats are digestible and wholesome, but did not know which sorts of meat are light, she or he would not produce health, but the person who knows that chicken is wholesome is more likely to produce health.

28. At *Posterior Analytics* II.19 100a7–8, Aristotle suggests that experience gives rise to the universal which when stabilized is the source of art and knowledge.

29. *Met.* I.1 981a5–30; *Post. Anal.* II.19 100b1–4.

30. Cf. *Nicomachean Ethics* VI.7 1141b14–21.

31. See S. Harding, *Science Question in Feminism*; J. Flax, "Postmodernism"; N. Scheman, "Though This Be Method."

32. In "Political Hierarchies and Family Structure," in *Aristotle's Political Philosophy: Proceedings of the Sixth International Conference on Greek Philosophy, Ierissos, 1994* (Athens: International Association for Greek Philosophy, 1995), I argue that Aristotle excludes women,

artisans and others from the rights of citizenship because their capacity for happiness is marginal at best. This political exclusion will have consequences for the acquisition of the theoretical sciences for the reasons discussed above.

33. For a discussion of *endoxa*, see Robert Bolton, "The Epistemological Basis of Aristotelian Dialectic," in *Proceedings of the La Rochelle Conference on Aristotle's Metaphysics and Philosophy of Science*, ed. P. Pellegrin and D. Devereux (Paris, 1990).

34. See Freeland, Chapter 3, this volume for further discussion of the way that *endoxa* are gendered.

35. Cf. Irigaray, Chapter 2, this volume, and Freeland, Chapter 3, this volume.

36. Daly, *Gyn/Ecology*.

37. This issue is also discussed at length in Witt, Chapter 5, this volume.

38. That definition in the strict sense is the *logos* expressing the essence and hence pertains primarily to substance is asserted in a number of other contexts in the *Metaphysics*; see, for example, V.8 1017b22, VII.7 1032b14.

39. See especially Chapters 3, 5, and 6, this volume.

40. Cf. Caroline Whitbeck's argument that the motifs embodied in psychology and philosophy reveal a masculist ontology of dualistic oppositions ("A Different Reality: Feminist Ontology," in *Women, Knowledge, and Reality*, ed. Garry and Pearsall).

41. De Beauvoir, *The Second Sex*.

42. Irigaray, Chapter 2, this volume, and *This Sex Which is Not One*; Daly, *Gyn/Ecology*.

43. *This Sex Which is Not One*, 26.

44. These differences in method are not limited to the differences between practical sciences such as ethics and politics and the theoretical sciences, for Aristotle adapts the principles of demonstrative science to the subject at hand in theoretical sciences as well. See Modrak, "Aristotle's Epistemology."

45. See above.

46. See Modrak, "Aristotle's Epistemology."

47. *On the Parts of Animals* I.1; see also Modrak, "Aristotle's Epistemology."

48. Cf. *N.E.* 1140b8–9: It is for this reason that we think Pericles and men like him have practical wisdom; namely, because they can see what is good for themselves and what is good for men in general.

49. See, for example, Sue V. Rosser, "Re-visioning Clinical Research: Gender and the Ethics of Experimental Design," *Hypatia* (1989) 125–39; Helen Longino, "Scientific Objectivity and Logics of Science," *Inquiry* 26 (1983): 85–106.

50. Helen E. Longino, "Can There Be a Feminist Science?" in *Women, Knowledge and Reality*, ed. Garry and Pearsall, 212.

51. For an especially clear discussion of the question whether the scientific norm of (assumed) objectivity is gendered and an argument for why feminists should reject this norm even if it is not strongly gendered, see Sally Haslanger, "On Being Objective and Being Objectified," in *A Mind of One's Own*, ed. Antony and Witt.

5

Form, Normativity, and Gender in Aristotle

A Feminist Perspective

Charlotte Witt

For surely it is not likely either that fire or earth
or any such element should be the reason why
things manifest goodness and beauty both in
their being and in their coming to be, or that those
thinkers should have supposed it was.
—*Met.* 984b10–14

Metaphysical and scientific theories are paradigms of objectivity. A metaphysical theory explains the basic constituents and structure of reality, and scientific theories explain the world, and predict its events. And, it is widely assumed that in order to be objective, true to reality or nature, metaphysics and science must be value-free or devoid of normativity. Yet, as feminist theorists, among others, have pointed out, the histories of metaphysics and science are rife with examples of theories that are infused with normative and political dimensions like gender.[1] Normative concepts like gender can appear in the language of a theory, in its assumptions or, more blatantly, in its core concepts. Feminists have argued that gender appears in all these ways in Aristotle's metaphysical theory of hylomorphism and his scientific theory of reproduction.[2]

Most feminist philosophers of science think that the values that appear in theory originate on the subjective side, in the theorizer.[3] They are the values of the scientist himself, projected and glorified in the name of science and objectivity. Hence, much feminist attention has been given to debunking the image of the disinterested scientist, and in detailing the covert political norms that guide modern scientific research. Objectivity itself, the preeminent norm of modern scientific practice, is seen by some feminists in psychological terms, as a projection of the self-image of the scientist, or alternatively, by others, as representing the aspirations of a class (bourgeois), gender (male) and historical period (post-Galilean science).[4]

Feminist developments of the thesis that objectivity, the cardinal norm of modern science, is androcentric has been varied. Borrowing Sandra Harding's terminology we can distinguish feminist empiricists, feminist standpoint theorists, and feminist postmodernists. Feminist postmodernists take the moral of the story to be that Enlightenment thought, including modern science and its norm of objectivity, are hopelessly implicated in patriarchy, and should be rejected, period. In contrast, both feminist empiricists and standpoint theorists think that feminist criticism will allow for an elimination of androcentric bias in science, and an emergence of genuine objectivity. Paradoxically, it is argued that it is precisely *because* of their explicit political concerns that feminists have been able to decrease distorted research results:

> Scientific knowledge-seeking is supposed to be value-neutral objective, dispassionate, disinterested, and so forth. It is supposed to be protected from political interests, goals, and desires (such as feminist ones) by the norms of science. In particular, science's "method" is supposed to protect the results of research from the social values of researchers. And yet it is obvious to all that many claims which clearly have been generated through research guided by feminist concerns nevertheless appear more plausible (better supported, more reliable, less false, more likely to be confirmed by evidence, etc.) than the beliefs they replace.[5]

Whether the political dimension of metaphysical or scientific theories renders them entirely suspect, makes them candidates for rehabilitation, or might bring them closer to the truth, is a matter of debate among feminist philosophers of science. What all parties to the debate share is the assumption that the values that pervade and shape purportedly value-neutral theory originate on the side of the theorizer.[6] Their task has been to show how feminist values, in contrast to masculinist or racist values, can help eliminate bias and achieve a genuinely value-neutral theory (feminist empiricism), or can help develop an enriched notion of objectivity that is compatible with, and indeed requires, the politically correct values of the feminist inquirer (feminist standpoint theory).[7]

What is never questioned in this debate is the assumption that the norms in a scientific or metaphysical theory originate entirely in the scientist or his culture (race, class, and so forth) and not in nature itself. This is because feminist philosophers of science generally work within the problematic of modern science in which nature is quantitative, devoid of quality and value.[8] Given this view of nature, the only available source of norms in a theory is the theorizer. Where else could they come from? However, this view of nature is itself historically and culturally locatable; it coincides with the rise of modern science, and is constitutive of the way that science has constructed its ideals of objectivity and value-neutrality.

In this essay, I use Aristotle's theory of hylomorphism to suggest an alternative view according to which nature itself contains norms and values. Perhaps the value-neutrality of the objective scientist, and his disinterested relationship to an inert quantitative nature are all of a piece, and part of the task for feminists is to reconceive a richer image of the objects of theory to go along with the richer description of the theorizer and their relationship.[9] And, if nature itself contains norms and values, then any adequate theory of it must include normative language or concepts quite independently of whatever values the theorist brings to it. This essay traces the complex interaction of political and cultural norms that Aristotle brings *to* his theory with the norms that he finds *in* nature itself. While it would be silly, not to mention futile, to recommend a reversal of the scientific revolution, it is neither to suggest that it might be profitable for feminists to be as skeptical of a nature devalued as they have been of its impartial, disinterested observer.[10]

In this essay I argue against an interpretation of Aristotle's metaphysics that conflates objectivity with non-normativity, and then condemns Aristotle for undermining the objectivity of his theories with normative associations and language, and, in particular, gender associations. In its place I propose an interpretation of hylomorphism (Aristotle's famous theory of matter and form) that emphasizes its inherently normative dimension, and I explain the way in which Aristotle attaches the gender norms of his culture to hylomorphism.[11] Hylomorphism is an inherently normative theory of reality because, for Aristotle, nature and reality are infused with value. For Aristotle, then, in order for a theory to be objective, in the sense of true to reality and nature, it must be a normative theory.

My essay treats hylomorphism as both a metaphysical thesis concerning the being (ontological makeup) of sensible substances (you, me, and the tree) and as principles Aristotle uses to explain events in nature like the generation, formation, and functional parts of natural entities (you, me, and the tree). Although I have argued elsewhere that Aristotle's metaphysics and biology are separate projects, there is little doubt that he employs the conceptual triad—matter, form, and substance—in both.[12] And, since the modern divide between metaphysics and science does not coincide with Aristotle's distinction between first philosophy and natural philosophy, it would be artificial to limit myself to one or the other in a discussion of contemporary criticism. Further, although most feminist criticism has been directed against the claims of science to be objective and value-neutral, the very same arguments can be made, and have been made, against the claim of metaphysics to be objective and true to reality.[13]

On the interpretation I develop, the normativity of nature and reality is constituted by two features of Aristotle's thought: his functional concept of form and the teleological framework of his metaphysics, which is articulated by the distinction between potential and actual being. I do not develop, therefore, the bizarre view that Aristotle thought that reality or nature was gendered, and that therefore an objective account of it must make reference to gender. Rather, I explain the way in which the normative aspect of a functional definition of form, and the norms inherent in a teleological view of metaphysics, readily lend themselves to more explicit and concrete political coloring (e.g., to gender associations).

Although Aristotle's normative metaphysical theory is a framework within which the inegalitarian gender norms of his culture are expressed, his thought offers feminists something far more interesting than an opportunity to deplore that result. Consider, for example, that the question of whether or not (and on what basis) there are values in nature is being debated today by ecologists and ecofeminists.[14] Aristotle's theory provides one important answer to that question, as well as an opportunity to explore the consequences of a normative view of nature. What if, as Aristotle thinks, nature and reality have a normative dimension? What if we cannot divorce scientific and metaphysical issues from questions of value because values and reality are intermingled?

These questions suggest interesting possibilities for feminist approaches to the connections among science, metaphysics, and values, but they also suggest certain difficulties. Isn't an inherently normative perspective on metaphysics and science more open to political distortion and oppressive uses than one that tries to maintain a distinction between the world and values? Consider, for example, the way in which the normative idea of what is natural can be used to limit possibilities for women. Moreover, since the kind of normative metaphysics that Aristotle develops is intrinsically hierarchical, isn't it just the kind of worldview that feminists ought to oppose?

In the first section of this essay I discuss the evidence that form and matter in Aristotle's theory of hylomorphism are gendered notions, and I develop the difficulties that follow for the coherence of hylomorphism given that evidence. I also discuss the standard diagnosis of Aristotle's mingling of metaphysics and gender, which assumes that hylomorphism is a non-normative theory. I then develop an alternative interpretation of hylomorphism. I explain how Aristotle's functional notion of form, and the teleological context of his metaphysics require that form and matter are inherently normative. Given that form, matter, and their relationship has a normative dimension, I explain the way in which Aristotle maps gender relations onto them. I next consider Susan Moller Okin's feminist critique of Aristotle's teleological understanding of nature and his functional understanding of form.[15] Okin's argument is important to consider because she claims that the teleological and functional norms in Aristotle's theory of nature provide direct theoretical support for the political status quo in Athens, including the inequality of women.[16] I then turn to the broader question of what value an Aristotelian approach to the issue of objectivity and norms might have for feminist theory.

Hylomorphism and Gender

Feminist readers of Aristotle have made the case that the notions of form and matter are gendered notions.[17] By a gendered notion I mean a notion that is connected, either overtly or covertly, either explicitly or metaphorically, with gender or sexual difference. Aristotle's writings, especially his biological and political texts, yield evidence that supports either overt and explicit connections between form and being male, and matter and being female, or covert and metaphorical connections (or both).[18] There are two types of evidence. First, there are texts in Aristotle's biology and natural philosophy that associate form with the male and matter with the female.[19] Second, there are texts, primarily in the *Politics*, that suggest that women's forms, or the way they have forms, are somehow defective.[20]

Let us begin by reviewing this evidence. Sexual difference colors form and matter in the biological writings, as in this text that gives Aristotle's explanation of why there are two sexes:

> And as the first moving cause, to which belongs the logos and the form, is better and more divine in nature than the matter, it is better also the superior one should be separate from the inferior one. That is why wherever possible and so far as possible the male is separate from the female, since it is something better and more divine in that it is the principle of movement for generated things, while the female serves as their matter. (*Gen. An.* 732a2–10)

Here sexual dimorphism is explained as a means of keeping form away from matter, the better from the worse, where it is clear that form is located in the male and matter in the female. Moreover, the female is virtually identified with matter.[21]

These associations are enriched and complicated by Aristotle's statement that women are, not simply, but "as it were" deformed males (*Gen. An.* 775a15); and by his view that there is something lacking in women's ability to deliberate, a function concerning which form is the cause or principle (*Politics* 1260a8–14). Here, the idea is not that women, or their reproductive organs are matter, but rather that there is something wrong with their forms. There is the vague implication that form is really and fully at home in men (in men who are not slaves to be precise), and not in women. In these statements Aristotle conveys that there is something compromised about the forms that women have, or about the way that they have forms.

The texts we have just considered provide strong support for the thesis that form and matter are gendered notions; form is somehow male and matter is somehow female.[22] Exactly how literal and explicit these gender associations are is a matter of interpretation, but their presence is indisputable. Form and matter are gendered notions; hence, it might seem, hylomorphism is a gendered, metaphysical theory.

This conclusion is puzzling and problematic for the simple reason that according to hylomorphism both men *and* women are composites of matter *and* form. If we think of Aristotelian form as male and matter as female in a straightforward sense, then human beings turn out to be hermaphrodites, and not men and women after all. Moreover, given that hylomorphism is a perfectly general theory concerning the structure of all composite substances, whatever intuitive appeal gender associations with matter and form might have in the case of human beings is much weaker in the case of plants and birds, and disappears entirely with houses and brazen spheres. That is, there is a striking tension between Aristotle's theory of composite substance according to which all human beings (indeed, all composite substances) are composites of matter and form, and the texts where sexual difference appears associated with matter and form. If all human beings are metaphysically identical, how can form and matter bear any gender associations?

Moreover, a substance's form is what secures its membership in a species or kind. It is by virtue of its form that we categorize a substance as a human being or a hummingbird. Since male and female human beings are the same species we would expect them to have the same form.[23] Given the role of form in securing species identification, it is deeply puzzling that Aristotle indicates quite clearly that men and women differ as to form (without, of course, being at all clear as to what that difference is)[24] but not in species. If all human beings share the same form, as Aristotle states in the *Metaphysics*, how can form be differentiated by gender? (1058A 29–b2). If human beings differ in form according to gender, why do they belong to the same kind?

The standard diagnosis of these puzzles is that Aristotle allowed his objective, non-normative scientific and metaphysical theory of matter and form to be influenced by the political and social beliefs of his culture. The beliefs can be seen in his remarks about the defective forms of women, even though, strictly and metaphysically speaking, all human forms are equal. Similarly, we can see the influence of his culture in his suggestion that form is male and matter female, even though they can be neither in his descriptive metaphysics. In short, the idea is that the political and social values of Aristotle's culture have shaped and infiltrated his purportedly descriptive, non-normative theory of hylomorphism.

This interpretation of gender in Aristotle's thought follows the pattern of feminist criticisms of the claim of objectivity of science and metaphysics. It seeks to show that Aristotle's purportedly value-neutral theories are infused with Aristotle's norms, the values and biases of his culture, including especially sexism. It assumes that nature, what Aristotle is theorizing about, is devoid of value and norms. On this interpretation, Aristotle becomes an example, a notorious example, of the way in which the values of the person who writes the books, appears inscribed in them— even when the book is metaphysics or science, the twin pillars of objectivity.

One might attempt a reformist interpretation of Aristotle, and argue that his limited scientific methods and tools and his cultural context make the presence of gender bias in his writing virtually inevitable. And one might think further that the removal of gender bias does not change hylomorphism except to rid it of the internal tensions created by Aristotle's false beliefs about women and men. Or one might take the opposite tack and campaign for the centrality of gender in Aristotle's theory by pointing out the systematic ways in which putatively metaphysical theories like hylomorphism always carry with them a subtext of gender. Form, matter, and hylomorphism, insofar as they purport to frame a general theory of composite substance, are necessarily undercut by sexual difference. Far from thinking of the gender associations of hylomorphism as external and eliminable, this approach uses them to point out the inevitable limits of universalism. While purporting to be universal, neutral, and objective, the categories of hylomorphism are revealed to be necessarily limited, sexual, and normative. I call this the *gendered interpretation* of hylomorphism.

In the next section I propose an alternative approach to Aristotle's intermingling of hylomorphism and gender, one that places that issue in the broader context of the question of form, matter, and normativity. Both the reformist and the gendered interpretation of hylomorphism share a common but mistaken assumption about Aristotle's notion of form: that form is a scientific or descriptive principle devoid of normativity. The reformist view thinks that form can emerge intact once we cleanse it of its extrinsic gender associations. The gendered approach also thinks that form is purportedly descriptive and non-normative, but adds that it is always subverted by norms like gender. On either interpretation Aristotle's intended notion of form is descriptive, scientific, and non-normative. This shared assumption is mistaken, and I think the issue of hylomorphism and gender can be best understood once we see that, and in what sense, Aristotelian form is inherently normative.

Form, Normativity, and Gender

What do I mean when I say that form is inherently normative? Before answering this question, I should say more about the alternative, standard interpretation. Many scholars of Aristotle (including, I have just claimed, feminist scholars) have assumed the objective or descriptive character of Aristotelian form. One reason to think of form this way is the role that it plays in classification. The idea that form is a principle of classification makes sense both in the context of Aristotle's metaphysics of substance,[25] and in the taxonomical project of his biological writings.[26] And, it is assumed that the answer to the Aristotelian question, What is it? in the metaphysical or biological context will not rely upon a normative principle. What something is, is a matter of fact or reality, not a question of value. Hence, it makes sense from this perspective to think that form is a descriptive, non-normative principle of classification.

On my view, Aristotelian form is inherently normative; hence, it is *not* a purely descriptive scientific principle of classification into kinds or species. Although form *is* a principle of classification into species, it is a principle that has normative content. However, the kind of normativity that infuses Aristotelian form is not the kind of concrete gender and political associations that feminist critics have pointed out, and that I discussed in the previous section. In saying form is normative I do not mean that it is metaphorically associated with being male, although I do think these associations are in the text. Rather, form is normative be-cause it is a functional concept that operates in the context of a teleologi-cal metaphysics. The normativity of form is, as it were, formal. Form would be normative in the sense I develop even if all the political associa-tions, both overt and covert, in the text were removed or never appeared.

Let me begin sketching out the case for the normativity of form. One way to see the normative aspect of form is to see that it is a functional notion for Aristotle. Soul, for example, is a principle and cause of an array of life functions; nutrition, reproduction and perception, movement and reasoning. So, form is a principle of species identification as the source of those functions that are characteristic of the species.

Form is a functional principle of species identification; what a thing is, for Aristotle, is determined by what it can do (and not, for example, by its morphology or reproductive history). What Aristotle says about the parts of organisms, that they are defined by their functions, is also true of whole organisms: "What a thing is is always determined by its function: a thing really is itself when it can perform its function; an eye, for instance, when it can see. When a thing cannot do so it is that thing only in name, like a dead eye or one made of stone, just as a wooden saw is no more a saw than one in a picture" (*Met.* IV 12 390a10–13).[27] So, for example, to say what a human being is, to define a human being, is to list the set of functions that are characteristic of human life. The human form or soul is the principle or cause of that array of activities.

The idea that form is a functional notion, that species identification is secured by what an entity can do, might seem paradoxical. What about animals or plants that cannot perform their characteristic species functions? What about human babies, for example, who are unable to reason and reproduce? Are they human or not? The answer to this puzzle weaves together Aristotle's functionalism, and his teleological metaphysics. An immature human being is potentially human because it is potentially capable of performing the characteristic human functions. Its identity is secured by its end, which is to be a (mature) human being; to be actually human, for Aristotle, is to be capable of doing the range of activities characteristic of creatures of that kind.

Moreover, for Aristotle the notion of a function is intrinsically normative in the sense that it carries with it the idea of what is good for the entity in question, and hence what that entity ought to do. Aristotle's *ergon* or function argument in the *Nicomachean Ethics* turns on the connection between the idea that there is a human function and that performing that function constitutes the good life for a human being.[28] "For with a flautist or sculptor or any craftsman—or anything that has a particular thing to make or do—it is in what it does that its good (and its doing well) seems to reside. And so it would seem to be with man too, if there is in fact anything for him to do" (Bk. I, 7 1097b25–29). Aristotle asserts that there is indeed a characteristically human function for which rational soul is the principle or cause. And it is the exercise of that function that constitutes the human good or excellence. For Aristotle, clearly, there is a normative dimension to functions, and, given his functional specification of form, a normative dimension to form.[29]

Normativity enters the realm of hylomorphism as well once we realize that form and matter are related to one another teleologically. Aristotle tells us that matter exists for the sake of form (*Met.* IX 8 1050a15–16). But, ends for Aristotle are goods (*Met.* I 983a31–32; 988b6–16). Moreover, the realization of form in matter, the process by which an organism becomes fully formed, in the sense of being able to perform the full range of its functions, is a teleological process. And the goal of that process, a fully formed, fully functioning animal or plant, for example, is not only that for the sake of which the process occurs, but it is also a good. The realization of a form in nature, as in art, is the realization of a good.

Further, Aristotle argues not only that actualities (forms) are prior in being and knowledge to potentialities (matter), but also that actualities are better than potentialities (*Met.* IX 9). Not only then are forms, as that for the sake of which natural processes occur, goods, but they are better than matter. Clearly, if we consider hylomorphism within the context of Aristotle's teleological metaphysics, the theory is embedded in a network of normative claims.[30]

I have argued that the intrinsic normativity of hylomorphism can be located in three aspects of Aristotle's theory of form. First, insofar as form is a functional notion it describes what an entity ought to do. Second, insofar as form is an end or goal it is a good. Third, form is prior to matter and better than matter. One of the themes of feminist critiques of both science and metaphysics has been the way in which political or normative concerns and categories shape and infiltrate purportedly descriptive, non-normative bodies of knowledge. Indeed, as I pointed out above, feminists have tended to interpret Aristotle's metaphysics (and his biological writings) in this way. Given my argument concerning the intrinsic normativity of form in Aristotle, however, this approach to his thought is clearly misguided. There is no purely descriptive, non-normative theory of hylomorphism to begin with, and hence no non-normative metaphysical theory to be illicitly subverted by norms.

This is not the occasion to consider in any detail the inherent merits or defects of Aristotle's teleological metaphysics.[31] I make a few comments on the perils and possibilities of an overtly normative metaphysics at the end. Here, I consider another issue, namely, how the kind of intrinsic normativity of form that I have been discussing is related to the gender associations that feminist historians of philosophy have noted.

The two striking examples of political language in Aristotle's theory of hylomorphism concern the way in which gender is associated with matter and form, and the fact that women (and slaves) seem not to have their forms fully; they are, in different ways, defectively rational. On the standard accounts, these statements reflect false beliefs about women (and slaves) and they also attach clearly political values to purportedly non-normative concepts. On my interpretation, Aristotle fills in, so to speak, the normative spaces in his theory with the categories of women (and slaves) in a way that reflects their status in his culture.

This essay began with the puzzling idea that form is somehow male and matter is somehow female. Our central evidence was a passage from the *Generation of Animals* that explained sexual dimorphism as a means of keeping the better, more divine principle (form) from the inferior, material principle. The better, more divine principle needs a location separate from the inferior material principle. Hence, the need for two sexes. On my interpretation the characterization of the two principles in this text simply restates the intrinsic normative features of form and matter in Aristotle's hylomorphism. Their respective locations (form in the male and matter in the female), however, is not an intrinsic feature of hylomorphism. The locations of the better principle and the worse principle reflects the value accorded to men and women in Aristotle's culture. Where would one locate a more divine, better principle than in the male, given the respective social and political positions of men and women?

The second example of Aristotle's tendency to describe form in political terms is the idea that women and slaves do not seem to have their forms fully because their capacity to reason is lacking. We should recall how this idea sits uneasily with the conception of form as a scientific, purely descriptive principle of species classification. Since it is not Aristotle's view that women and slaves are different species from male non-slaves, it is impossible to rid his statements about the deformations of women and slaves of blatant inconsistency with the standard understanding of form as a principle of species classification. The teleological, normative view of form fits much better with Aristotle's statements about form in women and slaves. On my view, having a form admits of degrees; one human being can be more fully formed (i.e., more capable of performing the human functions) than another. It might be helpful to recall my earlier discussion of immature substances, like a human baby, that cannot perform the full array of human functions. I pointed out earlier, and I have argued in detail elsewhere, that Aristotle would call the baby potentially human.[32] Becoming human is a process and the human form can be realized to different degrees just as becoming an oak tree is a process and the oak form can be realized to different degrees. The more fully realized the form, the better the entity is in that it is more fully able to perform its function.

I have argued that understanding form, matter, and hylomorphism as intrinsically normative concepts fits well with Aristotle's tendency to give them overt, political content. In particular I have argued that we find Aristotle reflecting the political realities of his day in the gender associations we find surrounding the notions of matter and form. Rather than indicting Aristotle for illicitly confusing the metaphysical and scientific with the normative and political, my interpretation pictures him as infusing his inherently normative metaphysics with the social and political realities and values of his time.

Like the revisionist interpretation I described above, the normative interpretation of Aristotle's metaphysics (and philosophy of nature) distinguishes between what is intrinsic to hylomorphism (functional and teleological norms) and what is extrinsic and, in principle, removable (inegalitarian gender associations).[33] But, the feminist political theorist Susan Moller Okin has argued that Aristotle's teleological and functionalist metaphysics were devised in order to justify the political status quo, including the oppression of women.[34] In the next section, I consider Okin's criticism, as well as the broader issue of whether or not a normative metaphysical theory is better suited to conservative political purposes than an objective, in the sense of non-normative, theory.

Metaphysics, Norms, and Sexism

A philosopher who sees reality and nature as structured by means of form and matter, a better and a worse, is susceptible to identifying these evaluations with whatever norms are dominant in his culture. If it is believed that men are better than women, then it is easy to find that judgment to be anchored in, and to exemplify, what is better and worse in reality or nature. Metaphysical norms and cultural norms are linked together and reinforce one another. I have suggested that this is what is happening when Aristotle associates gender with hylomorphism.

Susan Moller Okin has argued, however, that Aristotle's functionalist metaphysics justifies his social conservatism and his misogyny. "Thus Aristotle has established a philosophical framework [functionalism] by which he can legitimize the status quo. For the conventional function of any person determines that person's goodness, and a person's nature, or natural condition, is also equated with his or her goodness. Every person, therefore is naturally suited to his or her existing role and position in society."[35] Okin depicts Aristotle's functionalism as providing the theoretical framework that legitimizes the political status quo in Athens, including the institution of slavery and the inequality of women. If Okin is correct, then Aristotle's normative metaphysics can be of little interest to feminists.

By functionalism Okin means three different things, which she tends to conflate in her discussion of Aristotle's theory. First, she notes that Aristotle gives a functionalist account of the soul: "the soul of a thing is its capacity to fulfill its function."[36] This is the kind of functionalism that I discussed in explaining how values are intrinsic to Aristotle's metaphysics. I shall refer to this thesis as *functionalism*. Second, she uses functionalism to refer to a view of reality in which all entities stand in a hierarchy of instrumental relationships to one another. This position Okin derives from two assumptions: (a) if an entity has a function, then it must stand in an instrumental relation to some other entity; (b) that Aristotle believed that all entities are ordered by instrumental relationships into a natural hierarchy. I shall refer to this as the thesis of *universal instrumental relations*. Third, she uses functionalism to refer to Aristotle's sparse discussions of women's place in society, which is constituted by her reproductive and household functions—the very functions assigned to women in misogynist Athenian society. I shall refer to this as the thesis of *gender functions*. Okin's claim is that functionalism justifies, and is intended to legitimate, the thesis of gender functions. Aristotle's metaphysics provides legitimacy for the real-world functions of women in Athens, and their merely instrumental value in relation to men.

Okin's claim that Aristotle's metaphysics is a system of justification for the political status quo links together the first sense of functionalism to the third, or, in other words, ties the functional specification of form to the particular functions performed by Athenian women, which Okin characterizes as purely instrumental. The connection is secured by the second meaning of functionalism, the thesis of universal instrumental relations, which holds that all functions are instrumental, and argues that Aristotle's general teleology connects all beings instrumentally.

But the thesis of universal instrumental relations attributes views to Aristotle that he did not hold. First, Aristotle's functional specification of form does not hold that all functions are instrumental, if by that is meant "exist for the sake of another being's good." Soul is the principle or cause of an array of life functions; but those functions are not instrumental—for the sake of—*another* being's good. They are for the sake of the animal or plant itself; they are for *its* good or flourishing. So, Okin is simply wrong when she singles out man as the only being whose function and end is his own flourishing. "The proper activity of man alone among mortals has no end or aim outside of the actor himself."[37] On the contrary, for all natural substances—men, women, dogs and cats—the life functions whose principle is soul are for their own good. Hence, if Aristotle did think that women had only instrumental worth, he would need grounds other than his functional specification of form for thinking so.

The other piece of Okin's argument is also mistaken. On her view, "His [Aristotle's] entire universe, from the lowliest plant to the human race and beyond the human race to the heavenly bodies and the gods is arranged in strict hierarchy."[38] The purely instrumental relationship that Okin thinks relates all beings, does so in a strictly ordered, teleological hierarchy that encompasses the universe. But Aristotle's teleology did not operate to knit together all beings into a hierarchical union of instrumental relations. There is very little direct evidence to support a universal teleology in Aristotle.[39] This is because his teleological explanations of nature occur at the level of individual organisms; he does not develop a theory of how different species of plants and animals are instrumentally related to one another. Rather, he explains how their parts and processes are goal-directed, where the goal is their own ability to live and to flourish.[40]

Okin's argument that hylomorphism (the thesis of functionalism) legitimates the inegalitarian status and functions assigned to women by Aristotle fails because it rests upon two positions that Aristotle did not hold.[41] Without the thesis of universal instrumental relations, there is no connection between functionalism and the thesis of gender functions. Still, even if Aristotle's functionalist metaphysics does not justify his embrace of inegalitarian gender norms, it might be reasonable to think that a normative metaphysical theory is more open to political abuses than a theory that claims to be objective (in the sense of non-normative). Perhaps Aristotle's easy assimilation of cultural belief and metaphysical norms ought to persuade us that the modern world's bifurcation of values and nature is a good idea. Shouldn't feminist theorists above all insist upon the separation of norms and nature as perhaps the only way of avoiding the inscription into nature of our inequality?

Unfortunately, metaphysical and scientific theories that posit nature as a value-free zone are equally prone to their own insidious form of bias. One merely sees the actual political inequality as rooted in non-value-laden, objective facts or realities. Women simply have smaller brains or different brains—it's a fact proven by science! As I remarked at the beginning of this essay, feminist philosophers have written at length about the authority asserted by the idea of objectivity in science and metaphysics, and the abuses of that authority. What is really at issue for feminists in both Aristotle and his modern brethren is the attempt to connect social inequalities to some underlying scientific or metaphysical reality; not whether or not that reality is itself normative. So, while I do think that a normative metaphysics can reinforce actual political inequality, so, too, can theories that claim to be about an objective, value-less world. With regard to the question of using a theory of nature to enforce or encode inegalitarian political ideas, it makes no difference whether the object of inscription, nature, is conceived of as containing values or as value-free.

But if there is nothing to chose between them on this point, why should feminists be interested in the Aristotelian perspective? I think that it is of interest for two reasons. First, because it suggests that feminists engaged in rethinking the image of modern science and the scientist have ignored an important piece of that image: the image of nature, of what is known, of what is real. The feminist, critical evaluation of the ideal of objectivity, and the reinvention of a richer, more adequate notion is incomplete insofar as it does not consider one assumption of that ideal, namely, the way that nature is characterized. But it is only in considering an alternative view, like Aristotle's, that a particular view of nature can emerge as an assumption to be queried, rather than as simply the way things are.

There is a second point. Aristotle provides a useful reminder to those who are trying to articulate when and how norms and values enter into theory that locating them on the side of the theorist alone accepts uncritically the image of nature formed by modern science. Perhaps, as Aristotle asks us to believe, and as some ecofeminists argue, there are values in nature *and* on the side of the inquirer. If so, then the entire debate over values and norms in science (and theory in general) is too simple, and an adequate account is a complex weave of the theorizer's values and the norms of nature. Aristotle's hylomorphism provides a picture of how that might look. So I recommend Aristotle's normative metaphysics to feminists because it asks us to think critically about all the assumptions of modern science and metaphysics in a holistic fashion, rather than to focus exclusively upon the figure of the disinterested scientist or the view-from-nowhere metaphysician.[42]

Notes

1. For example, see the following essays in *Discovering Reality: Feminist Perspectives on Epistemology, Metaphysics, Methodology and Philosophy of Science*, ed. Sandra Harding and Merrill B. Hintikka (D. Reidel, 1983): "Have Only Men Evolved?" by Ruth Hubbard; "Evolution and Patriarchal Myths of Scarcity and Competition," by Michael Gross and Mary Beth Averill; "The Man of Professional Wisdom," by Kathryn Pyne Addelson; "Gender and Science," by Evelyn Fox Keller; "How Can Language Be Sexist," by Merrill Hintikka and Jaako Hintikka. Also see Cynthia Freeland's discussion of gendered concepts in the Introduction to this volume.

2. For a discussion of gender and hylomorphism see Cynthia Freeland's "Nourishing Speculation: A Feminist Reading of Aristotelian Science," in *Engendering Origins*, ed. Bat-Ami Bar On (New York, 1994), and Elizabeth Spelman's "Aristotle and the Politicization of the Soul," in *Discovering Reality*. Gender in Aristotle's theory of reproduction is discussed in Nancy Tuana's "Aristotle and the Politics of Reproduction," in *Engendering Origins*, and in Linda Lange's "Woman is Not a Rational Animal: On Aristotle's Biology of Reproduction," in *Discovering Reality*.

3. Evelyn Fox Keller is a possible exception in that she suggests changes in both the relationship between science and nature (from one of dominance to eros) and the way that nature is thought of. She suggests that Barbara McClintock has a richer, more complex view of nature than her fellow scientists—a view that contains qualitative, normative descriptions of nature. See Keller, *Reflections on Science and Gender* (New Haven: Yale University Press, 1985, 162–65. However, Keller is most concerned with describing a new, richer relationship between scientist and nature, and her comments on a new view of nature are sketchy.

4. In *Reflections on Gender and Science* Evelyn Fox Keller uses the theory of "object relations" to show how objectivity is constructed in a gendered way, and then argues that the objectivity that characterizes modern science is a projection of objectivity as it is developed in male psyches. In other words, scientific objectivity is androcentric, and is rooted in male psychological development (69–126). In *The Science Question in Feminism* (Ithaca, N.Y., 1986) Sandra Harding also argues that objectivity as value-neutrality is androcentric, but she provides a social constructivist account of its origin (227–28). These interpretations of objectivity as androcentric can be read together because Keller's psychological account can be housed within Harding's broader historical interpretation.

5. "Conclusion: Epistemological Questions" in *Feminism and Methodology*, ed. Sandra Harding (Bloomington, 1987), 182.

6. Postmodernist feminists would question the stability and identity of the theorizer, but we can overlook that wrinkle here, because they accept in general the thesis of the social construction of knowledge.

7. Lorraine Code's *Rhetorical Spaces: Essays on Gendered Locations* (New York, 1995) argues that the ideals of objectivity and value-neutrality are neither possible nor desirable. In her view "objectivity requires taking subjectivity into account" (44). The task for feminist epistemologists is to make the case that investigations guided by feminist political committment result in better knowledge than, for example, research guided by sexist or racist committment.

8. See Sandra Harding's description of the connection between the characteristics attributed to scientists and the objects of science in the modern period in *The Science Question in Feminism*, 227–28.

9. Both Evelyn Fox Keller and Lorraine Code have suggested new, richer images for the relationship between scientist and nature. Keller proposes an erotic relationship whereas Code thinks that the model should be knowing a person. It is interesting that in both cases the way that nature is thought of changes, away from the quantitative and inert and toward the qualitative and normative. The argument in this paper can be seen as supporting the idea that a reconsideration of the attributes of the theorizer, the objects of theory, and the relationship between the two is a wholistic endeavor. You just can't love a quantum.

10. Philosophers of social science, from a variety of perspectives, have argued that the objects of social science (humans, *Dasein*, us) have normative features like rationality, and that these features demand *Verstehen* rather than ordinary scientific explanation. Aristotle's view is broader in that he holds that all natural objects have normative features, and it is different in that the normativity of nature is not anchored in the rationality or self-consciousness of natural entities.

11. My essay does not argue that it is *because* of Aristotle's inegalitarian views on gender (and so forth) that he developed hylomorphism, his normative view of nature. That is, I do not assign a causal role to Aristotle's false beliefs about men and women in the development of his theory as Cynthia Freeland does in "Nourishing Speculation." I leave the causal question open.

12. In "Teleology in Aristotelian Science and Metaphysics," forthcoming in *Methodos in Ancient Philosophy*, ed. Jyl Gentzler (Oxford University Press).

13. For a feminist critique of the metaphysical tradition see Genvieve Lloyd's *The Man of Reason* (Minneapolis, 1984). For a discussion and evaluation of feminist criticisms of metaphysics see my "Feminism and Metaphysics," in *A Mind of One's Own: Feminist Essays on Reason and Objectivity* (Boulder, Colo.: 1992).

14. See *What is Nature? Culture, Politics, and the Non-Human* (Oxford, 1995) by Kate Soper, and *Radical Ecology*, by Carolyn Merchant (New York, 1992).

15. See *Women in Western Political Thought* (Princeton, 1979), chap. 4.

16. Along similar lines, Nancy Tuana in "Aristotle and the Politics of Reproduction" has argued that Aristotle's biological account of reproduction both was caused by, and provides theoretical support for, the belief that women are inferior to men. Marguerite Deslauriers argues against this interpretation in her contribution to this volume (Chapter 6).

17. In their contributions to this volume Cynthia Freeland maintains a gendered interpretation of form and matter, and Marguerite Deslauriers argues against a gendered interpretation (Chapter 6).

18. A distinct issue of concern to feminist philosophers and historians of science is the secondary role that Aristotle assigns to women in his account of reproduction. See Nancy Tuana's "Aristotle and the Politics of Reproduction" for a feminist perspective on the role of women in reproduction. Recent discussions among Aristotle specialists have stressed another issue: the difficulty posed to Aristotle's view that all formal determination is via the male semen by the phenomenon of inherited characteristics. In "Metaphysics in Aristotle's Embryology" (*Proceedings of the Cambridge Philological Society* 214 [1988]) John Cooper argues that Aristotle can provide an adequate, internally consistent explanation of inherited characteris-

tics that attributes all formal determination to the male. However, in "Biomedical Models of Reproduction in the Fifth Century B.C. and Aristotle's *Generation of Animals*" (*Phronesis* 41 [1995]), Andrew Coles provides compelling grounds for questioning the internal coherence of Aristotle's demotion of the female role. While I think that this is an important issue in evaluating Aristotle's attitude toward women, I do not explore it directly in this essay. Here, I am interested in his account of reproduction insofar as it contains gender associations with matter and form, and not insofar as it reveals Aristotle's inability to assign to women their proper reproductive role.

19. *Gen. An.* 732A2–10; 765b9–10; 775a15; 1, 22; *Phy.* 1 9 192a22–23.

20. *Politics* 1260a8–14.

21. The association of form with males and matter with females holds even if we pay attention to certain important details in this text. The first point is that Aristotle often uses "male" and "female" to refer to the reproductive organs of men and women (*Gen An.* 716b30; 732a1–716B30; 732a1–3; 766a19; 768a7). What is being called better in this text is, strictly speaking, the male sex organ and not the male person. Further, strictly speaking, the male (sex organ) is identified with the principle of movement that conveys the form to the matter and not with the form itself. However, even with these refinements in place there remains a set of gender associations with matter and form, as male sex organs are regularly found in men and female sex organs in women.

22. For a discussion of the way in which Luce Irigaray has treated the connection between women and matter in the Greek philosophical tradition, see Cynthia Freeland's contribution (Chapter 3).

23. For a full discussion of the evidence supporting the claim that male and female are not different species, see "Sex and Essence in Aristotle's Metaphysics and Biology," by Marguerite Deslauriers (Chapter 6).

24. For an interesting and persuasive interpretation of how women are defective see Deborah Modrak's "Aristotle: Women, Deliberation, and Nature," in *Engendering Origins*.

25. Two recent studies of Aristotle's *Metaphysics* that emphasize the role form plays in species classification are Frank Lewis's *Substance and Predication in Aristotle* (Cambridge, 1991), and *Primary "Ousia": An Essay on Aristotle's "Metaphysics" Z and H* (Ithaca, 1991) by Michael Loux.

26. Recently there has been a vigorous scholarly debate over the question of whether or not Aristotle's biology contains a taxonomical project. For a discussion of this issue from a feminist perspective, see Cynthia Freeland's, "Nourishing Speculation: A Feminist Reading of Aristotelian Science," in *Engendering Origins*. For a nonfeminist argument against taxonomy in Aristotle's biology, see *Aristotle's Classification of Animals: Biology and the Conceptual Unity of the Aristotelian Corpus*, by Pierre Pelligrin, trans. A. Preus (Berkeley and Los Angeles, 1986).

27. See also *Politics* 1 1253a; –*Gen An.* I 19 726b 22–24, II 1 734b 24–27; *De An.* II 1 412b 18–22.

28. Whether and in what way this argument is fallacious has been the object of debate among scholars. I am not concerned with this question here. Rather, I want to use this text as evidence that Aristotle thought that the notion of a function warranted an inference to a normative conclusion.

29. My interpretation of the *ergon* argument is widely accepted by scholars. It is criticized in Alfonso Gomez-Lobo's "The Ergon Inference," *Phronesis* 34, no. 2 (1989).

30. My evidence is intended to show that Aristotle used normative language in his account of form, matter, and their relationship. I do not address the further philosophical issue of whether or not "good" in this context is the moral good. Notoriously, Aristotle does not differentiate the moral good from other goods, so we can claim that forms are normative in the sense available to Aristotle.

31. I explain the way in which Aristotle's teleological metaphysics differs from teleology in his natural philosophy in "Teleology in Aristotelian Science and Metaphysics," in *Methodos in Ancient Philosophy*, ed. Jyl Gentzler (Oxford University Press, forthcoming). And I discuss Aristotle's reason for holding that actuality (form) is prior to potentiality (matter) in "The Priority of Actuality in Aristotle," in *The Identity and Unity of Aristotelian Substances*, ed. T. Scaltsas, D. Charles, and M. L. Gill (Oxford, 1994).

32. In the "Priority of Actuality in Aristotle."

33. Although I take the reformist position that the explicit gender associations in Aristotle's text are removable without compromising hylomorphism, obviously the theory that results will not reflect accurately Aristotle's ideas. I have never been interested in writing an apology for Aristotle, and I think the interest in his texts for feminists resides *both* in their unaltered states, *and* in the alternatives they offer to standard modern philosophical categories.

34. In *Shame and Necessity* (Berkeley and Los Angeles, 1993), Bernard Williams has argued a similar point with regard to Aristotle's attempt to justify the institution of slavery.

35. *Women in Western Political Thought*, 80.

36. Okin, 75.

37. Ibid., 77.

38. Ibid., 77.

39. For a discussion of this issue see John Cooper's "Aristotle on Natural Teleology," in *Language and Logos: Studies in Ancient Greek Philosophy*, ed. Malcolm Schofield and Martha Craven Nussbaum (Cambridge, 1982).

40. Reproduction is part of the function of individual animal and plants. But, for Aristotle, reproduction is for the sake of achieving whatever immortality is available to mortals; even in this case, the goal is a good of the individual animal or plant.

41. The other piece of Okin's case against Aristotle as the philosopher of the status quo concerns his philosophical method: dialectic. "Unlike Plato, he [Aristotle] does not argue, in dealing with ethics any more than with biology, that the world should be different from the way it is, but starts from a basic belief that the status quo in both the natural and the social realm is the best way for things to be" (*Women in Western Political Thought*, 74). Note that this view of Aristotle's method does not provide an argument that shows that his metaphysics of hylomorphism was intended to justify the political inequality of women. Rather, it points out that his method of dialectic, which considers the opinions of the wise and the many to be important data, has a conservative tendency. The question of how to understand dialectic has received a great deal of scholarly attention since Okin published her book, however, and her view underestimates the critical resources of Aristotle's method.

42. I am indebted to the editor of this volume, Cynthia Freeland, for her criticisms of an earlier version, and also to Mark Okrent for his helpful suggestions.

6

Sex and Essence in Aristotle's *Metaphysics* and Biology

Marguerite Deslauriers

Are women perceived to be different from men because women are economically, socially, and politically subordinate to men, or are women subordinate to men in these ways because they exhibit certain anatomical and physiological (or psychological) differences from men?[1] No one, I take it, denies that the anatomical and physiological differences exist. The question is why, given the myriad of differences exhibited by people, these are among those we consider significant or interesting. Why are these socially significant when, say, baldness versus hirsuteness or blood type differences, are not? One possible answer: because they are historically the foundation, if not the justification, of the political differences. Another possible answer: because suggesting that they are significant allows men to justify to themselves and to women the subordination of women.[2] Of course, the anatomical and physiological differences might justify subordination only if women are not merely different from men but somehow inferior to men. For whatever the difference, if women are different from men, men are just as different from women.[3] That is, to argue that the differences between men and women explain, even if they do not justify, the subordination of women, one must show not only that women are *different* from men, but that women are in some respect *worse* than men.

While my own sympathies lie with the arguments that demonstrate that the physical differences between men and women have become so-cially and politically significant because of the power differences between men and women, my aim here is not to argue for that position.[4] It is rather to re-assess Aristotle's views on the difference between male and female in light of two of the questions raised above: Do the physical differences between male and female allow us to explain in some way the political differences between male and female? And, if they do, wherein lies the inferiority or disadvantage of the female? Aristotle has long been associated with the position that sex differences not only explain but justify differences in political power between men and women.[5] I shall argue that Aristotle's philosophical claims and reasoning do not generally warrant such an association; nor does Aristotle himself argue for such a position. He is committed to the claim that there is no difference in species, and hence no essential difference, between male and female animals. On the other hand, Aristotle does insist on the deficiency of the female relative to the male. We shall need to consider the relation between the claim that there is no essential difference between male and female, and the claim that the female is deficient relative to the male.

Two creatures who do not differ in species cannot differ essentially.[6] Male and female animals are different, but their differences are material and do not constitute a specific difference. Aristotle does not, however, believe that maleness and femaleness are merely accidental attributes of the genus animal, as are, for example, pallor or darkness. This is because maleness and femaleness are attributes that belong uniquely to animals; nothing but animals has a sex.[7] So the difference that constitutes male and female belongs nonaccidentally and yet nonessentially to the genus animal. At the same time, we will see that maleness or femaleness belong to each individual accidentally, in just the way that eye-color or nose-shape belong.

The main question I shall address is, then, Just what sort of difference does Aristotle understand the difference between male and female to be? The evidence from his *Metaphysics*, the biological works, the *Categories*, and the *Analytics* is, I shall argue, entirely consistent, and shows that Aristotle believed male and female to be differences in the matter that are peculiar to the genus and that therefore belong nonaccidentally to the genus, but that belong accidentally to any particular individual animal (I do not mean to suggest that genera exist separately from the member species or—ultimately—the individuals that fall under the genera). Aristotle does not then argue for the subordination of women based on the claim that the female is essentially different from the male. Nor, on my view, does he *argue* for the subordination of women at all. Aristotle clearly believes that the female is biologically deficient relative to the male, and may even have philosophical reasons for believing that one sex *must* be biologically deficient relative to the other, but he does not have philosophical reasons for believing that it is the female who is deficient relative to the male.[8]

A second question then arises; namely, whether Aristotle's claims about sex differences in the *Metaphysics* and the *Generation of Animals* offer philosophical justification for the differences between male and female in "habits" that Aristotle believes are observable, or the difference between men and women in household (and hence political) status that Aristotle accepts as appropriate. I shall show here that Aristotle's philosophical views do not underlie these claims. That is, Aristotle considers the difference between male and female to be nonessential and generally less radical than is often supposed; and he does not explain the social habits or justify the political subordination of women by appeal to that difference. It is certainly true that Aristotle accepts as obvious that females are different, and worse, in their "habits" and that women ought to be subordinate to men in the household. He does not, however, *argue* for these claims.[9] More precisely, while one can find in Aristotle an argument that one sex must be deficient relative to the other, there is no argument to show that it is the female who is deficient—Aristotle regularly assumes rather than argues for that claim.[10] And insofar as he develops a theoretical account of the metaphysical and biological differences between the sexes, he tends to downplay the differences and emphasize the similarities.

There seem then to be two strains of thought concerning sex differences in Aristotle's work: one according to which Aristotle reasons that the differences are minimal; and another according to which he accepts without discussion, much less argument, that males and females differ manifestly, and that females compare unfavorably with males (in this latter strain the differences are many, although typically trivial; see, e.g., HA 2. 3 501b20, 4. 11 538a22, 9. 1 608a22). These strains can often be distinguished, and this might lead us to think that we can easily salvage an Aristotelian conception, and construction, of sex differences as minimal, by abandoning certain claims Aristotle makes that have little bearing on his philosophical doctrines. I shall show that the strains cannot be so readily distinguished in the case of Aristotle's identification of the female with matter, and that the tension between them in that case raises interesting questions about the relation of form and matter as well as about the construction of sex differences.

My aim is to provide an analysis of Aristotle's claims about sex differences, in effect his construction of sex differences, which I conceive to be preliminary but necessary to some of the feminist work on Aristotle that has already been undertaken, and some that remains to be done.

Metaphysics

In the *Metaphysics* we find that Aristotle argues that the male and female *principles* that make individual animals male or female are indeed opposites. He does not, however, argue that male and female *animals* are as a result opposites of one another; rather he insists on the sameness of male and female in species form, and minimizes the differences between them.

At *Metaphysics* X 9 1058a29ff. Aristotle directly addresses a question: Why are the male and female of a species not different in species (εἴδει)? That is, why do they not constitute species of the genus animal or subspecies within species?[11] Aristotle presents the argument that might lead one to believe that male and female are separate species. That argument is: male and female are contrary (ἐναντίου), and their difference is a contrariety (ἐναντιώσεως). It is not the case that *every* contrariety within a genus is such as to constitute species of that genus, since there are accidental contrarieties. Pallor and darkness, for example, is a contrariety that belongs to animals but does not divide the genus animal into species (dark and pale animals) because it does not belong to animals as such (καθ᾽ αὑτό). That is, while animals may be dark or pale, so may many other things; pallor and darkness are not peculiar to the genus animal.[12]

So, accidental contrarieties (i.e., contrarieties that do not belong to the genus as such) do not divide a genus into species. The difference that is a contrariety and distinguishes male and female, however, belongs to animal in virtue of animal itself (ᾗ ζῷον). So male and female ought to constitute species of the genus animal, since the difference that distinguishes them is a contrariety and belongs peculiarly to the genus.

Aristotle clearly takes for granted that male and female do not constitute species of the genus animal (or subspecies of any animal species).[13] At the same time, he accepts both that male and female are contraries, and that they belong to animal as-such. He needs, then, to show that it is possible for contrary attributes that belong to a genus as-such not to divide that genus into species. More particularly, he needs to show why some such attributes will divide a genus into species, and others will not.

We need to consider what it means for Aristotle to say both that male and female are contraries, and that they belong as-such to the genus animal.[14] Notice first that Aristotle does not argue that male and female are contraries; he takes this to be as obvious as that hot and cold are contraries.[15] The claim has implications. At *Metaphysics* X 3 1054a23–26 and at *Categories* 10 11b18–19 Aristotle identifies contraries as one kind of opposites (ἀντικείμενα or ἀντιθέσεις).[16] He defines opposites generally as those things that cannot be present together in that which is capable of receiving both (*Met.* V 10 1028a22–24). So the members of pairs of contraries exclude one another. Contraries are often characterized as what are "most different" (τὰ πλεῖστον διαφέροντα), although these may be items of various kinds: (1) of things that differ in genus, those that cannot be present in the same thing together, (2) the most different of things in the same genus, (3) the most different of things in the same receptive [material], (4) the most different of the things that fall under the same capacity, and (5) those things the difference between which is greatest either absolutely or in genus or in species (*Met.* V 10 1018a25–30). Now Aristotle is clear that male and female are qualities of substances, and not themselves substances. That is, there is nothing male or female except male and female animals; there is no male-in-itself or female-in-itself (*Met.* XIII 3 1078a7–8).[17] So male and female are contrary qualities in the same genus, namely, the genus animal. Male and female are not, then, contraries of the first sort, because they are in the same genus. We shall see that Aristotle characterizes them as different in capacity; so they are unlikely to be of the fourth sort. And since, as we have seen, Aristotle maintains that male and female fall within not only the same genus but also the same species, they cannot be contraries of the fifth sort. Are they the most different of things in the same genus? This is implausible, since surely whatever is most different in the same genus will be in different species. This leaves us with "most different of the attributes in the same receptive material." Since Aristotle will say of male and female precisely that they belong to the matter rather than to the form of the genus animal, we can conclude that male and female are contrary qualities that belong to the matter of the same genus.

That it is the *same* genus is important. It is of the nature of contraries (at least of contrary qualities) to belong to the same thing, that is, to something that is the same in species or in genus (*Cat.* 11 14a15). That is, it is of the nature of pairs of contraries to belong to the same thing. It is animals that are male or female, and numbers that are odd or even. The pair of contraries belongs at the same time to the same genus. Only one of the pair will belong at any given time to any given individual member of that genus. Any particular number will be odd *or* even, any particular animal male *or* female.[18]

While some contraries have intermediates, others do not. That is, some contraries are such that it is not necessary for one or the other to belong to the things to which they naturally belong, while others are such that it is necessary for one or the other to belong (*Cat.* 10 11b38–12a4). Odd and even, sickness and health (curiously) are offered as examples of contraries that do not have intermediates and one of which must belong in each case to that to which the pair of contraries naturally belongs, animal bodies in the case of sickness and health, and numbers in the case of odd and even. Male and female seem to be contraries that do not have intermediates, since Aristotle classes them with odd and even.[19] To say that male and female are contraries without intermediates is to say that they are qualities of the same genus that are as different as possible. This suggests a strong opposition, and a radical difference. We shall, however, see that while Aristotle is prepared to suggest that male and female as principles and as attributes of the genus animal are radically different, male and female animals, individuals qualified by those principles or attributes, are not radically different.

What does it mean to say that male and female belong as-such to the genus animal? The passage that explains the καθ᾽ αὑτό relation is at *Posterior Analytics* I 4 73a34–b24. Aristotle enumerates four senses of καθ᾽ αὑτό; for our purposes it is the first two that are of interest.[20] In one sense, X belongs to Y καθ᾽ αὑτό if X is in the essence (τί ἐστι) of Y

(73a34–37). So if it were part of the essence of animal to be male or female, then male and female would belong καθ' αὐτό to animal. As we know, however, Aristotle denies that male and female are essential attributes of animal. The second sense in which an attribute might belong to a subject is detailed at 73a37–b5. Aristotle says that when the subject must be mentioned in the account of the attribute, that attribute belongs καθ' αὐτό to the subject. In this sense X belongs to Y καθ' αὐτό if Y is in the essence of X. Aristotle does not use male and female as examples: his examples are straight and curved as attributes of line; odd and even, prime and composite, and equilateral and oblong as attributes of number.[21] But male and female satisfy the definition of such attributes, because to give an account of male and female one must mention animal. This amounts to saying that male and female are peculiar to animal, which is what Aristotle claims in the *Metaphysics*, when he says that we cannot explain what a female is without appeal to animal (*Met.* VII 5 1030b25). And this sort of as-such attribute then seems to be what Aristotle calls in the *Topics* an ἴδιον, a nonessential but necessary property of some substance. An ἴδιον, "does not make clear the essence [of something], but belongs to [that thing] alone and is predicated convertibly of that thing," (*Topics* I 5 102a18–19). Moreover, later in the same chapter of the *Posterior Analytics*, at 73b16–24, Aristotle goes on to say, "Whatever, therefore, . . . is said to belong to things as such in the sense of inhering in the predicates or of being inhered in, holds both because of themselves and from necessity. For it is not possible for them not to belong, either in absolute terms or as regards the opposites—e.g. straight or crooked to line, and odd or even to number. For the contrary is either a privation or a contradiction in the same genus—e.g. even is what is not odd among numbers, in so far as it follows. Hence if it is necessary to affirm or deny, it is necessary too for what belongs as such to belong." This passage clearly mentions contraries as καθ' αὐτό attributes in the second sense, and reiterates a claim we have already considered: that in the case of contraries without intermediates (including odd and even) the pair of contraries belongs necessarily to that which can receive it. That is, καθ' αὐτό attributes of the second sort are here linked to contraries without intermediates by the claim that in both cases one or the other of a pair must belong to every member of the genus to which the pair belongs as-such.

Since Aristotle wants to maintain that male and female are contraries, and that they belong to the genus animal as-such, while asserting that male and female do not constitute subspecies, he needs to show how all three claims can be consistent with one another. To do so, he distinguishes between contraries in the formula of the genus (ἐν τῷ λόγῳ) that do divide that genus into species, and contraries in the compound material thing (ἐν τῷ συνειλημμένῳ) that do not divide the genus (Met. X 9 1058a37–b3). To make this point Aristotle appeals by analogy to individual differences within a species. For example, although a pale animal is different from a dark animal, they are not different in species. This suggests that pallor and darkness as accidental contrarieties of the genus animal do not divide that genus into species. Similarly, Callias is different from Socrates but he is not different in species from Socrates; he is different in matter. Just as pallor and darkness are material accidents that distinguish one animal from another, so too it is accidents of the matter that distinguish one member of a species from another. Aristotle wants to extend the point to male and female. He wants, that is, to claim that just like the accidents that distinguish Callias from Socrates, or like pallor and darkness relative to animals, male and female are differences in the matter rather than the form.[22] In all these cases the person (or animal) that is qualified is the material person (or animal) (ὡς ὕλη γὰρ ὁ ἄνθρωπος (1058b5–6)); i.e., the compound thing (συνειλημμένον) rather than the form or formula of person.[23]

There is, however, a difficulty. While we can accept that Callias and Socrates differ in matter in the sense that they differ with respect to certain accidental attributes (but do not differ with respect to specific form), it cannot be the case that male and female are merely accidental attributes of animal as a genus, because they are attributes of animal as such. So Aristotle is proposing that male and female are differences in the matter that are nonaccidental. They are peculiar to the genus not because they are peculiar to its form, but because they are peculiar to its matter. At the same time, in saying, "therefore the same seed becomes male or female by being acted on in a certain way (παθόν τι πάθος)," (1058b23–24), Aristotle seems to suggest that the difference between male and female is like other accidental features of the individual. Male and female can be both accidental and nonaccidental features only because they belong in one sense (as a pair of contraries) to the genus, in which case they belong nonaccidentally, and in another sense (one or the other) to particular individuals that are members not only of the genus but always of some species of that genus.

The particular phrase Aristotle uses to describe the kind of attributes that are male and female in *Metaphysics* X 9 is οἰκεῖα πάθη (peculiar modifications) (1058b22). That male and female are πάθη suggests that they are not formal attributes, but material attributes, as we should expect; that they are οἰκεῖα means that they belong in virtue of the thing itself (or as-such) and are ἴδια of that thing. By "material attribute" here I mean an attribute that belongs as-such, but to the matter rather than the form of the genus in question. Male and female are then material attributes (and ἴδια) relative to the genus animal, because anything that is male or female will have to be an animal, but neither maleness nor femaleness are part of the form or essence of animal. So too pallor and darkness will be material attributes (and ἴδια) of surfaces, since anything that is pale or dark will have to be a surface, but neither pallor nor darkness belong to the essence of surface. And equal/unequal will be material attributes (and ἴδια) of quantities, since anything that is equal or unequal will have to be a quantity, but neither equal nor unequal are part of the essence of quantity.[24] At *Met.* XIII 3 1078a7 Aristotle refers to male and female, in a similar manner, as ἴδια πάθη. In this latter passage he says, "Many in-itself accidents (συμβέβηκε καθ' αὐτὰ) belong to things *qua* each such thing, since, for example, [with respect to] the animal, both *qua* female and *qua* male, there are peculiar attributes (ἴδια πάθη) (and yet there is no female or male thing separate from animals)." The point is that certain attributes, male/female or equal/unequal, bring with them certain other attributes (or are constituted by those other attributes) but remain attributes rather than substances.[25] This is significant because it emphasizes that male and female principles, which are radically different, can never be more than attributes of the animals that are then called male and female, and that as we shall see, are not so different.

By claiming that the sort of attributes of which male and female are an example are (seemingly paradoxically) both καθ' αὐτό and accidental, Aristotle turns out to mean that these attributes belong καθ' αὐτό to the matter, rather than the form. While then some of the καθ' αὐτό attributes of the second sort will be differentiae of the genus to which they belong, not all such attributes can be differentiae; some will belong to the form of the genus, but some will belong to the matter. The description of such attributes does not require that they be specific differences, although it does require that they be contraries without intermediates.[26] But again, this does not entail that every καθ' αὐτό attribute will be a differentia since it is not the case that every set of contraries divides the genus to which it belongs into species, even if it belongs peculiarly to that genus.[27]

Biology

In his biological works, particularly the *Generation of Animals*, we find once again that Aristotle denies there are essential differences between male and female animals of the same species. We find, moreover, that while Aristotle certainly reports anatomical and physiological differences between males and females he describes them as minor differences, usually differences in degree rather than kind, and emphasizes the parallel development and generative functions of male and female.

What exactly are the differences between male and female according to Aristotle? The differences that he gives some argued account of are anatomical and physiological, differences in both organs and capacities. Aristotle offers us a theoretical account of these differences in the *Generation of Animals*. He takes the difference in reproductive capacities that he identifies in male and female to be primary, and to explain the difference in organs. Of course, what is most readily observable (most knowable to us, in Aristotelian terms) are the differences in organs. The differences in capacities—concocting capacities, as it turns out—are less observable (less knowable to us) but more fundamental in the sense that these capacities explain the differences in organs (and are therefore more knowable in themselves).[28] (How exactly the concocting capacities are supposed to explain the difference in organs is a question to which I shall return.) When I say that the capacities are primary and supposed to explain the difference in organs, I mean that Aristotle believes the reproductive organs are *for the sake of* reproductive capacities (GA I 1 715a12–13). At GA IV 1 765b9–15 Aristotle says, "the male and the female are distinguished by a certain capacity and incapacity (δυνάμει τινὶ καὶ ἀδυναμίᾳ) (for the one who is able to concoct and form and ejaculate semen and who has the principle of the form is the male. . . . That which receives but is incapable of both forming and ejaculating [seed] is female." At 766a31–35 Aristotle spells out the capacity/incapacity that distinguishes male from female, and constitutes their primary difference: it is the ability or inability to concoct blood or the counterpart of blood (the "ultimate nutriment," τῆς ὑστάτης τροφῆς) up to the point where it becomes semen.

Both male and female animals produce something Aristotle calls "seed" (σπέρμα); but in the case of the male the seed is semen and in the case of the female it is menses. Both male and female animals concoct the food they eat into blood; they differ in that the male concocts the blood further into semen.[29] The ability to concoct blood into semen depends on the ability to produce a certain degree of "natural" heat in certain organs, namely the heart and the genitals. This is because (1) the heat in the heart (which at 766a35–37 is said to be the source of natural heat in the body) changes the residue of the nutriment as it enters the heart into blood through the addition of "pneuma," a special kind of air; and (2) in male animals with testes the residue of blood is concocted into semen during copulation when, because of the heat produced by friction, more pneuma is added (717b23–26, 718a5–10, 718a25).[30] In order, then, for the ability to concoct to be realized the body must have certain organs, and as male and female concocting abilities differ, so too their anatomy differs (766a23–24). Since the difference in concocting capacity is limited to the concoction that occurs in the genitals, males and females differ only with respect to genitals (and whatever differences genital differences entail). If the difference in concocting capacity amounts to a difference in the ability to add heat at the final stage, and if that difference is supposed (as we have seen) to explain the difference in organs, we must presume that male animals have the organs they do in order to make it possible to add the necessary heat by way of friction, and female animals have the organs they do in order that such heat will *not* be added.[31] Aristotle maintains that it is the difference in heat insofar as it produces a difference in concocting capacity that is the principle or cause of male and female, but adds that it is when an animal has the *parts* that distinguish the female from the male (as well as the principle or cause of those parts) that it *is* female or male (766b3–6).[32] At the same time, Aristotle is emphatic that the difference between male and female with respect to organs is *accidental*, and neither a principle nor a cause, but, presumably, a result of the underlying principle and cause, namely the difference in heat (764b36–765a4, 767b10–15).[33]

Aristotle does claim that the male has the principle of change (κινήσεως) and generation, the female the principle of matter (GA I 2 716a6–8). In general, the difference between moving causes and material causes is pronounced (consider the difference between the skill of the sculptor and the bronze). As a result we might be led to suppose that this claim posits a radical difference between male and female. We should remember, however, that in the case of male and female, the male is the moving cause of generation because he can concoct the residue of nutriment further than can the female. In this case being the moving cause rather than the material cause amounts to being able to concoct the residue one stage further. That the semen is the moving cause because it is further concocted is demonstrated by Aristotle's insistence that the ability of the semen to "prevail" (κρατέω) over the menses is a result of the further concoction of the semen (GA IV 1 766b12–17).³⁴ The prevalence of semen over menses occurs in the normal course of conception and its success or failure determine the characteristics of the individual (766b15–16). The difference between semen and menses that motivates Aristotle to speak of the former prevailing over the latter, and of the former as the moving cause, is simply the further concoction of the residue at the final stage. I say "simply" because, understood as seminal residue of the same kind at different stages of concoction the difference between the material contribution of the female and the formal contribution of the male seems slight; I shall, however, return below to the question of material and formal contributions to generation.

The question at hand is whether Aristotle understands this difference between male and female animals (the production of semen or menses) to be essential. Now, we know that male and female as *principles* are not accidental relative to the genus animal. And since Aristotle explicitly describes the difference between male and female *animals* with respect to their organs as accidental (as we have seen), this question is only pertinent to the difference in capacities in the case of individual animals. That is, is the capacity to concoct seed that is the efficient cause of generation accidental to any given individual animal? Now, at GA IV 1 763b27–30 Aristotle raises the question whether animals are male or female before they are perceptibly male or female. This question amounts to asking whether animals can have the principle of maleness or femaleness before they have the corresponding organs (since it is possession of the organs that makes an animal perceptibly male or female). His answer is that while there is a principle or capacity that is male or female, that capacity is acquired simultaneously with the organs that allow the individual animal to exercise the capacity. Animals become male or female when their organs of generation (male or female) are formed. "Nature gives each one its instrument simultaneously with its capacity, since it is

better done thus" (IV 1 766a5–7). If the capacity is acquired simultaneously with the organs, and the organs are accidental, we have some reason
to think that the capacity is accidental.

Moreover, if male or female capacities were essential, they would be
part of the form transmitted by the male seed to the female matter. Now,
the determination of sex in animals occurs after conception (GA II 3
736b2–5, together with II 4 737b11).[35] It is clear, then, that on Aristotle's view the contributions of the male and female parent to the embryo are not sexed prior to conception, and hence that the form
transmitted by the male parent does not include a principle of maleness
or femaleness.[36] The σπέρματα of the male and female parents do not
have a determinate sex not just in the sense that they do not already have
sex organs (as preformationist theories would have it), but in the sense
that they do not contain the potential to become one or the other
sex—or rather, they contain both potentials. Aristotle, as we have seen,
attributes the determination of sex in the embryo to the degree of mastery that the male seed exercises over the female matter; if the male seed
fails to prevail over the matter, the embryo will be female. This prevalence or failure to prevail is a question of the interaction of male and
female contributions; it is not a question of anything about either of
the contributions independently considered. Since the contributions of
neither the male nor the female parent are sexed, and since the sex of
the embryo is determined by the ability of the male contribution to prevail over the female contribution in a certain respect, Aristotle clearly
cannot have believed that male and female are different in essence (to be
different in essence or in form, the determining factor would have to be
the form transmitted by the semen).

I say this despite the passage at 767b16–23: "If the seminal residue in
the menstrual fluid is well-concocted, the movement derived from the
male will make the shape such as itself (καθ᾽ αὑτήν). . . . So that if this
movement prevails it will make a male and not a female, and a male
which takes after its father, not after its mother; if however it fails to
prevail, whatever be the capacity in respect of which it has not prevailed,
in that capacity it makes the offspring like [that capacity, i.e., deficient]
(κατ᾽ αὑτήν)." This passage is crucial to the debate about individual
forms in Aristotle, but that is not a debate I want to enter into here.[37]
The passage is of interest to the question at hand in that it might seem
to suggest that Aristotle *did* believe that the male contribution and the
female contribution are innately male prior to conception. What else can

we make of the claim that the movement from the male makes the off-spring "like itself"? The point Aristotle wants to make is that conception results in female offspring only when the female contribution is not well concocted (presumably, as well concocted as it can be; it is never, of course, as well concocted as the male contribution). As I read the passage the καθ' αὐτὴν in line 17 is parallel to the καθ' ὁποίαν . . . κατ' αὐτήν construction in lines 23–24. The claim is not then that in the first instance, when the "seminal residue in the menstrual fluid" is well concocted, the movement of the male (in the seminal residue of the male) is itself male; if that were true, when the seminal residue in the menstrual fluid is *not* well concocted the movement of the male would itself be *female*, and in general the innate maleness or femaleness of the movement of the male would be a function of the degree of concoction of the seminal residue in the female contribution. I take this to be absurd. The claim is rather that the offspring is "like" the movement in the male in the prevalence or nonprevalence of some capacity in that movement (Aristotle goes on to say at 767b23–768a3 that the "capacities" in question are the capacities of the individual male parent). The movement of the male seminal residue must then be potentially either male or female in every case. If it were only male, either actually or potentially, then every offspring would be male (or nothing).

It is important to notice that Aristotle has strong philosophical reasons for wanting to *deny* that the semen or the menses before their interaction already have a determinate sex. Those reasons have to do with his rejec-tion of the preformationist account of generation, according to which the contribution of the parent (generally the male parent) already con-tains the parts of the embryo, which are not then formed, but only devel-oped, *in utero*.[38] Just as Aristotle does not allow that the contribution of the male or female parent already contains, say, a liver or a heart, so too he does not allow that those contributions contain organs of generation. And since he insists that the capacity which is maleness or femaleness only comes into being with those organs, the capacities as well as the organs are determined, and come into being, after conception. Notice that Aristotle might both have rejected preformationism and argued that the sex of the offspring is determined by the contribution of the male, if he had been willing to posit two kinds or species of semen. He might, that is, have argued that although semen does not have a determinate sex in the sense of having sex organs or capacities, it does have a determinate sex in the sense that it carries with it a male or a female "form" or set of motions. Aristotle does not do this, presumably because he is committed to males and females not being subspecies, but he is as a result left with a problem. For while all animals of a given species will have the same organs other than generative organs—say, heart, liver, and so forth— Aristotle has to explain why some animals have female organs and some male organs: because some have the female principle and some the male principle. But then why does a given animal have, say, the female principle rather than the male? Because in some cases the form contributed by the male parent by way of the motions imparted by the semen masters the matter, and sometimes it does not. And this success or failure of mastery seems to be accidental (unlike, say, the development of the liver). It is accidental in the sense that the ability to master is not a determinate feature of the semen; ability to master does not belong καθ' αὐτό to the semen. So the differences that ensue on mastery or failure of mastery, differences in principle and ultimately in organs, are accidental to the individual.

There is, however, one passage that suggests that Aristotle does think that male and female are essential or formal differences. He says that male and female differ both with respect to their account (λόγον), and with respect to sensation (716a19–20): with respect to their account because they have different capacities and tasks, with respect to sensation because they have different parts or organs. The point has already been made: because male and female differ in their capacities or principles or tasks with respect to generation, they must have different organs of generation. The question is, In saying that insofar as male and female have different capacities and tasks they differ with respect to their *account*, does Aristotle means to say that they differ in essence? I argue that the claim is that male and female do differ in essence, but that the male and female in question are not male and female *animals*, but the male and female *principles*, which are attributes of animals. This means then that male and female animals are not different in essence any more than pale and dark animals are different in essence, although maleness and femaleness are different in essence just as pallor and darkness are different in essence.[39]

κατὰ μὴν τὸν λόγον is parallel to κατὰ δὲ τὴν αἴσθησιν. Male and female are said to differ in both respects. κατὰ δὲ τὴν αἴσθησιν is clearly a reference to the organs of reproduction: male and female animals differ perceptibly insofar as they have different organs. κατὰ μὴν τὸν λόγον, on the other hand, is a reference to the capacities that distinguish male and female. The principles that carry with them those capacities are different with respect to their account. The capacities as such are not observable. "Male" and "female" here then seem to refer not so much to male and female animals, but rather to the principles that make an animal male or female by determining that animal's capacity for concoction. So what are different κατὰ μὴν τὸν λόγον are not male animals and female animals, but the principles that make some animals female and some male. The point is one we have already seen made in the *Metaphysics*: male and female are not substances but attributes of substances; hence, it is not the account of the substances that is different, but rather the account of the attributes.[40]

That this is how we should take this phrase is confirmed by Aristotle's other references to male and female as διάφορα, or differences, in the rest of the GA. In a passage at 748a2 Aristotle refers to the male and female of a species being undifferentiated from one another in species (εἴδει). And in all other passages where Aristotle refers to male and female as διάφορα it is in the nontechnical sense of differences, not the differentiae of a species.[41]

There is, then, considerable evidence in the *Generation of Animals* as well as the *Metaphysics* that Aristotle is philosophically and consciously committed (quite sensibly) to the claim that male and female, while contrary principles of generation, are certainly not principles that entail essential differences between male and female animals. This is true even though male and female animals have different generative functions, and correspondingly different organs of generation. We have seen that the origins of male and female are not different; neither the male nor the female σπέρμα has a determinate sex. Moreover, the development of the generative organs and processes in male and female animals is parallel (and Aristotle maintains this despite observable differences): in the *History of Animals*, in describing the changes of puberty, Aristotle repeatedly remarks on the similar development of males and females, in the deepening of the voice, the swelling of breasts, the beginning of sexual desire, and changes in general health (HA VII 1 581a27ff., 581b6ff., b12ff., b24ff.). And the processes of concoction that determine whether an animal will produce semen or menses are parallel, not different in kind but only in the degree to which they are concocted (GA 727a2–9, 727a26–30, 737a27). In these respects Aristotle seems to be downplaying male

ɔmical and physiological differences, and relegating
ɔf the material and accidental.

ion I consider Aristotle's claim that male and female
abits (βίοι and ἔθη), and that women ought to play a
ɪold subordinate to men. In both these cases I maintain
attempt to found the claims of observable or appropriate
differences on any deep (physiological, anatomical, or psychological—
where by "psychological" I mean "with respect to the soul") difference.
That is, in these cases Aristotle simply asserts that there are differences,
or asserts the appropriateness of a certain social role for women, rather
than arguing for that deficiency, or the appropriateness of that social role.
We shall then have the evidence for the two strains of thinking about sex
differences that I identified earlier. I shall then return to the *Generation
of Animals* to consider the most troubling of Aristotle's discussions of sex
differences: the difference he posits between the material role played by
the contribution of the female to the process of generation and the formal
role played by the contribution of the male. It is there that we find Aristotle constructing a sex difference plainly tainted by male bias (a difference he claims to be observable), where that difference cannot easily be
excised from its philosophical context.

Difference and Misogyny

If, as I have argued, Aristotle is philosophically committed to a view of
sex differences as material and nonessential, how does this commitment
manifest itself in his views on the behavioral differences between male
and female or the political role of women? I shall show that in these areas
Aristotle does not have, or pretend to have, a philosophical or scientific
justification for his claim, variously expressed, that females are somehow
inferior to males. That is, Aristotle does not appeal to any psychological
or biological account of the differences between male and female to legitimate his view that females compare unfavorably to males in certain respects and realms.

Consider first the behavioral differences (differences of βίοι and ἔθη)
of male and female as documented in *History of Animals* IX 1 608a3–b19.
Aristotle says, for example: "the female is softer in disposition, is more
mischievous, less simple, more impulsive, and more attentive to the nur-

ture of the young; the male, on the other hand, is more spirited, more savage, more simple and less cunning" (608b1–5). Or, at 608a14–19, "the male is more courageous than the female, and more sympathetic in the way of standing by to help. Even in the case of the cephalopods, when the cuttlefish is struck with the trident the male stands by to help the female; but when the male is struck the female runs away."[42] The list of such differences in life and habits is extensive. Aristotle offers no theoretical account of these differences. He states them as matters of fact, available for observation.[43] Nowhere does he claim that they arise from or are produced by physiological or anatomical differences. Aristotle notes that while they are observable in most species, they are particularly evident in the case of people, whose character (or habits) is more developed. He seems, in fact, to stress these higher-order differences more emphatically than any difference he remarks at the level of anatomy or physiology. There, as we have seen, he typically stresses the *parallel* between male and female, in their origins, their development, and in the capacity to concoct. There is, then, no evidence that Aristotle wants to argue that the observable differences in habits he remarks are somehow founded on the differences of organs and capacities. On the contrary, there is reason to think that he believed the differences of organs and capacities were too slight to provide a foundation for the exaggerated differences of habits.

Consider next the passage in the *Politics* at I 13 1260a12–14 where Aristotle says that the authority of the male head of a household over his wife stems from the character of her deliberative faculty (τὸ βουλευτι-κον) as unauthoritative (ἄκυρος), and thereby suggests that the role of women in the household ought to be one of subservience to their husbands. Elizabeth Spelman, among others, has taken Aristotle to mean that the deliberative faculty of women is without authority in the sense that it is easily overruled by the nonrational element in her soul.[44] I do not find textual support for this reading. Aristotle has already said that the rule of men over women is like constitutional rule (1059b9–10), which he has described as a system in which "the ruler and the ruled interchange in turn (for they tend to be on an equal level in their nature and to have no difference at all)." What distinguishes the rule of men over women from the rule of some citizens over others in a constitutional state is that the former is continuous; that is, male and female do not take turns ruling. This strongly suggests that Aristotle does not have philosophical reasons for distinguishing the deliberative faculty of women from that of men; on the contrary, it suggests that he has reason to think their faculties are *not* different.[45] He does take for granted that a hierarchy must be established and that women ought to take the subordinate role because someone must. This is not, of course, a reason why *women* ought to take the subordinate role. Aristotle fails to suggest any difference between men and women that would justify the subordination of women. So insofar as he considers seriously the faculties of women and men, Aristotle posits no significant difference between them. This does not prevent him from maintaining the appropriateness of women's subordination to men in the household, but we should notice that he does not offer us reasons for that subordination.[46]

Consider finally Aristotle's attribution of the material cause of generation to the female, and of the moving and formal causes to the male. If Aristotle denies, in both the *Metaphysics* and the biological works, that male and female are essential differences, how can we account for his identification of the male with form and the female with matter, given that matter and form are so often opposed?[47] I have suggested in the previous section that in this context matter (menses) and form (semen) are not so radically different, that they are the same stuff at slightly different stages of concoction. While this is true, Aristotle's identification here of the male with form and the female with matter leads to his view that the female is not only different from the male, but deficient with respect to the male. Once Aristotle has attributed formal causation in generation to the male, given his explanation of resemblance to the parent in terms of the efficacy of the prevalence of the formal cause (the motions in the semen) over the material cause (the menses), the occurrence of female offspring becomes anomalous.[48] Hence his infamous remark in the GA at 775a15 that females are imperfections in a species, where males are perfections.[49] One sex or the other does have to be a natural imperfection given his theory.[50] But it is only because he has assigned the material cause to the female that it is the female rather than the male who is, according to Aristotle, a kind of imperfection. So the question becomes whether Aristotle has scientific or philosophical reasons for attributing material causation to the female rather than the male and formal causation to the male rather than the female.[51]

It is clear that Aristotle believes not only that there is a difference in the contributions of male and female to generation, but also that there is a hierarchy between those contributions, the hierarchy between matter and form. It is also clear that he places the female lower on that hierarchy by identifying her with matter rather than with form. Aristotle probably had philosophical reasons for believing that both parents cannot contribute form, and hence that one must contribute form and one matter (i.e., that there is a difference). Furth, for example, offers a persuasive account of Aristotle's commitment to the claim that the form must come from only one parent.[52] And Aristotle probably had philosophical reasons for believing that form is better than matter (i.e., for the hierarchy).[53] But we could grant him both those claims and still ask what reasons he has for attributing material causation to the female rather than the male and formal causation to the male rather than the female.

Some have proposed that innocent empirical observation would lead Aristotle to identify the female contribution as matter. Tress, for example, says, "The menstrual blood . . . , being heavier and bulkier, looks like a material contribution."[54] We may agree that "menstrual blood" looks like a material contribution; but then so does semen. On the supposition that we accept that only one parent can contribute matter, and that we already accept that matter is worse than form, can it be an innocent (objective) observation that one kind of matter is somehow more material than another? If it *were* an innocent observation, then even Aristotle's view that females are deficient relative to males would turn out to be free of male bias. This is possible, of course, but implausible, if only because, as we have already seen, Aristotle exhibits male bias in describing the appropriate political role for women and the alleged habits of the females of species. Given that he exhibits such bias, why should we believe that this observation is free of it?

One might suppose that Aristotle does have some kind of argument for the claim that women contribute matter and not form. Roughly, that argument reconstructed would be: (1) females are less hot; (2) creatures that are less hot are less able to concoct the seminal residue; (3) so, females are less able to concoct the seminal residue; (4) less well-concocted seminal residue is more material than well-concocted seminal residue; (5) so, females contribute the matter rather than the form. But Aristotle establishes that females are less hot by appealing to the claim that seminal residue in the female is less well concocted than seminal residue in the male, that is, that it is more material.[55] The argument would then be circular: in order to show that females have less well concocted seminal residue Aristotle must assume that females are less hot; and in order to show that females are less hot he must assume that they have less well concocted seminal residue. What seems important to me is not that this is a bad argument, but that in order to fix it Aristotle would have to be able to show independently either that the female is less hot than the male or that her seminal residue is less well concocted. One of these phenomena would have to be observable. Since Aristotle argues that because the seminal residue in the female is less well concocted the female must be less hot (GA IV 1 765b 16–19), I take it that he believes it to be observable that the seminal residue in the female is less well concocted (765b 9–14). We are back where we started: How could such an observation be innocent, given the philosophical commitments to the superiority of form and the separateness of form and matter that Aristotle already holds?

We find, then, on the one hand, that Aristotle manifests in the *Metaphysics* and the *Generation of Animals* a philosophical commitment to the sameness of the sexes with respect to essence. On the other hand, in various other discussions he exhibits male bias: in claims about the habits of males and females, in claims about the appropriate domestic roles for men and women, and in his claim that the female is biologically defective relative to the male. All of these claims are, or depend on, allegedly innocent observations of how things are: females just are less courageous, women just do not hold political power, females just are less hot. At the same time, in making these observations, Aristotle never suggests that they are in any conflict with the commitment to the sameness of the sexes in essence. In the next section I shall say something of the implications of the conflict between a commitment to the essential sameness of the sexes and a commitment to the deficiency of one sex relative to the other.

Conclusion

I have been arguing that there are two strains to Aristotle's thinking on differences between the sexes. Both begin with observations that Aristotle clearly takes to be evident: in the one case, that males and females do not differ in species; in the other, that females differ from males in a variety of ways, and in all of these ways are somehow inferior to males. My reason for saying that Aristotle is philosophically committed to the former observation is that he entertains, and tries to refute, an argument to the contrary, namely, the argument presented in *Met.* X 9 to show that males and females must be subspecies. In his claims about observable sex differences that clearly involve male bias (the claims that the female is in some respect inferior) he does not engage in any such philosophical justification. We can conclude, then, that Aristotle has a reasoned belief in the sameness of the sexes with respect to essence, together with an unreflective belief in the deficiency of the female with respect to the male in various respects. I now ask about the relation of those beliefs.

One might think that, because Aristotle is committed to the sameness in essence of male and female, whenever he speaks of deficiencies in the female he intends us to understand that these are nonessential deficiencies. That he does not appeal to differences in biology or psychology (I mean differences in the soul) as the origins of the behavioral and political differences that he claims to observe might seem to be evidence for this. And if Aristotle understands all the differences between male and female to be nonessential, in keeping with his metaphysical commitment, then one might think that the aspects of his work that exhibit male bias can be abandoned, leaving the philosophical content intact. This, I think, is not the case, on the evidence of his claim that the female contributes matter to the process of generation because she is less hot. I have focused on this claim in the preceding section because it leads Aristotle to the claim that only the female contributes matter in the generation of offspring, which then leads to the claim that female offspring are, as it were, defective, although naturally defective (ὥσπερ ἀναπηρίαν εἶναι τὴν θηλύτητα φυσικήν) (GA IV 6 775a15). They are defective in the sense that if the form from the male parent had been transmitted as it should have been, male offspring would have resulted (IV 3 767b16–23). (Had Aristotle observed that males were less hot than females and hence that they alone contributed matter, then male offspring would have proved to be defective by this reasoning.)

The question is whether this "deficiency" on the part of the female is material and nonessential. Given what Aristotle has said about sex differences in the *Metaphysics* and at other points in the *Generation of Animals*, the evidence we have already examined, we should expect the answer to be affirmative. But given the context, the discussion of matter and form, on even the most charitable reading this seems unlikely. That is, if the female is deficient finally because she is produced only when matter defeats form in some capacity, then it would seem to be a formal deficiency from which she suffers.

One might argue that a formal deficiency need not be an essential deficiency, if one takes the view that, at the level of the individual, form and matter are the same. David Balme, for example, says that, "A material accident . . . is a formal feature which is due to the proximate matter's own form: it is not itself a bit of matter qua matter."[56] On this view *all* differences are formal differences. As a result, not only are sex differences formal differences between animals, but so too are such differences as eye-color. One implication of this is that form is individual (and definition is of individual form): "taken out of change, as at a moment, the combined whole [i.e., the individual composite of form and matter] is entirely determined in a form which can be grasped and defined. This form necessarily includes all the matter, and is therefore individual."[57] On such a view animal form is distinguished from animal essence, because while the form includes the material accidents, the essence does not (and thus one does not have to concede that a particular eye-color, for example, is essential to some kind of animal). If this is right, male and female can be formally different without being essentially different.

If, however, we agree that at the level of the individual all differences are formal, then the blue-eyed person is just as formally different with respect to the brown-eyed person as the male is to the female. This does not seem to have been Aristotle's view. I have argued that he did not take this view because he believed male and female to be attributes that belong as-such to the matter of animal (blue or brown eye-color and other material accidents do not belong as-such to the animal at all), and *not* because he believed male and female attributes in the individual to be essential. I understand Aristotle's discussion at *Metaphysics* X 9 of male and female as as-such attributes of animals as an attempt to explain not only why male and female are not subspecies of animal species, but also why male and female as differences are not just like "material accidents."

This route of interpretation has, then, serious implications for Aristotle's metaphysical doctrines: not only does it commit Aristotle to a theory of individual forms, it also commits him to a willingness to blur distinctions between material accidents and as-such material attributes.[58] We cannot be warranted in taking it simply to save Aristotle from the charge of misogyny, given all the evidence that he did hold misogynist views (although one might think that we are warranted in taking them on independent grounds).

However we decide to interpret the claims about female deficiency, those claims make clear that at least on this issue the two strains of thinking on sex difference, the two ways in which Aristotle constructs sex differences, collide. Aristotle's philosophical commitment to the essential sameness of the sexes does not prevent his unreflective views on the differences between the sexes from intruding on other philosophical arguments that have implications for that commitment to the essential sameness of the sexes.[59]

Notes

1. Catharine A. MacKinnon argues that sex differences are in fact the result of, rather than the cause of, the subordination of women. See "Sex Equality: On Difference and Dominance," in *Toward a Feminist Theory of the State* (Cambridge: Harvard University Press, 1989), 215–34. She claims that the view that women are subordinate to men, or at any rate appropriately distinguished from men, because they exhibit certain biological sex differences is that of the "mainstream epistemologically liberal approach" ("Sex Equality," 218). She cites John Rawls as a philosophical proponent of this view (*A Theory of Justice* [Cambridge: The Belknap Press of Harvard University Press, 1971], 102).

2. In either case, the causality needs to be spelled out: How exactly do the anatomical and physiological differences account for the social, economic, and political differences? And how, exactly, do the social, economic, and political differences shape the perception of these anatomical and physiological differences?

3. MacKinnon, "Sex Equality," 224–25.

4. For such arguments, see MacKinnon, "Sex Equality."

5. See, for example, Lynda Lange, "Woman is Not a Rational Animal: On Aristotle's Biology of Reproduction," in *Discovering Reality*, ed. Sandra Harding and Merrill B. Hintikka (Boston: D. Reidel, 1983), 1–15. Lange claims that Aristotle argues not only that men and women are different, but that women are inferior, and it is this inferiority that justifies the subordination. Lesley Dean-Jones says, "the Aristotelian model used scientific theory to argue for the natural subordination of women to men in a way that had not been done before" (*Women's Bodies in Classical Greek Science* [Oxford: Clarendon, 1994], 21).

Thomas Laqueur, in *Making Sex: Body and Gender from the Greeks to Freud* (Cambridge: Harvard University Press, 1990), 28–30, does describe both the ways in which Aristotle minimizes or blurs the organic differences between the sexes (suggesting that male and female are more and less perfect versions of the same thing), and the ways in which he insists on sexual opposition in discussing the causal roles of male and female in generation. Linda R. Hirshman, in "The Book of 'A'" (Chapter 8, this volume), citing Laqueur, says that he (and others) "claim that Aristotle assumed the inferiority of women and from this assumption drew his biology and his politics separately. This still leaves the task of dealing with the politics intact, but at least jettisons the scientific-looking part of the enterprise. By this way of thinking, Aristotle's characterization of women as inferior natural instruments of the material of reproduction is neither necessary nor sufficient for his political misogyny." I agree that the misogyny we find in Aristotle's biology is not used as a foundation for the misogyny in the political theory, that these are two distinct instances of Aristotle's misogyny. Neither Laqueur nor Hirshman, however, makes the point that I insist on in what follows: that Aristotle does have a positive, reasoned, philosophical commitment to the essential sameness of male and female in any species, which works against any misogynist prejudice.

Martha Nussbaum, in replying to Hirshman ("Aristotle, Feminism and Needs for Functioning," Chapter 9 this volume), urges us not to conclude from Aristotle's empirical mistakes about women that there is "a deep defect in either his methodology or the substance of his scientific thought. It is simply a grossly flawed application of methods that, properly applied, would have ascertained that the capabilities of women were (as Plato already had argued) comparable to those of men." Is this too charitable a reading of Aristotle, suggesting as it does that we can skim off the "grossly flawed application of methods" and be left with both methodology and substance intact? Relative to Aristotle's political theory I think it is not too charitable. I shall, however, argue in the final section of this paper that Aristotle's misogyny does make a philosophical difference to his account of generation. For although Aristotle could argue just as easily that the male is deficient relative to the female in order to make his account of generation truly neutral as to the contributions of male and female he would have to abandon certain dearly held views about the relative value of form and matter.

6. It may be controversial to say that two such creatures do not differ in *form*, since some commentators, at least, believe that there are individual forms; if this is right every individual is different in form from every other.

7. Aristotle does of course recognize that there are animals that are not male or female; these are all those animals that do not reproduce sexually (GA I 1 715a20).

8. Gareth Matthews argues that the bulk of evidence suggests that Aristotle accepted what he calls a "Norm-Defect Theory" of gender differences over a "Complementarity Theory." According to the Norm-Defect Theory the characteristics of the male are the norm, and those of the female are the defect. Matthews thinks that Aristotle had some reason to adopt the Norm-Defect Theory, but that Aristotle had no philosophical reason to establish the male as normative and the female as defective. See Gareth B. Matthews, "Gender and Essence in Aristotle," *Australasian Journal of Philosophy*, supplement to vol. 64 (June 1986): 16–25.

9. See Daryl McGowan Tress, "The Metaphysical Science of Aristotle's *Generation of Animals* and its Feminist Critics," *Review of Metaphysics* 46 (December 1992): 307–41. Tress seems to think that because Aristotle does not *argue* for the inferiority of the female to the male he does not believe the female to be inferior. He does, however, allow that Aristotle's "commonplace views" (which include the view that females are somehow inferior to males) may have occasionally entered into his philosophical thinking (when Aristotle names the male as superior and the female as inferior) (330). In many respects I agree with Tress; I do not, however, accept his conception of the feminist understanding of essentialism (314), for which he cites no text, but against which he attempts to defend Aristotle. One of the questions I ask is, To what extent can the commonplace views of a philosopher remain separate from his or her philosophical work?

10. See Matthews, "Gender and Essence in Aristotle," 22–23 for a reconstruction of Aristotle's argument for one sex being deficient relative to the other.

11. The context of this discussion of sex differences in *Met.* X is a discussion of the one, and of the one and the many as contraries. This leads to a more general discussion of contraries, intended to support the argument that in some sense the many and the one are contraries. In chapter 8, Aristotle describes the difference between things that differ in species as contraries. Given that description, Aristotle has to consider cases where differences seem clearly to be contraries, but do not divide a genus into species. Male and female are among such differences. The point of raising the question about male and female is to show that while all differences that divide a genus into species will be contraries, it is not the case that all contraries divide a genus into species. The greater point is then perhaps that one and many can be contraries without dividing a genus into species, just as male and female are contraries that do not divide a genus.

12. At *Met.* VII 5 1030b18–22 Aristotle says, "it is not by accident that the nose has the attribute either of concavity or of snubness, but in virtue of its nature; nor do they attach to it as whiteness does to Callias, or to man (because Callias, who happens to be a man, is white),

but rather as 'male' attaches to animal and 'equal' to quantity, and as everything else which is said of something in its own right." This passage is pertinent here for two reasons. First, it confirms that Aristotle distinguishes attributes like "whiteness" from attributes like "female" on the grounds that the latter, unlike the former, belong as such to that to which they belong. Second, the analogy of "male" to "equality" suggests that certain mathematical attributes are attributes of matter (perhaps only intelligible matter?) like male and female, as we shall see. And if this is the case, then the suggestion that "one" is like "male" in being an attribute that belongs as such, but only to the matter, gains credence.

13. Although Aristotle does not here give us his reasons for thinking that male and female cannot be distinct species, presumably it is because the sexual union of male and female "naturally" and usually (although not always) produce offspring of the same species (GA II 7 746a29–33; HA 606b19ff.). Gareth Matthews argues that this is not sufficient reason to suppose that male and female cannot be distinct species, and that at any rate Aristotle has more complex reasons for believing that male and female do not constitute subspecies. See "Gender and Essence in Aristotle" (20–21) for the argument that taking the standard case of reproduction among animals to be one in which a female and male of the same species unite and produce offspring of that same species does not provide sufficient reason to believe that male and female cannot be distinct species; and (21–22) for the reconstruction of Aristotle's reasoning to the claim that nothing is essentially male, and nothing essentially female.

14. In at least one passage in the GA, at 724a35–b12, Aristotle speaks of generation occurring *from* (ἐκ) the contraries that are male and female. This passage is, however, perplexing, since Aristotle specifies the sense in which something comes to be "from" opposites as the sense in which one contrary is destroyed as the other comes into being from it (as, say, hot comes to be "from" cold). Offspring do not seem to come "from" male and female in this sense. But see GA IV 3 768a3–9 for a possible understanding of generation as occurring from contraries in this sense.

15. At Met. 986a23–b5 Aristotle lists sets of Pythagorean opposites, one of which is male and female.

16. The other kinds of opposites cited are relatives, privations and possessions, and affirmations and negations; this list is reiterated at Met. X 4 1055a38–39 and X 7 1057a33–37. In an earlier passage in the Metaphysics at V 10 1018a20–22, Aristotle lists the kinds of opposites as contradictories, relatives, privations and possessions, and "the extremes out of which and into which generation and destruction occur." See also Topics II 8 and V 6.

17. What sort of qualities? Perhaps the "shape or external form" of a thing (Cat. 10a11). Triangle and square and straight and curved are the examples Aristotle offers of such qualities. This description of one kind of quality reflects Aristotle's description of male and female as attributes or affections of the matter of animal, since the shape or external form is of course the shape that the matter of the animal takes. This is confirmed by Aristotle's terminology when he discusses eunuchs (εὐνοῦχος; ἐκτετμημένον) at GA 716b5, 766a24–30, 784a6, 784a12, 787b20–788a17 and HA 545a20–21, 540a1–2. In all of these passages except GA 766a24–30 Aristotle describes the change from male into "female" as a change in shape (μορφή). This description of the sort of quality male and female are might be adequate to the account of male and female as founded on the possession of certain organs, but what of the capacities the exercise of which these organs are supposed to make possible? Should we not rather suppose that male and female are among the qualities that Aristotle calls natural capacities or incapacities (Cat. 8 9a14–19)? If capacities and incapacities are understood to be opposites in the sense of privations and possessions, Aristotle seems committed to denying that male and female are a case of capacity/incapacity, because, for complex reasons, he wants to deny that they are a case of privation/possession (see note 19).

18. But see notes 7 and 19.

19. Aristotle consistently describes male and female as opposites in the sense of contraries, and not in the sense of possession and privation, despite his description in the GA of male and female as a certain capacity or incapacity. Possessions and privations, while they are opposites, are not contraries because they fit neither the description of contraries *without* intermediates nor the description of contraries *with* intermediates. They do not fit the description of contraries without intermediates because some possessions/privations do not belong (one or the other) to everything capable of receiving them; e.g., neither sight nor blindness belong (always) to everything capable of receiving them. On the other hand, privations/possessions do not fit the description of contraries with intermediates, because such contraries may *never* belong to what is capable of receiving them (some surfaces will never be black or white), but privations/possessions will belong at some time to that which is capable of receiving them (*Cat.* 10 12b26–13a3). If male and female are contraries without intermediates, then, on Aristotle's account, one or the other will have to belong *always* to every animal that belongs to a species that has different sexes (i.e., to everything capable of receiving male or female). Neither sight nor blindness, however, might belong to something capable of receiving sight or blindness. Aristotle, in saying this, seems to mean that a creature might have the organs without yet having the capacity for sight. Why, then, does he not believe that one might have the organs for generation without yet having the capacity? What reason is there, in other words, to distinguish the case of maleness and femaleness from the case of sight and blindness?

Another puzzling implication of Aristotle's classification of male and female as contraries is that contraries can change into one another (*Cat.* 11 13a19ff.). How might male change into female, or vice versa? Aristotle may have in mind cases of eunuchs (see note 17).

A difficult question is whether male/female admits of degrees. If they are contraries without intermediates, then they should not. Yet at GA 11 715b17–22 Aristotle speaks of certain animals and plants as though they have a small degree of maleness or femaleness. And at HA VIII 2 589b29 he seems to suggest that maleness and femaleness admit of degrees.

20. For recent discussions of the difficulties of this passage see Jonathan Barnes, trans., *Aristotle's Posterior Analytics*, 2d ed. (Oxford: Clarendon, 1994), 112–14; Michael Ferejohn, *The Origins of Aristotelian Science* (New Haven: Yale University Press, 1991), 96–108; Richard D. McKirahan Jr., *Principles and Proofs: Aristotle's Theory of Demonstrative Science* (Princeton: Princeton University Press, 1992), 87–90.

21. In Greek mathematics, numerical quantities were often treated as geometrical quantities. This probably began with Pythagoras, but became standard.

22. In this passage Aristotle says, "matter does not make a differentia, for [individual] people are not [different] species because of it, even though the flesh and the bones out of which this [person] or that [person] are made are other" (1058b6–8). "Species" could also of course mean "form"; so one might read this as evidence against a theory of individual forms.

23. Notice that, at *Met.* V 10 1018b2–3, in listing conditions that make two things other in species Aristotle mentions "if they have a contrariety in their substance (ὅσα ἐν τῇ οὐσίᾳ ἐναντίωσιν ἔχει)."

24. Not every ἴδιον will be a material attribute: in the passage in the *Topics* where Aristotle defines the ἴδιον the example he offers is the capacity in people to learn grammar; since this capacity belongs to our souls it is not a material attribute.

25. Again, notice the parallel between male/female and certain mathematical examples: Aristotle says that certain attributes will belong to certain things insofar as those things are planes or lengths (and yet being a plane or a length cannot be separated from being a quantity/magnitude).

26. Ferejohn seems to suppose that all καθ' αὑτό attributes of the second sort will be differentiae (*Origins*, 96). This is not implausible if one considers only the examples Aristotle offers in this passage, but when one considers other items that fit the description (e.g., equal/unequal) it clearly cannot be the case.

27. For an argument that we can find in the HA a search for those attributes that *do* divide genera into their species, see James G. Lennox, "Divide and Explain: The *Posterior Analytics* in Practice," in *Philosophical Issues in Aristotle's Biology*, ed. Allan Gotthelf and James G. Lennox (Cambridge: Cambridge University Press, 1987), 90–119.

28. See Anthony Preus, *Science and Philosophy in Aristotle's Biological Works* (New York: Hildesheim, 1975), 108.

29. The process of concoction of nutriment into "seed" (σπέρμα) involves several stages, beginning in the stomach, and moving on to the liver and the spleen, the heart, and the genitals (see PA 669b25ff, 670a20ff, 674a9ff, 678a4–6, 647b5; GA 717b23–6, 718a5–10, 719b2, 738a10–738b4, 766b7–12, 737b28–31). Andrew Coles outlines the process in some detail in "Biomedical Models of Reproduction in the Fifth Century BC and Aristotle's *Generation of Animals*," *Phronesis* 40, no. 1 (1995): 63. At every stage except the last the female concocts the nutriment in the same way as the male, and the only aspect of the male σπέρμα that the female σπέρμα lacks is "the source of soul" (GA II 3 737a27).

30. There is some debate about whether the pneumatization of the nutriment occurs only in the heart or also in the male genitals. Since the heart is the source of natural heat (766a35–37) and the difference in natural heat between male and female is ultimately responsible for their different capacities, if the heart is the only bodily site where pneuma is added to the residue of the nutriment, then the male and female heart must be somewhat different in their capacity to add pneuma. If, on the other hand, pneuma is also added in the male genitals, and it is this final addition of pneuma that differentiates semen from menses, then the organic differences between male and female need only be in the genitals. See Coles, "Biomedical Models," 64–67.

31. At 765b37–766a5 Aristotle says, "as there is an organ in the case of every capacity, in the case of that [capacity] which completes its [process?] better and that which completes it worse, and the male and the female [complete the same process, one better and one worse], since capacity and incapacity are said in many ways, it is necessary, therefore, that there are organs in the case of the male and the female; hence in the one case there is the uterus, in the other the περίνεός." In this passage I understand the capacity/incapacity of male and female to be their differing capacities of concoction. The περίνεός must refer to the penis and testicles, since the final concoction occurs there.

32. There is an embryonic stage during which the animal has the principle but does not have the parts and as a result is not actually male or female (763b27–28). The animal may not yet be an animal, however, so that there would be no time during which the animal is an animal but does not have a sex. See note 35.

33. One passage describing the difference between male and female animals particularly downplays the significance of that difference: "We call 'male' the animal that generates in another, and female the animal that generates in itself," (716a14–15). This seems to suggest that the difference is merely one of location of generation. This passage, however, appears in a discussion that is preliminary, so that it is not clear that it is Aristotle's considered opinion.

34. Coles argues that menses as well as semen has "movements" that impart form, although Aristotle claims that if all goes well the movements of the semen prevail over the movements of the menses and thereby impart form to the matter that is the menses. See Coles, "Biomedical Models," 69, 74–76, 83.

35. Sex is said to be determined after conception: at 736b2–5 Aristotle says that it is not the case that when an animal is formed a human or a horse or any other given species of animal is formed, because the end (τό τέλος) is formed last of all; 737b11 says that a fetus is complete (τέλειον) when it is either male or female. (In the next lines Aristotle speaks of male and female as differences in form, but it is clear from what follows that by "form" in this context he means "shape.") We should remark that the capacity that comes with the organs

will be analogous to the capacity in an infant to learn geometry, not immediately realizable; both organs and capacities are possessed only potentially until the onset of puberty (728b22–32). See also *Met.* 1058b23–24 where Aristotle says that *the same seed* (τὸ αὐτὸ σπέρμα) becomes male or female when acted on in a certain way.

36. Aristotle says as much in rejecting both Anaxagoras's explanation of the sex differences (the σπέρμα from male and female already have sex) and Empedocles' explanation of the same phenomenon (the contribution of the male is male and of the female is female, and one wins out over the other depending on the heat of the uterus) (GA IV 1).

37. See, as a starting point, the chapters by Lloyd, Balme, Cooper, and Furth in *Biologie, logique et métaphysique chez Aristote*, ed. Daniel Devereux and Pierre Pellegrin (Paris: Editions du CNRS, 1990).

38. I am indebted to Brian Fogelman for suggesting the importance of Aristotle's rejection of the preformationist view to his denial that maleness and femaleness are essential attributes of animals.

39. See *Met.* VIII 3 and 5 for a discussion of essence in "compound" items, i.e., items that are combinations of substance and accident, and of essence in items where the attribute is not an accident, but a feature peculiar to the matter.

40. For a different interpretation of this passage, see Dean-Jones, *Women's Bodies*, 182.

41. See GA I 1 715b17–22; GA II 4 737b11–13; GA IV 1 764a7–10 and 766a22–24; HA 538a2; HA 581a11; HA 589b29; HA 608a19; PA 648a11.

42. Passages I quote from the HA are translated by d'A. W. Thompson.

43. Evidence that he considers the habits he reports as empirically observable is at 608a10–12: "Of the animals that are comparatively obscure and short-lived the characters are not *so obvious to our perception* as are those of animals that are longer lived" (my emphasis). One might think that Aristotle attributes the differences of habits he claims to observe in male and female to differences in blood. He clearly does think that male and female blood differ: at HA III 19 521a1–3 he distinguishes the finest and purest (καθαρώτατον) blood from thick and black blood, then goes on at 521a24–25 to say that blood in the female is thicker and blacker than male blood. When then at PA II 4 651a13–16 Aristotle says that the nature of the blood affects the habits and sensory faculties of the animal, we should not be surprised that he adds at 651a23–25 that finer and purer blood is responsible for making the sensory faculties of animals more easily affected. Yet Aristotle associates more watery blood (which is characterized as "purer" [καθαρωτέραν]) not only with intelligence, but also with timidity (650b27–28). So the characterization of male and female animals' habits does not map neatly onto the characterization of male and female blood.

44. Elizabeth V. Spelman, "Aristotle and the Politicization of the Soul," in *Discovering Reality*, ed. Sandra Harding and Merrill B. Hintikka (D. Reidel, 1983), 17–30, 18. Spelman argues persuasively that there is an argument in the *Politics* for the subordination of women, albeit a circular argument. Her reconstruction of the argument depends on her gloss of "unauthoritative" said with respect to the deliberative faculties of women as "without authority with respect to the non-rational element in the soul," and it is this with which I disagree.

45. See my "Aristotle's Conception of Authority," in *Law, Politics and Society in the Ancient Mediterranean World*, ed. Baruch Halpern and Deborah W. Hobson (Sheffield: Sheffield Academic Press, 1993), 122–36, 129–31.

46. Thomas Laqueur suggests that Aristotle viewed the differences between men and women in the social and political sphere as, "indubitable facts, "natural" truths" (*Making Sex*, 28). Aristotle, however, certainly thought that natural phenomena were subject to explanation. If, then, he did take such a view, we should expect him to offer an explanation for these differences.

It is worth remarking that if Aristotle did simply assume the naturalness, or at least the appropriateness, of different social and political roles for women and men, this is not true of all his philosophical contemporaries. Plato, of course, in *Republic* V 453e–457c argues that there is no reason to assign men and women different roles in the city. Moreover, as Sarah Pomeroy points out, Xenophon recognized that "the qualities of the soul are neither immutable nor predetermined by gender"; *Xenophon. Oeconomicus. A Social and Historical Commentary* (Oxford: Clarendon, 1994), 37.

47. See GA 732a2–10, 765b9–10, 775a15.

48. For Aristotle's account of the resemblance of offspring to their parents, see GA IV 3–4.

49. Notice that Aristotle sometimes speaks of *both* male and female as perfections. See, e.g., 737b10ff.

50. See Matthews, "Gender and Essence in Aristotle," 22–23.

51. Some commentators clearly think Aristotle does not have such reasons. Dean-Jones, for example, says: "The allocation of different roles in conception was a direct consequence of Aristotle's unquestioned assumption of male superiority" (*Women's Bodies*, 181). Similarly, Matthews says: "That, as it turns out, males are supposed to be successes, and females failures, is, I think, better explained by psychological and sociological factors, than by philosophical ones" ("Gender and Essence in Aristotle," 23).

52. Montgomery Furth, "Specific and Individual Form in Aristotle," in *Biologie, logique et métaphysique chez Aristote*, ed. Daniel Devereux and Pierre Pellegrin (Paris: Editions du CNRS, 1990), 106–10.

53. See Charlotte Witt's contribution to this volume for the argument that Aristotle's hylomorphism is inherently normative. Witt also argues that we ought not to accept either the "reformist" or the "gendered" interpretation of hylomorphism, where the "reformist" interpretation considers it possible to remove gender bias from the theory of hylomorphism while retaining the theory, and the "gendered" interpretation considers the gender associations of matter and form to be an ineliminable aspect of the theory. On the "gendered" interpretation Aristotle's male bias enters in here, in the very formulation of the distinction between form and matter.

54. Tress, "Metaphysical Science," 326.

55. For an examination of the claim that the female is less hot, and a discussion of the arguments and evidence that are supposed to justify this claim, see Nancy Tuana, "Aristotle and the Politics of Reproduction," in *Engendering Origins: Critical Feminist Readings in Plato and Aristotle*, ed. Bat-Ami Bar On (Albany: State University of New York Press, 1994), 189–206.

56. David Balme, "Matter in Definition: A Reply to G.E.R. Lloyd," in *Biologie, logique et métaphysique chez Aristote*, ed. Daniel Devereux and Pierre Pellegrin (Paris: Editions du CNRS, 1990), 49–54, 50. See also "Aristotle's Biology Was Not Essentialist," in *Philosophical Issues in Aristotle's Biology*, ed. A. Gotthelf and J. G. Lennox (Cambridge: Cambridge University Press, 1987), 291–312.

57. Balme, "Matter in the Definition," 50. Balme presents this view as a reading of *Metaphysics* H.6 on p. 52.

58. For some concerns about individual forms, see G. E. R. Lloyd, "Aristotle's Zoology and his Metaphysics: The Status Quaestionis. A Critical Review of Some Recent Theories," in *Biologie, logique et métaphysique chez Aristote*, ed. Daniel Devereux et P. Pellegrin. See also my "Tensions and 'Anomalous' Passages: Aristotle's Metaphysics and Science, Method, and Practice," a review of *Biologie, logique et metaphysique chez Aristote*, in *Apeiron* 25, no. 3. (September 1993): 189–207.

59. I am very grateful to Angela Curran, Sophia Elliott, Brian Fogelman, Cynthia Freeland, Eric Lewis, and Stephen Menn for their comments on an earlier draft of this chapter. Charlotte Witt kindly provided me with a copy of the draft of her contribution to this volume, which both clarified and changed my own thinking on certain points. I also owe thanks to Mary Deslauriers and Rose Charles for taking excellent care of Théophile.

Part Two

Practical and Productive Knowledge

7

The Virtue of Care
Aristotelian Ethics and Contemporary Ethics of Care

Ruth Groenhout

Feminist criticisms of Aristotle are so extensive one might wonder whether a feminist should waste her time on his work. His ethical theory makes theoretical rationality necessary for the fulfillment of true human excellence, since "reason more than anything else *is* man."[1] When this conception is placed together with Aristotle's account of women's nature, which is characterized, in his view, by a defective capacity for rationality,[2] one finds an ethical theory that excludes women from ever exhibiting true human excellence. Aristotle's political theory is inherently hierarchical; he writes, "that some should rule and others be ruled, is a thing not only necessary, but expedient; from the hour of their birth, some are marked out for subjection, others for rule."[3] Even his metaphysics seems to rest on the fundamental inferiority and subjection of women to men since procreation itself, as Aristotle understands it, demonstrates that the male is the active principle, capable of generating a new being, while the female is the passive contributor of material.[4] All of Aristotle's theorizing seems infected by an objectionable hierarchy with women placed on a fairly low rung. Slaves, both male and female, fall even lower on this hierarchy, a further reason to eject Aristotle from the feminist canon. Given the pervasiveness of his ranking tendencies, it might seem surprising that any feminists would find anything of importance in Aristotle's philosophy.

There are feminists who find him a useful resource, however, for a number of reasons. For one thing, his ethical theory offers an account of ethical reasoning that incorporates the emotions as essential to adequate rationality, rather than assuming that the two are inevitably opposed.[5] Such an opposition has been harshly criticized by many feminist thinkers.[6] Aristotle also has an ethical theory that seems congenial to feminist conceptions of the self as situated, particular, and enmeshed in social relationships,[7] because his theory recognizes the particularity and situatedness of ethical decision-making[8] and because it recognizes the extent to which human nature is inescapably social.[9] In addition, Marcia Homiak has recently argued that Aristotle offers a useful corrective to a tendency in some feminist ethical theories to glorify self-sacrifice and subservience to others.[10] Given these features, a feminist might expect to find much of value in Aristotle in spite of the objectionable aspects of his thought mentioned earlier.

In this essay I shall argue for this latter claim: that Aristotle's thought, and its modern variation, virtue ethics, is a valuable resource for contemporary feminist philosophers, particularly those developing an ethic of care. An ethic of care arose out of the attempt to develop an ethical theory that recognizes and incorporates women's moral experiences and reasoning. The project originated with Carol Gilligan's work on a woman's voice in ethics, and Nel Noddings's discussion of caring.[11] Both thinkers began with a concern for how women experienced and conceptualized the ethical aspects of their lives, Gilligan from the standpoint of a sociologist, Noddings from a more philosophical standpoint. Several characteristics are common to the various theories that have been placed in the category of an ethic of care. First, such an ethic rejects universal absolutes as the basic moral principles, in favor of particularized, concrete moral responsibilities generated by relationships. Second, such a theory considers the emotions or passions to be central to any understanding of morality; third, it turns to the study of specific relationships, frequently the relationship between mother and child, in order to better understand moral responsibilities.

While many feminists have found an ethics of care attractive, as evidenced by the number of writers who have contributed to the topic, the theory has not been met with uncritical acclamation. Feminists have offered sharp criticisms of several features of an ethics of care, and some have argued that it should not properly be considered a feminist ethical theory at all.[12] There are two main feminist criticisms of care theories. The first is that such an ethics glorifies the very traits that traditionally have been used to justify the relegation of women to a private domestic sphere. If the distinctive features of a "woman's voice" are traits of caring and service, a theory based on those traits seems to offer little more than a return to the values of Victorian true womanhood, with women cast in the role to which "nature" has suited them, caring for the physical needs of those around them.[13] The second criticism generally raised against an ethics of care is that it is a theory that is unable to produce or advocate adequate concern for those who are outside the "circle of care."[14] The theory seems to lack a mechanism to protect the rights of one person against another, and when people meet as strangers (as surely they often must) the theory provides inadequate (moral) protection against the abuse of strangers for the sake of a "cared-for one."

In evidence for the continuing relevance of Aristotle's ethics for contemporary feminists I offer a synthesis of an ethics of care with an Aristotelian ethical framework. There are important ways in which the defects of an ethics of care can be overcome by the addition of an Aristotelian concern for self-improvement and for political participation. Conversely, Aristotelian tendencies to produce hierarchical, oppressive systems can be counteracted by the addition of an element of concern for the good of the other generated by an ethics of care. A synthesis of the two ethical traditions results in a theory that is both more adequate as an account of human experience and more attractive from a feminist point of view.

This essay first takes a feminist look at Aristotle's ethics. From there it turns to a consideration of an ethics of care, and then to a proposal for a synthesis of the two. Throughout I shall be assuming that it is possible to speak intelligibly about a feminist perspective, or feminist thought. This is a somewhat controversial assumption, since there is no unified group of people who constitute "the feminists." Moreover, there has been a tendency for a small class of women to assume that their beliefs are *the* feminist standpoint and to ignore the extent to which their position is structured by class- or ethnic-related biases.[15] I shall attempt to avoid this assumption of homogeneity. Nonetheless, since the focus of this essay is on Aristotle and ethics of care theories, I shall be leaving open the question of who counts as a feminist, and what beliefs they might have. There are a few central tenets I shall assume feminists share, such as the principle that women are not inferior to men either in worth or ability to live a full human life, that women's experiences are as representative of human experience as men's experiences, and that women deserve at least the same level of legal and moral protection as any other human deserves.

Aristotelian Ethics and Feminist Perspectives

Criticisms of Aristotle

Aristotle's ethical theory, and its modern offspring, virtue ethics, have both been criticized by feminist thinkers for several flaws. One is the implicit or explicit devaluation of women and women's roles that can be found in both theories. This can be easily demonstrated in the case of Aristotle. The human function, he tells us, is rational activity in accord with the good.[16] But women, he also remarks, are not fully rational, but are rather defective compared to men in their ability to exercise their rational potential.[17] The remark occurs in the context of a discussion of whether there are some humans who are naturally suited to be slaves, and hence properly relegated to the role of serving others. Women seem to him an obvious example, noted simply in passing. Since true virtue and complete flourishing as a human being depend on exercising one's rational capacity in an excellent manner,[18] women would seem to be excluded from both by their very nature. Aristotle assumes that the proper place for women is under the rule of men, devoted to service and care.

Aristotle's account of the respective natures of men and women should not be portrayed too simplistically, however. While he clearly believes that women in general are inferior to men in general, he is not so blind as to assume that every particular woman is always and in every way inferior to every man. In his discussion of household relationships in the

Nicomachean Ethics he comments that the proper relationship between husband and wife is one in which the husband "rules in accordance with his worth and in those matters in which a man should rule, but the matters which befit a woman he hands over to her."[19] Relationships in which the man rules over every matter, he continues, fail to reflect the respective worth of the parties. In specific cases, and particularly with respect to household duties, women may be capable of exhibiting a limited form of excellence.[20]

While Aristotle's views on women and their capacities do not reach the depths of misogyny demonstrated by Saint Jerome or Schopenhauer, they are clearly offensive and unacceptable. It is curious, then, that many commentators simply ignore his views as if they were irrelevant to his ethics.[21] The reader is left unsure whether Aristotle's views on women are left unremarked because they are so obviously wrong, or because they are so obviously right. When commentators do mention women, they do not always clear up this confusion. Richard Kraut's discussion of Aristotle's ethics mentions women only in passing, as examples of inferior human beings who are unable to achieve the full human good.[22] While this approach is perfectly in accord with Aristotle's own treatment of the topic it is hardly satisfying to the contemporary reader, particularly one who is quite convinced that she is, in fact, fully human. One exception to this general tendency is Francis Sparshott's discussion, which reaches the conclusion that if Aristotle had included women in his description of the good human life, Aristotelian ethics would have been radically changed.[23]

Aristotle's feminist critics do not treat his discussion of women as a peripheral matter, but instead see it as central to any understanding of his ethical theory. Some argue that Aristotle's account of human nature, relying as it does on the notion of function, is inherently hierarchical and forces human relationships into oppressive molds.[24] It has even been argued that female inferiority is a central, crucial component of the entire Aristotelian worldview, without which Aristotle's metaphysics is incoherent.[25]

Nor are contemporary appropriations of Aristotle free from sexist biases. Recent discussions of virtue ethics generally adopt an Aristotelian account of rationality and the virtues.[26] They also (not universally, but to a fairly high degree) adopt a communitarian or traditionalist position,[27] a natural result of accepting Aristotle's account of ethical reasoning. Because he assumes that only those who have been properly brought up and already accept the general rules that structure society are suitable candidates to engage in moral reflection, conformity with tradition is built into Aristotle's account of rational deliberation in ethics.[28]

Contemporary virtue ethics is marked by a similar respect for traditions. Alasdair MacIntyre, for example, turns to traditions to ground moral reasoning, and in particular argues for a return to a traditional Aristotelian conception of reasoning as that conception developed historically through the thought of Thomas Aquinas and subsequently the Scottish Moral Sense theorists.[29] Likewise Michael Sandel argues that political theory needs to be grounded in a rich conception of the good life, developed out of community values and ways of life.[30] Both Sandel and MacIntyre thus seem to endorse traditions (both social and religious) that have been oppressive to women and that incorporate that oppressiveness deeply within their understandings of reality, rationality, and human nature.

Elizabeth Frazer and Nicola Lacey criticize the virtue tradition for its tendency to ignore the impact that social and religious conventions have had on women's lives.[31] The sexist and ethnic biases of many traditional cultures are problematic for ethicists who hope to derive adequate ethical theories from tradition. On the other hand, traditions are rarely monolithic structures, and it is quite possible to use one aspect of a tradition to criticize another. The Christian tradition, for example, was used simultaneously to support and to criticize the practice of slavery; some traditions may have sufficient complexity to develop internal mechanisms of reformation. And Aristotle's own account of the relationship between justice and obedience to the law indicates that he was aware of the need for internal critiques of traditional mores. Toward the end of his discussion of the nature of justice he points out the tension between the equitable and the legally just, and indicates that traditional laws are themselves in need of criticism and philosophic evaluation.[32]

Nor is it entirely correct to claim that all virtue theorists are blind to the oppressive nature of traditions. The exclusion of women from Aristotle's conception of full human flourishing is recognized by MacIntyre, for example, and criticized as a typical ideology of domination. But MacIntyre goes on to argue that what Aristotle gets wrong is not the belief that the best kind of social organization will be hierarchical, but rather the belief that one can exclude either women or foreigners from that hierarchy because of a supposed inferior nature.[33]

This brings up a related criticism of Aristotle's ethics: that its objectionable nature lies not so much in its specific conception of women's nature, but rather in the political structures the theory necessarily produces. Because Aristotelian ethics is perfectionist, and because it makes political participation dependent on virtuous character, it also necessarily incorporates a hierarchical conception of politics. Such a conception, it is argued, is at odds with a central feature of feminist thought, namely a rejection of hierarchies, imbalances of political power, and a more general rejection of socially imposed moral standards altogether.[34]

These criticisms seem to be accurate. Aristotle's ethical theory is hierarchical, placing those who are more fully human in positions of control and domination over those who are less capable of rationality. It also justifies the use of those who are subordinate by those who are "naturally superior" as both natural and expedient.[35]

To evaluate these criticisms, however, it is important to keep several issues distinct. The question of whether any and all hierarchies are objectionable is separate from the question of whether a particular hierarchy is objectionable. Likewise, the question of how the various members of a hierarchy should be treated is separable from an evaluation of the very concept of a hierarchy. The concept of a hierarchy is simply the concept of the possibility of making value judgments; of evaluating some societies, or some humans, or some abilities as better than others. While this concept has been challenged by contemporary feminists, it is one that women should be wary of giving up. For one thing, the claim that hierarchies are bad, or wrongheaded, itself depends on the possibility of making evaluations (rankings) of social structures. If that possibility is rejected, then the evaluation of hierarchies themselves would seem to be impossible. Rejection of hierarchical structures simpliciter thus runs afoul of what Bernard Williams has called the paradox of vulgar relativism.[36]

Hierarchies should be evaluated on their own merits. Some are clearly objectionable (Aristotle's discussion of the relationship between husband and wife being a case in point), others are not. There is nothing wrong with ranking job applicants in a hierarchy based on their abilities and training. There is something wrong when people are systematically denied training, or are judged incompetent despite having obvious abilities solely on the basis of their gender or their race. But it is not the hierarchy itself that is objectionable, it is the morally objectionable criteria used to select places within that hierarchy.

Likewise, the fact that those who rank low in hierarchies are often mistreated is ample reason to change that treatment, but it may not be reason to reject the very concept of hierarchy in the first place. Mistreatment of the weak is wrong, but the solution to it is to build protection of the weak into the social system, not to pretend that they are not weak by denying hierarchical structures.

Any discussion of the hierarchical structure of Aristotle's ethics must include a discussion of Aristotle's advocacy of *theoria* as the activity characteristic of the highest pinnacle of human excellence. (*Theoria* is variously translated as contemplation, theoretic activity, theoretical contemplation, study, and, less commonly, self-immortalization, which is the realization of the presence in the soul of the Prime.)[37] There are two main interpretations of the place of *theoria* in Aristotle's ethics. In the first interpretation, *theoria* is understood to be an activity separate from the exercise of the moral virtues, so that one can choose either the life of political and ethical action or the life of contemplative inaction. On this account, Aristotelian ethics would appear to be inherently elitist, hierarchical, and designed only for those fortunate few (generally wealthy and male) who have the leisure and the wealth to live truly excellent lives; that is, lives which include the maximum amount of theoretical contemplation.[38] This understanding of the ultimate goal in human life rests on a conception of the human self as primarily intellectual, explaining why intellectual activity should be thought to be the crowning glory of human existence, rather than political or social activity.[39]

Given this intellectualist understanding of the highest human good, Aristotle's discussion of friendship rules out the possibility of friendship between those capable of full rational activity and those who are not. Those who cannot engage in the life of *theoria* are deficient, and the truly excellent person cannot love them in the sense she or he could love another "godlike" person.[40] They play a role in one's life, to be sure, but it is a role of service, and Aristotle thinks this is proper, since the worse person should serve the better.[41] When this intellectualist, exclusivist conception of the highest good for humans is paired with Aristotle's tendency toward constructing hierarchies, the result is quite bad for those who cannot achieve the highest good.

This understanding of *theoria*, however, seems to suffer from numerous problems. Among them are the fact that if intellectual activity (separate from a moral and political life) were the ultimate goal of all human activity it would be rather pointless for Aristotle to spend most of his discussion of the flourishing life explaining how to achieve moral excellence. Likewise Aristotle's account of friendship is unintelligible on this account of *theoria* since the intellectual life is not generally understood to incorporate social activity, and would presumably preclude the amount of time Aristotle feels is necessary for true friendship.[42]

Both Sarah Broadie and Anthony Kenny argue that an understanding of *theoria* that places it in opposition to a life fully expressing the moral virtues and containing ample room for the exercise of the capacity for friendship and political activity makes Aristotle's theory incoherent and fails to do justice to the nuances of his thought.[43] While in Aristotle we do find a conception of the moral life that places intellectual or rational activity as the ultimate goal that should structure all subordinate goals, this does not imply that the virtues could be dispensed with once one achieved the ability to engage in rational activity. Aristotle's conception of human nature is such that pursuit of intellectual goods is not possible when a virtuous character is not present, not least because the nonvirtuous person cannot possibly experience true friendship, and such friendship is an integral part of the intellectual life as well as a necessary component of any pleasurable human life.[44] Stephen White goes so far as to see rational activity as an integral part of all virtue, arguing that dignity, rather than theoretic or contemplative activity is the supreme virtue.[45] If the most fully flourishing human life is understood to include and incorporate all the virtues, as is argued by these latter thinkers, then the flourishing human being cannot leave social and political ties behind when engaging in rational activity. This does not remove the hierarchical aspect of Aristotle's thought, but it does soften it somewhat. While a truly good person cannot be friends at the deepest level with those who are inferior, such a person nonetheless has moral responsibilities, and perhaps ties of friendship of a different sort to these others, and this places constraints on how they are treated. Hence Aristotle's description of marriage, which involves (necessarily, he thinks) a relationship between unequals, is also of a relationship marked by pleasure and benefit to both parties.[46] This would seem to rule out at least the grosser forms of exploitation and oppression. On this more inclusive account of *theoria* the hierarchical elements in Aristotle are less exploitive and limited by the requirement that those on the top of the hierarchy have developed true moral excellence.

A final criticism that has gained prominence more recently with respect to Aristotle's ethical theory concerns its essentialist aspects, particularly Aristotle's use of an essentialist account of women's nature to justify their subordinate role in society.[47] Some feminists go further to criticize essentialist accounts of human nature as well, arguing that to be a human is to be free to be what one chooses, rather than to have certain essential characteristics such as rationality.[48]

An adequate response to the charge that Aristotle's theory is essentialist must be twofold. It is surely correct to point out, as Aristotle's critics do, that any theory that defines a particular gender or ethnic group as inferior or superior to other humans is a moral theory that should be rejected. Moral theorists need to recognize the extent to which all humans are capable of both virtuous and vicious behavior, and the extent to which bigotry and prejudice can be reified by various ethical theories.

However, there is a sense in which the proponent of an Aristotelian or virtue-oriented theory will need to accept some degree of essentialism with respect to human nature. A theory that relies on a conception of human flourishing for its development is dependent on some account of what humans ought to try to become if it is to have any content at all. Furthermore, it is not clear that this is a bad thing. Certain claims seem to be true about all human lives, for example, the claim that humans require relationships within which caring and the development of the ability to care are possible. This would seem to be a restatement of Aristotle's claim that humans are social creatures and need friends for full happiness.[49] It would follow from this that humans are (objectively) better off when they are able to experience reciprocal, loving relationships than when they are not. If this is true, certain determinants of the good life and characteristics of the good human will be determined in ways that individuals may not be able to choose. The individual cannot, by an act of free will, make a life lived in the absence of close, loving, constructive relationships as good a life as one lived in the presence of such relationships (all things being equal.)

Furthermore, one can acknowledge that there are truths about what lives are good ones for humans to live and still coherently criticize social structures that oppress women. Any criticism of oppresive social structures relies on an implicit or explicit claim that such structures make the full expression of women's humanity impossible, which presumes that women's lives can be assessed as better or worse.

Are there more concrete limitations on the life that can be called a good life for a human to live? Presumably there are. Martha Nussbaum has noted the extent to which human lives inescapably force human persons to choose certain ways of living, and in that choice to reject a thoroughgoing relativism in favor of the endorsement of one form of life over another. She then goes on to argue that in spite of cultural differences, there is a shared bedrock of human experience (she points to the experiences of mortality, the body, pleasure and pain, cognitive capability, practical reason, early infant development, affiliation, and humor as shared features of any human life) that limits the range of answers to the question of how humans ought to live.[50] But to begin to answer this question is to assume that there are unchosen, essential aspects of human life.[51]

What Aristotle Has to Offer to Feminist Theory

It might be possible to excise the more objectionable features of Aristotle's conception of women from his ethical theory. It has not yet been shown that there is any point in doing so. That argument has been made by a number of feminist theorists who argue that, even with all his flaws, Aristotle still has something to offer the contemporary feminist. Marcia Homiak, for example, has argued that an Aristotelian conception of the good life offers a useful corrective to women who too often define morality in terms of what they owe to others.[52] Aristotle provides theoretical room for the agent to be concerned with who she is and who she should become, and to reject others' claims on her when they would make self-determination impossible.

In his discussion of immoderate humility, for example, Aristotle points out that such humility has four detrimental effects. The person who is unduly modest robs herself of what she deserves, causes others to think badly of her because of her humility, lacks self-knowledge, and fails to perform the noble actions of which she might otherwise be capable.[53] This portrayal of humility as a vice, albeit a nonmalicious one, offers a healthy alternative to the complete self-effacement sometimes portrayed as "good mothering" in the popular press.

More than this, Aristotle offers an ideal for women that includes active participation in a political life.[54] He carefully rejects the notion that the political life involves the irrational use of force to control others,[55] but argues that properly understood, the life of virtue involves statemanship. Responding to those who renounce political power in favor of inactivity, in the *Politics* he reiterates the point, made originally in the *Nicomachean Ethics*,[56] that happiness requires activity.[57] Such an ideal would require a radical restructuring of society. If a full human life requires active social and political engagement, then social structures that prevent particular groups from such engagement are morally wrong. An Aristotelian conception of ethics, then, could serve as a force for societal change. This is an important feature of any ethical theory at a time when feminist are occasionally criticized for academic posturing devoid of practical content.

Other positive aspects of Aristotle's ethics have been noted by Martha Nussbaum, including the extent to which Aristotle incorporated emotions into his account of reason in ways important for contemporary feminist thought.[58] A common feminist complaint concerning contemporary philosophical and ethical thought is that both tend to denigrate or simply ignore the place of the emotions in human life and in human reasoning. Some thinkers attribute this denigration of the emotions to the influence of Descartes on contemporary moral thought; others locate its source in other areas. Wherever it originated, however, this rejection of the emotional part of the human self has tended to go hand in hand with an association of women with the emotions and a denigration of the moral capacities of women.[59] If morality depends solely on pure rationality, divorced from the emotions and the passions, those to whom society delegates the task of expressing and dealing with emotions will be considered less rational and less moral, and it is not surprising that women have thus been relegated to an inferior position with respect to moral reasoning and their capacity for disinterested ethical thought.

For Aristotle, however, the life of reason does not require a rejection or denigration of emotion. One of the attractive features of Aristotle's ethics is the extent to which rationality requires appropriate emotions. In his discussion of anger, for example, Aristotle recognizes that both too much and too little anger are vicious character traits.[60] A good human should feel angry when she is treated badly, and the absence of anger under legitimately provoking circumstances is seen as a mark of an inferior sort of person.

All of the moral virtues, in fact, involve the emotions.[61] But it is not simply the individual moral virtues that incorporate the passions; rationality itself is connected with one's experience of pleasure and pain, since one of the marks of the truly good human is that such an individual feels pleasure at doing what is right.[62] Moreover, the pleasure that is involved in the exercise of the rational faculties is ultimately held up as the paradigmatic human pleasure, not as something that tempts one away from intellectual activity.[63]

Aristotle's account of rationality has many affinities with feminist claims that knowledge itself is not separable from emotional engagement with the world. Virginia Held has pointed out the extent to which the activities women characteristically engage in, such as caring for children, preparing meals, and the like require careful reflection, theoretical interpretation, and all the other intellectual traits of a rational being.[64] Likewise, Lorraine Code's work on empathy as a way of knowing, or for that matter Edith Stein's discussion of empathy, both emphasize that the capacity humans have for understanding and relating to other human beings is an intellectual trait, not a "merely" emotional response.[65] Or, more properly, such understanding incorporates both intellectual and emotional response, as intellect and emotion are not exclusive concepts. Morwenna Griffiths has also recognized the extent to which an adequate account of knowledge must include emotional realities.[66]

Aristotle's general conception of rationality exhibits many of the features contemporary feminist thinkers consider important. His account of moral reasoning also has attractive features from a feminist point of view. Feminists have criticized contemporary moral theory for its limitation of moral reasoning to the production of abstract, universal, impersonal principles, often generated by a contractual model of human relationships.[67] Aristotelian accounts of moral reasoning, on the other hand, offer a model that recognizes the particularistic nature of ethical decisions, the importance of individual circumstances, and the rejection of abstract rules.[68] Practical wisdom is the intellectual capacity required for the presence of true (as opposed to merely instinctive or natural) virtue.[69] Aristotle describes it as concerned with variable matters and those that are the goals of human action. Because it deals with such a subject matter, it is also the intellectual capacity that brings together universals and particulars.[70] This aspect of Aristotelian thought is particularly important for contemporary feminist ethics of care theory. Seeing why it is important will require a discussion of the strengths and weaknesses of care.

Ethics of Care

There are a number of features that, together, characterize an ethics of care. The first, which was the original impetus for a new ethical theory involves an attempt to articulate a women's perspective in ethics. This can be seen in both Nel Noddings's *Caring* and Carol Gilligan's *In a*

Different Voice. Women's moral reasoning, Noddings and Gilligan argue, is marked by a concern for maintaining and nurturing relationships, rather than by a concern for protecting individual rights or obeying abstract ethical principles. This concern for relationships they termed *caring*. Placing caring at the center of the moral life produces an ethics that emphasizes special relationships rather than impartiality, the importance of contextual matters for moral judgment rather than a search for universal laws, and a recognition that moral agents always have a history, a body and a sociocultural background rather than (ideally) being disembodied, ahistorical "views from nowhere." These features are common to most of the writers who have developed an ethics of care further.[71] All these theorists agree that the core concept on which an adequate ethical theory should be constructed is the concept of caring (rather than rationality, justice, or an ideal contract situation.) This does not mean that they reject rationality or justice: Noddings emphasizes that caring is a component of rationality,[72] and Gilligan discusses the extent to which both justice and care orientations must be integrated in any adequate ethical theory.[73] But neither justice nor (pure) rationality are the foundation of these ethical theories, and both are limited by, and structured by, the demands of caring relationships in ways that are foreign to most Kantian or Utilitarian thinkers.

Caring is the characteristic that marks the relationships among members of healthy families, or among friends, and several of these theorists explicitly point to the mother-child relationship as the paradigm example of care.[74] The way in which a good mother responds to the needs of her child, both the short-term physical and emotional needs and the long-term social and developmental needs, tailoring her responses to the particular personality she cares for, is exemplary for all human relationships. Good persons, according to such a conception of ethics, are those with the character traits needed to provide care in appropriate situations, and good actions are those that one who cares would perform.

Unfortunately, this definition of caring remains fairly vague; it is circular to define caring in terms of good mothering and the good mother as one who cares. Without more specificity as to what exactly care is, it is not clear that the theory offers a compelling account of the moral life.

Furthermore, a conception of ethics that is based on special relationships, and on particulars rather than universal laws runs the risk of dissolving into an unprincipled relativism.[75] One needs some way of discerning who counts as an exemplar of caring behavior, or what actions serve as models for the one who wishes to care for another. Again, though many theorists point to the practice of mothering as the source of a paradigm of care, there are both good and bad mothers. In order to distinguish among abject subservience to the whims of others, rigidly controlling behavior, and proper concern for the good of the other, the theory needs more specificity and a better theoretical account of why certain mothers are good examplars while others are not.[76]

The lack of a definition of good caring is the central difficulty faced by ethics of care thinkers, but it is certainly not the only criticism the theory has faced. An ethics of care also has a tendency to limit the focus of the moral agent to those people in close proximity to her, and perhaps to blind her to the needs of those far away. Noddings has been criticized, for example, for limiting the responsibility to care to those who are inside the circle of care, those who are close enough to the moral agent to generate a caring response.[77] This is problematic from a feminist viewpoint, however, as it would allow blindness to the needs of those who are at a distance from oneself, socially, physically, or culturally. This leads to a weakening of respect for the rights of others, particularly those others whom we are most tempted to abuse because they are not like ourselves.

A third criticism engendered by an ethics of care is that the theory depends on, and provides support for essentialism with respect to women's nature. The theory begins with an attempt to observe women's experience of the moral life. What ethics of care thinkers seemed to discover was that women are nurturing, giving, self-sacrificing, and willing to maintain relationships even when the cost to them is high.[78] It is not too big a step from this point to the conclusion that women are naturally self-sacrificial and suited to a life of subordination to the needs of others. But this is a conception of women's "nature" that contemporary feminists have generally rejected for several reasons. One reason is that the traits identified as "feminine" are common to many people who are raised under oppressive circumstances, and are perhaps better understood as survival mechanisms than virtues.[79] This criticism is also raised by some who argue that gender is socially constructed rather than biologically based.[80]

A second, more political critique of this essentialist conception of women's nature points to the close similarity between women's caring nature as developed by ethics of care thinkers and the Victorian cult of true womanhood, which likewise described women as caring, self-sacrificing, and generally too good to engage in the rough-and-tumble world of commerce and competition. This Victorian conception of women provided a clear and compelling justification for restricting (upper-class) women to the home, restricting their right to own property, engage in intellectual pursuits, or develop any measure of autonomy. Not surprisingly, contemporary theorists suggest that feminists should be wary of any ethical theory that ascribes those same traits to women as a class.[81]

Finally, in a related criticism, some have criticized the extent to which an ethics of care seems to be of limited political efficacy. Noddings's account of the political role women are suited to take illustrates this well; she argues that since women have experienced oppression, but have also experienced love for those who oppress, they need to take on the role of mediator between oppressed and oppressor.[82] But the role of mediator hardly allows for political power. Noddings instead argues that it requires a recognition of powerlessness. For feminists who are concerned with working for political change, however, this role can hardly provide sufficient scope for an ethical theory. More recent discussions of an ethics of care have pointed out the extent to which such an ethics can provide the impetus for political change, and this seems an important modification of the theory.[83]

These criticisms pose a serious challenge for writers who work with an ethics of care. The Aristotelian tradition seems to offer suggestions for resolving some of these problems, and it seems one of the few traditions that could be utilized in this way.

There are limits on which theoretical frameworks a thinker might turn to in order to provide an account of what proper caring looks like. Contemporary versions of Utilitarian, Kantian, and Contract ethics almost universally define the moral reasoner as a disengaged, disembodied, ahistorical self—precisely the conception of moral agency which an ethics of care rejects. Postmodern criticisms of "Enlightenment rationality" are often valuable as criticisms but provide little in the way of a positive framework on which to build a substantive theory.[84] Ethical theories such as Joseph Fletcher's situation ethics likewise have little appeal from a feminist standpoint as they lack precisely the feature the theory needs, namely, some theoretically grounded way of distinguishing the better from the worse.[85]

There is another option, however, that offers a middle way between universal, timeless, laws and absolute relativism. In Aristotle's ethics one finds an acknowledgment of the contextual nature of moral reasoning and a recognition of a connection between reason and emotion (rather than an opposition between them). Aristotle also offers an account of human nature that recognizes the fact of embodiment and the social construction of the self. In many ways his theory would seem to be suitable for adaptation to feminist needs. At the same time, an ethics of care has the resources to resolve some of the more intractable problems of Aristotelian ethics; the two theories seem ideally suited to mutually modify each other.

A Gentler, More Caring, Aristotle?

Aristotelian ethics, both in its original form, and in its more modern form of virtue ethics, exhibits a problematic tendency toward essentialist hierarchies, exploitation, and a validation of oppression. Contemporary ethics of care avoids these problems while exhibiting others, particularly a tendency to reify women's self-sacrifice, and a lack of respect for abstract ethical qualities such as justice and rights with a concomitant tendency to drift into principle-less situationalism.

If the two theories could be brought together, however, the strengths of each might serve to avoid the defects of the other. It seems that a version of virtue ethics could be developed that did place care at the center of what it is to be fully and excellently human. Such an ethical theory would define the capacity to care, to fully develop relational capacities, and to live a life characterized by caring relationships as partially constitutive of true human excellence. To be fully human, on such a view, would involve having the capacity to develop close relationships with others, having the skills needed to recognize the other's self and empathize with her, and to express these capacities and skills in the context of a society that allows for the possibility of caring relationships.

This emphasis on relationships is not entirely foreign to Aristotle's ethics. His location of friendship as an essential component of the good life, as well as his account of the necessity of the moral virtues for a flourishing, fully excellent life both point to the centrality of human relationships of care for human excellence.[86] But the conception of care such a position would utilize does differ in important ways from the conception Aristotle uses.

Among other differences, contemporary proponents of an ethics of care often propose mothering as the practice that should guide our conception of what or who counts as an exemplary human being. Such an exclusive emphasis on mothering may be mistaken, because humans exhibit care for others in many different relationships. One might, however, reject an absolute maternalism while still holding that mothering is a central and invaluable part of a good human life. This view would vastly increase the extent to which women can be envisioned as excellent, flourishing human beings, providing the beginnings of a method for ridding Aristotelian ethics of its sexist bias. Much of the work that women have traditionally done, such as caring for children, and providing for the physical needs of others, would be seen as part of the definition of what it is to live a fully human life. As Virginia Held has pointed out: "Human beings engaged in giving birth and bringing up children are as capable of transcending what already exists as are most of those in government or the arts and sciences. Creating new human persons and new human personalities with new thoughts and attitudes is as creative an activity as humans are involved with anywhere."[87] If, in fact, this ability to engage in nurturing relationships with other humans were recognized as a fundamental characteristic of a flourishing human life, then presumably how one understood women's nature might fundamentally change. One might, for example, have to offer arguments against the conclusion that men are inferior to women, since they seem on the face of it so much less able in this central human activity.

Consider how such a change might affect an Aristotelian account of particular virtues. In his discussion of temperance, for example, Aristotle focuses on moderation and excess, while treating a deficiency with respect to pleasure in only one sentence. "People who fall short with regard to pleasures and delight in them less than they should," he writes, "are hardly to be found; for such insensibility is not human."[88] This seems too simplistic. Women frequently do exhibit insensibility, reacting to pleasure with guilt rather than enjoyment. The inclusion of women's experiences in an account of temperance provides a more nuanced picture of the virtue.

Or consider Aristotle's discussion of pride. He rejects undue humility as inappropriate and damaging, as was discussed earlier. His discussion of the nature of proper pride, however, shows unmistakable signs of a limited range of vision, considering a proper sense of self-worth exclusively as it functions in a largely self-centered, upper-class realm. As a contrast to this, consider Sarah Ruddick's discussion of humility:

> Mothers identify humility as a virtue when they recognize in
> themselves the delusive, compulsive efforts to see everywhere and

control everything so that a child will be safe. With "humility," a mother respects the limits of her will and the independent, un-controllable, and increasingly separate existences she seeks to pre-serve. A mother without humility would become frantic in her efforts to protect. But she cannot, out of degenerative humility or passivity, relinquish efforts to control.[89]

For Ruddick, a healthy humility that recognizes human limitations while also accepting responsibility for authority, is a hallmark of the virtuous person. Humility in this case is considered to be proper self-respect, but it is turned away from a concern with social rewards and honor, toward a concern for the good of another.

A second change that would accompany such an inclusive revision of Aristotelian ethics is that the very notion of hierarchy would change. As long as the trait that marks one as human is theoretical intellectual activ-ity, excelling as a human will involve maintaining a proper distance from other humans, particularly those who are unable to engage in such activ-ity. One has only to read Aristotle's description of pride, the "crown of the virtues" to recognize the extent to which the virtuous person looks on others with condescension and a clear sense of his own superiority.[90]

This is not to say that Aristotle's virtuous person is a monster of cru-elty. Even the proud person, after all, is quick to benefit others, and treats those who are significantly inferior to himself with gentleness.[91] But there is a sense in which the truly great person has no particular interest in those who are far inferior to him, either their assesment of him, their opinions of the world in general, or their lives. There is a distancing that occurs in Aristotle's theory here, due to his conception of what the ulti-mate good activity for humans must be. But this distance is in tension with the social, community-oriented aspects of Aristotle's thought, and this tension is not easy to resolve.

This hierarchical, elitist tendency is even more apparent in Aristotle's discussion of slavery. Aristotle does not advocate despotism in his discus-sion of authority over slaves, but instead argues that masters should incul-cate the proper amount of virtue in slaves so as to render them more useful. Such usefulness provides the limits to the virtues that are to be developed in slaves; Aristotle is careful to point out that the slave, "will obviously require only so much virtue as will prevent him from failing in his duty through cowardice or lack of self-control."[92] More virtue would blur the line between master and slave, and so be detrimental to the proper functioning of society. Likewise citizens are to remain aloof from the menial tasks that are appropriate to slaves, since the habitual performance of such tasks will again blur the master-slave distinction.[93]

If true human excellence involves caring, the virtuous life cannot be understood to require distancing oneself from those who are weak, needy, or less proficient. It is precisely in such relationships that one is able to develop part of what caring requires, namely, a concern for the needs of others. While caring is essential for any human relationship, including relationships among equals, some of its characteristics do appear in their clearest light precisely in the interactions between parents and children. As parents care for children, they discover abilities and excellences that they never knew they had, and learn to be far better people than they might otherwise have been. Human caring offers a conception of excellence in which concern for the good of the weaker generates an improvement in the character of the stronger as well.[94] This results in a very different sort of hierarchy than Aristotle's hierarchy of natural slavery, one not based on subordinating the needs of the weak to the development of the strong. If anything, this new conception provides reason for thinking that there may be a way for both the proficient and the needy to develop toward excellence together. Care is a concern for the good of the other, furthermore, so to stop the other's moral development at a point that suits him for one's own use is clearly immoral. Deliberately stunting another's moral growth is no longer an ethical option.

Turning to Aristotle's effects on an ethics of care, one can also see that such a theory would be improved by an infusion of Aristotelian blood. Theories of care often suffer from a too narrow focus on those close to the ethical agent. Noddings herself provided grounds for this criticism since she quite frankly acknowledged that there might be people for whom one could not care if they were too distant from one's own position. This is particularly problematic since general feminist concerns would encourage women of various cultures and ethnic heritages to work together to end women's oppression. Noddings's position, however, seemingly justifies a lack for concern for those who are too distant, either socially or physically, from one's own position.

Here the justification for turning to Aristotle becomes obvious. Aristotle's conception of justice offers an account of the proper relations between people unconnected by ties of affection, without lapsing into the fiction of purely self-interested, rational agents resorted to by contemporary contract ethicists. Aristotelian justice, for example, is closely bound up with such character traits as gratitude, friendship, and love, and closely connected to benevolence[95]—hardly the traits to be looked for in the abstract individuals who cluster behind the veil of ignorance.

As can also be seen in an examination of Aristotle's discussion of justice, Aristotelian theory offers an alternative to the abstract principles approach to ethics that many feminists find objectionable, without sliding into a relativistic situationalism. The latter is clearly unacceptable, since it provides no grounds for the absolute rejection of practices and actions that destroy women's lives. But the former has been rejected as well, since abstract universal principles seem to conflict with the particularistic, relational mode of perception that is made central to an ethics of care. Aristotle's conception of moral reasoning, which recognizes that moral choices can be right or wrong, and offers criteria for judging them, while rejecting any attempt at universal, scientific lawlike rules, seems to offer just the proper mean between two unacceptable extremes here, as has been pointed out by several thinkers.[96]

But there is another aspect of Aristotle's ethics important for generating political principles. Humans by themselves cannot produce true excellence. They rely on parents to bring them up properly, on a society that is structured to assist parents, on social structures that allow for the education and development of such talents as they may be able to develop and so on.[97] Since this is the case, no ethical theory is complete that lacks some conception of how society should be structured to ensure the development of true excellence.[98] Stephen Salkever presents an extended argument for the claim that Aristotle is properly read as an opponent of the politics of virility (that is, an understanding of political theory that glorifies participation in the political sphere to the denigration of the private sphere and the activities and excellences proper to that realm). "Family life," he writes, "provides a separate focus of attention and care . . . which can check the danger of excessive civic-mindedness that seems always to threaten to turn the most tightly-knit cities into armed camps."[99] Structures of care are essential parts of a well-run polity, and must be included if the citizens are to become virtuous.

So in the *Politics* Aristotle provides for the physical needs of the citizens, with a special concern for the poor,[100] provides legislation dealing with the health of the citizens,[101] the education of children,[102] and so on. The conviction that care for the well-being of the citizens is an integral part of the well-ordered state could add a balance to an ethics of care by turning the focus of such an ethics away from individuals who care and toward the social structures within which care takes place.

An ethics of care is also frequently criticized for its regressive, potentially oppressive account of women's nature. Listening to the woman's voice and hearing special concerns about caring and nurturing appears to be nothing more than the old Victorian notion of the "angel in the house" and is likely to be put to much the same political use. In other words, this criticism accuses ethics of care proponents of glorifying the traits that have been used in the past to justify relegating women to a subordinate sphere of selfless service to others. And there is some justification to this criticism. Ethics of care proponents have developed their theories by listening to women and recognizing their concerns. The women they listen to are often in a position of subordination. By defining the ethical concerns of such women as the "voice of care" such theories seem to encourage women to continue to play the role of the silent servant, a far from liberating call.

As was mentioned briefly above, moreover, without a definition of what constitutes good caring, as opposed to submissive or self-effacing servitude to the whims or arbitrary claims of others, an ethics of care could easily be used in the service of reactionary political movements. But what is needed is not the rejection of caring as an ideal so much as a more specific definition of what exactly caring is. Caring is the character trait that allows one to promote, encourage, or develop human excellence in others.[103] Human excellence consists in the development of the moral and intellectual virtues. Among the moral virtues, it should be noted, is the ability to care, so this particular virtue is one that reproduces itself in others.

Given an Aristotelian account of the moral virtues and intellectual virtues, ordered by practical wisdom, but one that includes care as one of the virtues, one is able to offer at least a sketch of the flourishing human life. One who lives well exhibits excellence in reasoning and doing, and part of doing well involves an openness to and concern for the good of others. This concern is particularly strong in the case of others who stand in a close relationship to the moral agent. This concern for the other's good will manifest itself in concrete assistance toward the development of the virtues in the other, both by education and habituation. Caring is thus partly defined by its ability to reproduce itself as a characteristic in the other.

Among the virtues Aristotle discusses only friendship seems to have this reflexive and other-directed character. Friendship is characterized as willing the good of the other, and to consist more in loving than in being loved (and it is interesting that Aristotle cites mothers and children to support this latter claim.)[104] The other virtues do not directly produce virtue in another except by way of imitation,[105] but friendship involves wishing and doing the good for the sake of the friend, including caring for the good character of the other.[106]

One rarely sees Aristotle's discussion of friendship accused of requiring too much subservience or unthinking devotion to the other at one's own expense. The reasons for this are obvious: friendship involves a mutuality of concern and well-wishing, and it occurs in the context of a full development of all the virtues. These features should be incorporated into a theory of care. Care cannot be conceived of as exclusively unidirectional. It involves mutuality and reciprocity in the same way as friendship, although in specific cases such as caring for small children the reciprocity only becomes apparent over time. But if caring is a part of human excellence, then one who cares cannot act in such a way as to preclude the development of excellence in another. Care does not require subservience to the whims of others for the simple reason that such subservience develops selfishness in the other. The very definition of care requires that others be encouraged to care in return, and so develop their own potential for human excellence.

The good life is an ideal for all humans. As such it should not be used to relegate women to a separate sphere, but should instead encourage all humans to develop their ability to care. There is a recognition of this in several recent care theorists, most notably Rita Manning and Joan Tronto, both of whom use a concern for care as the basis for a call to greater support and protection for those who care in society as well as a more equal sharing of the burden of care.[107] And as Marcia Homiak has argued, an Aristotelian conception of the importance of the intellectual flourishing of the individual offers a useful balance to the moral call to care.

Ethics of care theorists generally find it difficult to produce a nonarbitrary limit to the extent to which one should care. If caring is the central feature of one's ethical theory, it would seem that only care itself, either for others or for one's self, could limit one's obligation to care for another, and this is essentially the conclusion many thinkers draw.[108] It would be preferable, however, to have some way of limiting the obligation to care short of complete self-sacrifice. As Marcia Homiak points out, Aristotelian conceptions of the rational life allow us to distinguish healthy relationships of care from unhealthy relationships of subordination and self-sacrifice.[109] Concern for the agent herself, and her own development, needs to play a central role in a feminist ethics. It should not be dependent on, or derived from, the need to provide care for others. An Aristotelian account of each individual's need for intellectual development and civic engagement provides needed limits on the obligation to care.

Again, Aristotle's discussion of friendship is helpful here. Friendship, according to Aristotle, is characterized by the same marks as a person's relationship to herself. Not only does the good person love what is good in herself, and strive to develop it, but the good person is also particularly concerned about her intellectual development and her individuality. As Aristotle puts it, "For existence is good to the virtuous man, and each man wishes himself what is good, while no one chooses to possess the whole world if he has first to become some one else."[110] The good of the other, central as it is to Aristotle's account of friendship, never slides into subservience.

As one might expect, feminists have no need for Aristotle to play the role of Prince Charming, riding to the rescue on the white horse of virtue ethics. Fairy-tale relationships have no place in the adult world. But there is ample room for a relationship of mutual respect between feminism and Aristotle, and such a relationship would be of benefit to both parties. Aristotelian ethics needs a more well-rounded, less intellectualistic conception of human flourishing. In particular, Aristotle's blindness to the extent to which women's activities are constitutive of the good human life provides a skewed picture of human excellence. An incorporation of caring provides Aristotelian ethics with a more complete, less oppressive conception of how humans should live together.

At the same time, an ethics of care could draw on Aristotelian resources to develop a theory that does not require self-sacrifice or an unhealthy lack of self-respect. These resources could also be used in the development of political critiques, and offer a model of moral reasoning that is well suited to an ethics of care. This is not to say that an ethics of care should become the mirror image of Aristotelian ethics, but instead to recognize that his ethics offers resources that are of value to contemporary feminists.

Notes

1. *Nicomachean Ethics* X 7, 1178a 7–8.
2. *N.E.* VIII 9 1160b 32–37, *Politics* I 5 1254b 12–15.
3. *Pol.* I 5, 1254a 21–23.
4. *De Generatione Animalium* I 21, 7296 8–20.
5. *N.E.* II 3, 1105a 14–16.
6. See, for example, Morwenna Griffiths, "Feminism, Feelings and Philosophy," in *Feminist Perspectives in Philosophy*, ed. Morwenna Griffiths and Margaret Whitford (Bloomington: Indiana University Press, 1988), 131–51; Genevieve Lloyd, *The Man of Reason: "Male" and "Female" in Western Philosophy* (Minneapolis: University of Minnesota Press, 1984); and Susan Bordo, *The Flight to Objectivity: Essays on Cartesianism and Objectivity* (Albany: State University of New York Press, 1987).
7. In addition to the articles mentioned in note 6, this conception of the self is discussed by Lorraine Code, *What Can She Know? Feminist Theory and the Construction of Knowledge* (Ithaca: Cornell University Press, 1991); Seyla Benhabib, "The Generalized and the Concrete Other: The Kohlberg-Gilligan Controversy and Moral Theory," in *Women and Moral Theory*, ed. Eva Feder Kittay and Diana Meyers (Totowa, N.J.: Rowman and Littlefield, 1987), 154–77; Carol Gilligan, *In a Different Voice* (Cambridge: Harvard University Press, 1982); and Virginia Held, *Feminist Morality: Transforming Culture, Society, and Politics* (Chicago: University of Chicago Press, 1993).
8. *N.E.* I 3, 1049b 12–28.
9. *N.E.* I 7, 1097b 9–12, *N.E.* VIII 1, 1155a 5–30, *Pol.* I 2, 1253a 1–10.
10. Marcia Homiak, "Feminism and Aristotle's Rational Ideal," in *A Mind of One's Own: Feminist Essays on Reason and Objectivity*, ed. Louise Anthony and Charlotte Witt (Boulder, Colo.: Westview, 1993), 1–18.
11. Carol Gilligan's *In a Different Voice* and Nel Noddings's *Caring: A Feminine Approach to Ethics and Moral Education* (Berkeley and Los Angeles: University of California Press, 1984).
12. Rosemarie Tong, for example, considers such an ethical theory to be "feminine" rather than feminist. She also draws distinctions among ethics of care, relational ethics, and maternalist ethics that I shall not be drawing. All three types of theories exhibit the features with which I am concerned here, so I shall not separate them. See *Feminine and Feminist Ethics* (Belmont, Calif., Wadsworth, 1993).
13. For examples of such a criticism, see Patricia Ward Scaltsas, "Do Feminist Ethics Counter Feminist Aims?" in *Explorations in Feminist Ethics*, ed. Eve Browning Cole and Susan Coultrap McQuin, (Bloomington: Indiana University Press, 1992), 15–26; John Broughton, "Women's Rationality and Men's Virtues: A Critique of Gender Dualism in Gilligan's Theory of Moral Development," in *An Ethic of Care: Feminist and Interdisciplinary Perspectives*, ed. Mary Jeanne Larrabee (New York: Routledge, 1993), 112–39; Laura Duhan Kaplan, "Woman as Caretaker: An Archetype that Supports Patriarchal Militarism," *Hypatia* 9, no. 2 (Spring 1994): 123–33; Claudia Card, "Must We Mean What We Say?" *Ethics* 99, no. 1 (October 1988): 125–36; and Catherine A. MacKinnon's contribution to "Feminist Discourse, Moral Values and the Law—A Conversation," 1984 James McCormick Mitchell Lecture, *Buffalo Law Review* 34, no. 1 (Winter 1985).
14. Seyla Benhabib, for example, argues that while care for particular others is an important part of ethics, it must always be contained within the limits of universal respect for the rights and dignity of others. See her "The Debate over Women and Moral Theory Revisited," in *Situating the Self: Gender, Community and Postmodernism in Contemporary Ethics* (Cambridge: Polity Press, 1992), 178–202.
15. See, for examples, the essays collected in chap. 9, "Perspectives on the Intersections of

Race, Class and Gender," of *Feminism and Philosophy: Essential Readings in Theory, Reinterpretation, and Application*, ed. Nancy Tuana and Rosemary Tong (Boulder, Colo.: Westview, 1995).

16. *N.E.* X 8, 1178a 6–8.

17. *Pol.* I 5, 1254b 5–19.

18. *N.E.* I 7, 1098a 1–18.

19. *N.E.* VIII 10, 1160b 32–35.

20. *Pol.* I 13, 1260a 15–31.

21. John M. Cooper, *Reason and Human Good in Aristotle* (Indianapolis: Hackett, 1986); Anthony Kenny, *The Aristotelian Ethics: A Study of the Relationship Between the Eudemian and Nichomachean Ethics of Aristotle* (Oxford: Clarendon Press, 1978) and *Aristotle on the Perfect Life* (Oxford: Clarendon Press, 1992); Sarah Broadie, *Ethics with Aristotle* (Oxford: Oxford University Press, 1991); Stephen Clark, *Aristotle's Man: Speculations upon Aristotelian Anthropology* (Oxford: Clarendon Press, 1975); and C. D. Reeve's *Practices of Reason* (Oxford: Clarendon Press, 1992) are examples of contemporary commentaries on Aristotle's ethics that completely ignore Aristotle's discussion of men's and women's nature. Curiously, Reeve's book does include (as an appendix) a discussion and criticism of Aristotle's discussion of male and female natures in the *Generation of Animals* but ignores such issues in the main body of the text.

22. Richard Kraut, *Aristotle on the Human Good* (Princeton: Princeton University Press, 1989), 99 n. 28, 110 n. 42.

23. Frances Sparshott, *Taking Life Seriously: A Study of the Argument of the Nichomachean Ethics* (Toronto: University of Toronto Press, 1994), 21–23.

24. Susan Moller Okin, *Women in Western Political Thought* (Princeton: Princeton University Press, 1979), chap. 4, "Woman's Place and Nature in a Functionalist World"; and Jean Bethke Elshtain, *Public Man, Private Woman: Women in Social and Political Thought*, 2d ed. (Princeton: Princeton University Press, 1981), 41–54.

25. Judith Green, "Aristotle on Necessary Verticality, Body Heat, and Gendered Proper Places in the Polis: A Feminist Critique," *Hypatia* 7, no. 1 (Winter 1992): 70–96.

26. I am not including Natural Law theorists in the category of virtue ethicists. Natural Law, based as it is on a concept of timeless, universal, and general moral rules, is in direct opposition to Aristotelian conceptions of moral reasoning. For a discussion of the relationship between virtue ethics and Natural Law, see Joseph Boyle, "Natural Law and the Ethics of Traditions," and Russell Hittinger, "Natural Law and Virtue: Theories at Cross Purposes," both in *Natural Law Theories: Contemporary Essays*, ed. Robert P. George (Oxford: Clarendon Press, 1992). For an argument that Thomas Aquinas is better understood as an Aristotelian virtue theorist than a Natural Law theorist, see Daniel Nelson, *The Priority of Prudence: Virtue and Natural Law in Thomas Aquinas and the Implications for Modern Ethics* (University Park: Pennsylvania State University Press, 1992).

27. An exception is Philippa Foot's *Virtues and Vices and Other Essays in Moral Philosophy* (Berkeley and Los Angeles: University of California Press, 1978).

28. *N.E.* I 3, 1095b 4–6.

29. See Alasdair MacIntyre, *Whose Justice? Which Rationality?* (Notre Dame: University of Notre Dame Press, 1988).

30. Michael Sandel, *Liberalism and the Limits of Justice* (New York: Cambridge University Press, 1982). See also Michael Walzer, *Spheres of Justice* (New York: Basic Books, 1983), and Charles Taylor, *Sources of the Self: The Making of the Modern Identity* (Cambridge: Harvard University Press, 1989).

31. Frazer and Lacey, *The Politics of Community: A Feminist Critique of the Liberal-Communitarian Debate* (Toronto: University of Toronto Press, 1993). See also Marilyn Friedman's "Feminism and Modern Friendship: Dislocating the Community," *Ethics* 99, no. 2 (January 1989): 275–90.

32. *N.E.* V 10, 1137b 27–29.

33. MacIntyre, *Whose Justice? Which Rationality?* 105.

34. Kathryn Pyne Addelson, Martha Ackelsberg, and Shawn Pyne, "Anarchism and Feminism," in *Feminism and Philosophy*, ed. Tuana and Tong, 330–52.

35. *Pol.* I 5, 1254a 20–23; VII 9, 1328b 34–1329a 2.

36. Bernard Williams, "An Inconsistent Form of Relativism," in *Relativism: Cognitive and Moral*, ed. Michael Krausz and Jack Meiland (Notre Dame: University of Notre Dame Press, 1982), 171–74. Williams points out that one cannot coherently adopt a complete cultural relativism with respect to ethics and still assert that people should be tolerant of other cultures, since such tolerance is itself a (culturally relative) moral principle.

37. The terms are those used, respectively, by Richard Kraut, Sarah Broadie, John Cooper, C. D. C. Reeve, and Stephen R. L. Clark.

38. For a defense of this understanding of *theoria* see Richard Kraut's *Aristotle on the Human Good* (Princeton: Princeton University Press, 1989), and John Cooper's *Reason and Human Good in Aristotle* (Indianapolis: Hackett, 1986).

39. See Cooper, *Reason and Human Good*, 168–77.

40. *N.E.* VIII 3, 1156b 6–17.

41. *N.E.* VIII 7, 1158b 24–28.

42. *N.E.* VIII 5, 1157b 19–24.

43. Anthony Kenny, *Aristotle on the Perfect Life* (Oxford: Clarendon Press, 1992), and Sarah Broadie, *Ethics With Aristotle* (Oxford: Oxford University Press, 1991). See also the articles by Ronna Burger, Susanne Hill, and Timothy Roche in *The Crossroads of Norm and Nature: Essays on Aristotle's Ethics and Metaphysics*, ed. May Sims (Lanham, Md.: Rowman and Littlefield, 1995) and Amélie Oksenberg Rorty's "The Place of Contemplation in Aristotle's Nicomachean Ethics," in *Essays on Aristotle's Ethics*, ed. Amélie Oksenberg Rorty (Berkeley and Los Angeles: University of California Press, 1980), 377–94.

44. *N.E.* IX 9, 1170a 13–15.

45. *Sovereign Virtue: Aristotle on the Relation Between Happiness and Prosperity* (Stanford: Stanford University Press, 1992), IV III, "Honor and Dignity."

46. *N.E.* VIII 12, 1162a 15–28.

47. See, for example, Susan Moller Okin's *Women in Western Political Thought* (Princeton: Princeton University Press, 1979), chap. 4 "Woman's Place and Nature in a Functionalist World."

48. See, for example, Donna Haraway's "A Manifesto for Cyborgs: Science, Technology and Socialist Feminism in the 1980s," in *Feminism and Postmodernism*, ed. Linda Nicholson (New York: Routledge, 1990), 190–233. Haraway's article argues for the confusion of all boundaries between human and machine, body and world, between humans and animals. Presumably such a position precludes any essential difference between these groups.

49. *N.E.* IX 9, 1169b 18–22.

50. Martha Nussbaum, "Non-Relative Virtues: An Aristotelian Approach," *Midwest Studies in Philosophy* 13 (1988): 32–53.

51. For a very helpful article on the varieties of essentialism with respect to women, see Natalie Stoljar's "Essence, Identity and the Concept of Woman," *Philosophical Topics* 23 (1995): 261–93.

52. Homiak, "Feminism and Aristotle's Rational Ideal."

53. *N.E.* IV 3, 1125a 19–28.

54. Homiak, "Feminism and Aristotle's Rational Ideal," 10.

55. *Pol.* VII 2, 1324b 26–36.

56. *N.E.* I 8, 1098b 30–1099a 6.

57. *Pol.* VII 3, 1325a 30–32.

58. Martha Nussbaum, *Love's Knowledge* (Oxford: Oxford University Press, 1990), 27.

59. Genevieve Lloyd, *The Man of Reason: "Male" and "Female" in Western Philosophy* (Minneapolis: University of Minnesota Press, 1984); Andrea Nye, *Feminist Theories and the Philosophies of Man* (London: Croom Helm, 1988).

60. *N.E.* IV 5, 1126a 2–8. Martha Nussbaum has an interesting discussion of this point in *The Therapy of Desire* (Princeton: Princeton University Press, 1994), 93–96.

61. *N.E.* II 6, 1106b 24–27. See also L. A. Kosman's "Being Properly Affected: Virtues and Feelings in Aristotle's Ethics," in *Essays on Aristotle's Ethics,* ed. Rorty, 103–16.

62. See particularly Aristotle's discussion of temperance, *N.E.* III 10, 11 and 12.

63. *N.E.* X 7, 1177a 24–27.

64. Virginia Held, *Feminist Morality: Transforming Culture, Society, and Politics* (Chicago: University of Chicago Press, 1993), chap. 6.

65. See Code's *What Can She Know?* and Edith Stein's *On the Problem of Empathy,* trans. Waltraut Stein (Washington, D.C.: I.C.S. Publications, 1989).

66. Griffiths, "Feminism, Feelings and Morality."

67. Brenda Almond, "Women's Right: Reflections on Ethics and Gender," in *Feminist Perspectives in Philosophy,* ed. Griffiths and Whitford (Bloomington: Indiana University Press, 1988), 42–57; Annette C. Baier, "What do Women Want in an Ethical Theory?" in *An Ethic of Care: Feminist and Interdisciplinary Perspectives,* ed. Mary Jeanne Larrabee (New York: Routledge, 1993), 19–32; Virginia Held, *Feminist Morality.* Feminists have not been alone in making these criticisms. They have been offered by others, most notably Bernard Williams.

68. Sarah Broadie offers a good discussion of abstract principles and Aristotle's ethical thought. See *Ethics with Aristotle,* 17–21.

69. *N.E.* VI 13, 1144b 14–16.

60. *N.E.* VI 7, 1141b 8–16.

71. Among these are Sarah Ruddick's *Maternal Thinking: Towards a Politics of Peace* (New York: Ballantine, 1989); Nel Noddings's *Women and Evil* (Berkeley and Los Angeles: University of California Press, 1989); Jeffrey Bluestein's *Care and Commitment: Taking the Personal Point of View* (New York: Oxford University Press, 1991); Rita Manning's *Speaking from the Heart: A Feminist Perspective on Ethics* (Lanham, Md.: Rowman and Littlefield, 1992); Virginia Held's *Feminist Morality.* For a discussion of the relationship between feminist ethics and an ethics of care see "Toward a Feminist Conception of the Moral Life," by Eve Browning Cole and Susan Coultrap-McQuinn, in *Explorations in Feminist Ethics,* ed. Eve Browning Cole and Susan Coultrap-McQuinn (Bloomington: Indiana University Press, 1992), 1–11 and Rosemarie Tong, *Feminine and Feminist Ethics.*

72. Noddings, *Caring,* 36.

73. See Gilligan, "Moral Orientation and Moral Development," in *Women and Moral Theory,* ed. Kittay Meyers, 19–33.

74. Ruddick, Held, and Noddings all consider this the paradigmatic caring relationship.

75. Lorraine Code has argued that feminists should be relativists, but her relativism is one that allows for the possibility of adjudicating among knowledge claims, is held to high standards of correspondence with the world, and so on. "Must a Feminist be a Relativist After All?" in *Against Patriarchal Thinking,* ed. Maja Pellikan-Engel (Amsterdam: VU University Press, 1992), 141–47. The term *relativism* will be used in the more traditional sense in this essay.

76. Jean Grimshaw points this out in *Philosophy and Feminist Thinking* (Minneapolis: University of Minnesota Press, 1986), 243–48; as does Allison Bailey in "Mothering, Diversity and Peace Politics," *Hypatia* 9, no. 2, (Spring 1994): 188–98. This is a particularly problematic aspect of most ethics of care theories because many theorists assert that contemporary Western society is not an optimal situation in which to mother. But they nonetheless seem to think

that women's experience of mothering under such conditions does provide the grounds for developing an ethical theory.

77. Noddings, *Caring*, 108–13. Rita Manning makes this point in *Speaking from the Heart*, 72.

78. Gilligan, *In a Different Voice*, chap. 6, "Visions of Maturity"; *Maternal Thinking*, chaps. 3, 4, and 5.

79. Sandra Harding, "The Curious Coincidence of Feminine and African Moralities," in *Women and Moral Theory*, ed. Kittay and Meyers, 296–315.

80. Judith Butler, "Gender Trouble, Feminist Theory, and Psychoanalytic Discourse," in *Feminism/Postmodernism*, ed. Linda Nicholson (New York: Routledge, 1990), 324–40; Monique Wittig, "One is Not Born a Woman," *Feminist Issues* 1, no. 2 (1981): 47–54.

81. John Broughton, "Women's Rationality and Men's Virtues: A Critique of Gender Dualism in Gilligan's Theory of Moral Development," in *An Ethic of Care*, ed. Larrabee, 112–39. Lorraine Code also makes a similar point in *What Can She Know?* 89–97.

82. Noddings, *Women and Evil*, 166–70.

83. See Julia Wood's *Who Cares? Women, Care, and Culture* (Carbondale: Southern Illinois University Press, 1994), chap. 7, "At a Cultural Crossroad: The Future of Care in the United States"; and Joan Tronto's *Moral Boundaries: A Political Argument for an Ethic of Care* (New York: Routledge, 1993).

84. Held, *Feminist Morality*, 16. Postmodern philosophy is criticized as subverting a feminist critique of society by Nancy Hartsock in "Foucault on Power: A Theory for Women?" and Susan Bordo in "Feminism, Postmodernism and Gender Scepticism," both in *Feminism/Postmodernism* ed. Nicholson. The postmodern tendency to undermine effective moral or political critique of the status quo is also noted by Seyla Benhabib in *Situating the Self: Gender, Community, and Postmodernism in Contemporary Ethics* (Cambridge: Polity Press, 1992).

85. Fletcher argues that "doing the loving thing" is sufficient as a rule for action, but it seems clear that this is not sufficient. One still needs some specification of what counts as love and what does not, and Fletcher seems to lack the capacity to offer such specification. See *Situation Ethics: The New Morality* (Philadelphia: Westminster, 1966).

86. See John Cooper's "Aristotle on Friendship," in *Essays on Aristotle's Ethics*, ed. Rorty, 301–40; and Paul Schollmeier's *Other Selves: Aristotle on Personal and Political Friendship* (Albany: State University of New York Press, 1994).

87. Held, *Feminist Morality*, 129.

88. *N.E.* III 11, 1119a 5–7.

89. Ruddick, *Maternal Thinking*, 72.

90. *N.E.* IV 3.

91. *N.E.* IV 3, 1124b 15–24.

92. *Pol.* I 13, 1260a 33–1260b 7.

93. *Pol.* III 4, 1277b 3–6.

94. Virginia Held makes this point in *Feminist Morality*, 208–9.

95. See, for example John Casey's *Pagan Virtue: An Essay in Ethics* (Oxford: Clarendon Press, 1990), chap. 5, "Justice."

96. See, for example, Martha Nussbaum's *Love's Knowledge*, chap. 2, "The Discernment of Perception: An Aristotelian Conception of Private and Public Rationality"; Nancy Sherman's *The Fabric of Character* (Oxford: Clarendon Press, 1989); and Joan Tronto's *Moral Boundaries: A Political Argument for an Ethic of Care* (New York: Routledge, 1993).

97. *Pol.* VII and VIII.

98. For an example of what such a conception might look like, see Held, *Feminist Morality*, chap. 10, "Noncontractual Society: The Postpatriarchal Family as Model."

99. Stephen Salkever, *Finding the Mean: Theory and Practice in Aristotelian Political Philosophy* (Princeton: Princeton University Press, 1990), 191.

100. *Pol.* VII10, 1330a 1–17.

101. *Pol.* VII 16 and 17.

102. *Pol.* VIII 1, 1337a 11–20.

103. In saying this I am disagreeing with Rita Manning, who extends caring to human-animal relationships. I would be willing to call such "tending to the good of another" caring only in an analogous sense. Properly speaking, care occurs between humans.

104. *N.E.* VIII 8, 1159a 26–37.

105. The virtue of justice, if it is equated with statecraft, may be somewhat like caring in its political sense. Part of the virtue of the good citizen is the ability to produce the virtues of the good citizen in others, through education and training.

106. *N.E.* IX 4, 1166a 3–6; IX 3, 1165b, 18–20.

107. See Manning's *Speaking From the Heart: A Feminist Perspective on Ethics* (Lanham, Md.: Rowman and Littlefield, 1992), and Tronto's *Moral Boundaries: A Political Argument for an Ethic of Care* (New York: Routledge, 1993). A similar point is made by Julia Woods in *Who Cares?*

108. See Manning's discussion in *Speaking from the Heart*, 72–73, and Noddings's discussion in *Caring*, 52–55.

109. Homiak, "Feminism and Aristotle's Rational Ideal," 14–15.

110. *N.E.* IX 4 1166a 19–21.

8

The Book of "A"

Linda Redlick Hirshman*

Introduction

I suppose that, in light of Harold Bloom's claim that a woman wrote the Bible, my contention that Aristotle was a feminist should be positively

*Distinguished Visiting Professor of Philosophy and Women's Studies, Brandeis University, J.D., University of Chicago Law School; Ph.D., University of Illinois. Thanks to Professors Ronald Allen, John Ayer, Randy Barnett, Richard Kraut, Jane Larson, and Richard Posner for reading and criticizing the drafts, and to the participants in the New York University Law School Legal Theory Workshop, the University of Chicago Law School Legal Theory Workshop, and the Arizona State Law School Faculty Workshop for their communal consideration and individual suggestions. ("[T]he activity of wisdom is admittedly the pleasantest of excellent activities." 2 ARISTOTLE, *Nicomachean Ethics, in* THE COMPLETE WORKS OF ARISTOTLE uncontroversial.[1] Nonetheless, as in Bloom's work, it is the apparent per-versity and actual richness of the juxtaposition between feminism and the ancient understandings that I wish to explore. This effort springs from the contemporary revision of moral philosophy, which poses a morality of virtue—particularly as expressed in Aristotle's ethical writings—against the modern tradition of a morality of rules.[2] As set forth below, contemporary feminism powerfully invokes and instantiates that revision; it is a puzzle that the relationship to the Aristotelian source has not been more fully explored. The role of Aristotelian misogyny must not be underestimated, but the effort is eminently worth making, because Aristotle's writings on virtue ethics are the most ambitious work in the philosophical tradition addressing the critical question facing femi-nism—and contemporary political theory generally—today: the purpose and limits of equality.

Accordingly, I will first try to draw feminism and Aristotelianism to-gether by emphasizing the similarity in their assumptions about human nature and philosophical method. Next, I will try to draw some insights from classical philosophy, specifically from Aristotle's work, for contem-porary issues of law and feminist jurisprudence, particularly the issues like surrogacy and the selective service, which have puzzled—if not stymied—liberal theorists. In the end, I will focus on the hard differences between a philosophy characterized by overt misogyny and by the affirmative pos-iting of answers on the one hand and a jurisprudence of liberation and the tolerance of differences on the other. I will conclude that Aristote-lian "tough-mindedness"[3] on the varieties of the human condition, cou-pled with the unifying classical vision of citizenship, breaks the liberal frame and provides a model of a good life unavailable in other moral traditions, a model from which answers to the puzzles of modern feminism may be drawn.

Feminist Jurisprudence and Classical Philosophy

Can a study of Aristotle's writings add to feminist jurisprudence? I think the answer is clearly "yes," in at least three ways. First, Aristotle's meth-

X.7.1177a23–24, at 1729 1861 ([Bollingen Series No. 71, Jonathan Barnes ed., 1984] [Revised Oxford Translation]).

ods and the attendant epistemology presage and support feminist methods and epistemology; each is also importantly linked to the recent revival of interest in oral learning from the methods of literary analysis. Second, Aristotle's writings make explicit and defend a view of the human condition as naturally political that is central to most important contemporary feminist thought. Finally, and I hope most interestingly, the Aristotelian vision of an ideal of the good life for citizens may be the best source of substantive answers about politics and the political community to which liberal equality has been inadequate and which feminism, like any normative theory, must ultimately produce.

Feminist Methods and Classical Methods

To take the easy subject first, consider feminist methods. Since Catharine MacKinnon's pathbreaking work ten years ago,[4] feminist jurisprudence has pursued several avenues of analysis, reasoning, and criticism. First, and perhaps earliest, feminists began "asking the 'woman question,' " meaning challenging legal doctrines and methods on the grounds that they disadvantage women.[5] Having found legal doctrines and methods that purported to be just and appeared to be neutral, but produced results that grossly disadvantaged women, feminists perceived a hidden male viewpoint first in the rules and then in the process of liberal legalism itself.[6] Feminist scholars countered with methods of feminist practical reasoning, which resembles traditional practical reasoning,[7] in approaching problems "with multiple perspectives, contradictions, and inconsistencies"[8] which precludes as undesirable the "reduction of contingencies to rules by which all disputes can be decided in advance."[9] In order to be able to gather the information necessary for feminist practical reason, feminists turned to the well-established social feminist method of consciousness raising:[10] "collaborative or interactive engagements with others based upon personal experience and narrative."[11]

Feminist methodology also implicates and invokes feminist epistemology. As feminist scholar Katharine Bartlett points out, methods must ultimately be evaluated according to the defensibility, and even rightness of the answers they generate.[12] Here, too, there are several schools of thought. The first, rational empiricism, pretty much tracks traditional modes of truth-finding.[13] Corresponding to the liberal assumptions of the "early contemporary legal feminists," rational empiricism is a tool for bringing women up to the purported neutrality of equal treatment.[14] When rational empiricism failed to address the truth claims of women with different life experiences than men,[15] feminists responded to the inadequacy of rational empiricism with theories of standpoint epistemology, which challenges rational empiricism as hopelessly tied to the existing male power structure, and with claims for women's unique access to understanding, based on their particular life-experiences.[16] A third school, corresponding to trends of deconstruction in other disciplines, sees each of the prior claims to knowledge as fatally foundationalist and asserts the pure social, local, and provisional nature of all truth.[17]

Recently, several feminist scholars have been trying to modify the parochial epistemologies of postmodernism and standpoint epistemology.[18] Bartlett, for example, calls her more general epistemology "positionality."[19] Positionality recognizes the existence but situated and partial quality of truth, which emerges from relationships and involvements and is subject to variation depending on the social context, a variation which is the product of an effort to examine truth, particularly in light of other viewpoints.[20] Within this realist, yet flexible, approach to knowledge, feminists ask the next question, which Deborah Rhode characterizes as "the difference makes."[21] In answering this question, she makes an epistemological claim similar to Bartlett's: "To disclaim objective standards of truth is not to disclaim all value judgments. We need not become positivists to believe that some accounts of experience are more consistent, coherent, inclusive, self-critical, and so forth."[22]

Margaret Radin similarly seeks a middle ground by linking feminism to the revived interest in pragmatism.[23] As a result of her confrontation with the "double bind"[24] of lost freedom or bad choices in the context of commodified sexuality,[25] she sees pragmatic choice of the "less bad" alternative (and constant revision of choice) as the only path to a positive outcome.[26] According to Radin, pragmatism, like feminism, is characterized by a strong linkage to actual experience and a capacity to seek workable choices rather than an idealized hypothetical.[27]

Radin's feminism is greatly strengthened by its linkage with pragmatism: one of the founders of pragmatism, William James, cogently articulated the linkage between the idealization of rationalism and weak-mindedness. Instead he claimed the (male language) superior ground of "toughness" for people who can live with incompleteness and uncertainty.[28] The converse is also true since pragmatism, dependent as it is on real experience, is often criticized for its epistemological and normative conservatism.[29] Linked to feminism in Radin's vision, however, pragmatism must include the viewpoints and experience of persons rather removed from the social-epistemological hegemony, who provide a much-needed source of alternative vision.[30]

Bartlett's positionality and Radin's pragmatism are hardly a breakthrough in epistemology; the solution to epistemological regression by the social positing of knowledge is at least as old as On Certainty[31] and as new as the work of Charles Taylor.[32] Indeed, I am going to claim that feminism actually instantiates methods and answers dating back to antiquity. Yet, as set forth below, this linkage of late contemporary legal feminism to Aristotelianism, while not assuming to create the world anew,[33] is actually quite a political and epistemological asset.[34]

How do these feminist methods recapitulate classical methods? For these answers, I turn to the work of one of the leading scholars of the classical revival, Martha Nussbaum. Nussbaum's writings bring together two of the strands in the tapestry I wish to weave herein: the analysis of classical philosophy and the moral role of fiction.[35] Nussbaum has long written from the joint perspective of a classical scholar and a student of fiction,[36] but her recent work has focused increasingly on the latter.[37] As I will show, each perspective embraces and illuminates contemporary feminism.[38]

First, in the method of consciousness raising, feminists are using two very traditional Aristotelian methods: canvassing the appearances and conversing about justice with people who speak the same language about justice the questioner does.[39] As in consciousness raising, the appearances are also set forth in their confusion and disarray,[40] and, in trying to order them, thinkers must avoid the seduction of abstract theorizing[41] but ultimately come to see the fundamental quality of our everyday behaviors, or, as Nussbaum puts it, to the "ability to give accounts."[42]

In her recent essay The Literary Imagination in Public Life,[43] Nussbaum described the process in rich detail:

> When we read a novel such as Hard Times, reading not as literary theorists asking about theories of interpretation, but as human beings who are moved and delighted, we are not skeptics . . . we are, in effect, being constituted by the novel as judges of a certain sort—as Aristotelian equitable women and men. . . .[the ensuing judgments] are not based on transcendent standards; indeed, our experience as readers leads us to think that such standards would

> be both unnecessary for and irrelevant to our search. For as con-
> cerned readers we search for a human good that we are trying to
> bring about in and for the human community; . . . we move back
> and forth, as readers, between concrete experience and general
> principle, seeking for the best and most comprehensive fit be-
> tween principles and concrete perceptions, sorting out all the "ap-
> pearances," as Aristotle said, and producing a view that will "save
> the greatest number and the most basic." We attempt, in effect,
> to know ourselves, and what is deepest in ourselves, regarding the
> novel as *about us*, our hopes and fears.[44]

Not only is the Aristotelian judge sensitive to the human, as compared
to the transcendent, she is also anchored to the concrete, as opposed to
the abstract. Thus, "the novel also directs our attention to the historical
and local particularities of the characters' world, making us see ways in
which it differs from our own. We think about human flourishing not
abstractly, but in relation to that concrete context, asking about the material and social conditions of the characters' daily lives, and the relation
of those concrete conditions to their hopes and fears."[45]

The second and most obvious parallel between the classical methods
and feminist methods is the feminist invocation of practical reason—a
concept inextricably intertwined with the Aristotelian method—as it
emerges from the procedure linked to consciousness raising set forth
above. Thus, assuming that the appearances are all we have to deal with,[46]
ethics must be centered in human discourse, as well. From this immersion
in the human, Nussbaum elicits the basic structure of what she calls
Aristotle's "non-scientific deliberation."[47] Like human situations, rules
must be particular enough to be concrete and flexible. Thus,

> the good judge is one who regards general principles as summaries
> of wise decisions in the past, whose judgment respects that tradi-
> tion of judgment, but who is also keenly perceptive of the con-
> crete context and prepared to extend her historical tradition in
> order to meet the new context in an appropriate way.[48]

In order to do so, we must take account of the changeability, context-
dependency, and variety of life.[49] Nussbaum invokes Aristotle's image of
the flexible ruler: one cannot use a straight edge to measure a fluted
column.[50] She contrasts this Aristotelian methodology with

the aim of the law to become a simple and systematic science—an aim that has been around since Bentham, . . . a mistaken aim, . . . a simple pseudo-scientific algorithm (or a deductive system) represent[ing] not the achievement of order and rationality, but a falling off from the order and the rationality that are there to be found in human life.[51]

All of this sounds very like the description of feminist practical reason set forth above.

The hardest fit is of course asking the woman question. Actually, as some recent Straussian[52] rereadings of the works reflect, Aristotle did ask the woman question;[53] like most feminists, I just don't like the answer he gave. Yet, asking the question remains constant. Like the feminists of the current generation, he noticed the differences between women's lives and men's lives and asked why they were different. He noted that women resemble men in their capacity for speech and hence for justice. As a contemporary feminist described it, "judging by the number of references to the question, Aristotle considered the existence and nature of women to be one of the features of life that most compellingly called for an explanation."[54] His answers were physical, ethical, and political. Now, obsession can hardly qualify as support, or Hitler would be considered a Jewish scholar. But within the parameters of rational discourse on the range of matters that attracted Aristotle's attention, his concern with the issue is noteworthy and, compared with modern treatments, the complexity of his answers commendable. The value of Aristotle's approach might be described as taking the subject seriously, even if getting it somewhat wrong, as opposed to treating it as of no moment.[55]

For example, recent work on the construction of human gender highlights the difference between the two approaches and illuminates Aristotle's inquiry about women with much new light. In the opening words of Making Sex,[56] historian Thomas Laqueur lays out the issue: "The first thing that strikes the careless observer is that women are unlike men. They are 'the opposite sex' (though why "opposite" I do not know; what is the "neighboring sex"?). But the fundamental thing is that women are more like men than anything else in the world."[57]

Laqueur musters an impressive array of evidence to demonstrate that the opposition of the genders is substantially modern, a construct of the eighteenth century.

For two millennia the ovary, an organ that by the early nine-teenth century had become a synecdoche for woman, had not even a name of its own. Galen refers to it by the same word he uses for the male testes, *orcheis*, allowing context to make clear which sex he is concerned with. Herophilus had called the ovaries *didymoi* (twins), another standard Greek word for testicles, and was so caught up in the female-as-male model that he saw the Fallopian tubes—the spermatic ducts that led from each "testi-cle"—as growing into the neck of the bladder as do the spermatic ducts in men. They very clearly do not. Galen points out this error, surprised that so careful an observer could have committed it, and yet the correction had no effect on the status of the model as a whole. Nor is there any technical term in Latin or Greek, or in the European vernaculars until around 1700, for vagina as the tube or sheath into which its opposite, the penis, fits and through which the infant is born.[58]

Under the old model, "men and women were arrayed according to their degree of metaphysical perfection, their vital heat, along an axis whose telos was male."[59] Here, as in so much of human learning, Aristotle is a critical source. As I will set forth in more detail below,[60] Aristotle of course recognized the existence of men and women and their differences. The critical points are two: first, much of Aristotle's vision of the two genders is based on the naturalness of social behavior (passivity, house-holding, etc.)—not solely or even primarily the naturalness of physical or biological fact.[61] Second, as to physical-biological fact there is serious textual evidence that:

> though Aristotle certainly regarded male and female bodies as specifically adapted to their particular roles, he did not regard these adaptations as the signs of sexual opposition. The qualities of each sex entailed the comparative advantage of one or the other in minding the home or fighting. . . . But these adaptations were not the basis for ontological differentiation. In the flesh, therefore, the sexes were more and less perfect versions of each other.[62]

Accordingly, Aristotle not only asked the "woman question," he asked it with a particular intensity, because the answers were:

framed . . . to valorize the extraordinary cultural assertion of patriarchy, of the father, in the face of the more sensorially evident
claim of the mother. The question for the classical model is not
what it explicitly claims—why woman?—but the more trouble-
some question—why man?[63]

Laqueur's presentation of Aristotle's inquiry is most interesting because it stands in such marked contrast to the modern view. Compare it,
for instance, to Susan Okin's description of contemporary theories of
justice:

> superficial appearances can easily lead to the impression that they
> are inclusive of women. In fact, they continue the same "separate
> spheres" tradition, by *ignoring* the family, its division of labor, and
> the related economic dependency and restricted opportunities of
> most women.[64]

As the deep contextualization and concrete orientation of Aristotelian
methods suggest, Aristotle's epistemology also turns out to be markedly
similar to the modified contextuality of the recent feminist worldview.
Aristotle's theories of education begin with early childhood and emphasize heavily the role of parents in habituating children to virtuous behavior:[65] his virtues are largely social virtues.[66] Of great importance—and as
yet undervalued by contemporary feminism—Aristotle made an important point of expressing the social or learned component not only of
reason, but of emotions.[67] To take just one of numerous examples, as
Aristotle saw it, an emotion like anger includes a judgment about the
objects for anger and a belief that the object injured the angry person in
a relevant way.[68] Distinguishing offenses suitable for anger, for example
by criteria of intentionality, from those which are not is an obvious exercise of judgment and is easily distinguishable from more primal urges like
hunger.[69] Aristotle's clear expression of the social construction of belief,
combined with his methods of exploring ethics through the device of
looking first at the appearances of familiar, or at least accessible, societies,
supports the particularity of Aristotelian positionality.

Yet, as Martha Nussbaum has pointed out in a recent essay, there are
strong indications of an ultimate recognition of the limits on relativism
throughout Aristotle's work.[70] Here, the parallel to Radin's and Bartlett's
work is illuminating. First, and most importantly, Aristotle's ethics delin-

eates those aspects of human life to which any system of ethics must apply, regardless of the cultural context. The "list" is characterized by the possibility of choice (for instance, no discussion of the possibility of choosing immortality plays a role) and, usually, the debatability of the choices; that is, no one right answer immediately emerges. The relativism is immediately limited, Nussbaum notes, because all ethical systems at least have these spheres of choice in common.[71]

The ensuing debate over choices may produce competing versions of the good life for human beings, but the allowable answers will not be completely open-ended, either. At least some solutions will be discarded entirely, leaving at most a plurality of competing solutions.[72] As example of this is Aristotle's writing on the issue of management of one's property where others are concerned. Noting the human tendency to neglect the common on the one hand, yet committed to the concept of the superiority of citizenship to mere productivity on the other, he suggests a variety of virtuous schemes for sharing property.[73] His discussion excludes, however, Platonic communism on the one hand and unbridled dominion on the other. Nussbaum acknowledges the objection that immediately arises to examples such as this: that even the human tendency to neglect the common is grounded in a bedrock of human experiences that are themselves socially shaped.[74] Nonetheless, here again there is no need to choose between moral authoritarianism and moral anarchy. Indeed, after the long exercise in the *Politics* of examining the appearances of existing states, Aristotle ultimately devotes the last two chapters of the book to the ideal state and the even more abstract question of the best human life.[75]

This purchase, however tenuous, is essential, if feminism is going to defend itself against legitimate claims of unmanageable particularism.[76] Robin West's recent work exalting contextual empathy in defense of paternalistic judging reflects the problem. Although she carefully confines herself to decisions in particular cases,[77] more and more legal governance is statutory.[78] Moreover, although she notes the resemblance between the act of empathic recognition and the recognition of precedent,[79] she does not confront the fact that decisions in particular cases still play a role in predicting what future decisions will be; in that context, the empathic judge of the present will be influencing outcomes for persons not before her in any guise. By contrast to pure contextuality, Aristotle's ethical theory provides the possibility for preliminary assessments of preferred reality; cross-cultural comparison is also available to test the reality.[80]

Thus, as I will set forth more fully below, Aristotelian epistemology, like feminist positionality, limits the possibilities of idealism and its earthly companion, radical social change.[81] Whether that similarity is good or bad, and I will contend its desirability, it is sufficient at this point to note the effect.

Feminist Politics and Classical Politics

Having described the parallels between Aristotle's philosophy and feminist jurisprudence, I turn to the substantive inquiry. I thought to make scholarly history by being the first feminist writer in a decade to produce a whole article without citing Carol Gilligan's book, but here it is.[82] Gilligan opened the hottest debate in contemporary human psychology by differing with Lawrence Kohlberg's taxonomy of moral development, which culminates in the capacity for justice,[83] by accusing him of reproducing male norms for the morality of the whole species. Gilligan asserted that women grow up and develop a moral voice that emphasizes, at its fullest, relational values, seeking to maintain the community ties, rather than to satisfy abstract notions of justice.[84] Catharine MacKinnon, at the other pole of feminist theory, has been noteworthy for her relentless emphasis on the power of the existing social relationships of male domination, exposing " 'woman' as a social construction."[85] This includes the construction of Gilligan's appealing nurturing female, and MacKinnon is admittedly "agnostic" on what female moral development would look like in a transformed world.[86]

Two interesting insights emerge from these two leading schools of feminist thought. First, if male moral norms and behaviors of separateness support a political philosophy of people as naturally separate with the attendant consequences, including the liberal ideal of the "non-aggression treaty,"[87] the Gilligan model supports (at least for half of humanity) the philosophy of people as naturally social. Or, as Aristotle put it twenty-four hundred years ago, man is a political animal.[88]

Second, there is a deep level at which Gilligan and MacKinnon agree; if people are naturally political, it is predictable and understandable that they establish morality socially. (And vice versa. That is, if they create their morality socially, there is at least one sense in which sociability is natural and prior: in the creation of reality.) Where else would naturally political creatures get their norms?

Not surprisingly, Aristotle, also believing people to be naturally sociable, consistently asserted the social element of important aspects of the human self:

> But he who is unable to live in society, or who has no need because he is sufficient for himself, must be either a beast or a god: he is no part of a state.[89]

There are numerous examples of Aristotle's position, and each one of them corresponds to a current claim of feminist politics. In education, children must be told to engage in virtuous behaviors.[90] After long years of such coerced or shamed behaviors, they may become habituated to such behavior, which, for Aristotle, was the foundation of a virtuous character.[91] For students of good character, of course, virtue can be studied through philosophy, including Aristotle's lectures.[92] Moreover, and here is a critical core of Aristotle's ethics, friendship of good persons enhances one's self-understanding,[93] providing "another self before us whose similar actions and traits we can study."[94]

Much less familiar to modern and feminist ears, however, is Aristotle's (and the general classical) belief that even private and familial efforts do not suffice; Aristotle explicitly and repeatedly invokes the laws as the necessary and proper source of moral tutelage.[95] Indeed, it is to enable its citizens to lead a virtuous life that the city exists.[96]

So What?

Although many feminist theorists have broken the assumption of the neutrality of private orderings and revealed that the private-public distinction preserves the hegemony of private oppression, most of their work has sought to invoke the public authorities in the interests of equality, rather than virtue.[97] But, as recent feminist writings so powerfully reveal, equality—which always contains a more or less hidden image of the actual norm—constantly threatens to collapse into limoralism,[98] the introduction of the male norm in the guise of a universal neutral norm. Moreover, and as the debates over issues like abortion and the draft reveal, there are real differences related to gender which generate real social costs to a political effort to construct a genuinely egalitarian regime.[99] Where equality is seen as a social construct,[100] the discussion should change, and issues of political virtue and the definition of a good common life are unavoidable.[101] It is at this point that contemporary feminist jurisprudence stops.

As will be set forth immediately below, this hesitation at the door of substance is understandable, yet, as Drucilla Cornell's recent dissent from MacKinnon's vision makes explicit, both li*moral*ism and feminist oppositionism suffer from the same flaw: a failure to articulate a flourishing life suitable for women.[102] Cornell invokes the recent work of welfare economist Amartya Sen—a theory Sen calls equality of "capability and well being"[103]—to enrich the discussion. The problem is that the focus has been on equality rather than on the much harder and more important work of describing well-being.

The publication of Cornell's essay signifies, I hope, the beginning of an explicit acknowledgement that feminism cannot be neutral on the good, and it is at this point that the classical tradition, long neglected in legal philosophy, can play such a powerful role. Evidence of dissatisfaction with this failure has been surfacing in many places. For instance, in the recent literature, it is the moral claim against commodification of childbearing, not just the inequality claim, that supports withholding enforcement of or even criminalizing the act.[104]

Both Radin and Nussbaum articulate the problem, and in almost the same way, by comparing their solutions to Dworkin's superficially pragmatic-Aristotelian method of legal decision making as expressed in *Law's Empire*.[105] Dworkin's Herculean judge, the reader may recall, tries to find an interpretation of new events coherent with the previous products of the legal system after the fashion of the authors of a chain novel.[106] Critics since *Law's Empire* have used this conservative technique to tag Dworkin with impotence before the claims like those ultimately vindicated in *Brown v. Board of Education*.[107] In essence, the critique is that the legal system cannot be a source of change toward the ideal; it usually simply carries forward the past. In the best of circumstances it only brings legal institutions into conformity with social change from the outside.[108]

As noted above, Radin invokes the dialogic solution strongly associated as well with the Minow-Michelman school.[109] Bring the voices of the oppressed into discourse in the legal system, and change can occur consistent with conceptual coherence, because the social concept of a legal system includes the as yet unreconciled claims of the oppressed. Nussbaum's answers from the Aristotelian tradition are much more substantive about the good:

> My reader/judge operates with a general conception of the human being and human flourishing, treating some aspects of the person and some activities as essential, others as more peripheral. She has, in connection with this, a rich conception of human agency that she brings to bear in concrete cases. . . . I see no such clear guidance emerging from Dworkin's commitment to general ethical principles—and indeed it is clear from other writings that Dworkin's liberalism makes him suspicious of having any such conception of the human being and the human good, even at a very high level of generality.[110]

Furthering Nussbaum's project, I hope that by sowing the methodological and epistemological similarities between Aristotle's work and contemporary feminist thought, I have made legitimate an inquiry into the substantive answers about the human good Aristotle provided for feminist legal issues in particular. Rather than letting this important move rest on implication, however, let me reiterate in a nutshell how Aristotle's virtues reflect and support the substance of contemporary feminism. Since Aristotle, like many contemporary feminists, assumes the natural sociability of the species, his teleological virtues are directed to the end of society. Thus: "Since the end of individuals and of states is the same, the end of the best man and of the best constitution must also be the same. . . . Courage and endurance are required for business and philosophy for leisure, temperance and justice for both."[111]

How might a canvas of Aristotle's political virtues illuminate issues confronting contemporary feminism? Two examples come immediately to mind. They are not only the two most visible contemporary feminist issues; they are and have been, I would claim, issues at the core of human ethics since ethical theory began. They are but current variations of the old questions of citizenship.[112] In present terms, we ask whether feminists should press for the inclusion of women in mandatory military service and why, and whether feminists should support women's freedom to contract for surrogate motherhood or should resist state enforcement of such contracts, or, at the other extreme, contend for the criminality of such arrangements.

The Garden of the Finzi-Contini

In an extraordinary movie[113] a few years ago, director Vittorio de Sica depicted the last years before the extermination of the centuries-old Jewish community in Italy. The movie takes place after Mussolini had ascended to power but before the Jews were deported. In what was for me the most telling scene of the movie, the young, draft-age boy in the Jewish family is riding somewhere on a train when a group of soldiers—all boys of a similar age and in uniform—gets on. Nothing overtly violent or even threatening happens, but the juxtaposition of that Jewish boy in his civilian clothes to the community of soldiers chillingly foreshadowed the fate of those excluded from the community's norms and rites of citizenship.

In his recent Nimmer lectures, Professor Kenneth Karst articulated the liberal egalitarian claims for women (and gays and racial minorities) to be fully included in military service, as a part of their overall claim for equal citizenship under the Fourteenth Amendment.[114] The article, a noteworthy example of the possibilities for a liberalism free of limoralism, systematically dismantles the supposedly neutral arguments of efficiency against integration of the armed services, leaving bare the actual dynamic of a military establishment in the service of the social construction of gender.

As with so much of Karst's writing, his insights and proposals would do most of the work on any feminist political agenda.[115] I seek to add to his invaluable work a different perspective: I am asking why feminists should support the full participation in the armed services from without, not why a sincere liberal of any gender should from within. In the context of that inquiry, I am asking how concepts of virtuous citizenship inform that enterprise—not how concepts of equality of citizenship do. As set forth above, my theory of equality constructed for citizenship would support gender integration of the armed services, even against appealing claims of efficient screening or diminished effectiveness.

Courage is a personal virtue, in Aristotle, the mean between fear and confidence.[116] But tempting as it is to translate classical concepts of military virtue into things like courage in the face of disease or loss of status,[117] Aristotle quite clearly directs our attention to the concerns of the classical order:

> With what sort of terrible things, then, is the brave man concerned? Surely with the greatest; for no one is more likely than

> he to stand his ground against what is dreadful. Now death is the
> most terrible of all things; for it is the end, and nothing is thought
> to be any longer either good or bad for the dead. But the brave
> man would not seem to be concerned even with death in *all* cir-
> cumstances, e.g. at sea or in disease. In what circumstances, then?
> Surely in the noblest. Now such deaths are those in battle; for
> these take place in the greatest and noblest danger. And this
> agrees with the ways in which honours are bestowed in city-states
> and at the courts of monarchs.[118]

Courage in defense of the city, moreover, is so central to the community
that it even supports the claim of the many to political justice based on
their sharing in the risk of defending it. In Aristotle's polity form of
regime, for example, citizens are defined as those who can bear heavy
arms.[119] This is, of course, another example of the linkage between personal virtue and political virtue described above.[120]

Interestingly, critical as participation in defending the city in battle is,
ultimately Aristotle is going to relegate war to the category of the necessary, rather than the good in itself.[121] This diminution of enthusiasm is
among the most important evidence for what many scholars regard as the
role of classical philosophy in moderating the war culture of Homeric
Greece.[122] Aristotle supports this argument in his usual way, by referring
to the experience before his readers—the defeat of the warlike
Sparta[123]—as well as to commonsense arguments, like the riskiness of an
expansionist policy[124] and ultimately to oral claims like the injustice of
subordinating people to slavery (unless, of course they are natural
slaves).[125]

The critical thing to notice here, however, is that military virtue is not
abandoned; it is simply transferred from the individualistic honor culture
to the collectivity. Political theorist Jean Elshtain expresses the transition
well:

> When Socrates steps onto the stage, a new discourse—cast in
> the form, first, of Plato's dialogues, then of Aristotle's sustained
> analyses—takes shape as the pre-eminent narrative of and for the
> city, the real and the ideal polis. The shift thus marked as the
> polites supersedes the warrior is not one from war to peace. What
> is at stake instead is collective understandings of war as a human
> undertaking and an object of reflection. . . . War may bind the

body politic, but only as a regularized collective activity, undertaken from civic necessity, not from an individual search for glory
or vengeance or lust to annihilate. There is not room in Plato's
Republic for the war lover. But there is ample space and need for
the Guardian-warrior, a zealous defender of the autonomy of the
city, wholly devoted to its good and cut off from "selfish" pursuits.[126]

If additional evidence were needed of the linkage of military virtue and
communal life, the crucial claim of community (and against the individu-
alism of private property that pervades the Politics)—the common
table—is an ancient Homeric war custom.[127]

Interestingly, in the debate among feminists before the Supreme Court
turned away the equality challenge to the single sex draft law,[128] this
argument never really got made. Instead, the debate centered on an assimilationist versus alienationist ground in which no one was willing to
speak up for the military virtues. The alienationist position was that
women should reject the draft as a part of a fundamental critique of
American foreign and domestic policy and "reject the war reflex as an
instance of male hysteria; in its essence, feminism is opposed to violence."[29] The assimilationist position, as well articulated by liberal feminist Wendy Williams, tracks the basic argument of liberal autonomy:

> To me, Rostker never posed the question of whether women should
> be forced as men now are to fight wars, but whether we, like them,
> must take the responsibility for deciding whether or not to fight,
> whether or not to bear the cost of risking our lives, on the one
> hand, or resisting in the name of peace, on the other.[130]

Now there are things that could be said. For instance, feminists who
believe in the abstract primacy of community might argue that they will
not serve a society that is oppressive root and branch. Or communitarian
feminists might defend their consistency by asserting that the community, whether of women or all humanity, is not defined by national borders and thus they are being faithful to their communitarianism in
refusing to participate in rending the community with arms.

But for those who invoke, as many—perhaps most—American feminists do, the ideals of equality[131] and of a share in American prosperity,[132]
the absence of serious discussion of the virtues of service is trouble-

some,[133] and the common features of feminist and classical assumptions quite helpful. Thus, when military service is seen as one of the rites by which the moral force of the law is brought to command the shaping of a virtuous self, the classical and feminist recognition of the role of the state in creating norms of self would lead feminists to address the larger question of the value of such service in the shaping of a self. Then, when military service is seen as the quintessence of participation in the community, the common ground of the primacy of the political would urge feminists in the direction of mandatory military service.[134]

Nor is this the only way in which consideration of the issue would change. Jean Elshtain speculates that the historical construction of war has left room for only two characters: the male "just warriors" and the female "beautiful souls," who suffer and support and sometimes protest, but are always the "other."[135] Within this dichotomy, there is no room for any moderate stance. Women are caught in a double bind of participating in acts of military aggression they feel to be wrong or of being found unfit to defend their country.[136] In the world of the double bind, one must seek the second-best solution. Elshtain sees the escape for women as resting on a revitalization of civic identity and connection in the defense of the state. The concept would include the role of private conscience and the recognition of incommensurability and conflicting claims in the making of military policy.[137] Like Nussbaum's Aristotle, Elshtain's politician would see the morality on large issues, but preserve decision making for a flexible measure that includes irony about the prospects of war and the tolerance of defeat in its engagement.[138] Under this measured view, the admixture of Aristotle's householding, life-preserving female would moderate the Athenian military norm to one more like a "large, dreamy beast. . . . Real courage has nothing of savagery about it, but goes 'rather with the gentler and more lion-like characters.' "[139]

The Case of Baby S(emen)

Laqueur asserts that Aristotle, like most thinkers before the eighteenth century, posits a model of the species as "one sex." "What we would take to be the basic facts of sexual difference . . . were for Aristotle contingent and philosophically not very interesting observations about particular species under certain conditions."[140] Thus, Thus, Aristotle discounted the identity of maleness and the existence (or size) of sexual organs, aligned the sex organs with the alimentary system, common to all species, and used a term for sex organs (*kaulos*) that was the same for both genders.[141] Even semen and menstrual fluid, so important for the hierarchy of reproduction, were, for Aristotle, but levels on a common hierarchy of blood.[142]

As reflected in the description of Aristotle's reproductive theory herein, Aristotle's thought is substantially less consistent than Laqueur's thesis permits.[143] While assuming at least proximity to the genders, if not identity as Lacqueur would have it still, Aristotle is also the author of the most hierarchical of theories about reproduction—and hierarchy of necessity implies some distinction. Aristotle's theory centers on "semen," defined not as the fluid which is its carrier, but as whatever it is that initiates the growth of a new life sort of in the way that a craftsman molds matter.[144] For reasons that do not matter here, he concludes that semen must come from one parent or the other, rather than both.[145] He further concludes that it comes from the male, because, *inter alia*, "the emission of even a small quantity of semen is exhausting."[146] Because women exist, however, and produce a sort of fluid, and because nature makes nothing in vain, according to Aristotle, the woman must also contribute something; Aristotle concludes that the something is the material of the child.[147]

This theory had some pitfalls for Aristotle, because, insofar as the semen contains no material, all the material elements of the new entity would need be in the material, and this provides a potentially preemptive role for the female. But Aristotle resolves this problem, too, in favor of the male, on the ground that the rational soul exists separate from the body. Thus, the father, producer of the semen, can be responsible for ensouling the mother's material contribution into the new individual. And is.[148]

Many things follow from this assertion. As the soul is higher than the body, which it shares with the lower animals, the male is higher than the female in Aristotle's taxonomy. Because the male is higher, the female exists to facilitate sexual (rather than hermaphroditic) reproduction. She is instrumental to species reproduction: "The actuality of her human potential is the incubation of a male child."[149] Thus, Aristotle's writings on reproduction contain the seeds of both the hierarchy and proximity of the genders. A lot of Aristotle's biology is clearly circular or nonsense or both. Aristotle is severely hampered by his lack of a microscope, to say nothing (since his semen theory also rests heavily on a notion of vital heat) of the lack of a thermometer. Commentators of this school, of whom Thomas Laqueur is the latest, claim that Aristotle assumed the inferiority of women and from this assumption drew his biology and his politics separately.[150] This still leaves the task of dealing with the politics intact, but at least jettisons the scientific-looking part of the enterprise. By this way of thinking, Aristotle's characterization of women as inferior natural instruments of the material of reproduction is neither necessary nor sufficient for his political misogyny. Not necessary, because Aristotle's debasement of the status of women, including his science, was the result of his methodology of reproducing as truth the opinions about virtue common in his society. And not sufficient, because his science was nonsense. So, until recently, Aristotle lay safely twice buried by the Enlightenment.

About fifteen years ago, people in the United States began engaging—not in great numbers, but in increasing numbers and with increasing visibility—in the practice of hiring surrogate "mothers"[151] to bear children to be taken away and raised in a separate family unit. The practice has generated enormous controversy, and there are numerous responses ranging from proposals to criminalize the practice, to treating it like a protected constitutional right.[152]

That's the thing about Aristotle. Just when his critics think they have him safely buried in a liberal overcoat of Enlightenment assumptions about equality and Enlightenment discoveries about science, up he pops. Before embarking upon what insights, if any, can be drawn from Aristotle's views on the production of offspring and gender relationships, I will make two preliminary points. First, unlike the discussion of courage set forth above,[153] the lessons from Aristotle's hierarchical biology for the politics of surrogacy bear largely not on the ends of a good human life, but on a preliminary issue for feminists: the means to claim such a life. If any lesson about the teleological concept of citizenship emerges from a return to the ancient writings, it is such assumption as existed of similarity between the genders. Second, I will discuss the moral-political wisdom of surrogacy from the standpoint of women's interests in aspiring to full citizenship separate from the question of whether and to what extent the coercive power of the state should be used to enforce an outcome. This disclaimer is not because classical learning has no wisdom on the role of the state as a force for virtue. As set forth above, this is one of the most neglected, but important, aspects of the classical revival.[154] Rather, it is because the role of the state in surrogacy arrangements has been much discussed in the last few years,[155] while the citizenship aspects of the undertaking have been less extensively explored. Insofar as they have been explored, it has been within a debate framed by liberal assumptions of sale and exchange, concerns that reflect the liberal focus on freedom rather than the classical focus on virtue.[156] Perhaps once the virtue issues are raised to the surface, the debate about avenues of effectuating the superior arrangement will go easier.[157]

In the debates about the wisdom of the practice of surrogacy, feminists on both sides of the issue have argued about a lot of things: whether surrogacy turns women into a commodity, thus debasing them in some unspecified commercial way or whether commodification is desirable, because women should be glad to make money from their childbearing capacities, otherwise sadly undervalued in the market place; whether reproductive technologies simply treat women as walking wombs, caring much more expensively and elaborately for the fetus than the woman, which could be solved by changing the power relationships with the medical establishment; whether claiming rearing rights would relegate women to the home again or raise them from the abased state in which children were entirely the father's domain,[158] as part of the common-law unity between man and wife, being man.[159] But, in all of the discussion of surrogacy—even the feminist debates over surrogacy—no one seems to have noticed that modern science has managed to reproduce the most oppressive parts of both classical and modern biology: the hierarchy of classical thought and the dualism of the modern.

1. *The Hierarchy of Surrogacy.*   In both common forms of surrogacy, a woman submits herself to a man's reproductive plans. In ordinary surrogacy, a man who wishes to "have"[160] a baby (reproduce himself) may obtain a female womb and material for his purposes. In gestational surrogacy, where the surrogate does not contribute the egg, two women contribute to the man's child.

As Aristotle's writings make clear, it is the soul of the new human that matters. Although we products of modern science now know that both genetic parents contribute to all aspects of the new human, insofar as we moderns also recognize the possibility of contributing by choice to the development of a human soul, it is in the form of rearing and educating the child. By taking it away at birth, the father can claim that domain exclusively. The best illustration of this dynamic is the paradigmatic surrogacy case, *In re Baby M.*[161] There, as the opinion reflects, "the family's only survivor [William Stern] very much wanted to continue his blood-line."[162] That end was accomplished the day Baby M was born. Yet he fought relentlessly—not for his physical "bloodline"—but to gain custody and raise the child. Interestingly, the hierarchy of the spiritual-intellectual over the physical also replicated the hierarchy, long familiar to feminist critics of liberalism, of the public over the private.[163] Thus, the production of the child in the hidden womb is valued less than the visible education and rearing.

The counterarguments on behalf of surrogacy do not overcome this fundamental political lesson. Insofar as the father delegates his authority to a woman not the mother he is simply exercising his judgment about the efficient way to accomplish his ends. Insofar as he is sharing the child with the egg donor, he is claiming at least half of the surrogate's service, which leaves the proportion of women to men in the enterprise at two to one, with one female still functioning entirely as the material cause.

Now simply replicating Aristotle's misogynistic biology is perhaps not a "discussion stopper"[164] about the wisdom of the procedure. But it should at least make one pause. This is so, because, as set forth above, the allocation of roles in reproduction is at least circular with, if not causal of, a powerful analogy with every other political role. For all of these reasons, the resemblance between the present fad for surrogacy and Aristotle's picture of the female providing the physical matter for a male to endow with a soul in the *Generation of Animals* is chilling.

2. The Dualism of Surrogacy.   In defense of the regime, liberals would say, that between members of opposite sexes the most optimistic prospect is sale—the nonaggression treaty.[165] In this market economy, the argument goes, selling what you have and purchasing what you want is the quintessential autonomous act. The emphasis on the dignity of the exchange is critical, because, without such a show of respect, being an instrument to someone else's purposes is an abased posture, with political consequences not only for the individual involved, but for all who resemble her in the relevant way.[166] Opponents of surrogacy have made the counterarguments against sale, of course:[167] arguments over freedom of will[168] and arguments over appropriate political limitations on free will, such as those contained in the Civil Rights Act of 1964.[169] In response, proponents of unregulated surrogacy also invoke the superficial equality of the sperm bank and all its variations like testicular implants.[170]

One conclusion to the argument is that the issue does not exist in the ideal world. The reports reflect that there is almost no controversy over sperm banks.[171] One assumes that sperm banks don't get anyone excited in part because the imposition on the male is so much less onerous, but also because these scenarios just don't happen all that often. And the reason they don't is the same one that supports confronting surrogacy as it exists. In American society, women are in a reduced position of social, political, and economic power. In that framework, surrogacy is a practice that disadvantages women for the symbolic and political reasons set forth above. If, in an Amazonian never-never-land, the larger purpose were truly a shared one, like the well-being of the city in which all live, the alienation and instrumentalism discussion would change. So probably would so many other factors that the discussion becomes science fictional.

But Laqueur's work fuels a much more powerful attack on the liberal defense of surrogacy: that it rests not on a fact of the matter, but on a social construct imposed upon the natural world and therefore subject to revision. As Laqueur describes the development, "[S]ometime in the eighteenth century, sex as we know it was invented. The reproductive organs went from being paradigmatic sites for displaying hierarchy, reasonant throughout the cosmos, to being the foundation of incommensurable difference."[172] Moreover, and most interestingly, the new paradigm did not rest on breakthroughs in natural science: important techniques in the measurement of hormones are a twentieth-century phenomena; there was no consensus on the functions of sperms and eggs until the nineteenth, and the two-sex model predicted all sorts of unprovable consequences, like qualitative differences in skeletal formation or uniform sexuality throughout nature (including, for example, plants).[173]

Cultural historians speculate, and it seems difficult to refute, that the newly discovered sexual difference was invented to justify continued male domination of the public sphere, after the universalistic claims for liberty and equality characteristic of the Englightenment.[174] Many writers have examined the politics of liberal exclusion, which Laqueur sums up as follows:

> Social-contract theory at its most abstract postulated a body that, if not sexless, is nevertheless undifferentiated in its desires, interests, or capacity to reason. In striking contrast to the old teleology of the body as male, liberal theory begins with a neuter individual body: sexed but without gender, in principle of no consequence to culture, merely the location of the rational subject that consti-

tutes the person. The problem for this theory is how to legitimate as "natural" the real world of male dominion of women, of sexual passion and jealousy, of the sexual division of labor and of cultural practices generally from such an original state of no-gender. The answer to making their "natural beings recognizable," . . . was for social-contract theorists to "smuggle social characteristics into the natural condition." However the argument works in detail, the end result is that women are absent from the new civil society for reasons based in "nature." A biology of sexual incommensurability offered these theorists a way of explaining—without resorting to the natural hierarchies of the one-sex model—how in the state of nature and prior to the existence of social relations, women were already subordinated to men. Therefore the social contract could then be created between men only, an exclusively fraternal bond. Ironically, the genderless rational subject engendered opposite, highly gendered sexes.[175]

Then, as now, absent such an explanation, liberal equality would have threatened profoundly the other critical item of the liberal agenda: limited government.[176]

The construction of the sexes as opposites is essential to the defense of commodification. For, as Radin so graphically expresses it, universal commodification is the default drive of even liberal pluralism:

> Prominent principles in liberal pluralism include negative liberty, the person as abstract subject, and a conceptual notion of property. These principles are basic to the free market and its institutions, private property, and free contract. Negative liberty and the subjectivity of personhood underlie convictions that inalienable things are internal to the person, and that inalienabilities are paternalistic. Conceptualism finds alienability to be inherent in the concept of property. These convictions make the case for liberal pluralism uneasy, always threatening to assimilate to universal commodification.[177]

The most important lesson to draw from this recital is that the arguments about surrogacy are good arguments, but they all exist within the "double bind" choice between free alienation and political disfigurement,[178] a choice which stems directly from the dichotomization of the genders themselves.

What the classical revival does here is break the liberal frame within which the debate has been waged in a way that even the arguments against commodification have failed to accomplish. The classical revival can do so because it reveals that the commodification of reproduction simply locks in the construct of opposite sexes; it shows that the more women behave and/or are categorized as distant and exotic variations on the species, the harder it's going to be to claim citizenship in the common polity. Already founded on a biology of little epistemological legitimacy, a regime of distance from all the social and emotional ties that can surround somewhat more intimate[179] reproduction is just widening the liberally (and limorally) constructed gulf between women and men. One alternative is of course the relationships of love and altruism associated with the family.[180] But critics of the family model have rightly pointed to its inadequacy as a matrix for free personal development[181] and for the resolution of conflict.[182]

Here, too, the revival of classical learning offers visions of an alternative world, long repressed under the limoral regime. Martha Nussbaum teases out the balance between separateness and unity in the political state, where the Aristotelian flexible measure can reflect degrees of difference and contexts of difference free of the Manicheanism of modern thought.[183] More specifically, Aristotle writes of political friendship: the relationship between citizens equal in important ways and valuing one another for the good in each other.[184] Such citizens are separate, but intimate in spending time together and knowing one another, even to the concrete details of their existence.[185] Such a friendship, even though linked to mutual advantage and thus not of the elevated nature of virtue friendship, still approaches a mean between the indifference of commercial relationships[186] and the authoritarianism of the family.[187] As the classicist John Cooper expressed it:

> civic friendship involves mutual good will, trust, and well-wishing, and the mutual interest that fellow-citizens have in one another's characters is part of that good will and well-wishing. . . . Each expects his fellow-citizens in their dealings with him (political, economic, and social) to be motivated not merely by self-interest (or other private particular interest) but also by concern for his good for his own sake.[188]

Although Aristotle clearly associated gender relationships with the household, he explicitly included them in his descriptions of kinds of friendships:

> Between man and wife friendship seems to exist by nature; for man is naturally inclined to form couples. . . . [B]oth utility and pleasure seem to be found in this kind of friendship. But this friendship may be based also on excellence, if the parties are good.[189]

Drucilla Cornell's recent dissent from MacKinnon's vision of hopeless alienation between the genders may mark the birth of such a vision in legal feminism.[190] Steven Salkever has also started to explore the implications of Aristotle's wisdom for the genders specifically, with an eye to constructing relationships of neither hierarchy nor alienation.[191] The good news is that the debate over surrogacy may open the way for revision of the relationship between the genders on a much broader front.

The Dog at the Gate

Opposition

As my two examples reflect, both the structure and the substance of the classical tradition[192] contain familiar modes of thought and much wisdom for the issues of feminist legal theory. However, there is surprisingly little evidence of this richness in contemporary writing. Although a feminist scholar, Katharine Bartlett disclaims the assertion of complete originality,[193] and her references at this point are all to the liberal underpinnings of feminist theory.[194] Thereafter, with the exception of one brief reference to Aristotle as the source of practical reasoning, one might read Bartlett's entire essay and conclude that the feminist modes and orders sort of sprang full-armored from the forehead of Catharine MacKinnon.

One exception would seem to be Suzanna Sherry's *Civic Virtue and the Feminine Voice in Constitutional Adjudication*, which broke very important ground in illuminating the similarities between the civic republican revival of classical concepts of community and feminist psychology.[195] Even

Sherry's excellent work, however, emphasizes heavily (and, one assumes, consciously) the later civic republican tradition rather than the classical sources. Moreover, in her consideration of substantive outcomes (the article is about Justice O'Connor's decisions), she focuses on the divergent results produced by a feminine sensibility in cases with no feminist substantive implications, rather than addressing her classical insights to the woman question.

There are at least three explanations for the feminist neglect of classical theory. One is that the revived interest in classicism has been highly overrated. Another is that, in fact, there is little or nothing to be gained from tracing a philosophical tradition to its roots. Finally, one might conjecture that the association of classical philosophy with the aforementioned bias is so poisonous that it reduces the utility of the relationship, indeed, perhaps, renders it counterproductive.

As to the first explanation—ignorance—the philosophical and political literature is replete with evidence of the depth and breadth of the revived interest in ancient philosophy.[196] In any case, the explanation of ignorance is the least interesting one because it is remediable. If, on the other hand, either one of the other explanations—irrelevance or indigestibility—holds true, education in the classics will still be of no moment.

Addressing the second objection—that a relationship to ancient philosophy sheds no light on current thought—there are at least four arguments for exploring the relationships between ancient philosophy and any contemporary discussions of the good life. First, as I hope the above discussion of substance reflects, ancient philosophy may have answers, even right answers according to some epistemology, as to how to lead a good life. Aristotle's theory is "rich in practical consequences as well as in theoretical insights."[197] Second, as is powerfully illustrated by Laqueur's exploration of the history of gender, there is the critical and comparativist function of exotic subjects. Scholars have returned to Aristotle out of "a sense of the impoverishment of recent moral philosophy."[198] An ancient tradition can serve as a point from which to criticize an otherwise solipsistic intellectual regime.[199] Third, the unsinkability of the tradition is interesting. Assuming the wide spread of the process of reflective equilibrium, a two-and-one-half millennium survival of a body of philosophic work has a certain market appeal. And finally, there is the aspect of stability. As feminist theorist Jean Elshtain put it, one must "forge links between the Western tradition and feminist thinking" in order to avoid "[w]ildly visionary futures" with "no cogent way to move from the horror

of the present to the heaven of the future."[200] If feminism, which seems
in so many ways to be prescribing an entirely new regime, can be shown
to have its roots in familiar traditions that did not have either uniformly
disruptive nor uniformly negative consequences, the risks inherent in revising society from above according to a theoretical formula are reduced.

Now it is true that "[w]hen we turn to the great tradition of Western
political thought with questions about the justice of the treatment of the
sexes in mind, it is to little avail."[201] But perhaps this is to ask the wrong
questions. The issue addressed here is what the ancient traditions have
to say about the deeper structure of feminist thought and social thought,
structures which, when separated from the immediate context of the answers they produced in ancient times, illuminate contemporary feminism
with quite a different light.

But, as is so often the case in the Greek world, there is a dog at the
gate: the third objection referenced above. Unlike liberal modernity,
which basically defined women away or at best ignored us,[202] Aristotle is
the original bad actor. The conservatism of his method, which dictated
that he start with the prevailing moral views, the functionalism of his
theory, according to which things had value only in relationship to their
ends, and his assumption that certain social ends were superior—the en-
abling of some of society to live the good life—are all blamed for producing his explicit conclusion that women are naturally inferior and for
setting in motion twenty-four-hundred years of philosophical misogyny.[203] If this is true, and if Aristotle's philosophy cannot be separated
from its objectionable associations, perhaps its similarity to contemporary
feminist theory is reason for concern, rather than celebration.[204] Or at
least for irony.

Starting with the core problem of classical misogyny, one must ask
whether the linkage can be broken. What of Aristotle's structure depends
upon its misogyny? Even if the misogyny is a product, rather than a process, are there elements critical to Aristotle's structure that inevitably produce that result?

Reconciliation

In contrast to feminist legal theorists, as the above discussion reflects,
feminist philosophers have been wrestling with Aristotle for quite a
while[205]—holding on, perhaps, for a blessing. The problem is set forth

quite graphically by Susan Okin: "Aristotle asserts that women are 'naturally' inferior to men, and that they are therefore 'naturally' ruled by them."[206] As Okin describes the problem, what is natural to any entity in Aristotle's world is inextricably intertwined with its function. Thus, an eye is to see; in its natural condition, it will perform this function. In society, according to Aristotle, a woman's function is to reproduce and to run the family men need for their well-ordered political life. Those aspects of her being compatible with that function are natural.[207] The whole structure rests, in turn, upon the superiority of the Greek political life and the essentiality of subordinating women to it. Once that hierarchy is established, the virtues can be allocated according to function; thus, for instance, women's virtues will be seen as subordination and industrious habits, and men's virtues as courage and the capacity to rule. Two things flow from this: the men's virtues will be automatically classified as superior, and any female manifestations of those virtues will be unnatural.

It is easy to see the points of attack. On the grandest level, one might discard, as has so much of modern thought, Aristotle's teleology: his assertion that things, or at least that people, have a purpose. Or one might attack the connection between teleology and nature, asserting the flexibility or social construct of either teleology or nature. Finally, one might get off at the level of hierarchy—a ranking of ends or natures—or at the positing of the hierarchy of virtue from the existing hierarchy of society at any particular social time. All of these techniques and more have been tried.[208] It is also easy to see that, depending on the level of attack, all, most, or only some of Aristotle's structure would have to go.

Most of the work to date focuses on the second and third points—Aristotle's nature and Aristotle's hierarchy. If, for example, as Laqueur has persuasively argued, "nature" is actually a political construct,[209] the whole scheme rests on Aristotle's political decision to assign women (or, more likely, his acceptance of the social reality that women were assigned) to the household and then assign the household to a lower rank in the "natural" hierarchy leading to the polis.[210] Here the concept of "nature" gets fuzzy, because it drifts from physical biology, however ill-conceived, toward a meaning of orderly or good.[211] As to this aspect of Aristotle's theory of the state, Elshtain says, Aristotle is never clear on what should be the orderly relationship of household and state, simply asserting that the household is "prior" to the state and a part of the state.[212] Elshtain further illuminates the disjuncture between Aristotle's misogyny and his larger theory: that Aristotle saw the basis for human political association in the capacity for speech,[213] and yet there is "no evidence that women in Aristotle's time had been struck dumb."[214] Accordingly, Aristotle is reduced to arguing that women lack the capacity for "reasoned" speech, which he supports in a perfectly circular way by their relegation to the (inferior) household, because they lack the capacity for reasoned speech. Arlene Saxonhouse suggests a more positive reading, arguing for Aristotle's recognition of friendship between the genders and his explicit rejection of slavery as the model for gender relationships.[215] She tempers his relegation of women to second best by noting that, to Aristotle, almost everyone was second best.[216]

Nussbaum attempts to use Aristotle's methods to attack the second aspect of classical misogyny—hierarchy. Starting with the fundamentality of the principle of noncontradiction,[217] she postulates a feminist challenging Aristotle's answer to the woman question by showing him that "a progressive position actually preserves certain deep human beliefs about the equal humanity of other human beings better than his own political theory does."[218] But Nussbaum's egalitarian Aristotle[219] is far from the only figure who might emerge. Freed from the misogyny and the false hierarchy of gender, Aristotle would be forced to confront the structural foundations of human hierarchy. Perhaps the work supports Nussbaum's leveling vision. As set forth above, I think that Aristotle would come closer to Hannah Arendt's resolution: that there is an arena in which naturally unequal players construct equality for extrinsic purposes.[220] Much of his writing, including his reference to the superior wisdom of many opinions on issues of governance[221] and the stability of a polity with a large middle class,[222] reflect this inclination. In a post-Enlightenment regime, civil peace might be such an extrinsic purpose.

Steven Salkever suggests a third reading: stripped of its gender hierarchy, Greek philosophy cannot equate virtue with virility, seen as military courage and the associated high-spiritedness, and other virtues, like temperance and ultimately contemplation-philosophy might emerge as the governing political paradigm.[223] Salkever offers this vision as an interesting alternative to the modern dichotomy of classical militarism versus liberal commercialism.[224]

This reading rests on the heavily contested Straussian presumption that a great philosopher, like nature, makes nothing in vain.[225] Be that as it may, the readings that ensue are sufficiently strained so that wholesale adoption of them would, I think, inevitably undermine the larger structure of Aristotle's thought, which does direct our attention to the polis as the final and most self-sufficient end of human enterprise and which does contain explicit descriptions or explanations of at least a moderately privatized and subordinated female role. Yet, as set forth above, these close readings are valuable for highlighting how Aristotle's thought might appear and develop, if the easy assumption of misogyny were removed.[226]

Regardless of which reading one adopts, lacking a grounding in physical biology, the naturalness of the subordination of women must rest on its normative meaning of well-ordered. Here, the Aristotelian picture fits together somewhat better, because Aristotelian society needed the household (and the institution of slavery)[227] to support the political activity he saw as best. But if, because of modern claims of equality, which would block the automatic assignment of any group to the subordinated role of household, or, if, as Nussbaum suggests, because of a change in the notion of leisure, or simply because of technological changes, the role of the household in Aristotle's order is no longer needed to support political activity, the foundation for the abased role of women in his philosophy is further undermined.[228] Nor is the opening of these questions the only beneficial result of excising Aristotle's misogyny. As the dialogists correctly assert, women in any society are uniquely both a part of the society and, to the extent that the society is a patriarchal one, not a part of it. If women are to participate in the dialogue over justice, different opinions about justice will no doubt emerge—as recent Western political history reflects—if only from their different sizes and their vulnerability to childbearing. Although difference—particularly difference based on separateness—is neither reliable[229] nor inherently valuable, in the Aristotelian mode of inquiry if everyone articulated the same position, there would be little play for philosophy.[230]

Thus, the way is somewhat cleared for the exercise outlined above: to show how these works of feminism generally and feminist jurisprudence, which is the more familiar legal variant, clearly and provocatively raise many of the large issues and are enriched by the answers available from antiquity.

Conclusion

[E]verybody knows values are the BMWs of the nineties and that you're just nobody if you don't have some.[231]

It always worries me when my ideas start to crop up in fashion magazines, especially when feminism has already gone through two whole phases (early contemporary and late contemporary) in the current incarnation, to say nothing of those poor benighted souls around 1920 who only wanted to vote. Yet there is a sense in which the movement from the beginning has been driving toward a consistent single goal, well expressed by the classical writers: the goal of citizenship. Put another way, woman is a political animal.

Notes

1. See HAROLD BLOOM, THE BOOK OF J (David Rosenberg trans., 1990). Of course, the assumption of human authorship of the Bible is already heresy. For the most recent of the several millennia of authority, see Richard Bernstein, A Perennial Scrapper Takes on God and the Bible, N.Y. TIMES, Oct. 24, 1990, at C11.

2. The beginning of the development is generally attributed to the path-breaking work of G.E.M. Anscombe. See 3 G.E.M. ANSCOMBE, Modern Moral Philosophy, in THE COLLECTED PHILOSOPHICAL PAPERS OF G.E.M. ANSCOMBE 26, 26–42 (Basil Blackwell ed., 1981).

3. The phrase is from William James through Margaret Jane Radin. See Margaret J. Radin, The Pragmatist and the Feminist, 63 S. CAL. L. REV. 1699, 1713 (1990).

4. See Catharine A. MacKinnon, Feminism, Marxism, Method, and the State: An Agenda for Theory, 7 SIGNS 515 (1982) [hereinafter MacKinnon, Agenda for Theory]; Catharine A. MacKinnon, Feminism, Marxism, and the State: Toward Feminist Jurisprudence, 8 SIGNS 635 (1985) [hereinafter MacKinnon, Toward Feminist Jurisprudence].

5. MacKinnon, Toward Feminist Jurisprudence, supra note 4, at 638; see Katharine T. Bartlett, Feminist Legal Methods, 103 HARV. L. REV. 829, 837 (1990).

6. Scratch the consciousness of any female law school graduate since the publication of Betty Friedan's The Feminine Mystique in 1963, and you will hear a story to illustrate this. Mine involves "vital heat." See infra text accompanying note 59. Sometime around the middle of my first year at (we'll call it the University of Chillcago) law school in the mid-sixties, I noticed that I was freezing all the time I was in the school building and suffering from an unusual number of colds. A preliminary inquiry into the matter sent me to, we'll call him Shel B. Nameless, a senior faculty member whose specialty and institutional role did not immediately suggest him as a candidate for control of the thermostat.

"Professor Nameless," I inquired, "why is it always so cold in the law school?"

"Well," he replied, "it's actually just the right temperature. If you'd wear a jacket and vest like a real law student, you wouldn't be cold at all."

"Plus ça change, plus c'est la même chose." A woman of my acquaintance was being considered for appointment to the faculty of one of the twenty "top ten" law schools this year. In urging his colleagues not to appoint, a faculty member (since he conflates the relevant norm with resemblance to himself, we'll call him Professor Moral) attempted to discount the publication of two of her scholarly articles in two top ten law reviews during the previous two years. "Not analytical enough," he explained. "If she'd write doctrinal scholarship like a real law professor, she might be good enough for our faculty."

It is this confusion of the species with the particular speaker—the replacement of the purported neutrality of liberalism with what I will hereafter call "limoralism"—that has fueled so much of the feminist disenchantment with the project generally. *See* Drucilla Cornell, *Sexual Difference, the Feminine, and Equivalency: A Critique of MacKinnon's* Toward a Feminist Theory of the State, 100 YALE L.J. 2247, 2258–59 (1991) (maintaining that feminist arguments, which suggest that the impact of gender hierarchy limits thinking about equality, are not given the weight they deserve). For very recent expositions of the phenomenon in legal academe, see Peter M. Shane, *Why Are So Many People So Unhappy? Habits of Thought and Resistance to Diversity in Legal Education,* 75 IOWA L. REV. 1033 (1991); Margaret J. Radin, *Affirmative Action Rhetoric,* 85 SOC. PHIL. & POL'Y 130 (1991). For a further explanation of *limoralism,* see *infra* text accompanying note 98.

7. Bartlett explicitly refers to "a classic Aristotelian model of practical deliberation." Bartlett, *supra* note 5, at 850.

8. *Id.* at 851; *see* Radin, *supra* note 3, at 1706–07 (invoking "feminism and pragmatism," meaning the "theory that truth is inevitably plural, concrete, and provisional" and noting that the two share "the commitment to finding knowledge in the particulars of experience").

9. Bartlett, *supra* note 5, at 853.

10. *See id.* at 831; MacKinnon, *Agenda for Theory,* supra note 4, at 519; Nancy Hartsock, *Fundamental Feminism: Process and Perspective,* 2 QUEST 67, 71 (1975).

11. Bartlett, *supra* note 5, at 831; *see* Radin, *supra* note 3, at 1707; Martha L. Fineman, *Challenging Law, Establishing Differences: The Future of Feminist Legal Scholarship,* 42 FLA. L. REV. 25, 38 (1990).

12. Bartlett, *supra* note 5, at 867.

13. *See id.* at 868.

14. Wendy W. Williams, *Equality's Riddle: Pregnancy and the Equal Treatment/Special Treatment Debate,* 13 N.Y.U. REV. L. & SOC. CHANGE 325, 370–74 (1984–85) (discussing the merits of equal protection as opposed to special treatment for women in the workplace).

15. *See, e.g., supra* note 6.

16. *See* Deborah L. Rhode, *Feminist Critical Theories,* 42 STAN. L. REV. 617, 622 (1990); Bartlett, *supra* note 5, at 868–87.

17. *See* Bartlett, *supra* note 5, at 878; *see also* Rhode, *supra* note 16, at 620–21 (discussing the irony of how feminist adherents of deconstruction may acknowledge gender oppression exists, but because of the tenets of deconstruction such oppression would not be able to be documented); DRUCILLA CORNELL, *The Feminist Alliance with Deconstruction, in* BEYOND ACCOMMODATION: ETHICAL FEMINISM, DECONSTRUCTION, AND THE LAW 79, 79–82 (1991) (discussing the implications of deconstruction for Lacan's foundationalist framework of the feminine and arguing for an alternative approach to the feminine as an allegory rather than as a fact). In her recent essay, *Sexual Difference,* Cornell seems to be proposing a more compelling vision of true concerns, defending the claims of female sexuality as essential to any proper "conception of the person," asserting affirmatively that "we cannot rise above our empirical selves of the flesh in order to be *free.*" Cornell, *supra* note 6, at 2267 (emphasis in original). Robin West is currently offering an epistemology of "empathy." *See* Robin West, *Taking Preferences Seriously,* 64 TUL. L. REV. 659, 701 (1990).

18. *See, e.g.,* Bartlett, *supra* note 5, at 880 (discussing "positionality," which acknowledges the existence of empirical knowledge and its contingency, as a modification of postmodernist and standpoint epistemology); Martha Minow, *The Supreme Court 1986 Term—Foreword: Justice Engendered,* 101 HARV. L. REV. 10, 74–82 (1987) (arguing against impartiality and standpoint theories in favor of an epistemology which will embrace multiple alternative realities); Rhode, *supra* note 16, at 626 (discussing the different theoretical approaches employed by feminists, while noting that each theorist's desire to locate judgments within the patterns of social practice served as a unifying commitment).

19. Bartlett, *supra* note 5, at 880.

20. *See id.* at 880–83.

21. Rhode, *supra* note 16, at 625.

22. *Id.* at 626.

23. Radin, *supra* note 3, at 1706.

24. *See id.* at 1699–1704. Radin defines the double bind to be the fact that "both commodification and noncommodification may be harmful." *Id.* at 1700.

25. *See* Margaret J. Radin, *Market-Inalienability*, 100 HARV. L. REV. 1849, 1921–36 (1987).

26. *See* Radin, *supra* note 3, at 1700.

27. *See id.* at 1706–9.

28. *See* Radin, *supra* note 3, at 1712 (citing WILLIAM JAMES, PRAGMATISM 13 (1975)). For tough-minded tolerance of uncertainty, see, *e.g.*, Robert C. Post, *The Constitutional Concept of Public Discourse: Outrageous Opinion, Democratic Deliberation, and* Hustler Magazine v. Falwell, 103 HARV. L. REV. 601 (1990) (finding tensions between unbridled expression and the community necessary for discourse both fruitful and troubling); Cass R. Sunstein, *Pornography and the First Amendment*, 1986 DUKE L.J. 589 (suggesting the revival of a sliding scale of protection with less deference for speech of low value, such as pornography). Compare, for example, the intolerance of uncertainty in Martin H. Redish & Gary Lippman, *Freedom of Expression and the Civic Republican Revival in Constitutional Theory: The Ominous Implications*, 79 CAL. L. REV. 267, 304 (1991) (arguing that Post's variety of civic republicanism is "the equivalent of communitarian vigilantism," and that "[o]nce one accepts the basic premise that the violation of communitarian sensibilities may be grounds for the punishment of expression, it is difficult to find *any* principled stopping point for application of that premise" (emphasis added)).

29. *See* Radin, *supra* note 3, at 1708–9.

30. *See id.* at 1719–20.

31. LUDWIG WITTGENSTEIN, ON CERTAINTY (G.E.M. Anscombe & G.H. von Wright eds. & G.E.M. Anscombe & Dennis Paul trans., 1969).

32. CHARLES TAYLOR, SOURCES OF THE SELF: THE MAKING OF THE MODERN IDENTITY (1989).

33. *Cf.* Joan C. Williams, *Deconstructing Gender*, 87 MICH. L. REV. 797 (1989) (stating that pragmatism is the product of male philosophy and thus not attributable to feminism).

34. *See infra* text accompanying notes 182–95.

35. I have explored these ideas previously. *See* Linda R. Hirshman, *Brontë, Bloom, and Bork: An Essay on the Moral Education of Judges*, 137 U. PA. L. REV. 177 (1988) [hereinafter Hirshman, *Moral Education*]; Linda R. Hirshman, *The Virtue of Liberality in American Communal Life*, 88 MICH. L. REV. 983 (1990) [hereinafter Hirshman, *Virtue of Liberality*]. For the explicit tie between literary morality and feminism, see Carolyn Heilbrun & Judith Resnick, *Convergences: Law, Literature, and Feminism*, 99 YALE L.J. 1913 (1990).

36. MARTHA C. NUSSBAUM, FRAGILITY OF GOODNESS: LUCK & ETHICS IN GREEK TRAGEDY AND PHILOSOPHY (1986) [hereinafter NUSSBAUM, FRAGILITY]; Martha C. Nussbaum, *Non-Relative Virtues: An Aristotelian Approach*, in ETHICAL THEORY: CHARACTER AND VIRTUE 32 (Midwest Studies in Philosophy Vol. 13, Peter A. Finch et al. eds., 1988) [hereinafter Nussbaum, *Non-Relative Virtues*]; Martha C. Nussbaum, *Shame, Separateness, and Political Unity: Aristotle's Criticism of Plato*, in ESSAYS ON ARISTOTLE'S ETHICS 395 (Amélie O. Rorty ed., 1980) [hereinafter Nussbaum, *Separateness*].

37. *See, e.g.*, MARTHA C. NUSSBAUM, LOVE'S KNOWLEDGE: ESSAYS ON PHILOSOPHY AND LITERATURE (1990); Martha C. Nussbaum, The Literary Imagination in Public Life, Alexander Rosenthal Lectures, Northwestern University Law School (April 8–10, 1991) [hereinafter Nussbaum, Literary Imagination]. Revised and reprinted in Nussbaum, *Poetic Justice: The Literary Imagination in Public Life* (1995). Chapters 1 and 2 of Literary Imagination correspond to chapter 1 of *Poetic Justice;* chapter 3 corresponds to chapter 2; chapter 4 corresponds to chapter 3.

38. It is certainly no coincidence that feminist Robin West articulates the case for legal paternalism in terms almost identical to Nussbaum's *See* West, *supra* note 17, at 664–65 (arguing that the "moral as well as motivational basis for paternalistic judicial intervention . . . is the judge's sympathetic understanding of the subjective well-being, aspirations, goals, values, and plights of the litigants before her").

39. Nussbaum quotes Aristotle's description of his philosophical method in the *Nicomachean Ethics:*

> [W]e must set down the appearances (*phainomena*) and, first working through the puzzles (*diaporēsantas*), in this way go on to show, if possible, the truth of all the beliefs we hold (*ta endoxa*) about these experiences; and, if this is not possible, the truth of the greatest number and the most authoritative. For if the difficulties are resolved and the beliefs (*endoxa*) are left in place, we will have done enough showing.

NUSSBAUM, FRAGILITY, *supra* note 36, at 240 (quoting and translating Aristotle, *Nicomachean Ethics* VII.1.1145b1–8); *cf.* RICHARD KRAUT, ARISTOTLE ON THE HUMAN GOOD 343 n.27 (1989) ("In defending the political and the philosophical lives, Aristotle is not simply recording 'Common Sense Morality,' for both lives were objects of criticism, and Aristotle's response to these criticisms is not merely an appeal to what most people think." [citations omitted]).

40. NUSSBAUM, FRAGILITY, *supra* note 36, at 246.

41. *See* Daniel A. Farber, *The Case Against Brilliance*, 70 MINN. L. REV. 917, 929 (1986) (arguing that brilliant, counterintuitive theories are undesirable in fields such as law and economics, which are dedicated to "understanding purposive human behavior"); Suzanna Sherry, *An Essay Concerning Toleration*, 71 MINN. L. REV. 963, 964 (1987) (noting that the adoption of a rights-based legal system has adversely affected society, encouraging the use of an entirely abstract method of discourse and creating a moral vacuum with serious practical consequences); Daniel A. Farber, *Brilliance Revisited*, 72 MINN. L. REV. 367, 376–81 (1987) (arguing that too much emphasis is placed on abstract theorizing in current scholarly standards and maintaining that common sense and truth may be of primary importance).

42. NUSSBAUM, FRAGILITY, *supra* note 36, at 251.

43. Nussbaum, Literary Imagination, *supra* note 37. A revised version of the first of these three lectures was recently published as Martha C. Nussbaum, *The Literary Imagination in Public Life*, 22 NEW LITERARY HIST. 877 (1991). As the title indicates, Nussbaum is discussing not Aristotelianism and feminism, but Aristotelianism and the literary imagination—but the similarities are striking.

44. Nussbaum, Literary Imagination, *supra* note 37, lecture 3 (emphasis in original).

45. *Id.* lecture 1. *Compare id. with* West, *supra* note 17, at 684 ("By seeing the individuality, the particularity, of the other, we can assume the feel of her burdens and by doing so we come to sympathetically understand them.").

46. *See* NUSSBAUM, FRAGILITY, *supra* note 36, at 240, 291. This is, of course, one of the crucial points on which philosophies, including ancient philosophies, divide. Compare the Aristotelian method described here with, for example, the theory-building Socrates in the *Protagoras* or Book VI of the *Republic*. *See* NUSSBAUM, FRAGILITY, *supra* note 36, at 241 ("The appearances—by which Plato and his predecessors usually mean the world as perceived, demarcated, interpreted by human beings and their beliefs—are taken to be insufficient 'witnesses' of truth. Philosophy begins [according to Plato] when we acknowledge the possibility that the way we pre-philosophically see the world might be radically in error."); *see, e.g.*, PLATO, THE REPUBLIC 176 (Benjamin Jowett trans., 1901) (asserting that, in Book VI, Socrates argues that "philosophers only are able to grasp the eternal and unchangeable, and those who wander in the region of the many and variable are not philosophers").

One might argue that the fault line doesn't even run between ancient and modern philosophy. *Compare* John Rawls, A Theory of Justice 1–17 (1971) ("My aim is to present a conception of justice which generalizes and carries to a higher level of abstraction the familiar theory of social contract. . . . [T]he guiding idea is that the principles of justice for the basic structure of society are the object of the original agreement.") *with* John Rawls, *Justice as Fairness: Political not Metaphysical*, 14 Phil. & Pub. Aff. 223, 225 (1985) ("Whether justice as fairness can be extended to a general political conception for different kinds of societies existing under different historical and social conditions, or whether it can be extended to a general moral conception, or a significant part thereof, are altogether separate questions. I avoid prejudging these larger questions one way or the other."). Insofar as *A Theory of Justice* is an exercise in the Aristotelian method of theorizing from the observed human condition in Rawls's world—as Rawls seems to be suggesting in his later work—Rawls's subject, in his metaphysical autonomy and separateness, seems like a powerful example of the solipsism of limoralism, which feminism has so powerfully unveiled. I am indebted to Lawrence Sager for reminding me of this Aristotelianism of (at least) late Rawls.

47. Nussbaum, Fragility, *supra* note 36, at 290; *see id.* at 290–317; *see also* Nussbaum, *supra* note 43, at 902–3 (distinguishing between the pseudoscience of economic rationalism and the truth claims of novelistic complexity).

48. Nussbaum, Literary Imagination, *supra* note 37, lecture 3.

49. *See* Nussbaum, Fragility, *supra* note 36, at 298–306.

50. *Id.* at 301.

51. Nussbaum, Literary Imagination, *supra* note 37, lecture 3. In rejecting the pure, but thin, air of liberal philosophy, feminism adopts one part of the communitarian critique of the metaphysics of liberalism. *See, e.g.*, Michael J. Sandel, Liberalism and the Limits of Justice (1982). See *supra* notes 6 and 46 for the critique of the solipsism, as well as the descriptive inadequacy of the enterprise.

52. "Straussian" refers to the (now quite various and even gender-integrated) followers, students, and interpreters of the works of Leo Strauss. Strauss was, for twenty-five years, the Robert Maynard Hutchins Distinguished Service Professor at the University of Chicago. For the most thorough review of his role in modern political philosophy, see *Special Issue on Leo Strauss*, 53 Rev. Pol. 3 (1991).

53. *See* Steven G. Salkever, *Women, Soldiers, Citizens: Plato & Aristotle on the Politics of Virility*, 19 Polity 232, 238–42 (1986); Harold L. Levy, *Does Aristotle Exclude Women From Politics?* 52 Rev. Pol. 397 (1990).

54. Lynda Lange, *Woman is Not a Rational Animal: On Aristotle's Biology of Reproduction, in* Discovering Reality: Feminist Perspectives on Epistemology, Metaphysics, Methodology and Philosophy of Science 1, 2 (Sandra Harding & Merrill B. Hintikka eds., 1983) [hereinafter Discovering Reality].

55. Modern American jurisprudence may not have progressed so far. *See, e.g.*, Geduldig v. Aiello, 417 U.S. 484, 496 n.20 (1974) (holding that California's failure to include pregnancy in its disability insurance scheme did not violate the Equal Protection Clause because it did not exclude women from coverage on the basis of gender but "merely removes one physical condition—pregnancy—from the list of compensable disabilities. While it is true that only women can become pregnant, it does not follow that every legislative classification concerning pregnancy is a sex-based classification"); Personnel Administrator of Massachusetts v. Feeney, 442 U.S. 256, 275 (1979) (holding that a statute which favored veterans for civil service jobs was not discriminatory even though it excluded "significant numbers of women from preferred state jobs," since it excluded them not as women but as nonveterans).

56. Thomas Laqueur, Making Sex: Body and Gender from the Greeks to Freud (1990).

57. *Id.* at 1 (quoting Dorothy L. Sayers, *The Human-Not-Quite-Human, in* Are Women Human? [1971]).

58. *Id.* at 4–5 (emphasis in original) (footnote omitted).

59. *Id.* at 5–6.

60. *See infra* text accompanying notes 146–54.

61. *See* LAQUEUR, *supra* note 56, at 28–29 ("What we would take to be ideologically charged social constructions of gender—that males are active and females passive . . . were for Aristotle indubitable facts, 'natural' truths. What we would take to be the basic facts of sexual differences . . . males have a penis and females a vagina . . . were for Aristotle contingent and philosophically not very interesting."); SUSAN M. OKIN, JUSTICE, GENDER, AND THE FAMILY 14 (1989) (arguing that "Aristotle, whose theory of justice has been so influential, relegated women to a sphere of 'household justice'—populated by persons who are not fundamentally equal to the free men who participate in political justice, but inferiors whose natural function is to serve those who are more fully human"). Laqueur's claims are, of course, not incontestable. *See, e.g.,* Katharine Park & Robert A. Nye, *Destiny is Anatomy,* THE NEW REPUBLIC, Feb. 18, 1991, at 53, 54 (noting that the "distinction between the [one sex and two sex models] blurs into a haze of contradictions"). Yet even Laqueur's success in blurring the modern dichotomy is instructive.

62. LAQUEUR, *supra* note 56, at 29.

63. *Id.* at 20.

64. OKIN, *supra* note 61, at 9 (emphasis added).

65. *See* M.F. Burnyeat, *Aristotle on Learning to Be Good, in* ESSAYS ON ARISTOTLE'S ETHICS, *supra* note 36, at 69, 74 (noting that for Aristotle, parents play a role in telling the child what is "noble and just" and in guiding his conduct "so that by doing the things [he is] told are noble and just [he] will discover that what [he has] been told is *true*" [emphasis in original]).

66. *See* NANCY SHERMAN, THE FABRIC OF CHARACTER: ARISTOTLE'S THEORY OF VIRTUE 1 (1989).

67. *See* WILLIAM W. FORTENBAUGH, ARISTOTLE ON EMOTION 45–49 (1975). Bartlett distinguishes as particularly feminist the recognition of diverse human experiences and the role of emotion or passion. *See* Bartlett, *supra* note 5, at 857–58.

68. *See* FORTENBAUGH, *supra* note 67, at 14–15.

69. *See* Nussbaum, Literary Imagination, *supra* note 37, lecture 2.

70. *See* Nussbaum, *Non-Relative Virtues, supra* note 36, at 33. Philosopher Rosalind Hursthouse recently described cabined Aristotelian relativism:

> We should not automatically assume that it is impossible that some other communities could be morally inferior to our own; maybe some are, or have been . . . [b]ut in communities in which life is a great deal tougher for everyone than it is in ours, having the right attitude to human life and death, parenthood, and family relationships might well manifest itself in ways that are unlike ours.

Rosalind Hursthouse, *Virtue Theory and Abortion,* 20 PHIL. & PUB. AFF. 223, 240 (1991).

71. Nussbaum, *Non-Relative Virtues, supra* note 36, at 32–36. Nussbaum's list of Aristotle's spheres of choice includes (1) fear of important damages; (2) bodily appetites; (3) distribution of limited resources; (4) management of personal property where others are concerned; (5) management of personal property where hospitality is concerned; (6) attitudes and actions with respect to one's own worth; (7) attitudes to slights and damages; (8) association and living together and the fellowship of words and actions; (9) attitudes to the good and ill fortune of others; (10) intellectual life; and (11) planning of one's life and conduct. *Id.* at 35–36.

72. Readers familiar with the monism of the liberal legalist position in, for example, the debate over pornography or the regulation of campus hate speech will recognize the utility of the Aristotelian middle ground of a plurality of approaches. *See supra* text accompanying note

28. For some other recent work on the range of possible middle grounds, see Kenneth L. Karst, *Boundaries and Reasons: Freedom of Expression and the Subordination of Groups*, 1990 U. ILL. L. REV. 95, 117 (arguing that members of a subordinated group "need the freedom to express their liberation in ways that are likely to fall outside the [F]irst [A]mendment's most generous interpretations"); Mari J. Matsuda, *Public Response to Racist Speech: Considering the Victim's Story*, 87 MICH. L. REV. 2320, 2321 (1989) (stating that in an effort to protect both the victim and the First Amendment, "formal criminal and administrative sanction . . . is an appropriate response to racist speech"); Richard Delgado, *Campus Antiracism Rules: Constitutional Narratives in Collision*, 85 Nw. U. L. REV. 343, 383 (1990) (arguing that "speech by which society 'constructs' a stigma picture of minorities may be regulated consistently with the [F]irst [A]mendment"); and Thomas C. Grey, *Civil Rights and Civil Liberties of a Discriminatory Verbal Harassment*, 8 Soc. PHIL. & POL'Y 81, 83 (1991) (arguing for a harassment policy which recognizes the concerns of civil rights and civil liberties).

73. 2 ARISTOTLE, *Politics*, in THE COMPLETE WORKS OF ARISTOTLE I.4.1253b24–.1254a17, at 1986, 1989 (Bollingen Series No. 71, Jonathan Barnes ed., 1984) (Revised Oxford Translation) [hereinafter *Politics*].

74. See Nussbaum, *Non-Relative Virtues*, supra note 36, at 41–42. We have already seen how vulnerable even the physical facts of gender are to this kind of construction. See supra text accompanying notes 56–64.

75. See *Politics*, supra note 73, VII.1.1323a15–VIII.7.1342b34, at 2100–29.

76. See Frederick Schauer, *Harry Kalven and the Perils of Particularism*, 56 U. CHI. L. REV. 397, 413 (1989) (noting that "law's traditional aversion to contextualism is contingent and not inexorable, and that it involves political and psychological presuppositions that ought to be exposed to more critical analysis"); Frank J. Michelman & Margaret J. Radin, *Pragmatist and Post-Structuralist Critical Legal Practice*, 139 U. PA. L. REV. 1019, 1049 (1991) (noting that "feminists can be tempted into disabling radical particularism").

77. West, supra note 17, at 693 (focusing on a contract dispute and a person affected by an antisodomy statute).

78. See GUIDO CALABRESI, A COMMON LAW FOR THE AGE OF STATUTES 1 (1982) (noting that statutes are the primary source of law in the legal system).

79. West, supra note 17, at 701 (arguing that the decision to follow precedent is a sympathetic choice: "[w]e must understand the subjectivity, the equities, and the 'feel' of the parties involved" in the case relied upon before declaring it is a controlling precedent for the case at hand).

80. See Nussbaum, *Non-Relative Virtues*, supra note 36, at 45–46.

81. See id. at 50 ("Aristotle likes to point out that an inquiry into the human good cannot . . . end up describing the good of some other being, say a god, a good, that on account of our circumstances, it is impossible for us to attain." (citation omitted)).

82. CAROL GILLIGAN, IN A DIFFERENT VOICE (1982).

83. Lawrence Kohlberg, *Stages of Moral Development as a Basis for Moral Education*, in MORAL DEVELOPMENT, MORAL EDUCATION, AND KOHLBERG 15, 62–66 (Brenda Munsey ed., 1980) (arguing that the final stage of development is "recognizing the primacy of justice over all other moral considerations"); see LAWRENCE KOHLBERG ET AL., MORAL STAGES: A CURRENT FORMULATION AND A RESPONSE TO CRITICS 122 (Contributions to Human Development Vol. 10, John A. Meacham ed., 1983) (noting that Gilligan pointed out "the possibility of sex bias in Kohlberg's theory" and postulated "a second moral obligation different from a justice orientation").

84. See GILLIGAN, supra note 82, at 24–63.

85. MacKinnon, *Agenda for Theory*, supra note 4, at 530. Here, Laqueur's work powerfully buttresses, as well as draws on, MacKinnon's insight. See supra text accompanying note 58; infra text accompanying notes 174–75.

86. *See Feminist Discourse, Moral Values, and the Law—A Conversation*, 34 Buffalo L. Rev. 11, 27 (1985) (remarks of Catharine A. MacKinnon).

87. *See* Bernard Williams, Ethics and the Limits of Philosophy 103–4 (1985).

88. *Politics*, *supra* note 73, I.2.1253a3, at 1987. Actually, unlike his translator, Aristotle didn't even get the gender completely wrong. The Greek word is ἄνθρωπος, meaning human being, although most translators regard it as most comparable to the pre-feminist English usage of "man" to include both genders. Susan M. Okin, Women in Western Political Thought 77 (1979). I am indebted to Richard Kraut for help with the usage.

89. *Politics*, *supra* note 73, I.2.1253a28–30, at 1987.

90. 2 Aristotle, *Nicomachean Ethics*, *in* The Complete Works of Aristotle, *supra* note 73, X.9.1180a1–5, at 1729, 1864 [hereinafter *Nicomachean Ethics*]; *Politics*, *supra* note 73, VIII.1.1337a10–32, at 2121; *see* Matsuda, *supra* note 72, at 2350 (noting the importance of education in the battle to combat racism).

91. *Nicomachean Ethics*, *supra* note 90, I.4.1095a31-b13, at 1731; *id.* II.4.1105b5-11, at 1746. This is, of course, the answer to Jon Macey's astute (but pessimistic) criticism of the civic republican revival of concepts of public virtue, that only the virtuous can deliberate virtuously. *See* Jonathan R. Macey, Comment, *The Missing Element in the Republican Revival*, 97 Yale L.J. 1673, 1674 (1988). Macey distinguishes rationality from virtue, a profoundly modern assumption. Reason, construed classically as including the reason of the emotions, *see supra* text accompanying note 67, and the cabined moral pluralism of practical reason would probably be all the virtue required for a civic republic. But I have suspected Macey for some time of virtuous longings. *See* Linda R. Hirshman. *Postmodern Jurisprudence and the Problem of Administrative Discretion*, 82 NW. U. L. Rev. 646, 704 (1988) (citing Jonathan R. Macey, *Promoting Public-Regarding Legislation Through Statutory Interpretation: An Interest Group Model*, 86 Colum. L. Rev. 223, 224 (1986)). (Macey's canons of statutory construction support the role of the judiciary as leading society to a public-regarding outcome in regulatory matters. Macey, *An Interest Group Model*, *supra*, at 262.).

92. *See* Burnyeat, *supra* note 65, at 81.

93. *Nicomachean Ethics*, *supra* note 90, IX.9.1170a13–b18, at 1849–50.

94. Sherman, *supra* note 66, at 143.

95. *See Nicomachean Ethics*, *supra* note 90, X.9.1179b4–80a21, at 1864–65.

96. *Politics*, *supra* note 73, III.9.1280a24–.1281a6, at 2031–33; *Nicomachean Ethics*, *supra* note 90, V.1.1129a7–12, at 1781.

97. The intransigence of gender inequality under a liberal regime is most graphically expressed in the work of Catharine MacKinnon, *see* MacKinnon, *Agenda for Theory*, *supra* note 4, and as collected in Catharine A. MacKinnon, Feminism Unmodified (1987); Andrea Dworkin & Catharine A. MacKinnon, Pornography and Civil Rights (1988); and Catharine A. MacKinnon, Toward a Feminist Theory of the State (1989).

98. *See supra* note 6.

99. I have dealt with this problem elsewhere. *See* Hirshman, *Moral Education*, *supra* note 35, at 223 (noting that in the abortion debate "the hard question [is] whether, against all of these contrary indications of [equality], an upright state must still intervene because of a moral claim on behalf of the potential life"). Even the authors of the bold egalitarian defense of the Equal Rights Amendment would only assert that there would be "many" women capable of meeting the weight requirements of armed combat eligibility. Barbara A. Brown et al., *The Equal Rights Amendment: A Constitutional Basis for Equal Rights for Women*, 80 Yale L.J. 871, 977 (1971). The most recent manifestation of the phenomenon is United Automobile Workers v. Johnson Controls, 111 S.Ct. 1196, 1206–7 (1991) (holding that Johnson Controls' fetal-protection policy which excluded fertile female employees from jobs with a high risk of exposure to lead violated the Civil Rights Act of 1964, because it was not justified as a bona fide occupational qualification).

100. It is interesting to note how this insight has lagged behind the widely accepted concept of the social construction of property.

101. The notion of constructed equality comes from Hannah Arendt. *See* HANNAH ARENDT, ON REVOLUTION (1963).

102. *See* Cornell, *supra* note 6, at 2248–51 (criticizing MacKinnon's inability to view "feminine sexual difference as other than victimization" as a stumbling block to her program for reform through state intervention into traditional gender hierarchy and identity, and proposing instead a program for "equivalent rights").

103. Amartya Sen, *Inequality Reexamined: Capability and Well-Being* (paper delivered at Conference on Quality of Life, Helsinki, Finland, July 1988), *cited in* Cornell, *supra* note 6, at 2251. Martha Nussbaum also relies on the same source. *See* Nussbaum, *supra* note 43, at 910.

104. *See* Radin, *supra* note 25, at 1925–27 (suggesting that society's aversion to the selling of babies may be based upon "a moral prohibition on market treatment of . . . babies").

105. Indeed, both Radin and Nussbaum articulate this imperative in nearly identical terms. *See* Radin, *supra* note 3, at 1723; Nussbaum, Literary Imagination, *supra* note 37, lecture 3.

106 *See* RONALD DWORKIN, LAW'S EMPIRE 228–32 (1986).

107. 347 U.S. 483 (1954); *see* Radin, *supra* note 3, at 1723; *cf.* Allan C. Hutchinson, *Indiana Dworkin and Law's Empire*, 96 YALE L.J. 637, 659–60 (1987) (criticizing Dworkin's analysis of legal integrity in the face of precedent perceived as immoral).

108. *See* DWORKIN, *supra* note 106, at 379–89. Ronald Dworkin has added greatly to the bootstrap effect of his already conservative technique by advocating in the New York Review of Books—a non-technical forum for the formation of social opinion—outcomes dictated by positive law, as if they were thereby entitled to moral weight. *See* Ronald Dworkin, *Liberty and Pornography*, N.Y. REV. BOOKS, Aug. 15, 1991, at 12, 15 (arguing that "[f]reedom of speech, conceived and protected as a fundamental negative liberty, is the core of the choice modern democracies have made" and that it is "a choice we must now honor").

109. *See* Frank J. Michelman, *Law's Republic*, 97 YALE L.J. 1493, 1524–32 (1988) (arguing for a move to a dialogic constitutionalism); Minow, *supra* note 18, at 90–95 (stating that one can decide when moved by competing views because "immersion in the particulars does not require the relinquishment of general commitments"); Frank J. Michelman, *The Supreme Court 1985 Term—Foreword: Traces of Self Government*, 100 HARV. L. REV. 3, 73–77 (1986) (arguing that "[o]ne can usefully describe, and significantly criticize, particular judicial performances in terms of their apparent degrees of commitment to the pursuit of mediative practical reason through normative dialogue").

110. Nussbaum, *Poetic Justice*, *supra* note 37.

111. *Politics*, *supra* note 73, VII.15.1334a11–15, at 2216–17.

112. *See* Susan Rose-Ackerman, *Inalienability and the Theory of Property Rights*, 85 COLUM L. REV. 931, 967–68 (1985) (discussing military service and jury duty as inalienable duties of citizenship); Kenneth L. Karst, *The Pursuit of Manhood and the Desegregation of the Armed Forces*, 38 UCLA L. REV. 499, 523–24 (1991) (discussing military service as an aspect of citizenship); Hirshman, *Moral Education*, *supra* note 35, at 180 (discussing freedom to control reproduction as an aspect of citizenship).

113. *The Garden of the Finzi-Contini* (Columbia Pictures 1980). Jean Elshtain suggests that movies are the bearers of the war culture in our time. *See* JEAN B. ELSHTAIN, WOMEN AND WAR 12 (1987). It may be that this relationship is explainable by the linkage between the flowering of the novel form and the feminization of culture. *See, e.g.*, ANN DOUGLAS, THE FEMINIZATION OF AMERICAN CULTURE (1977). *But see* NORMAN MAILER, THE NAKED AND THE DEAD (1948). I am indebted to Richard Posner for reminding me of the male war novels of World War II.

114. The concept of equal citizenship is the heart of Karst's constitutional jurisprudence and

comes as close as any modern liberal theory to articulating a rich claim to political life. *See* KENNETH L. KARST, BELONGING TO AMERICA: EQUAL CITIZENSHIP AND THE CONSTITUTION 2 (1989) [hereinafter KARST, BELONGING TO AMERICA]; *see also* Kenneth L. Karst, *The Supreme Court 1976 Term—Foreword: Equal Citizenship Under the Fourteenth Amendment*, 91 HARV. L. REV. 1, 5 (1977) [hereinafter Karst, *Equal Citizenship*] (defining the "essence of equal citizenship [as] the dignity of full membership in the society" and including within this principle "not only . . . equality of legal status, but also . . . a greater equality of . . . rank on a scale defined by degrees of deference or regard"). For a recent vindication of Karst's instrumentalist version of military service, see Charles Moskos, *How Do They Do It? Why the Military is the Only Truly Integrated Institution in America*, NEW REPUBLIC, Sept. 5, 1991, at 16, 20 (concluding from a look at the military that "race relations can best be transformed by an unambiguous commitment to non-discrimination coupled with uncompromising standards of performance" and that the change in the military was motivated by a realization that the military's race problem "was so critical that it was on the verge of self-destruction").

115. This is so even when Karst comes out in opposition to the main line of contemporary feminist politics, as for instance when Karst opposes regulation of pornography by articulating the advantage to the oppressed group of not restraining passionate and unreasoning speech. *See* Karst, *supra* note 72, at 138–39 (suggesting that "[i]t is dangerous for . . . women in particular . . . to define expressive behavior [pornography] outside the freedom of expression because the behavior is effective in conveying its message" because women, as an oppressed group, use this type of speech to further their cause).

116. *Nicomachean Ethics, supra* note 90, III.6.1115a7–8, at 1760.

117. *See* Salkever, *supra* note 53, at 244 (discussing Plato's treatment of *andreia* (virility) in the *Republic* and Plato's statement that "[t]rue courage . . . has nothing to do with soldiering or citizenship; it is best seen as persistence in following abstract arguments wherever they lead (*Republic* 6, 503b–504a)").

118. *Nicomachean Ethics, supra* note 90, III.6.1115a23–32, at 1760 (emphasis in original).

119. *See Politics, supra* note 73, III.7.1279b3–4, at 2030. Karst picks up this important point, too, although he does not trace it back to Aristotle. *See* Karst, *Equal Citizenship, supra* note 114, at 1.

120. *See supra* text accompanying notes 97–101.

121. *Politics, supra* note 73, VII.2.1325a6–7, at 2103.

122. *See* TERENCE IRWIN, PLATO'S MORAL THEORY: THE EARLY AND MIDDLE DIALOGUES 15–19 (1977); *see also* ELSHTAIN, *supra* note 113, at 54 (observing that a "tempering of the warrior ideal occurs in the work of Aristotle"). In his extraordinary essay on the *Iliad*, J.B. White has suggested quite another interpretation: that the revision of attitudes toward war begins in the last book of the *Iliad*, with the voice of Homer as the source. *See* JAMES B. WHITE, WHEN WORDS LOSE THEIR MEANING 50–58 (1984). *But see* SIMONE WEIL, THE ILIAD, OR, THE POEM OF FORCE 3 (Mary McCarthy trans., Pendle Hill 1956) ("The true hero, the true subject, the center of the *Iliad* is force. . . . In this work, at all times, the human spirit is shown as modified by its relations with force.").

123. *Politics, supra* note 73, VII.14.1333b21–23, at 2116.

124. *Id.*

125. *Id.* VII.14.1333b39–43, at 2116.

126. ELSHTAIN, *supra* note 113, at 53.

127. *See id.* at 54. Elshtain refers to the role of the common table in the Republic, which is, of course, far removed from Aristotle's views on private property. The significance of the practice in Aristotle's writings seems much greater, since the presumption is against sharing. *See* Hirshman, *Virtue of Liberality, supra* note 35, at 1024–25.

128. Rostker v. Goldberg, 453 U.S. 57 (1981).

129. The opposition is contained in *A Feminist Opposition to the Draft* (authors unidentified), collected in Catharine MacKinnon's unpublished materials for a course taught at the Stanford Law School, Fall 1980, and reported in Wendy W. Williams, *The Equality Crisis: Reflections on Culture, Courts, and Feminism*, 7 Women's Rights L. Rptr. 175 (1982); *see also* Cynthia Enloe, Does Khaki Become You? The Militarisation of Women's Lives 7 (1983) (stating that women's groups opposing militarism "have deliberately devised actions that have avoided top-down relationships . . . because they saw the qualities of equality, spontaneity, and connectedness as the opposites of the quintessential characteristics of both patriarchy and militarism" (citation omitted)).

130. Williams, *supra* note 129, at 190.

131. *See* Ann C. Scales, *Feminist Jurisprudence*, 95 Yale L.J. 1373, 1402–3 (1988) ("My admission that feminism is result-oriented does not import the renunciation of all standards. In a system defined by constitutional norms such as equality, we need standards to help us make connections among norms, and to help us see 'family resemblances' among instances of domination.").

132. *See* Williams, *supra* note 129, at 175 (asserting that women must look to legislatures rather than courts if they wish to share fully in American prosperity).

133. Elshtain sees some pro-military stance in the bellicose writings of the feminist separatists and in the National Organization for Women's brief on behalf of the petitioners in *Rostker*. *See* Elshtain, *supra* note 113, at 238–39. A decade earlier, the most influential piece of legal scholarship supporting the Equal Rights Amendment included some references to the connection between military service and citizenship. *See* Brown et al., *supra* note 99, at 968–69. The separatist writings are, of course, utopian, and of limited interest to an inquiry into community on this earth. The NOW brief, like the Brown article, basically instantiates the liberal claim to equality, stressing the importance of military service to equality, but not addressing in any meaningful way the virtue-citizenship issues of substance. In this, Karst's work is the best example of the genre. *See* Karst, Belonging to America, *supra* note 114 and accompanying text.

134. Note how this discussion differs from Karst's recitation of the virtues of combat service for women: "access to 'society's legitimate, organized, planned, rewarded, technological use of force' is a historically validated road to power in society." Karst, *supra* note 112, at 525. Women's voices are habitually denied authority, which comes automatically with military roles. *Id.* at 528.

135. Elshtain, *supra* note 113, at 3–13.

136. *See generally* Radin, *supra* note 3.

137. Elshtain, *supra* note 113, at 248.

138. *Id.* at 251–52.

139. Salkever, *supra* note 53, at 251 (quoting Aristotle, *Politics* VIII.4.1338b19). Compare, for instance, the supposed liberal "tough-mindedness" about war portrayed in David Halberstam, The Best and the Brightest (1976), with pragmatic tough-mindedness about the nuances and limits of power. *See* Radin, *supra* note 3.

140. Laqueur, *supra* note 56, at 28–29.

141. *Id.* at 34.

142. Laqueur, *supra* note 56, at 42. Laqueur refers chiefly to the *Generation of Animals* and the *History of Animals*. His references are accurate; although he acknowledges some debate about the authenticity of Book X of the *History of Animals*, Barnes reflects none. *See* Jonathan Barnes, *Note to the Reader* to 1 Aristotle, *supra* note 73, at xiii.

143. *See supra* note 61.

144. Lange, *supra* note 54, at 3.

145. *See* 1 Aristotle, *Generation of Animals*, *in* The Complete Works of Aristotle, *supra* note 73, I.19.727a26–30, b6–11, at 1129 [hereinafter *Generation of Animals*].

146. *Lange, supra* note 54, at 4 (citing Aristotle, *Generation of Animals*, I.18.725b6–8). I kid you not. Other reasons are that semen is more "concocted," which I take to mean concentrated, and that women have less vital heat than men. *Id.*

147. *See Generation of Animals, supra* note 145, I.20.729a29–31, at 1132.

148. *Id.* II.3.737b27–32, at 1144.

149. Lange, *supra* note 54, at 12.

150. Lange, *supra* note 54, at 13. For much of this line, we are indebted to the pathbreaking work of Michel Foucault. MICHEL FOUCAULT, HISTORY OF SEXUALITY (Robert Hurley trans., 1985). But Laqueur expands the social positing of sexuality with a lot of impressive research revealing the social construction of the body—a much less flexible notion, one would think, than sexuality. He thus strongly buttresses Foucault's insights. *See generally* LAQUEUR, *supra* note 56.

151. To judge from the readings and responses to drafts of this paper, vocabulary is critical in this debate. Readers have suggested "so-called" surrogacy, "contracted pregnancy," and "surrogate wombs." As Martha Field points out, however, in most surrogacy situations, the women are actual mothers, contributing both egg and womb. MARTHA FIELD, SURROGATE MOTHERHOOD 5 (2d ed. 1990). I'll use the popular term, as Field does, for ease, if not clarity.

152. *Id.* at 7–9.

153. *See supra* notes 116–20 and accompanying text.

154. *See supra* text accompanying notes 95–96.

155. *See* FIELD, *supra* note 151, at 229–38. Field's citation of writings on the subject occupies ten pages in the book. *Id.*

156. For an interesting recent instance of this methodology with more evidence of the relationship between feminism and virtue ethics, see Hursthouse, *supra* note 70.

157. Unless, of course, one buys into the "ominous" totalitarian scenarios of liberal legalism, in which case, of course, issues of the good life are too scary to consider. See *supra* note 6 for the hidden agendas of liberalism.

158. I am indebted to John Ayer for reminding me of the importance of this point; rearing children is indeed a two edged sword in gender relationships; it is traditionally private, yet critical to the public enterprise. *Compare* PLATO, *supra* note 46, *with* NANCY CHODOROW, THE REPRODUCTION OF MOTHERING: PSYCHOANALYSIS AND THE SOCIOLOGY OF GENDER (1978).

159. *See* FIELD, *supra* note 151, at 25–32.

160. Radin, *supra* note 25, at 1929–30 (noting that "the would-be father is 'producing' a baby of his 'own' ").

161. 537 A.2d 1227 (N.J. 1988).

162. *Id.* at 1235.

163. I am grateful to Cass Sunstein for suggesting this alternative reading of the hierarchy.

164. Lange, *supra* note 54, at 10.

165. *See supra* note 156 and accompanying text.

166. That's one reason why the oft-cited hypothetical about the altruistic surrogate bearing the sister's child is flawed. If the surrogate gives the child to her sister to raise, the instrumentalization factor is reduced a lot; in part, it's her own family history and line she's serving. *See* Shari O'Brien, *Commercial Conceptions: A Breeding Ground for Surrogacy*, 65 N.C. L. REV. 127, 131, 152–53 (1986) (using examples of this "altruistic surrogacy" to argue that it does not carry the same risks of exploitation and commodification as the commercial version, and therefore should not be regulated).

167. FIELD, *supra* note 151, at 151–52 (arguing that the choice by a pregnant surrogate to break the birthing contract and keep the baby as her own must be respected, trumping the prior autonomous acts of selling and purchasing the birthing services).

168. *See, e.g.*, Anita L. Allen, *Privacy, Surrogacy, and the Baby M Case*, 76 GEO. L.J. 1759,

1786 (1988) (arguing that economic duress, among other factors, makes the "role of individual free will in the formation of legal obligation in modern life . . . easily exaggerated"); Robin West, *Authority, Autonomy, and Choice: The Role of Consent in the Moral and Political Visions of Franz Kafka and Richard Posner*, 99 HARV. L. REV. 384, 386 (1985) ("[G]ood and evil, and right and wrong, lose all meaning when all that matters is whether and to what extent people get exactly what they think they want.").

169. *See, e.g.*, Margaret D. Townsend, Comment, *Surrogate Mother Agreements: Contemporary Legal Aspects of a Biblical Notion*, 16 U. RICH. L. REV. 467, 476–77 (1982) (addressing but ultimately rejecting a suggestion by the Assistant Attorney General of Virginia that surrogacy agreements violate the Thirteenth Amendment and the Civil Rights Act).

170. *See* Marjorie M. Shultz, *Reproductive Technology and Intent-Based Parenthood: An Opportunity for Gender Neutrality*, 1990 WISC. L. REV. 297, 330 n.93. (This source relates the story of a testicular implant in Europe. But the report is hearsay, and it may be apocryphal.).

171. Radin, *supra* note 25, at 1930 n.277, 1932 n.285 (noting that, given the present gender structure, men are less likely to be considered "fungible" in carrying on the female genetic line, despite the practice of artificial insemination).

172. LAQUEUR, *supra* note 56, at 149. Laqueur's critics, Park and Nye, are substantially less critical of Laqueur's reading of the modern literature than the ancient. *See* Park & Nye, *supra* note 61, at 54.

173. LAQUEUR, *supra* note 56, at 152–73.

174. *See id.* at 194.

175. *Id.* at 196–97 (footnote omitted) (quoting CAROLE PATEMAN, THE SEXUAL CONTRACT 41 (1988)); *see supra* note 6.

176. For a good discussion of the sources of modern liberalism in this context, *see* JULES STEINBERG, LOCKE, ROUSSEAU, AND THE IDEA OF CONSENT: AN INQUIRY INTO THE LIBERAL-DEMOCRATIC THEORY OF POLITICAL OBLIGATIONS 23–51 (1978).

177. Radin, *supra* note 25, at 1887–88.

178. *See supra* note 166.

179. Hirshman, *Moral Education*, *supra* note 35.

180. *See, e.g.*, ALLEN E. BUCHANAN, MARX AND JUSTICE: THE RADICAL CRITIQUE OF LIBERALISM 13, 86 (1982) (arguing that "Marx cannot appeal to the family as a model for . . . communist society because for him the family as it has existed throughout the history of class-divided society is a microcosm of alienation and exploitation").

181. *See* Jeremy Waldron, *When Justice Replaces Affection: The Need for Rights*, 11 HARV. J.L. & PUB. POL'Y 625, 645 (1988) (arguing that the ability to distance oneself from, analyze and even sometimes repudiate intimate relationships is a good thing because it can often enhance individual autonomy and lead to social change).

182. *See, e.g.*, WILL KYMLICKA, CONTEMPORARY POLITICAL PHILOSOPHY (1990).

183. *See* Nussbaum, *Separateness*, *supra* note 36, at 396–97, 410, 421 (discussing Aristotle's "attack" on Plato's vision of unity, and criticizing Plato's denial of the importance of separateness).

184. *See Nicomachean Ethics*, *supra* note 90, VIII.1.1155a1-IX.12.2.1172a16, at 1825–52 (concluding that the most perfect friendship occurs where both persons are good and resemble each other in their virtue); *see also* Salkever, *supra* note 53, at 242 (arguing that Aristotle understood political relationships as facilitating the development of the potential values that are peculiar to each sex); Carnes Lord, *Aristotle*, *in* HISTORY OF POLITICAL PHILOSOPHY 118, 129–30 (Leo Strauss & Joseph Cropsey eds., 1987) (asserting that for Aristotle, "[t]he political significance of friendship consists fundamentally in its mitigation of men's attachment to their private interests in favor of a spontaneous sharing with others of external goods").

185. *See Nicomachean Ethics*, *supra* note 90, IX.12.1171b29-.1172a8, at 1851–52; *id.* IX.10.1170b33-.1171a11, at 1850–51.

186. *Politics, supra* note 73, III.9.1280a25–b12, at 2031–32.

187. *See supra* notes 181–82.

188. John Cooper, *Political Animals and Civic Friendship, in* ARISTOTELES' POLITIK AKTEN DES XI 220–41 (Symposium Aristotelicum, 1990).

189. *Nicomachean Ethics, supra* note 90, VIII.12.1162a16–29, at 1836 (cited in ARLENE W. SAXONHOUSE, WOMEN IN THE HISTORY OF POLITICAL THOUGHT: ANCIENT GREECE TO MACHI-AVELLI 84 (1985)).

190. *See supra* note 102 and accompanying text.

191. *See infra* notes 223–24 and accompanying text.

192. *See* William A. Galston, *The Use and Abuse of the Classics in American Constitutionalism,* 66 CHI.–KENT L. REV. 47 (1990).

193. *See* Bartlett, *supra* note 5, at 834 ("Feminists acknowledge that some important aspects of their methods and theory have roots in other legal traditions. Although permeated by bias, these traditions nonetheless have elements that should be taken seriously.").

194. *See id.* at 834 n.10 ("Although existing legal tools limit the scope of possible change, I think it important not only to critique our traditions, but to acknowledge their useful—and in some respects subversive—features." (citations omitted)).

195. *See* Suzanna Sherry, *Civic Virtue and the Feminine Voice in Constitutional Adjudication,* 72 VA. L. REV. 543, 584–87 (1986).

196. *See, e.g.,* Ronald Dworkin, *The Foundations of Liberal Equality, in* THE TANNER LECTURES ON HUMAN VALUES 3 (Grethe B. Peterson ed., 1990); GEORG HENRIK VON WRIGHT, THE VARIETIES OF GOODNESS (1963); PETER GEACH, THE VIRTUES (1977); NUSSBAUM, FRAGILITY, *supra* note 36; ALASDAIR MACINTYRE, AFTER VIRTUE (1981); WILLIAMS, *supra* note 87.

197. Amélie O. Rorty, *Introduction to* ESSAYS ON ARISTOTLE'S ETHICS, *supra* note 36, at 1, 3.

198. *Id.* at 1.

199. *See generally* Ronald Beiner, *The Liberal Regime,* 66 CHI.–KENT L. REV. 73, 86–92 (1990).

200. JEAN B. ELSHTAIN, PUBLIC MAN, PRIVATE WOMAN: WOMEN IN SOCIAL AND POLITICAL THOUGHT 298–99 (1981).

201. OKIN, *supra* note 61, at 14.

202. *See id.* at 74–109; *see also* OKIN, *supra* note 88, at 198–202.

203. *See* OKIN, *supra* note 88, at 73–96; OKIN, *supra* note 61, at 52–55.

204. *See* Thomas R. Pangle, *The Classical Challenge to the American Constitution,* 66 CHI.-KENT L. REV. 145 (1990).

205. *See, e.g.,* OKIN, *supra* note 88, at 73–96; ELSHTAIN, *supra* note 200, at 41–54; ARLENE W. SAXONHOUSE, WOMEN IN THE HISTORY OF POLITICAL THOUGHT 63–91 (1985); Arlene Saxonhouse, *Aristotle: Defective Males, Hierarchy and the Limits of Politics, in* FEMINIST INTER-PRETATIONS AND POLITICAL THEORY 32 (Mary L. Shanley & Carole Pateman eds., 1991) [here-inafter Saxonhouse, *Aristotle*]; GENEVIEVE LLOYD, THE MAN OF REASON: 'MALE' AND 'FEMALE' IN WESTERN PHILOSOPHY 7–10 (1984); Lange, *supra* note 54, at 1–14; Elizabeth V. Spelman, *Aristotle and the Politicization of the Soul, in* DISCOVERING REALITY, *supra* note 54, at 17, 17–30.

206. OKIN, *supra* note 88, at 79.

207. *Id.* at 79–88.

208. *See generally* RICHARD SORABJI, NECESSITY, CAUSE, AND BLAME: PERSPECTIVES ON ARIS-TOTLE'S THEORY 163–65 (1980) (discussing six "[m]odern criticisms of teleological explana-tion," including "(1) the supposed exclusion of explanation in terms of necessitating causes"; "(2) the idea that [necessitating causes] are not genuinely explanatory"; (3) "the supposition that a teleological explanation must invoke a conscious agent at work"; (4) the "suspicion . . . that teleological explanations are all very well, but only because they are reducible to some-thing else"; (5) the "distinct doubt [as to] whether anything distinctively teleological actually

plays a role in explaining the presence of an organ"; and (6) the "final suspicion that teleological explanations are only second best, that they are rendered otiose by purely causal explanations with no teleological element" (citations omitted)).

209. See LAQUEUR, supra note 56, at 151–52 ("Aristotle did not need the facts of sexual difference to support the claim that woman was a lesser being than man; it followed from the a priori truth that the material cause is inferior to the efficient cause. Of course males and females were in daily life identified by their corporeal characteristics, but the assertion that in generation that male was the efficient and the female the material cause was, in principle, not physically demonstrable; it was itself a restatement of what it meant to be male or female." [emphasis in original]).

210. Nicomachean Ethics, supra note 90, VIII.12.1162a15–30, at 1836; see Politics, supra note 73, III.4.1277b25, at 2027 (arguing that it is men's role to acquire for the household while women's role is to preserve the household).

211. See OKIN, supra note 88, at 80–81.

212. Politics, supra note 73, 1.2.1253a19–20, b1–2, at 1988.

213. ELSHTAIN, supra note 200, at 48.

214. Id.

215. Saxonhouse, Aristotle, supra note 205, at 40.

216. Id.

217. See NUSSBAUM, FRAGILITY, supra note 36, at 252 (citing Aristotle, Metaphysics IV.4.1006a2–5) ("[C]ontradictory predicates cannot belong to the same subject at the same time").

218. Id. at 258.

219. See, e.g., Nussbaum, Separateness, supra note 36, at 417 (emphasizing Aristotle's claim that political association is an association of peers and equals).

220. See ARENDT, supra note 101, at 30–31; see also MARGARET CANOVAN, THE POLITICAL THOUGHT OF HANNAH ARENDT 68–69 (1974) (stating that "Arendt sets the view that all that is necessary for the existence of politics is a public space in which men can meet as equals and begin to act").

221. See Politics, supra note 73, III.11.1281b1–3, at 2033.

222. Id. at III.11.1282a30–41.

223. See Salkever, supra note 53, at 251–53.

224. See id. at 251. The dichotomy is graphically set forth in Galston, supra note 192, at 66 ("[T]here is no moral equivalent of war." (emphasis in original)).

225. Cf. Thomas L. Pangle & Nathan Tarcov, Epilogue: Leo Strauss and the History of Political Philosophy, in HISTORY OF POLITICAL PHILOSOPHY 907, 914 (Leo Strauss & Joseph Cropsey eds., 3d ed. 1987) (noting that the most controversial aspect of Strauss's approach to the history of political philosophy was his suggestion that many past philosophers engaged in "exoteric" teachings ["political teachings which were merely desirable or necessary under their particular (historical) circumstances"] as well as "esoteric" teachings [those that "they considered to be the political truth always and everywhere"]).

226. I am indebted to Ron Allen for suggesting this line of inquiry.

227. This is truly a subject for another paper, if not another lifetime.

228. Whether or which of these developments is either necessary or sufficient for the political changes is beyond the scope of this paper. At this point I assert merely that, as Laqueur has so graphically demonstrated regarding gender, the so-called natural is often less intransigent than the political.

229. MacKinnon quite properly takes on Gilligan, asserting in effect that the different voice may result largely or entirely from having a pillow over one's face. See MACKINNON, FEMINISM UNMODIFIED, supra note 97, at 38–39; MACKINNON, TOWARD A FEMINIST THEORY OF THE

STATE, *supra* note 97, at 51–52. For a graphic illustration of this concept, see GIUSEPPE VERDI, OTELLO, act 4, sc. 2.

230. *See* NUSSBAUM, FRAGILITY, *supra* note 36, at 240.

231. Colin McEnroe, *Was It Ethical for You, too?* MIRABELLA, Nov. 1990, at 130.

9

Aristotle, Feminism, and Needs for Functioning

Martha C. Nussbaum*

Was Aristotle a feminist? In her complex and vigorous essay, Linda Hirshman argues that, despite the evident misogyny and inaccuracy of his hierarchical biology, Aristotle does have a good deal to offer to a feminism that is struggling to surmount the limitations it perceives in

*Ernst Freund Professor of Law and Ethics; Law School, Philosophy Dept. & Divinity School U of Chicago. B.A. 1969, New York University; M.A. 1971, Ph.D. 1975, Harvard University. I am grateful to Linda Hirshman for generating this opportunity to discuss these issues, and to Richard Posner for allowing me to read his response to Hirshman before I wrote mine. For discussions of "Aristotelian feminism," I am grateful to the participants in the 1991 World Institute for Development Economics Research (WIDER) conference on *Human Capabilities: Women, Men, and Equality* and especially to Seyla Benhabib, Marty Chen, Nancy Chodorow, David Crocker, Jonathan Glover, Cathy Lutz, Susan Okin, Onora O'Neill, Amartya Sen, Cass Sunstein, and Susan Wolf.

contemporary liberalism.[1] I am in general agreement with this conclusion: some of the elements of Aristotelian thought that Hirshman singles out for praise are also those that I would endorse. On the other hand, it seems to me that the most profoundly important contribution Aristotle has to make to feminism—which, for me, is his view of the material conditions necessary for truly human functioning—would take feminism in a political direction rather different from that suggested in Hirshman's essay, with its emphasis on problems of surrogacy and abortion. For Aristotelianism, as I conceive it, insists on an exhaustive scrutiny of all existing distributions and preferences in the name of the basic needs all human beings have for functioning. It therefore takes as its starting point (for both females and males) the problem of providing basic welfare support, including food, shelter, and medical care—although it also attends to questions of education, employment, and citizenship. Since one of the greatest defects in American bourgeois feminism is, in my view, its failure (for the most part) to attend to the fact that a great many of the world's women are at risk from hunger and disease, and many more labor (like many males) in conditions inimical to truly human functioning, I think contemporary feminism does indeed have a great deal to learn from Aristotle[2]—who lived, after all, in a developing country, and knew that it was all too easy to be hungry. This sort of feminist (and also humanist) concern does not seem to me to appear prominently enough in Hirshman's account of Aristotle or of feminism.

I shall return to this central point at the conclusion of my argument. First, however, I shall offer a brief account of five ways in which Aristotle seems to me to make a potential contribution to feminist thought. Several of these will be in areas that Hirshman also discusses. I shall then discuss the relationship of these contributions to liberalism, arguing that the contrast is more subtle than Hirshman suggests, and that, indeed, a viable contemporary Aristotelianism must incorporate some elements of liberalism, in particular an account of basic rights of the person.

First, however, a point about biological misogyny. I believe that Aristotle's biology is, as Hirshman says, both misogynist and silly.[3] But its sheer silliness, in a man who was one of the greatest researchers in the history of biology,[4] is evidence that it was not a topic to which he devoted much effort. That a man whose knowledge of marine life was not surpassed until after Harvey should assert that women have fewer teeth than men and that the gaze of a menstruating woman turns a looking glass red—these are facts that call for some sort of explanation.[5] But whatever ultimately explains the fact that Aristotle said stupid things without looking, despite his evident genius for looking, whatever the reason why the body of a starfish elicited from him a greater wonder and attention than the body of the sort of creature with whom he lived, made love, and bore children, we should conclude, I think, that this is not a deep defect in either his methodology or the substance of his scientific thought. It is simply a grossly flawed application of methods that, properly applied, would have ascertained that the capabilities of women were (as Plato already had argued)[6]—comparable to those of men.

Nor should Aristotle's allegedly conservative ethical methodology bear the blame for this failure: for the allegedly conservative method actually prompts a sweeping and highly critical scrutiny of all existing regimes and their schemes of distribution, as well as of the preference that result from and support these distributions.[7] It leads, among other things, to the hardly conservative conclusion that money and possessions are merely tools of human functioning, a conclusion that was almost as radical in ancient Greek society as it would be in Western capitalism. So here again, the failure with respect to women is a failure to argue well, to apply his methods of scrutiny well. And this means, I think, that while we should not forget what Aristotle said here, we may proceed to appropriate other elements of his thought without fear that they are logically interdependent with his political and biological misogyny.

When I single out certain portions of Aristotle's thought as of special interest to feminism, I do not mean to suggest that other aspects of his ethical theory are not also of interest. Feminism needs a comprehensive ethical and political theory; and, thus, any plausible contribution made by Aristotle in these ares is *eo ipso* of interest to feminism.[8] As Hirshman argues, however, feminism has frequently wished to draw attention to aspects of ethical theory and practice that have not been sufficiently discussed in liberal political thought. And in some of these areas it does find, in Aristotle, a valuable ally.

The Rationality of the Emotions

As Hirshman briefly states, Aristotle, above all in the *Rhetoric*, offers a subtle analysis of emotions such as anger, fear, and pity, showing that they depend upon certain sorts of beliefs or judgments. Indeed, I believe

that it can be cogently argued that in every case an emotion has a judgment as one of its constituent parts. These judgments can then be assessed as any judgment is assessed; they can be true or false, and they
can be (with regard to their process of formation) rational or irrational.
Aristotle does not, in fact, go as deeply into this question as the Hellenistic thinkers who followed him—the Stoics above all. And I believe that
someone who wants a good philosophical understanding of this whole
matter should turn to Stoic accounts of the passions, in preference to
any other subsequent philosophical account, for illumination. But what
Aristotle does offer, in contrast to the Stoics (who hold that the judgments on which the emotions are based are all *false*) is a subtle defense
and justification of many emotions, as playing a crucial role in the rational and virtuous response to many of life's events. He argues that one
cannot think well or act virtuously without having the passions appropriate to the situation; and in some cases these will include intense responses of anger, grief, or even fear.[9]

This is a contribution to feminist thought, so far as the contemporary
world is concerned, since in our world women are frequently socialized to
be in some respects more emotional than men. And the fact of women's
greater emotionality is then very often used against them, where citizenship and employment are concerned, as indicating a lack of rationality.[10]
Aristotle reminds us that certain true beliefs about the way the world is
can be sufficient conditions for a response of, for example, anger or grief.
And if this is so, then it is the person who does *not* grieve or get angry in
such circumstances who is irrational. Reflection on his arguments would
force us to call into question the all-too-simple dichotomy between emotion and reason; this, in turn, would lead us to reexamine the strictures
our society has frequently applied against the emotional.

The Separate and the Communal

Another too-simple dichotomy that Aristotle helps us to question, to our
benefit, is the dichotomy between personal separateness and communal
affiliation. Early in Hirshman's essay I find evidence of the simple form
of this dichotomy: she suggests that a commitment to personal separateness as a salient ethical fact is in tension with a commitment to friendship and community.[11] Later, however, she does acknowledge Aristotle's

more complex way of seeing things.[12] Aristotle holds that each human being is, and is necessarily, a "this" and "one in number"—i.e., a definite individual, countable as a single unit apart from others, and living a separate life, with his or her very own track through the world, his or her very own pleasures and pains located in his or her separate body. And he holds that this fact has ethical and political consequences: in particular, that it is a bad thing to pretend (as he thinks Plato does)[13] that the city is one great organism in which the satisfactions and pains of all are fused. Such a pretense leads all too easily—as in fact it does in Plato[14]—to the conclusion that it is all right for some parts of the city to make choices of life-content on behalf of other parts, just as it is all right for my head to make choices about what my feet are going to do next. But people are not like that, Aristotle correctly argues. And because they are separate, each person's life-content does not have truly human worth unless it is selected, in each case, by their very own reflection and choice. This means that societies that exclude their citizens from choosing their own life plan are depriving them of their full humanity. And it also means that society must ask whether *each and every one* of its members has been enabled to live well—not only about the total or average welfare of the population.

On the other hand, human beings are not separate in a hard and impenetrable way, the way billiard balls are separate. They do not go through life simply bouncing off of one another. They need, love, care for, depend on one another in many ways; among the ends dearest to each of them, as they make their life plans, are ends that they share with others, ends connected with their membership in friendships, families, and cities. Indeed, Aristotle is prepared to say that a human being who did not regard his or her life as, in a very fundamental way, a life lived with and toward others, would not even be counted as properly human, much less as good.[15] Properly understood, Aristotle argues, this commitment to affiliation is not in tension with the commitment to the separateness of choice, for the deepest and most valuable affiliations are between persons each of whom is a separate chooser of a life plan, and who respect one another as such.[16]

Here again, Aristotle has much to offer to feminism.[17] Not that he does not have at least as much to offer to males as to females—for males in our society have perhaps been more ready than females to deny their dependency upon others, and the fundamental role of affiliation and interaction. Aristotle insists that to live in interdependence and with shared ends is valuable for every human being,[18] and I believe that he is right. But this is a contribution to feminism in the sense that his arguments can be used to support certain ethical claims that feminists have wished to press against models of the person that stress nonaffiliated independence and self-sufficiency as proper human goals.

Balance of Particular and General

Here I arrive at an area on which I have written frequently;[19] so in order to avoid boring the reader I shall be extremely brief. Aristotle holds that good practical judgment is informed by a detailed understanding of the whole context and history of the problem, including the histories and characters of the people involved, their cultural traditions, and so forth.[20] This means, in his view, that general rules alone cannot offer very good guidance in a concrete situation. On the other hand, it is very important to insist that what the good judge is trying to do, in approaching a particular context, is to realize, in and for that context, a very general view of the human good, which is taken to be applicable to all human beings in all places, in virtue of their human similarities. The view is, then, particularistic without being in the least relativistic; in this it differs sharply from postmodernist ethical views of the sort mentioned briefly by Hirshman and also, though less sharply, from at least some forms of pragmatism.[21] The general view of the human being must be held in a flexible and open-ended way, subject not only to fleshing out from the concrete circumstance, but also to revision in the light of new information or large-scale historical change. Nonetheless, it is a general view; and in most cases the conclusions it generates will be (if specified fully enough) fully universalizable. This aspect of Aristotle (and my own Aristotelianism) is, I think, perhaps insufficiently emphasized in Hirshman's account. Emphasizing it clearly makes the contrast between Aristotle and liberalism more subtle than it at first might appear, and makes plain the difference between Aristotelianism and many more relativistic brands of feminism.

The Ethical Relevance of Contingency

Not mentioned by Hirshman, but fundamental to my attempt to revive Aristotelianism, is Aristotle's insistence that the circumstances of life, including many that human beings do not control, have importance for their attempts to live well.[22] For Socrates, as for the later Stoics, a good and virtuous person cannot be harmed by any of the circumstances of life. Loss of health, loss of children and friends, loss of citizenship, even imprisonment and torture—none of these events can derail the sage from the flourishing life.[23] Aristotle is more realistic and, in William James's sense, more tough-minded. For he knows that a flourishing life requires activity and that it is possible to be prevented from acting well by hunger, illness, injury, loss of political rights, enslavement, or torture.[24] He knows, too, that the flourishing life requires friends and loved ones, and that it is possible for a good person to lose these to death, distance, or betrayal.[25] He therefore places great emphasis on the role of society in distributing these things. Political distribution comes to play a deep role in human life that it could not play in the Socratic-Stoic view: for the things that politics distributes are not just extras, they are things that are really necessary for *eudaimonia* (flourishing life).

This Aristotelian point has, I think, profound importance for feminism. For in Stoicism, and in those Christian views strongly influenced by it, it is possible to separate the discomfort and frustration and deprivation suffered by many of the world's women from the question of their ethical and spiritual achievement. Just as (in *Anna Karenina*) Tolstoy's peasants are almost better off than Levin, on account of the simplicity and poverty of their existence, so too with women's unequal situation wherever it is found: they are not the worse for it morally, and indeed they will, being meek and humble, no doubt get their heavenly reward.[26] Aristotle's this-worldly view tells us that the body is the scene of all our ethical achievements and that the deprivation of resources has not just material, but also ethical significance. It therefore makes it harder to justify inequalities in distribution or to ignore them as if they did not matter to the most important things.

The Account of Human Functioning

Closely connected with this interest in external conditions, we find in Aristotle an account of the most important human functions and what it is to perform them in a truly human way. This is among the parts of Aristotle that most deeply influenced the young Marx, who found there a basis for his criticism of the ways in which labor conditions prevent workers from using their faculties in a truly human way.[27] I have argued, along with Amartya Sen and others, that we can use Aristotle's account as the basis for an account of the "quality of life" of a country, asking what governments are doing to make it possible for their citizens to function in all these ways.[28] There are many complexities in this enterprise: one must justify the list of functions chosen; one must explain the role that personal choice plays in the account, showing that it does not neglect questions of freedom; one must show how certain more basic capabilities of persons give them a claim to capability-development, a claim that plays in the view a role very close to that played by the notion of basic rights in liberalism. All this I have tried to do elsewhere, and I shall not recapitulate here.

The relation of the Aristotelianism we get if we pursue all these questions to liberalism is subtle and complex.[29] It is not the simple opposition suggested at times by Hirshman. It has a particularly close and complicated relationship to Kantian liberalism of the sort defended by John Rawls, both in A Theory of Justice[30] and in other more recent writings in which he articulates further the role played by a concept of the good in his theory.[31] Both Kantian liberalism and Aristotelianism have a fundamental respect for choice; both hold that satisfactions without choice have no moral worth. Both insist on the importance of the separateness of persons and criticize utilitarianism for its neglect of separateness. Both insist, too, on the fundamental role of affiliation and community—for Rawls imagines his deliberating parties as building a society in which they intend to live together in community. I believe that Aristotelianism, with its greater willingness to take a stand on the goodness of certain basic human functions, offers a superior account of the role that commodities, wealth, and income actually play in human lives. I believe that it promises deeper and more accurate criticisms of many situations in which human beings live lives of frustration and functional inequality— including many labor situations and the situation of the family. I also believe that Aristotelianism can, on the whole, answer the questions the liberal will put to it about its openness to diverse choices of the good.

But in one area Aristotelianism must get help from the liberal. For in Aristotelianism, although there is a very general conception of separateness and personal choice, and although there is a rights-like conception of the basic capabilities as exerting a claim that they be developed, there is no account of the limits of government and legal interference with personal choices. Liberalism is well equipped to provide this, and I argue that Aristotelianism should be supplemented with a liberal account of basic liberties, such as the one offered in the United States Constitution. I think that feminism would be very ill-advised to jettison rights-talk or to try to get everything it needs from notions of community and affiliation that exclude rights. I see no reason at all why one should think rights-talk inherently masculine or hostile to the feminist interest in friendship, community, and affiliation. Indeed, I think that careful protection of rights protects friendships and affiliations of many kinds and constructs a morally valuable sort of community. Aristotle's failure to ask what limits on speech, association, or sexual activity a government might legitimately impose is among his greatest failures as a political thinker—and, I would say, as a feminist.

Hirshman's feminism is concerned with issues of importance to contemporary American women, and, above all, middle-class women. It focuses on issues such as surrogacy, abortion, equal treatment in the professions, and the structure of contemporary American gender relations.[32] But we are living in a world in which around one hundred million women who would be alive if they had received nutrition and health care equal to that of males are, in fact, "missing"—victims of unequal nutrition and health care.[33] We are living in a world in which women are starving because their traditions will not let them go outside of the house to seek employment, even though employment is their only hope of obtaining food.[34] We are living in a world in which even women who do seek and find employment are frequently not in law school buildings, suffering from the somewhat unequal temperature, but in the fields, moving forty cubic feet of earth per day to earn a bare subsistence wage.[35] I believe that Aristotle's account of human functioning does offer us a promising way of criticizing such situations, more promising in certain respects than Rawlsian liberalism. But of course, seen this way, Aristotelian feminism ceases to be concerned with gender issues solely; it becomes a branch of the larger critique of poverty, oppression, inequality, and the frustration of capability in the lives of human beings the world over. It becomes concerned not just with gender, but also with class. Its goal becomes the general goal of capability equality, its enemies whatever structures—economic or cultural or political or religious—prevent equality from being realized. This, I think, is as it should be, since I think that American feminism is too much propelled by questions of narrow self-interest, too little by a more generous and general concern for human functioning.

Notes

1. Linda R. Hirshman, *The Book of "A,"* 70 TEXAS L. REV. 971 (1992); reprinted this volume (Chapter 8).

2. *See* Martha C. Nussbaum, *"Human Capabilities, Female Human Beings" in* WOMEN, CULTURE, AND DEVELOPMENT: A STUDY OF HUMAN CAPABILITIES (Martha C. Nussbaum & Jonathan Glover, eds., 1995); Martha C. Nussbaum, *Aristotelian Social Democracy, in* LIBERALISM AND THE GOOD 203 (R. B. Douglas et al., eds., 1990); Martha C. Nussbaum, *Human Functioning and Social Justice: In Defense of Aristotelian Essentialism, in* 20 POLITICAL THEORY (1992): 202–46 [hereinafter Nussbaum, *Human Functioning*]. For a discussion of Aristotle's influence on Marx's idea of truly human functioning, see G. E. M. DE STE. CROIX, THE CLASS STRUGGLE IN THE ANCIENT GREEK WORLD FROM THE ARCHAIC AGE TO THE ARAB CONQUESTS (1981).

3. *See* Hirshman, *supra* note 1, at 997 ("Aristotle's writings on reproduction contain the seeds of both the hierarchy and the proximity of genders. A lot of Aristotle's biology is clearly circular or nonsense or both").

4. *See* G. E. R. LLOYD, SCIENCE, FOLKLORE AND IDEOLOGY 54–56 (1983) (describing Aristotle's work as, in many ways, "the high-water-mark of zoology in antiquity"); Martha C. Nussbaum, *Aristotle, in* ANCIENT WRITERS 377, 392–95 (T. J. Luce ed., 1982) (explaining Aristotle's philosophy of nature).

5. For one sociopolitical explanation, see LLOYD, SUPRA note 4, at 94–111 (discussing Aristotle's writings on the subject in detail and pointing out his ideological presuppositions on male superiority).

6. Plato, *The Republic* 451d–56e. All citations to classical sources refer to the original Greek texts.

7. For a general discussion of his methodology, arguing that it does not rule out radical criticism in either science or ethics, see MARTHA C. NUSSBAUM, THE FRAGILITY OF GOODNESS: LUCK AND ETHICS IN GREEK TRAGEDY AND PHILOSOPHY 240–63 (1983) [hereinafter NUSSBAUM, THE FRAGILITY OF GOODNESS]. Examples of its radical critical potential are given in Nussbaum, *Aristotelian Social Democracy, supra* note 2, and Martha C. Nussbaum, *Nature, Function, and Capability: Aristotle on Political Distribution, in* OXFORD STUDIES IN ANCIENT PHILOSOPHY 145 (Julia Annas ed., Supp. 1988).

8. This is seen clearly in the best recent "feminist" treatment of Aristotle, NANCY SHERMAN, THE FABRIC OF CHARACTER: ARISTOTLE'S THEORY OF VIRTUE (1989), which, accordingly, conducts a comprehensive survey of his accounts of moral development, virtue, friendship, and practical reasoning.

9. For my view of Aristotle's accounts, see MARTHA C. NUSSBAUM, THE THERAPY OF DESIRE: THEORY AND PRACTICE IN HELLENISTIC ETHICS (1994), and, more briefly, NUSSBAUM, THE FRAGILITY OF GOODNESS, *supra* note 7, at 307 ("Far from seeing them as obstacles to good reasoning, [Aristotle] makes proper passivity and passional responsiveness an important and necessary part of good deliberation."). For an excellent treatment of the topic, see Stephen R. Leighton, *Aristotle and Emotions,* 27 PHRONESIS 144 (1982) (examining Aristotle's conception of the interaction of emotions and judgment). On Hellenistic views, see Martha C. Nussbaum, *The Stoics on the Extirpation of the Passions,* 20 APEIRON 129 (1987) (examining Stoic arguments that emotions are forms of judgment).

10. For examples of this phenomenon, see CATHERINE LUTZ, UNNATURAL EMOTIONS:

EVERYDAY SENTIMENTS ON A MICRONESIAN ATOLL AND THEIR CHALLENGE TO WESTERN THEORY 74 (1988) ("When women are said to be emotional, their inferiority is generally asserted, given the general cultural devaluation of emotion."); SUSAN M. OKIN, WOMEN IN WESTERN POLITICAL THOUGHT 238–46 (1979) (discussing theorists who have asserted that women's nurturing nature compels them to put their family first and to play an "expressive" role in the family rather than an "instrumental" role in the world outside). For a pertinent analysis of women's emotions, see NANCY CHODOROW, THE REPRODUCTION OF MOTHERING: PSYCHOANALYSIS AND THE SOCIOLOGY OF GENDER 10 (1978) ("Women's mothering determines women's location in the domestic sphere and creates a basis for the structural differentiation of domestic and public spheres."). I discuss these questions in Martha C. Nussbaum, *Emotions and Women's Capabilities*, in WOMEN, CULTURE, AND DEVELOPMENT: A STUDY OF HUMAN CAPABILITIES, *supra* note 2.

11. *See* Hirshman, *supra* note 1, at 985–86 (noting conflict between the traditional "male" concern with independence, and the feminine desire to preserve the fabric of social relationships).

12. *See id.* at 1003–4 (referring to Aristotle's notion of "political friendships" in which individuals' social interaction is based on valuing individualistic qualities of others).

13. *See* Plato, *The Republic* 464a–e (on the community of pleasures and pains in the organically unified state). For Aristotle's criticism, see *Politics* II.1261a10–62a24.

14. *See* Plato, *The Republic* 590c–591a (concluding that most citizens should be the "slaves" of the philosopher-rulers, so that their lives will be governed by reason).

15. *See* Aristotle, *Politics* I.1253a2–18; Aristotle, *Nicomachean Ethics* VII.1145a15–27 (both arguing that social responsiveness is an essential characteristic of the human being).

16. *See* Aristotle, *Nicomachean Ethics* VIII.1156b8–1158a1 (arguing that the best friendships are based on respect for character and choice).

17. This issue is well discussed in SHERMAN, *supra* note 8, at 118–56 (observing Aristotle's proposition that since friends are necessary to a self-sufficient life, self-sufficiency is relational and the good life is dependent upon and interwoven with others).

18. *See supra* note 15.

19. *See, e.g.*, NUSSBAUM, THE FRAGILITY OF GOODNESS, *supra* note 7, at 290–317 (discussing Aristotle's belief that any judge of the human condition should base his deliberations on practical experience rather than general scientific principles); MARTHA C. NUSSBAUM, LOVE'S KNOWLEDGE: ESSAYS ON PHILOSOPHY AND LITERATURE (1990) (arguing that the most comprehensive and precise conception of ethical understanding involves emotional as well as intellectual activity and gives priority to the perception of particular people and situations, though still guided by general rules); Martha C. Nussbaum, POETIC JUSTICE: THE LITERARY IMAGINATION AND PUBLIC LIFE (1996) (describing how the novel portrays the complexity and inner mysteriousness of individuals, which theories of political economy too often omit).

20. *See* Aristotle, *Nicomachean Ethics* V.1137a31–1138a2, VI.1143a25–1143b6 (arguing that ethical reasoning requires a refined grasp of concrete particulars and that this is given by experience).

21. On the relation of Aristotelian thought to relativism, see Martha C. Nussbaum, *Non-Relative Virtues: An Aristotelian Approach*, in ETHICAL THEORY: CHARACTER AND VIRTUE 32 (Midwest Studies in Philosophy Vol. 13, Peter A. Finch et al. eds., 1988), and, in an expanded version, *in* THE QUALITY OF LIFE 242 (Martha C. Nussbaum & Amartya Sen eds., 1992). Nussbaum, *Human Functioning*, *supra* note 2, also deals with these issues.

22. *See* NUSSBAUM, THE FRAGILITY OF GOODNESS, *supra* note 7, at 1–21 (discussing the role of luck in the good life).

23. For an excellent account of Socrates' position, see GREGORY VLASTOS, SOCRATES: IRONIST AND MORAL PHILOSOPHER 200–232 (1991).

24. *See* NUSSBAUM, THE FRAGILITY OF GOODNESS, *supra* note 7, at 318–42 (discussing the vulnerability of the flourishing life to external forces).

25. *Id.*

26. Here I am, of course, giving the Christian version of this argument; the Stoic version would, instead, stress virtue and self-command, and would not promise any extrinsic reward.

27. *See* STE. CROIX, *supra* note 2, at 71.

28. *See* Nussbaum, *Non-Relative Virtues: An Aristotelian Approach, in* THE QUALITY OF LIFE, *supra* note 21, for representative work in this area and a comprehensive bibliography.

29. This relationship is the topic of Nussbaum, *Aristotelian Social Democracy, supra* note 2.

30. JOHN RAWLS, A THEORY OF JUSTICE (1971).

31. *See* John Rawls, *The Priority of the Right and Ideas of the Good,* 17 PHIL. & PUB. AFF. 251 (1980) (discussing several areas of his theory in which he uses a concept of the good).

32. This is not to say that abortion, equal employment, and gender relations in the family and the workplace are not urgent concerns for poor women in the United States and elsewhere. *See generally* SUSAN M. OKIN, JUSTICE, GENDER, AND THE FAMILY (1989) (discussing gender-related injustices in modern American society). But this part of the picture is not stressed in Hirshman's account.

33. *See* Amartya Sen, *More than 100 Million Women are Missing,* NEW YORK REVIEW OF BOOKS, Dec. 20, 1990, at 61, 61 (analyzing the fact that there are approximately 100 million women who have died because of unequal nutrition and healthcare in Asia and Africa). *See generally* JEAN DRÈZE & AMARTYA SEN, HUNGER AND PUBLIC ACTION 46–64 (1989); Amartya Sen, *Gender and Cooperative Conflicts, in* PERSISTENT INEQUALITIES: WOMEN AND WORLD DEVELOPMENT (Irene Tinker, ed., 1990); Amartya Sen, *Gender Inequalities and Theories of Justice in* WOMEN, CULTURE, AND DEVELOPMENT: A STUDY OF HUMAN CAPABILITIES, *supra* note 2.

34. *See* Martha Chen, *A Matter of Survival: Women's Right to Work in India and Bangladesh, in* WOMEN, CULTURE, AND DEVELOPMENT: A STUDY OF HUMAN CAPABILITIES, *supra* note 2.

35. *See id.*

10

Tragedy, Citizens, and Strangers
The Configuration of Aristotelian Political Emotion[1]

Barbara Koziak

Two issues that confront citizens with strangers—immigration and welfare—are often said to be highly emotional. U. S. Congressional debates
about transforming Aid to Families with Dependent Children and Food
Stamps have included emphatic declarations of the programs' failure, of
their monstrous lure, and of the enormous and frightening escalation in
teenage sexual activity and illegitimate children. Such declarations are
clearly meant to stir emotion, but what emotions are involved and what
is their origin? Do these debates manipulate a latent ingrown human
contempt for those less fortunate? Do they evoke ineradicable misogyny
and racism? Or do they rightly evoke moral indignation at laziness and
sexual misconduct? Or, perhaps, does emotion simply mask interest cal-
culations, so that we should read through the emotional disguise hiding

the rational, though self-interested, reality? Answering any one of these questions would assume much about the nature and role of emotion in political life.

The political realm, however, has often been construed as open only to those who possess reason. In various ways Plato, Aristotle, Hobbes, Locke, and Kant all built their political constructions on a demand for a society governed by reason, apparently maligning emotion. But, as has long been argued, the ancient and modern conceptions of reason are astoundingly different. While for Plato and Aristotle reason is an end in itself, linked to contemplation of the cosmos, in the seventeenth and eighteenth centuries, rationality is instrumental, tied to calculation and material self-interest.[2] Likewise, the conception of emotion has hardly remained static. Early modern rational self-interest was formulated as a strategy to withstand the force of dangerous passions.[3] The emotions were indeed typically called "passions," phenomena inherently disruptive of and distinct from reason. So while there was no denial that the political is often emotional, the hope was to create a more rational political realm and to outfox emotion.[4] Contemporary political theory has not yet substantially left this modern legacy behind. As has been increasingly evident, some political philosophers, Aristotle among them, had a more favorable and judicious understanding of the emotion-reason relationship. As a consequence, the self-conception and contemporary practice of political theory may need to be seriously amended.

Many feminists are skeptical of this legacy's unflattering portrayal of emotion, including the dichotomy of reason and emotion, since philosophers across time have purported that women are unequal due to their emotionality, their inability to reason. If women are not so incapable as some men thought them, then perhaps emotions are not so incapable either.[5] In fact feminist work has contributed to the contemporary burgeoning of work on the social and moral significance of emotion.[6] But in political theory work has just begun on the normative political purpose of emotion.[7] My claim, in this essay, is that a well-founded feminist politics should address how to incorporate and educate the emotional capacities of citizens.[8] This need arises because gender structures the emotions that matter in political life, including the institutions and practices fostering them. In turn, this structuring justifies the gender divisions we still see in social life. Anger, especially, but also greed or interest, have often appeared as the province of men and the animus of political life. The institutions that train and direct these emotions, such as the military for anger and the language and practice of interest politics for greed, delegitimate or inappropriately configure the emotions and practices needed for feminist transformation.

The debate surrounding welfare or social policy in particular, an issue with serious implications for gender, is also a debate about the proper institutionalization of our benevolent emotions, about the possibilities of public, reflective determination of benevolent practices. While some argue that charity and civil society can best handle care for the needy, this remedy often comes down to relying on women's care labor and legitimating the irresponsibility of men.[9] Good citizens, in their capacity as *citizens* not just as private individuals, require both emotion and reason. In the tradition of political theory two options exist for arguing that citizenship requires emotion; one is the civic humanistic or republican, while the other is the Aristotelian.[10] Among the differences between the two discourses is their approach to what has been called "spiritedness," or in Greek, *thumos*. While the civic republican tradition emphasizes patriotic fervor and love for the fatherland, and Greek spiritedness before Aristotle largely designated an aggressive, irascible attachment to honor and justice, Aristotle significantly transforms the traditional meaning.

Elsewhere, I show how Aristotle's work figures in the history of the Greek concept of *thumos*, for *thumos* has been the usual entree for a rather covert discussion of emotion in Greek political philosophy.[11] Although *thumos* is usually translated as spiritedness in the writing of political theorists, I claim that Aristotle's most innovative use of *thumos* is as the name for a general capacity for emotion, rather than the name of one emotion, such as anger, or for one drive or desire such as for honor or recognition, as "spiritedness" implies.[12] Such a *thumos* is an educable capacity that must be trained and organized for the sake of moral virtue—even more for political virtue. In Book 7 of the *Politics*, Aristotle stipulates that the good citizen requires both *logos* and *thumos* and comments on what kinds of things *thumos* does—expressing anger and affection. On my interpretation, a *thumos* tuned to the best political regime would support a particular activity: the benefaction of fellow citizens from a particular emotional disposition. It is the purpose of this essay to describe this emotional disposition by delineating more overtly the political *thumos* as a name for the characteristic emotional response of citizens for one another, one that is inculcated by laws, by the way of life of the regime, and by the regime's cultural production.

In so doing the essay builds on an incipient demasculinization of Aris-

totle. While there are good reasons for categorizing Aristotle as misogynist, there are equally good reasons for discovering in him sources of
resistance to dominant gender modes of his time and ours.[13] The expansion of *thumos* should be seen as part of Aristotle's critique of traditional
Greek masculinity. In earlier writers such as Homer and Plato, *thumos*
most characterizes the warrior, battle is its paradigmatic stage, anger or
indignation its most active emotions. In contrast, Aristotle's expansion
diminishes its militaristic and masculinist overtones. This shift hardly
transforms Aristotle into a protofeminist. Instead I contend that thinking
through Aristotle on these matters can alter our view of the authoritative
place of rationality in the philosophical tradition and illuminate emotional aspects of political life buried and silenced by modern history.

To find the emotional disposition of the citizen's *thumos*, I interpret
one clue located in the Book 7 passage—Aristotle's admonition that citizens should not be cruel to those who are unknown or strangers. One of
the ways to understand how citizens regard one another is to see how
they regard strangers. The way this is put implies that citizen and stranger
are mutually exclusive categories, but a citizen can be a stranger to another citizen, while a noncitizen, an immigration or resident alien, will
be a stranger in a different way. Under what conditions a noncitizen
becomes a citizen, and how foreigners are treated at home and abroad,
reveals what the essential bond or stamp of citizenship is. The characteristic attitude among citizens and that toward foreigners and strangers in
both classes appear for Aristotle to be mutually reinforcing. This is why
it is crucial for him to address the politics of foreign domination, as he
does in Book 7, not so much for how it intrudes on the lives of those
dominated, but for how it distorts the life of the dominators.

In the first part of this essay I describe one mode of cooperation in
Homeric society and propose that Aristotle, in his concern for emotion
and tragedy, addresses the problem of the new form of city cooperation
between relative strangers and between cities, a problem tragedy had itself
posed, but that Aristotle thought had not been adequately solved. This
discussion informs my later interpretation of the role of pity, recognition,
and *katharsis*. In contrast to Stephen Salkever's and Carnes Lord's readings of the political meaning of the *Poetics*,[14] I argue that pity, without
being a derivative of self-regarding fear, represents an opening for friendship; that the plot-device of recognition or *anagnorisis* has particular political significance as the recognition of kinship in strangers, at least as
important as the fear of reversal; that *katharsis* is one path to the configu-

ration of the thumotic capacity; and that this can be best seen by examin-ing one of Aristotle's two favorite tragedies, Euripides' *Iphigenia in Tauris*. Finally, I suggest ways in which this Aristotelian approach to political emotion can inform a feminist politics of emotion.

Strangers, *Xenia*, and the *Polis*

The imagery of strangers is rich in ancient Greek political culture. *Xenos* can mean foreigner, stranger, guest, host, or a friend established through *xenia* or ritualized friendship.[15] Zeus Xenios is protector of the guest/host relationship, itself often part of the greater relationship of *xenia*.[16] Preva-lent among the male aristocrats of the Homeric world, *xenia* was a "bond of solidarity manifesting itself in an exchange of goods and services be-tween individuals originating from separate social units."[17] As a method of creating artificial kinship ties it emulated kinship in several details. For example, *xenoi* would name sons after each other or even become foster parents. The outward manifestation of affection between *xenoi* was im-portant, and genuine feeling often resulted. You could depend on your *xenos* to ransom you, to support you with shelter and food, to provide dowries for your daughters, and to celebrate your memory after your death. *Xenia* was a process of turning important strangers into friends, of, as Herman explains, creating cooperation where none would ordinarily or "naturally" exist. It was a process of creating primitive "political" co-operation that often involved extra-kin and extra-tribal relations and a sharing of resources in a particularly equal fashion. The rise of the polis might be deemed a way for more people to have such sharing of resources and reciprocity relations outside of kin and clan. That is, the drive toward the polis was partly based on the example of *xenia*. At the same time, however, because of its territoriality and greater homogeneity of mem-bers, the polis stood in opposition to *xenia*. A Persian and a Greek may be *xenoi*, but they were not part of the same polis. And, as time went by, *xenia* alliances by splitting loyalties threatened the polis. Alcibiades' infamous reputation as a traitor is a later misunderstanding of an aristo-crat sustaining his *xenia* ties, while trying to preserve his polis popular-ity.[18] The city-states attempted to reconcile the conflict of loyalties by establishing *proxenia*, a decree naming a member of another city as *pro-xenos*, a sort of lobbyist for the granting city in his own community. Often these relations replicated the lines of *xenia* association, since an aristocrat would be asked to nominate a potential *proxenos*, for which role a *xenos* was ably fit. Fifth-century Athens, for example, named ninety-four such *proxenoi*.

The heroic warrior ethos, in which *xenia* originated, figures prominently in ancient Greek tragedy. Jean-Pierre Vernant has written that one of the social conditions of fifth-century tragedy was the conflict of hero and citizen revealed in the opposition of protagonist and chorus.[19] With tragedy the hero had become a problem, a subject of debate for a chorus that expresses anxiety and uncertainty about him. The urge to grapple with the heroic past was indeed the "mainspring" of tragedy.[20] One tension between the citizen and the hero was over the hero's often unrestrained pursuit of personal, usually war-related, honor.[21] The city's attempt to assimilate aristocratic zeal for glory to its own interests is seen in funeral orations after military expeditions, but it is the city and its excellences that are celebrated and not that of the individual dead warriors.[22] Simon Goldhill, who sees tragedy as a "genre of transgression" in which the "tragic texts seem to question, examine, and often subvert the language of the city's order," explores a fascinating contrast between the pre-play ceremonies and the text of *Ajax*.[22] He describes four such ceremonies, but the last, the presentation of state-educated orphans, now young men, as uniformed soldiers, connecting entry into manhood with becoming a citizen and warrior, contrasts with the heroic extremism of Ajax, the Homeric warrior. The ceremonies celebrate the assimilation of the warrior ethos into the city, while the play dissects the threat of manly heroism to social and political cooperation.

Another tension between the hero and the polis, not so often noted, is over the terms and types of cooperation, affiliation, and attachment. The same tension appears in the challenge of gender in tragedy. Both the hero with his *xenia* relations and the family, with its disputes over mother and father right displayed in the *Oresteia*, and with its challenge to political-military values played out in the *Antigone*, continued to bedevil the polis. We in our own time tend to assume there is an obvious complementarity or symbiosis between families and public spheres, except of course when women are no longer able or willing to devote themselves to child-rearing. The polis, with its concentrated and more numerous population, with its aspiration to include more people in cooperation on equal terms, had to develop new terms for attachment with relative strangers as well as new terms for alliance with foreign peoples and cities. One of the

problems for the polis was to judge how to establish new ties of cooperation, on what basis, to what ends. This meant, as Herman notes, "new
ideals of behavior, new points of reference for interpreting the world, and
. . . a way of thinking which took the city as its point of departure." Such
development in the city "prompted its members to remodel their own
personalities to meet these standards."[24]

Aristotelian political theory addresses the problem of the heroic warrior, the more recent problem of the politician seeking public honor, and
the equally recent problem of citizens negotiating the character of political cooperation. With the development of the city-state, aristocrats were
no longer the only class with their own well-developed ties of resource
distribution and security, two tasks accomplished by *xenia*. Cooperation
was simultaneously more widely encompassing and more centralized in
the city center, and increasingly so in the fifth and fourth centuries.
These problems created by these social and political developments required an innovative strategy. All three problems are handled partly
through the question of how to organize the political *thumos*. Aristotle's
concern for emotion indicates that practical excellence (moral virtue)
depends upon right feeling. As a result, questions about how any regime
is to be just, well-arranged, and sociable require deeper answers than
those posed in terms of the right distributive principles, the best relations
of production, or the traditions we should emphasize. A deeper answer
must investigate the question of "personality" in Herman's terms, of the
"self" in modern terms, or of the "soul" in Aristotle's, and especially the
place of emotions. Only then can we address the quality of citizenship
interaction. In particular, the centrality of emotions helps citizens to
determine if, what, and how much they are willing to share with other
citizens and strangers. It helps to determine whether citizens are disposed
to give time or resources to acts that aid fellow citizens or strangers, and
so in what manner they give recognition to others.[25]

Pity

The question of the importance of emotion in tragedy has emerged with
a particular forcefulness in recent years. One author complains that much
has been written about how tragedy reduces and expels emotion, but
little about how it stimulates and sustains emotion.[26] Another claims that

criticism's approach to tragedy has had an "intellectualist bias" neglecting its "emotive purposes."[27] Of course, the subject of tragic emotions has
existed ever since Plato's critique of them and Aristotle's characterization
of tragedy as "the representation of an action which is serious, complete,
and of a certain magnitude . . . through the arousal of pity and fear
effecting the *katharsis* of such emotions" (*Poetics* 1449b25–29).[28] But
since the most influential interpretation of *katharsis* regarded it as purgation of emotions, little later modern work had been done on the point of
the positive value of emotion.[29]

Just as the problem of the emotional is now reappearing in commentary on tragedy, appreciation of the *Poetics'* role in Aristotelian political
philosophy has only recently been renewed. Stephen Salkever and
Carnes Lord produce two divergent political readings of the *Poetics* that
nonetheless agree on the primacy of fear over pity.[30] Salkever maintains
that the context for reading the *Poetics* politically should be sought in
Aristotle's debate with Plato over the educability of the *dēmos*. Unlike
Plato, Aristotle believes the *dēmos* can undergo a *paideia* supplied by tragedy.[31] The nature of this education I shall discuss later; right now I want
to consider the emotive means of that teaching. Salkever believes pity
and fear are the only tragic emotions and that they are particularly "hu-
manizing" because they encourage deliberation. Fear is effective this way
because of the nature of the audience: "those whose self-understanding
and social situation are in a middle position (*hoi metaxu*) between heroic
self-sufficiency and wretched desolation." Such people are not subject to
excessive anger, either *orgē* or *thumos*; they are not "the very proud, the
very angry, and the very manly."[32] Thus, for Salkever, the emotional
constitution emerging from tragic spectatorship relies on a low incidence
of arrogant anger (note *thumos* is understood as anger) and on a high
susceptibility to fear with auxiliary pity.

But it is fear that is central while pity is derivative, in fact the "function or goal of tragedy is to arouse the sort of fear that makes political
deliberation possible."[33] As Salkever admits, this emphasis on fear can
make Aristotle sound much like Hobbes without explaining how Aristotle differs in his view of political emotion. What this essay contends
makes Aristotle different, and what Salkever underplays in his account
of the *Poetics* is the role of pity and fellow-feeling.

Similarly, attention to anger and to fear of anger's excesses predomi-
nates when Lord analyzes Aristotle's account of tragedy's educational effect. He makes the important connection between *thumos* and *katharsis*,

arguing that through *katharsis* tragedy moderates the *thumos*, yet he is incautious about the various meanings of *thumos*. In one instance, he describes *thumos* as connected to the class of passions associated with pain, as having a "simple" meaning of anger. In another instance, he claims the "spirited passions" include fear, pity, indignation, anger, jealousy, and the love of honor or "passions bearing on men's social and political relationship—moral indignation, friendship, the desire for honor and superiority."[34] And finally, he thinks of *thumos* as a singular drive—the "impulse to protect, preserve, extend, and exalt what is one's own as against what is alien or foreign."[35] Such spiritedness without qualification threatens the "predominance in politics of prudence or reason," but moderate spiritedness is the "reasonable assertion of one's rights and interests."[36] Ultimately, Lord scarcely alludes to the emotional experience of tragedy, preferring to rely on the notion of "moderation" of anger and the desire for domination in particular. As in Salkever there is little role for pity; it is only because the "gentlemen" of the regime are kept out of trouble by their taste for culture that they cease their marauding.[27]

In order to correct these interpretations I illustrate the part played by pity and the smaller role played by fear in Aristotle's political theater by considering a play Aristotle uses as a central example. Aristotle finds that Euripides "makes the most tragic impression of all poets" (*Poet.* 1453a29–30), and in his explanation of the kinds of plot devices that elicit the most emotional reaction he lists Sophocles' *Oedipus the King* and Euripides' *Iphigenia in Tauris* as containing the most affecting recognition scenes. Far less written about than *Oedipus*, *Iphigenia* is perhaps too strange, a tragedy with a happy ending, a story set in a non-Greek land that practices human sacrifice. To an unusual degree the play makes pity its causal agent and its subject. Pity and fear equally may have been felt by the audience, but pity alone propels the characters' action.

In the play, Euripides imagines what really happened to Iphigenia, the daughter of the Homeric Agamemnon, after she was sacrificed to allay the gods and the winds before the Greeks sailed against Troy. Some versions of the myth say that just as the knife was over Iphigenia's neck, Artemis substituted a deer for the young girl, whisking her away to the barbarian land of Tauris. The play begins with Iphigenia lamenting her fate as a priestess for Artemis, condemned to perform the sacrifices of any foreigners who land in Tauris. Her brother, Orestes, whom she has not seen since he was an infant and whom she believes is dead, arrives in Tauris pursued by Furies after killing their mother, Clytemnestra, but

Iphigenia does not recognize him. Just before she is to kill the newly arrived foreigner, Iphigenia discovers he is her brother; together they devise a plan for escape from the Taurian King, and Athena intervenes for a happy ending.

The *Iphigenia* begins with the main character in remorse, accepting what she believes is the extinction of her family line and opening onto a community of grief. Iphigenia has had a dream of her family's house being destroyed by a thunderbolt which she interprets as revealing the death of her brother. Her female assistants ask her: "What care is yours, / O daughter of Agamemnon [?]" She responds, "O my attendant women, hard mourning melodies are my task / discordant signing of sorrows / lyreless complaints / the tears of pity" (137; 143–145).[38] They respond with "I will sing you an answering song, / . . . the melody used in lamentation" (179–183), empathizing with the grief for the serious harm of losing a family line when the last male member has died. Despite their sympathy, Iphigenia reveals herself to be changed by her dream's revelation— she can no longer give sympathy. "O wretched heart of mine, you were considered / toward strangers formerly, and always pitied them [*galenos estha kai philoiktirmōn aei*] / . . . But now, by reason of my dream . . . you who arrive from this time forth will find me harsh" (344–52). Before her dream, when she obeyed both divine command and ancient Taurian custom to sacrifice foreigners, she felt sorrow for her victims; now, because of her misfortune, her capacity to acknowledge her acts through emotion is hampered. There is no more woe in her for the woe of victims.

Real danger threatens in Iphigenia's sensing that she will be uncompassionate, yet that sense is not realized. When Orestes appears, long before they recognize one another, his first words to Iphigenia—"O woman, why do you lament . . . ?" (483, my translation)—tell us that, contrary to her declaration, she in fact shows pity toward the strangers. The danger is past and her return to pity moves their encounter. As she speaks, she evokes first the family he will lose, arbitrary fate, and his distance from home, his alien status in an alien land. But Orestes dismisses this pity since her emotive acknowledgment of him makes his predicament harder for him: it threatens to infect him, to make him a coward, unmanly, to evoke his own feeling in the face of death: "Why, mistress, whoever you are, these words of pity [*ti taut odurei*], / thus adding to the pain we must look forward to?" (482–83). Iphigenia does not directly confront Orestes' rejection of her concern; instead, she continues to question him for details of his and Pylades' life, first their names, their relationship, their provenance. Orestes resists being drawn into giving his story since that would lead him into pity and human understanding. Instead of giving his name, he offers, "The right name to call me would be Unlucky Man," Iphigenia replies "Give that name to your fate." Since he wants nothing to do with pity, Orestes retorts, "If we die nameless, no one can insult our names" (503). Instead of revealing his town of origin, he says "It will do not good to answer. I am going to die" (506). But he cannot utterly withstand Iphigenia's questioning and is drawn at least to disclose some news from Argos, and ultimately that Agammenon's only son, though far from home, is alive. Through this encounter, where both want to deny pity, Iphigenia because she believes she has suffered her own misfortune and Orestes because he believes it will leave him incapable of facing his fate, the impulse of pity propels them toward recognition. They reach recognition because Orestes remains loyal to his *xenos* Pylades, who has accompanied him on his journey to Tauris. When Iphigenia offers to release Orestes without Pylades if he promises to deliver a letter to Argos, he refuses. Instead Orestes stays to die, while Pylades will return with the letter to Argos, accepting the risk of being accused of betraying his friend and *xenos* in order to obtain his inheritance through Electra, Orestes' sister and Pylades' wife.

The female attendants point out that both fates constitute serious harms, neither of which is clearly more pitiable. Indeed, the play implies a sort of organization of judgments of pity, just as Aristotle suggests that good men declining and bad men both rising and declining in fortune are not pitiable. Orestes, for example, is pitiable to Iphigenia, for killing his mother (559), while Agammenon is not pitiable (860–67) partly because he himself was without pity. In contrast to the demands of Orestes not to be pitied, the play emphasizes the efficacy of a related emotion, mutual sympathy in collective efforts. Orestes recognizes the women's strong capacity for pity: In order to convince her female attendants to stay silent about their escape plans, Iphigenia tells them: "We are women, a gender disposed kindly to one another / and most loyal in protecting our common affairs" (*gunaikes esmen, philophron allēlias genos / soizein te koina pragmat' asphalestatai.*)" (1059–61; my translation). Even the strong Orestes cannot escape Tauris by swift running or fighting, he must depend on Iphigenia's clever ruse, after he has depended on her pity.

Thus the play revels in the power of pity and friendship to overcome ignorance and oppression. Fear and anger are less dominant features of the narrative. The one eruption of anger by Thoas at the escape of the two protagonists is quickly stifled by the intervention of Athena. It is no wonder, then, that Aristotle emphasizes fear *and* pity as the most overt audience reactions to tragedy. Aristotle sees a congruence between the pity of the characters and the pity of the audience, and the *Iphigenia*, I propose, he regards as paradigmatic for the role of pity in tragedy and in the emotional constitution of citizens. But even if we have a better grasp of Aristotle's preferred emotional orientation for citizens, how is this orientation, especially the occurrence of pity, effected? Here we must look to his discussion of tragedy's plot techniques.

Recognition

"Recognition (*anagnōrisis*) is unquestionably the least respectable term in Aristotelian poetics"[39] and by extension in his politics. Scenes in which someone recognizes their long-lost sister, brother, father, mother, friend, lover, are considered the stuff of melodrama and romance. Just as there is little political analysis of poetics, so there is paltry attention to recognition as an honest dramatic device. If in literary theory and practice, as Cave argues, recognition has become more respectable, there is a similar return to recognition in politics and political theory.

While modern political theory stresses the recognition of individuality, uniqueness, or achievement, Aristotle's handling of recognition involves finding kinship in the identity of the other. The stress is on recognizing someone else rather than winning recognition for yourself, although in recognizing the other you recognize yourself. The failure of recognition is not in being misrecognized, or in not being recognized, but in not recognizing. One may object that the use of recognition, a term from the techniques of tragedy, in a political context has no support in Aristotle even if the tragedy is conceived as offering political lessons or guides. But separating the supposed lesson from the means of its production would be artificial. Nevertheless, there is no simple correspondence between the viewing of tragedies structured by recognitions and political life. The significance can only be disclosed within the context of political *thumos*.

In the *Poetics*, along with the other plot elements of reversal and pathos that induce fear and pity leading to *katharsis*, recognition is "a change from ignorance to knowledge, bringing the charters into either a close bond, or enmity, with one another, and concerning matters which bear on their prosperity or affliction" (*Poet.* 1452a30–31). The fear, pity, and *katharsis* are audience phenomena; they provide the intention, purpose, or telos of the tragic genre. What the audience experiences is crucial for deciding what the best tragedy should be like, but in the first instance recognition is something that occurs for a character. What becomes known is the identity of a person: "recognition involves people" though in the lesser kinds it "can relate to inanimate or fortuitous objects," or to deeds committed (*Poet.* 1452a35). In chapter 14, Aristotle differentiates plays according to the protagonist's extent of knowledge: Medea acts in full knowledge; Oedipus without knowledge; Iphigenia acquires knowledge just as she is about to act. Medea knows who her children are; Oedipus did not know that the man he met on the road was his father and that the man's widow was his mother. Thus what characters know or fail to know is the relatedness, the kinship of someone to themselves. They mistake them for strangers, whereas their kinship dwells inside.

Also important is the dramatic means employed to achieve recognition. A sign such as a scar, a memory returning, and reasoning, may all precipitate recognition, but the best kind occurs as a result of the plot itself. In the *Iphigenia*, one of Aristotle's examples in this passage, it is reasonable that Iphigenia should want to smuggle back home a letter asking for rescue, and through reading aloud the letter she is recognized. The less skillful method of direct questioning allows Iphigenia to recognize her brother.

With the best method, characters "undergo" a recognition in much the same way spectators undergo a *katharsis*. They are seized by events, seized in a moment of shock when they suddenly know their relation to a stranger, know the story of their own lives. Characters become spectators, seeing the life they have led for the first time. The former story of their lives is revealed as false; now they can proceed on the truth of their relationships, their acknowledgment of kinship.

In *Iphigenia*, the two recognitions of course bring great joy, since both Orestes and Iphigenia had been seeking each other (unlike Oedipus who had been desperately seeking to stay away from his mother and father); but they also create the occasion for more spectatorship and simultaneously for extraordinary cooperation. Just after their recognition of one another, Iphigenia begins to imagine a narrative of happiness in Argos, but then the narrative of her unhappy false sacrifice at her father's hand intrudes. Orestes becomes a sympathetic spectator: "Oh, I can see you, though I was not even there" (854). Iphigenia wonders how they can escape, how they can create their own ending: "But now, what will be the end of it all? / What chance will come my way? (873–74). It is now the chorus who become spectators to the unfolding action: "As witness, not from hearsay, I will testify / to these events, marvels and past the power of words" (900–903). Sister and brother tell each other more stories, but the centerpiece is Orestes' recounting of his fate: "I can tell you. Here is how my many toils began" (939). In his tale he reveals that his trial for matricide, narrated in the Oresteia, failed to placate all the Furies. In Delphi, Orestes says, Apollo offered him freedom from the persecution of these chthonic goddesses if he would retrieve a wooden statue of Artemis housed in the Taurian temple. Thus, brother and sister are both spectators, telling each other tales, reliving what the recognition has shown. As Sheila Murnaghan has argued, tragedy and Aristotle's theory of tragedy are true to each other in their mutual emphasis on the displacement of horror, on the "indirection" with which both represent terrible events.[40] With the preference for recognitions that avert imminent deeds, with mimesis understood as mediated representation rather than direct enactment, Aristotle turns plays into "representations of spectatorship."[41]

But in Aristotle's conception the characters are not only spectators; tragedies are after all representations of actions. In Iphigenia at least, spectatorship leads to action. Because narratives evoke emotion, spectators act. Because they were brothers "in friendship but not by birth" (498; my translation), Pylades and Orestes embarked on the journey to capture the statue of Artemis for which they have come to Tauris. Because they created a narrative of friendship through xenia, they are impelled to act together. But the action at the end of the play is Iphigenia's. With Iphigenia's joy upon their mutual recognition comes fear that they will not escape, so her turn comes for heroism, heroism with the cooperation of her female companions. Although she has already said the job of escaping is too big even for a man, and that her death would not hurt their family while the death of the first son would seal their family's extinction, she is urged by Orestes to come up with a plan. He immediately recognizes the alchemic abilities of women with "Women are terribly clever in inventing schemes" [deinai gar hai gunaikes heuriskein technas] (1032), and of their talent for pity with "A woman has the power to work on pity" [echei toi dunamin eis oikton gunē] (1054). It is as though Iphigenia is sketching a model of cooperation with distinctly political overtones. She appeals to the women: "We are women, a gender disposed kindly to one another /

and most loyal in protecting our common affairs" (1059–61; my translation). She acts partly by weaving a narrative, using fiction to put on a
spectacle for Thoas. She claims that because one of the Greek strangers
was discovered to have committed matricide, the statue has been polluted
and must brought along with the strangers to an oceanside purification.
This feigned spectacle allows the party to board the Greek ships and
escape Thoas's anger. Pointing to this aspect of Euripides' play is obviously not meant to suggest we can agree with the character's essential
conception of women or that Aristotle had any interest in the gender
delineations, but that for Euripides pity and sympathy are recognized by
female characters as essential to saving life.

   If characters become similar to spectators by undergoing recognition,
do spectators undergo recognition? And if so, where does this lead them?
I have examined the effect of the recognition on the character in a play
and specifically on the characters in *Iphigenia*. Now I want to draw out
the effect of recognition on the play's audience, its true spectators. At
the beginning of the *Poetics*, Aristotle briefly considers the natural foundation for the historical development of tragedy: humans are typically
mimetic animals who take pleasure in recognizing representations of objects, a pleasure extending to the dramatic representation of human action. The reason for this propensity is that humans enjoy using their
understanding (*dianoia*) "identifying such-and-such as a man, for instance" (*Poet.* 1448b17). Humans take pleasure in detecting the familiar
in the strange; even when we cannot identify an object or person per se,
we take pleasure in the colors or craftsmanship. The natural desire to
recognize the familiar supports the more specific enactment of tragic recognition. The theme of familiarity ties together the ontological propensity for recognition and the characters' recognition of a stranger as a kin.
Although general recognition appears as essentially cognitive, spectators
react to its mimesis with emotion, since reversal and recognition are tragedy's "greatest means of emotional power" (*Poet.* 1450a34). They react,
first of all for Aristotle, with fear and pity, each of which depends upon a
judgment of similarity between the spectator and a character.

   Yet as spectators we do not respond primarily to the psychic life of the
stage characters, we do not "identify," but we respond to events, to plot
structure and in this case to very particular plot structures of reversal and
recognition. This reaction is consistent with Aristotle's claim that fine
tragedy as a whole is concerned with action above all, especially above
character, because "happiness and unhappiness rest on action. . . . The

goal is a certain activity, not a qualitative state; and while men do have certain qualities by virtue of their character, it is in their actions that they achieve, or fail to achieve happiness" (*Poet.* 1450a14–20). In their responses, spectators become almost the characters themselves, but in ways that differ from a simple identification between them. Spectators, like characters, are subject to and affected by the turn of events and the acquisition of sudden new knowledge. Their emotions respond to action and events just as they were required to respond. I say almost like them because spectators are both like characters and not like them; they respond to events with fear as if they were the same and they respond with pity as if they were different or other (we do not pity ourselves primarily). In the same way friends, for Aristotle, are other selves, both other and self (*NE* 1170b7). Our responses are not identical with the characters partly because the playwright plans the story to lead to *katharsis*.

Despite ourselves, Aristotle wants us to see, events often bring us to recognition: in *Iphigenia* a recognition that averts catastrophe, in *Oedipus* a recognition of what one has really done and so of what one was and now is consigned to be. The implication is that other sorts of recognitions, those effected through signs like birthmarks or simply by memory, are contrived and require unusual efforts or tricks. Recognition leads characters to see who a stranger really was, to see their own lives anew, to become a kind of spectator of their own and other lives, and then to act. For the audience, general recognition is a natural inclination that is reinforced by the recognition undergone by characters through the emotions felt at events enacted.

Katharsis

In contrast to the tragic emotions and recognition, *katharsis* has been so much discussed it might easily win the international prize for the secular concept most subject to exegetical interpretation. Almost everyone who has taken up the subject has their own view. Fortunately Stephen Halliwell has been able to discern six broad varieties of *katharsis* interpretation:

1. *Didactic*, emphasizing self-regarding fear over pity;
2. *Emotional fortitude*, a "loosely stoical" view in which the agent is

inured to misfortune, and experiences a reduction in emotional susceptibility.

3. *Moderation*, in which the experiences and actions one sees in tragedy help to shape future capacities for the same experiences and
   actions, related to the doctrine of the mean and of habituation;
4. *Outlet*, consisting in a pleasurable expending of pent-up emotions;
5. *Intellectual*, a clarification, for example a removal of false opinion
   and so of pity and fear for the tragic agent;
6. *Structural*, as an internal feature of the work itself.[42]

Recent scholarship including Halliwell's has completely rejected the
nineteenth-century preference for the outlet understanding, especially
because of its ill fit with Aristotle's cognitive view of emotion, but this
scholarship has not settled on a consensus that would incorporate the
psychological, aesthetic, and political aspects to an equal degree.[43]

Salkever's and Lord's views are distinguished by their attention to the
political goals of undergoing *katharsis* but are less well developed on the
actual process of *katharsis*, eve though they devote more time to it than
to pity or recognition. Salkever's view on the process is particularly suggestive, but I discuss both because they reveal how easily one can stray
from the emotional nature of tragedy's effects. In Lord's analysis, *katharsis*
happens through a partial, rather than total, purgation of pity and fear[44]
and later a "purification" rather than a purgation,[45] but this seems to be
the result of intellectual reflection. *Katharsis* is said to occur when the
audience reacts to the hero, whose story demonstrates the dangerous excesses of spiritedness.[46] Rather than feeling with the characters, it appears
from Lord's language that we learn a lesson cognitively by seeing overly
spirited characters punished. What is crucial is not what we feel during
the play, but what we apprehend, and later what we do with the apprehension or lesson. We learn to see what in the protagonist's character is
responsible for initiating the tragedy; we learn that he or she has the
hamartia (fault) of an excess of anger or spiritedness.[47] The lesson acts to
"fortify the audience" against their own future excesses of spiritedness.
Although he mentions that Aristotle acknowledges that the punishment
is disproportionate to the vice, Lord does not say how, given the lack of
fairness, the lesson is a good one.

Salkever has several alternative ways of describing *katharsis*. First, he
lists three lessons learned via *katharsis* but he then disavows the idea that
tragedy is overdidactic, explaining the educative effect as a "focusing of

concern rather than a direct teaching or admonition."[48] Or, *katharsis* can be understood in terms of Aristotle's distinction between form and matter as the "unobtrusive imposition of a certain form upon a certain kind of matter (the democratic audience) by encouraging acceptance of a certain opinion about what is truly fearful."[49] Finally he offers Aristotle's actuality-potentiality theory as a basis for saying that what needs *katharsis* is not "something requiring purge or lustration, but rather that which is primarily potential and in need of being shaped."[50] Unfortunately the subject of this *katharsis* is referred to only as "that which lacks *katharsis*" never as anything more specific. The ideas of concern-focusing, form imposition, and actuality-shaping are useful, but not without a clearer understanding of the nature of emotion and the emotional capacity.

Salkever's version of *katharsis* generally corresponds with the intellectual type described by Halliwell, while Lord's mixes the moderation and the intellectual type. Their versions differ from all those Halliwell mentions in their specifically political results and in their reference to particular political classes. Salkever's gains credence from the historical association of tragedy and democracy, while Lord's is more plausible if we stress the *Poetics* as elucidating tragic theater for the *Politics'* ideal aristocratic regime. Yet this context would mean that the class of the spirited (in Lord's terms) men are equivalent to the entire citizen class as Aristotle describes it in Book 8. Who then are the nonspirited men? Surely the laborers and farmers do not count as a comparison, and neither do the female quasi-citizens. If spiritedness retains the image of the desire for preeminence, among whom of worth would the spirited be preeminent when everyone in the citizen class was spirited—in Lord's terms? Does he mean that only the best, who are also the spirited, will be sophisticated enough to go through the *katharsis* of tragedy, while the rest of the audience will gain certain peripheral and more vulgar pleasures? But he does not say this. Neither Salkever nor Lord claims that Aristotle thought tragedy could only effect its *katharsis* in democracies or highly limited democracies equivalent to aristocracies of spirited men. Nor do they claim that different types of *katharsis* fit with different regimes. Neither thinks of *katharsis* as an expulsion of unsalutary emotion, but they also do not consider the experience a positive training in emotion.

Yet all that Aristotle says about *thumos* should make an alternative view more plausible. Since it appears there is a general emotional capacity, *thumos*, one that has an optimum ethical and therefore political arrangement, and since the *Poetics* appears to be a prescriptive work, *katharsis* should be seen as ethical and political configuration or shaping, one involving a clear object: the *thumos*.[51] The movement in the *thumos*, the teaching or alteration the *katharsis* is supposed to accomplish, does not involve the acceptance of any opinion, although emotions can be altered or aroused by opinion, as the *Rhetoric* attests. What we must ask here is: How is virtue or *hexis* learned? How is the *hexis* of *thumos* learned? That is, how is the "condition, either good or bad, in which we are, in relation to the emotions" (*NE* 1105b26) learned? Aristotle's first answer is that moral virtue results from habits (*NE* 2.1). We develop *hexeis* by corresponding activities; we become just by performing just actions, courageous by performing courageous actions. Likewise, we feel appetites and emotions in the right way "by reacting in one way or in another to given circumstances" (*NE* 1103b19).

But we also learn or continue to learn by spectatorship. One of the reasons that even a supremely happy person will need friends is his "moral purpose or choice is to observe actions which are good and which are his own, and such are the actions of a good man who is his friend" (*NE* 1170a3–4). In fact, "we are better able to observe our neighbors than ourselves, and their actions better than our own" (*NE* 1169b34). Virtues and their local applications in the right manner, at the right time, are learned by watching a person of practical wisdom, by being a spectator of another person's actions. Unlike elementary schooling, learned discussions, and philosophy, tragedy appeals to us in our capacity to feel emotion, because that is how we primarily react to other people when we watch the stories of their lives. Philosophy can use this, but by itself rational discussion, even when infused with emotion, cannot substitute for a mimesis of responding to people in actual life. Although there are similarities, watching a tragedy is more concentrated and more structured than watching a person of practical wisdom. We do not learn rules of conduct, but patterns of conduct, patterns of emotion, of what can happen when we feel in this way, at that time, toward this person, on account of this reason. We learn, in other words, emotional scenarios.[52]

The distance that mimesis creates, even as it brings us into touch with the other, allows us to reflect on those emotions so that although we may be engulfed by pity, fear, or anger, we start to wonder why this situation, fictional and yet possible, makes us feel this way. We learn that, in a serious consideration of human action, pity is as efficacious and as necessary as fear and that recognition should lead one to feel benevolence. *Katharsis* is that distancing that allows reason and emotion to work closer together in order to reaffirm the efficacy and need for pity and fear as an opening for friendship or metaphorical kinship. As Salkever maintains, *katharsis* is a shaping, but one that acts to shape the general emotional capacity of the spectator through an interplay of distance and presence. *Katharsis* is one means to coax the *thumos* to react habitually well in political situations.

Lessons and Configuration

So far I have compared the treatment of pity, recognition, and *katharsis* in the two prominent commentators with the treatment in the *Poetics* and in the *Iphigenia*. Yet these elements of tragedy converge in the political lessons of tragic spectatorship. Salkever and Lord's treatment of this final issue is governed by their assumptions about the socioeconomic class of the audience.

Salkever's key premise is that, for Aristotle, tragedy is directed to a moderately democratic audience, that it is a democratic audience which is both most susceptible and most in need of tragedy. The focusing of concern constituting *katharsis* enables the audience to "act well, or at least not to act badly" by being protected from a universal inclination to act unjustly, and to learn:

> First, that serious mistakes are possible, and one must therefore act with caution; second, that wealth, social prestige, and the power to do whatever we want do not necessarily bring happiness, and one must therefore resist the tendency to identify freedom and happiness with power; third, that the familial order is as fragile as it is precious, and so requires the support of institutions such as the laws if it is to be maintained.[53]

"[T]ragic art is crucial to the successful actualization of a good democracy,"[54] since it reinforces the disposition to respond to threats with deliberation rather than resignation or revenge on the part of those of "mediocre fortune."[55] Again the dominant emotion is fear.

Salkever's emphasis on training for deliberation accords with Carnes Lord's on *phronēsis* (or, as he calls it, political wisdom or prudence), but they clearly differ on the nature of the audience. Lord argues that Aristotle views tragedy as a lesson for aristocrats: "Particularly for gentlemen who are disposed to be susceptible to the spirited passions and to condone and even to admire such susceptibility in others, tragedy provides, as it seems, a salutary demonstration of their dangerous excesses."[56] More positively, tragedy is an "education par excellence of spirited gentlemen in political virtue or prudence."[57]

Thus, while Salkever believes tragedy's political lessons are directed toward moderate democrats, Lord finds them directed toward moderate aristocrats. Yet the lessons are similar. For the democrat, excessive love of power and wealth are shown to be unstable guides to happiness, while for the aristocrat, the same excessive love of power, glory, and wealth, though euphemistically called spiritedness, is shown incompatible with social order. These counsels clearly involve the arousal of fear, for we fear the repercussions of such excesses, but less clearly explain how tragedy involves pity and recognition.

Neglecting pity and recognition has consequences for a feminist reappraisal of Aristotle. Elsewhere Salkever has argued that Aristotle, along with Plato, deprecates the ancient Greek connection of politics, war, and virility.[58] In so doing Salkever opposes the civic republican, and sometimes feminist, interpretation of Aristotle as a proponent of a public, political sphere superior to a private, economic, and familial sphere. Instead, for Salkever, Aristotle counsels "moderate alienation" from politics, minimizing the public sphere of aggression, domination, and spiritedness (*thumos*), while recommending attention to family, personal friends, and philosophy. In his *Poetics* article, Salkever similarly stresses the moderately semipolitical audience. Lord, on the other hand, believes that the aggressive, spirited, and political quest for honor—read virility and masculinity—can be successfully managed but will inevitably persist.

Yet Aristotle accomplishes something more thoroughgoing than either Salkever or Lord propose. He theorizes a way to reorient political life by educating the emotional repertoire of citizens. So virility or spiritedness is no longer a constant, natural feature of political life, however capable of moderation. Nor is the answer immersion in apparently nonpolitical activities or the tragic spectator's experience of fear. Rather Aristotle, after rejecting conventional Greek virility, incorporates an emotional orientation or configuration into the ideal political psyche, which in retrospect we can claim for a woman-friendly polity.

My account, then, of the configuration of Aristotelian political emotion builds on an interpretation of *thumos* as open to such training and on Aristotle's keen sense that the treatment of strangers was the rub of the problem of polis cooperation. Athenian tragedy pondered the problems associated with the development of the polis, overshadowed as it was by the persisting social values of Bronze Age heroic society. Rituals of xenia had once provided for cooperation between strangers; now the new institutions of polis cooperation needed refinement. For this task, Aristotle addressess the emotions and tragedy.

If we use the *Iphigenia* to understand the *Poetics*, we have to change our sense of the effect of tragedy on the *thumos* or a person's emotional capacity. Pity in the *Iphigenia* accomplishes the recognition; more pity accomplishes the escape that in turn accomplishes the quelling of anger and the institution of a new ritual. The *hamartia* or mistake is not an excessive anger (Lord) or a failure to fear the mistakes of the powerful (Salkever), but the failure to recognize the kin in the stranger. While watching *Iphigenia* the *katharsis* allays our fear of overlooking our kinship, leaving a keenly attuned pity and sympathy as a way of averting disaster. We might be prone to see the scene of encountering strangers in our daily lives as a dangerous moment when we may miss similarity and fail to incorporate them into the system of cooperation supporting the development of the good life. For rulers and citizens these are crucial orientations, since through pity or compassion both must perceive the nature and extent of human suffering, be disposed through recognition to seeing kinship, and act to reinforce the necessary dependency of citizens on each other. While fear and reversal may be half the story, pity and recognition are the other half.

Thus the *thumos* of good Aristotelian citizens, that is, their emotional capacities, should be shaped to feel pity, meaning to feel a kinship with citizens and strangers. Without this configuration of emotional habits, political friendship is very difficult. Among the key institutions that shape the *thumos* are dominant forms of narrative art or cultural production. This lesson is learned through a political reading of the *Poetics* and *Iphigenia in Tauris* in the context of a revised view of *thumos*. Whether anything Aristotle has to say is particularly relevant to modern liberal democratic politics may be disputed.[59] Yet I have claimed that Aristotle is unusually able to trace the workings of emotion in political life, not in the service of helping us to become less emotional and so more rational, but to align our rational and emotional political capacities.

What feminist theoretical purchase can Aristotle's political emotion have? Here, I can merely suggest an answer. Feminist have long investigated the cultural production of masculinity and femininity, themselves a complex of tastes, desires, and social practices. A politics that keeps apart private benevolence and public action reproduces the separation of two spheres: the masculinized world of politics and business and the feminized world of family care and charity work. Issues of welfare, then, are central to the transformation of traditional gender distinctions.

The feminist political theorists who have come closest to handling welfare and emotions are care feminists and maternalists such as Joan Tronto and Virginia Held.[60] Although this genre superbly challenges the central concepts of our dominant political philosophies, it harbors two flaws relevant to the issues of this essay. First, it lacks a theory of emotion that would be able to explain how social emotions and dispositions attain dominance, how they vary historically and culturally, and most important, how political relationships depend on emotional dispositions. Second, it lacks a sustained justification of the ethics it supports and often of the practices that it praises. A full justification would require evaluating normatively to what extent a social and political structure should be organized to nurture particular capacities of human beings, what emotional dispositions are beneficial in a political regime, and under what conditions a regime should cultivate emotions other than those implicit in care, emotions such as anger, grief, envy, and fear.

For the first flaw, Aristotle certainly doesn't provide the only or best answer; indeed, he is far closer to giving a universalist account of human psychology. Recent work in philosophy, history, sociology, and anthropology have made enormous contributions to a historicist account of emotion. But his political philosophy is an inspiration in its continual engagement with emotion concepts and with his sense of the interrelationship of character, regime, and institutions. When he writes that the capacity for virtue is implanted in human nature but needs proper habituation to be activated, he treads the margin among biological, universalist, and constructivist accounts of soul/mind. Tragedy was the narrative civic medium par excellence; it had enormous religious and political authority. For Aristotle, then, it was natural to theorize its emotional effects. If we want to evaluate why caring or mutual aid or benefaction is not a more prevalent concern of our regime, then we should do more than attempt to redraw the boundary between morality and politics as Tronto does. One of the obstacles to valuing caring is the contemporary understanding of the "emotional" and its particular configurations. Feminists should evaluate the specific operations of emotional scenarios not just in popular narrative mediums such as film or television, but also in our underlying political theories, in political rhetorical strategies, and in our actual practice of welfare state provision.

For the second flaw, Aristotle allows us to resist a narrow enthusiasm for care and compassion and to contemplate the ultimate justification for particular configurations of emotional and practical dispositions. He supplies a genuine evaluative language of human capacities, excellences, and flourishing capable of sorting through our various social and political emotions. In his commendation of pity and fear, his identification of the failure to recognize the kinship as a central failing of political emotion, Aristotle ends a debate with the Platonic and Homeric configurations of *thumos*. Anger in particular was overemphasized in these configurations. For Aristotle, while anger remains necessary, and expected as a guarantee of independence and pursuing what is rightly one's own, excessive use of it in domination of other peoples contravenes the essence of a good political regime.

Care feminism, perhaps for strategic reasons, excessively values caring to the detriment of other humanly valuable practices—artistic and intellectual achievement for example. Held's focus on the relations of mother and child leads to her claim that of "all the human capacities, it is probably the capacity to create new human beings that is most worth celebrating" and that the "central task" of a society should be the "creation and nurturing of the next generation."[61] Even if a good feminist regime must revere the labor of nurturing or caring more than most regimes historically have done, it is unclear why it should be central and how it can be reconciled with other potential aims such as economic prosperity, ecological health, and protection of human rights.

Should, however, feminists use not just the form of Aristotelian philosophical argument but also its content, not just the search for contemporary configurations of political emotion, but Aristotle's own preferred configuration? Again, it is impossible even to begin a persuasive argument in this space, but let me suggest for the moment that they should. Where would this lead? Using this account of the *Poetics*, a feminist political theorists should ask, How do we beget public institutions that encourage public benevolence and public recognition of essential similarity?[62] How can recognition and *katharsis* happen in apparently non-narrative institutions? Although our current connotations of pity make it seem a sign of superiority and a mere aesthetic indulgence without consequence, some such disposition is indispensable to any moral action, as I believe care feminists have insisted. Whether we call it pity, compassion, sympathy, empathy, goodwill, friendship, or a disposition of care, one of these configurations of the recognition of kinship with strangers must underlie both a good feminist regime and specifically an understanding of welfare. On the other hand, this emotion/practice is not sufficient for a flourishing life or regime. Fear, anger, envy, curiosity, or wonder, may all in some form need their recognized place. Here, then, Aristotle is clearly a friend of care feminism, but one who considers an expanded spectrum of morally and politically necessary emotion and suggests possible avenues of renewed justification.

For feminist theory, then, Aristotle helps to connect ethical innovations to possible political innovations through his valuation of emotion. If feminist theory interests itself in an ethics that integrates emotion and sees the other-directed expression of virtue in justice and friendship and if it savvy to the social, political, cultural formation of emotion through paradigm scenarios, then Aristotle provides the beginning of an apt analytic and evaluative language. While no one can resurrect tragic drama or any of the Greek institutions that Aristotle lauded, feminists can start to think how, in a greatly historically altered period, we might identify, evaluate, and reconfigure political emotions.

Notes

1. I am grateful to the National Endowment for the Humanities for research support and to Sarah Winter and Romand Coles for perceptive comments. A version of this article was presented at the 1996 American Political Science Association Annual Meeting.

2. See Charles Taylor, *Sources of the Self: The Making of the Modern Identity* (Cambridge: Harvard University Press, 1989).

3. This history is explored in Albert O. Hirschman, *The Passions and the Interests* (Princeton: Princeton University Press, 1978).

4. This is particularly true of liberal political theory, see Stephen Holmes, *Passions and Constraints* (Cambridge: Harvard University Press, 1985).

5. Mary Daly, *Gyn/Ecology: The Metaethics of Radical Feminism* (Boston: Beacon, 1978) and *Pure Lust: Elemental Feminist Philosophy* (Boston: Beacon, 1984); Susan Griffin, *Woman and Nature* (New York: Harper and Row, 1980); Joan Cocks, "Wordless Emotions: Some Critical Reflections on Radical Feminism," *Politics and Society* 13, no. 1 (1984); Alison Jaggar, "Love and Knowledge: Emotion in Feminist Epistemology," in *Gender/Body/Knowledge: Feminist Reconstructions of Being and Knowing*, ed. Alison Jaggar and Susan Bordo (New Brunswick: Rutgers University Press, 1989); Arlene Russell Hochschild, *The Managed Heart: Commercialization of Human Feeling* (Berkeley and Los Angeles: University of California Press, 1983); Genevieve

Lloyd, *The Man of Reason: "Male" and "Female" in Western Philosophy*, 2d ed. (Minneapolis: University of Minnesota Press, 1993).

6. See, for example, Robert C. Solomon, *The Passions* (New York: Doubleday, 1977); William Lyons, *Emotion* (London: Cambridge University Press, 1980); Amélie Rorty, ed., *Explaining Emotions* (Berkeley and Los Angeles: University of California Press, 1980); Cheshire Calhoun and Robert Solomon, eds., *What is an Emotion? Classic Readings in Philosophical Psychology* (New York: Oxford University Press, 1984); Rom Harre, ed., *The Social Construction of Emotions* (Oxford: Basil Blackwell, 1986); Carol A. Stearns and Peter N. Stearns, *Emotion and Social Change: Toward a New Psychohistory* (New York: Holmes and Meier, 1988); Ronald de Sousa, *The Rationality of Emotion* (Cambridge: MIT Press, 1990); Justin Oakley, *Morality and the Emotions* (New York: Routledge, 1992); Joel Pfister and Nancy Schnog, eds., *Inventing the Psychological: Towards a History of Emotional Life in America* (New Haven: Yale University Press, 1997).

7. For some exceptions see Susan Okin, "Reason and Feeling in Thinking about Justice" *Ethics* 99, no. 2 (1989): 229–49; and Joan Tronto, *Moral Boundaries* (New York: Routledge, 1993); Morwenna Griffiths, *Feminisms and the Self: The Web of Identity* (New York: Routledge, 1995); Robert Solomon, *A Passion for Justice: Emotions and the Origins of the Social Contract* (Reading, Mass: Addison-Wesley, 1990); Stephen Holmes, *Passions and Constraints*; Albert Hirschman, *Passions and the Interests* (Princeton: Princeton University Press, 1977); Michael Ignatieff, *The Needs of Strangers* (New York: Penguin, 1982).

8. Although I shall continue to use the words "emotion" and "reason" suggesting two separate capacities, I certainly allow for a great deal of interrelationship or even identity between the two. Whether these categories are philosophically, psychologically, or historically adequate, or whether we should significantly blur if not renounce the distinction is a huge question. I can say that in the cognitivist interpretation of emotion, which traces its beginnings to Aristotle, emotions are partly distinguished by their rational beliefs whether factual or evaluative. See Lyons, *Emotion* and De Sousa, *The Rationality of Emotion*.

9. While middle- and upper-class women are encouraged to do charity work by a gender ideology, lower-class women and men and women of color do care work more due to material necessity. According to Lori Ginzberg, in the United States nineteenth-century culture particular merged femininity and charity: "[M]iddle- and upper-class women of the antebellum era shared a language that described their benevolent work as Christian, their means as fundamentally moral, and their mandate as uniquely feminine." See *Women and the Work of Benevolence: Morality, Political, and Class in the Nineteenth-Century United States* (New Haven: Yale University Press, 1990). See also Joan Tronto, *Moral Boundaries: A Political Argument for an Ethic of Care* (New York: Routledge, 1993), on the prevalence of women and men of color and of working-class women in care-giving.

10. For the central text in the contemporary revival of civic republicanism, see J. G. A. Pocock, *The Machiavellian Moment: Florentine Political Thought and the Atlantic Republican Tradition* (Princeton: Princeton University Press, 1975).

11. Barbara Koziak, *Retrieving Political Emotion: Thumos, Aristotle, and Contemporary Gender* (University Park: Penn State Press, forthcoming). For an earlier treatment of *thumos* in political theory see Catherine Zuckert, ed., *Understanding the Political Spirit: Philosophical Investigations from Socrates to Nietzsche* (New Haven: Yale University Pres, 1988).

12. Up until very recently the only work to examine Aristotle's view on emotion was W. W. Fortenbaugh, *Aristotle On Emotion: A Contribution to Philosophical Psychology, Rhetoric, Poetics, Politics and Ethics* (London: Duckworth, 1975). Then came Martha Nussbaum's *Fragility of Goodness: Luck and Ethics in Greek Tragedy and Philosophy* (Princeton: Princeton University Press, 1986) and later her *Therapy of Desire: Theory and Practice in Hellenistic Ethics* (Princeton: Princeton University Press, 1994). Just recently a wealth of new work has appeared. See the

articles by Leighton, Cooper, Frede, and Striker in *Essays on Aristotle's Rhetoric*, ed. Amélie Oksenberg Rorty (Berkeley and Los Angeles: University of California Press, 1996). From a feminist perspective see Deborah Achtenberg, "Aristotelian Resources for Feminist Thinking"; and Marcia Homiak, "Feminism and Aristotle's Rational Ideal," in *Feminism and Ancient Philosophy*, ed. Julie K. Ward (New York: Routledge, 1996).

13. See the revisionist views of Stephen Salkever in chapter 4 of *Finding the Mean: Theory and Practice in Aristotelian Political Philosophy* (Princeton: Princeton University Press, 1990); and in Arlene Saxonhouse, *Women in the History of Political Thought: Ancient Greece to Machiavelli* (New York: Praeger, 1985).

14. Stephen Salkever, "Tragedy and the Education of the Demos: Aristotle's Response to Plato," in *Greek Tragedy and Political Theory*, ed. J. Peter Euben (Berkeley and Los Angeles: University of California Press, 1986); Carnes Lord, *Education and Culture in Political Thought of Aristotle* (Ithaca: Cornell University Press, 1982).

15. For this account, I rely on Gabriel Herman, *Ritualised Friendship and the Greek City* (Cambridge: Cambridge University Press, 1987).

16. See Walter Burkert, *Greek Religion: Archaic and Classical*, trans. John Raffan (Cambridge: Harvard University Press, 1985), 130 and 248; and Jon D. Mikalson, *Honor Thy Gods: Popular Religions in Greek Tragedy* (Chapel Hill, University of North Carolina Press, 1991), 77ff.

17. Herman, *Ritualized Friendship and the Greek City*, 10.

18. Ibid., 159.

19. Jean-Pierre Vernant and Pierre Vidal-Naquet, *Myth and Tragedy in Ancient Greece*, trans. Janet Lloyd (New York: Zone Books, 1990), 24–25 and 242.

20. Ibid., 28.

21. Ajax is such a character; see David J. Bradshaw, "The Ajax Myth and the Polis: Old Values and New," in *Myth and the Polis*, ed. Dora C. Pozzi and John Wickersham (Ithaca: Cornell University Press, 1991), 99–125; and Wm. Blake Tyrrell and Frieda S. Brown, *Athenian Myths and Institutions* (Oxford: Oxford University Press, 1991), 73–98.

22. See Nicole Loraux, *The Invention of Athens*, trans. Alan Sheridan (Cambridge: Harvard University Press, 1986).

23. Simon Goldhill, "The Great Dionysia and Civic Ideology," in *Nothing to do with Dionysos?* ed. John Winkler and Froma Zeitlin (Princeton: Princeton University Press, 1990), 97–129. For similar views see J. Peter Euben, "Introduction," in *Greek Tragedy and Political Theory*.

24. Herman, *Ritualised Friendship and the Greek City*, 159.

25. Plato himself is concerned about the disintegrative effects of private families and private property among the ruling classes. Yet his goal is less to allow all to flourish and more to guarantee the rule of reason. Aristotle who articulates the telos of flourishing on the shoulders of Plato, appropriately criticizes the *Republic's* elimination of personal possession and responsibility.

26. W. B. Stanford, *Greek Tragedy and the Emotions* (London: Routledge and Kegan Paul, 1982), 2.

27. Malcolm Heath, *The Poetics of Greek Tragedy* (Stanford: Stanford University Press, 1987), 79.

28. Quotations are from *The Poetics of Aristotle: Translation and Commentary*, trans. Stephen Halliwell (Chapel Hill: University of North Carolina Press, 1987).

29. J. Bernays, "Aristotle on the Effect of Tragedy," trans. J. and Barnes from *Zwei Abhandlungen über der aristotelische Theorie des Drama* (Berlin, 1880, first published Breslau, 1857) in Barnes et al., *Articles on Aristotle*, vol. 4 (New York, 1979).

30. Stephen Salkever, "Tragedy and the Education of the *Demos*," in *Political Theory and*

Greek Tragedy, ed. J. Peter Euben (Berkeley and Los Angeles: University of California Press, 1986), 274–303; Carnes Lord, *Education and Culture in the Political Thought of Aristotle* (Ithaca: Cornell University Press, 1982).

31. Salkever, "Tragedy," 301.

32. Ibid., 295.

33. Ibid., 294 and 295.

34. Lord., *Education and Culture*, 161.

35. Ibid., 195.

36. Ibid., 164 and 193 n. 16.

37. Ibid., 202.

38. Translations, unless otherwise noted, are from Euripides, *Iphigeneia in Tauris*, trans. Richmond Lattimore (New York: Oxford University Press, 1973). For the Greek I rely on *Euripides Fabulae*, vol. 2, ed. John Diggle, (Oxford: Oxford University Press, 1981). Hereafter cited by line numbers referring to the Greek text.

39. Terence Cave, *Recognitions: A Study in Poetics* (Oxford: Clarendon Press, 1988), 1.

40. Sheila Murnaghan, "Sucking the Juice without Biting the Rind: Aristotle and Tragic Mimesis," *New Literary History* 26 (Autumn 1995): 755–73.

41. Ibid., 770.

42. See Stephen Halliwell's excellent summary in *Aristotle's Poetics* (Chapel Hill: University of North Carolina Press, 1986), 350–56. He himself favors the moderation view, which involves "psychological attunement or balance, not one of simple or invariable reduction" (352). It rests on Aristotle's theory of habituation and may result in some cases for those who need it in a "heightened capacity for emotion."

43. See also the recent views of Jonathan Lear, "Katharsis"; Richard Janko, "From Catharsis to Aristotelian Mean"; and Alexander Nehamas, "Pity and Fear in the *Rhetoric* and the *Poetics*," in *Essays on Aristotle's Poetics*, ed. Amélie Oksenberg Rorty (Princeton: Princeton University Press, 1992). Nussbaum also discusses *katharsis* in *Fragility of Goodness*; see note 49.

44. Lord, *Education and Culture*, 159.

45. Ibid., 164.

46. Ibid., 173.

47. Ibid., 171.

48. Salkever, "Tragedy," 300.

49. Ibid., 300.

50. Ibid., 301.

51. In the *Fragility of Goodness*, Martha Nussbaum likewise stresses the emotions as keys to understanding *katharsis*. On her reading, *katharsis* is a "clarification" through the emotional response of pity and fear of our common vulnerability (390). She adds that it would be a mistake to take this definition as implying an instrumental use of emotion to reach rational enlightenment. Emotions are necessary for perception and good judgment (307–9). My account builds on hers, adding to clarification the notion of emotional shaping, or configuration, through the habituation of emotions.

52. See de Sousa, *The Rationality of Emotion*, for an account of "paradigm scenarios" and Catherine A. Lutz, *Unnatural Emotion: Everyday Sentiments on a Micronesian Atoll and their Challenge to Western Theory* (Chicago: University of Chicago Press, 1988) where she writes: "In each cultural community there will be one or more 'scenes' identified as prototypic or classic or best examples of particular emotions. . . . The scenes each emotion concept evokes are most typically social scenes involving relations between two or more individuals. The emotions can be seen as sociocultural achievements in the fundamental sense that they characterize and create a relationship between individuals and groups" (211).

53. Salkever, "Tragedy," 300.

54. Ibid., 303.

55. Ibid., 295–96.

56. Lord, *Education and Culture*, 173.

57. Ibid., 164.

58. See chapter 4 of Salkever's *Finding the Mean*.

59. For critics of such relevance see Stephen Holmes, "Aristippus in and out of Athens," *American Political Science Review* 73 (March 1979): 113–28; and John Wallach, "Contemporary Aristotelianism," *Political Theory* 20 (November 1992): 613–41. For supporters see Steven Salkever, *Finding the Mean*, and Martha Nussbaum, "Aristotelian Social Democracy" in *Liberalism and the Good*, ed. R. Bruce Douglass, Gerald M. Mara, and Henry Richardson (New York: Routledge, 1990).

60. Joan Tronto, *Moral Boundaries: A Political Argument for an Ethic of Care* (New York: Routledge, 1993); and Virginia Held, *Feminist Morality: Transforming Culture, Society, and Politics* (Chicago: University of Chicago Press, 1993).

61. Held, *Feminist Morality*, 81 and 159.

62. This suggestion might be startling in the midst of a trend in feminist theory, and to some extent in feminist practice, that converges on "difference" rather than similarity. Feminists have argued that 1970s American feminism neglected race, class, and ethnic difference, with some additionally arguing that the category "woman" itself is part of a heterosexual matrix, without a stable, unified content. In effect, the experience and hopes of women are so different that the future existence of "feminism" itself is questioned. Although I believe this is a deeply important issue, in this space I can only say that a median must be struck. Some issues—"welfare," for example—require both respect for differential needs and a capacity to feel the moral impact of these needs. This capacity, in turn, arises from emotively crossing perceptions of difference to find similarity. For support, I recommend Anne Phillips's cogent "Universal Pretensions in Political Thought," in *Destabilizing Theory: Contemporary Feminist Debates*, ed. Michelle Barrett and Anne Phillips (Stanford: Stanford University Press, 1992).

11

Feminism and the Narrative Structures of the *Poetics*[1]

Angela Curran

> Of all things which are living and can form a judgment
> We women are the most unfortunate creatures.
> —Medea, from Euripides' *Medea*.[2]

In fifth-century Athens a good woman was expected to live confined to the household, devoting herself to it and to her family's well-being.[3] Ancient Greek tragedy, however, showed women acting and speaking in ways that departed from the norm in real life. In Sophocles' *Antigone*, for example, a female character is shown criticizing the male world for failure to balance family and civic interests. In Aeschylus's *Agamemnon*, Clytemnestra redresses her husband's sacrifice of their daughter Iphigenia. And to take a more extreme example, Euripides' *Medea* dramatizes a woman who avenges her husband's infidelity by killing his mistress and her own children.

Despite these examples of strong women characters, ancient Greek tragedy has come under heavy criticism by feminists, who find that it presents views of women that are problematic. As Helene Foley comments, "For every action a tragic woman takes in her own interest—every action outside of self-sacrifice for family or community—receives explicit criticism within the plays as unfeminine and has destructive consequences."[4] Feminist drama critic Froma Zeitlin questions whether Greek tragedy contains any strong women characters at all, arguing that from the point of view of plot, women are always introduced not as characters-in-themselves but as plot-devices who "play the roles of catalysts, agents, instruments, blockers, spoilers, destroyers and sometimes helpers or saviors for the male characters."[5] Yet classicist Bernard Knox suggests that ancient Greek tragedy has a subversive potential for feminism, arguing that it presents, "a picture of the wife and mother in that confined space where she is both queen and prisoner very different from that suggested by the bland eulogies of the funeral inscriptions. It suggests, what one would in fact have suspected, that in many cases the result of confining a wife to the house, the slaves, and the children was to create a potentially dangerous, explosive force."[6]

Knox's remarks point to a reading of Greek tragedies with women protagonists that I develop in this paper. My proposal involves, first, a feminist critical response to Aristotle's famous discussion of best tragic plot patterns in *Poetics* 13 and 14; and second, the presentation of a feminist alternative reading of ancient Greek tragedies with women protagonists. This proposal, which I call a "feminist re-reading" of Greek tragedy, reverses the tradition initiated by Aristotle of selecting as best tragedies ones that involve the *hamartia* (error) of an individual, and instead looks at how these women's tragedies focus on the social context of patriarchy as a source of misfortune for the women protagonists and at how the action of the tragedy reveals that this is so.

This "re-reading" proposal is similar in its spirit to Bertolt Brecht's famous criticisms of Aristotelian "dramatic" theater and to Brecht's own view of "epic" theater, in its emphasis on producing readings by the viewer, which highlight the social context rather than particular actions of an individual. Brecht's criticisms of Aristotle's view and his own aesthetics of drama can be seem in the following passage:

> The dramatic theater's spectator says: Yes, I have felt like that too—Just like me—its only natural—It'll never change—The sufferings of this man appall me, because they are inescapable—That's great art; it all seems the most obvious thing in the world—I weep when they weep, I laugh when they laugh. The

epic theatre's spectator says: I'd never have thought it—That's not the way—That's extraordinary, hardly believable—It's got to stop—The sufferings of this man appall me, because they are un-necessary—that's great art; nothing obvious in it—I laugh when they weep, I weep when they laugh.[8]

Here Brecht criticizes "dramatic" theater for having a form and content that deflects the viewer's critical attention away from considering how oppressive social structures make for human suffering, rather than human nature or a course of events outside the tragic protagonist's control. Be-cause Brecht thought that empathy with characters led the viewer to "submit uncritically" to the social messages contained in a drama, he says that rather than empathizing with the tragic characters, it is necessary for the spectator to "distance" herself from the characters and situations represented—"weeping when they laugh"—to maintain a critical atti-tude toward the events and social messages the drama represents. In con-trast, Brecht's own Marxist "epic" theater aimed for plays with form and content that aided viewers in considering how capitalism's social hierar-chies make for human misery and conflict, thereby readying them for political action.

My feminist re-reading proposal is Brechtian in spirit insofar as it sug-gests that it is the social context, rather than individual error, that is the source of tragedy for women protagonists. I also use Aristotle to make a feminist correction to Brecht's view that drama cannot engage both our emotions and our capacity for reflection, while faulting him for preferring tragedy that deflects critical attention onto the individual and away from oppressive social structures as the source of misfortune in tragedy.[9]

I first examine Aristotle's view of best tragedy, look at why tragedies with women protagonists get eliminated from his preferred tragedies, and critically examine his view that the best tragic plots—the ones that en-gage us the most—are those in which the tragic protagonist's *hamartia* contributes to her misfortune. I then present my proposed feminist method of "re-reading" Greek tragedy. I contrast it to other feminist approaches to tragedy, discuss some methodological principles involved in producing this reading, and illustrate my proposal with some readings of Greek tragedies about women. In my conclusion, I discuss the connec-tion between the aesthetic tradition Aristotle initiated and recent discus-sions in feminist aesthetics.

Aristotle's Theory of Best Tragedy

Aristotle's preferred plot-patterns

In *Poetics* 6 Aristotle defines tragedy as an imitation or representation (*mimesis*) of action and life. The end of all human life is happiness (*eudaimonia*) and it depends upon people's actions (50a19), so plot—which Aristotle defines as the representation of action—will be the most important feature and is "the originating principle and soul of tragedy" (50a38–39). On the analogy with biological organisms, he says that tragedy has a final purpose or end (*telos*) and that is to inspire a catharsis (literally "purification") of pity and fear by means of representation (53b12) and to give pleasure from experiencing their relief (49b25).

In *Poetics* 4, Aristotle suggests that poetry, of which tragedy is a subgenre, gives pleasure through dramatizations that involve some kind of learning or understanding (1448b4–19). Although we shall need to get clear on Aristotle's view of just what kind of learning tragedy gives, for now let us note that he suggests that poetry gives some kind of pleasurable learning through its representations of human actions and the misfortune and suffering that can accompany them.

In *Poetics* 13 and 14, Aristotle tells us which plot-patterns on his view are the best ones for achieving a catharsis of emotions in the audience. With this comes his view about the proper sort of *hamartia* or error that brings about (or threatens to bring about) the tragic misfortune. The meaning of Aristotle's use of *"hamartia"* is hotly contested, even though much has been written on this. Commentators have suggested that by *hamartia*, Aristotle means "character flaw," "mistake of fact," or a range of error that includes moral failure as well as mistake of fact.[10] Part of the difficulty in interpreting Aristotle's meaning of *"hamartia,"* I believe, comes from the fact that the two chapters seem to be inconsistent in characterizing tragic error. Aristotle's discussion of tragic error in Chapter 13 links tragic error with character, whereas his remarks in Chapter 14 suggest that *hamartia* is ignorance of fact. This tension seems to arise because Aristotle is trying to address two different concerns in each chapter.

Chapter 13 begins by saying that the worst plot-pattern is one that shows a person superior in virtue (*epieikes*)[11] going from good to bad fortune. Aristotle eliminates this plot-pattern for the reason that it is *miarion*, morally shocking or confusing. Aristotle's rejection of this plot-pattern suggests he holds that a good plot will make a connection between good character and happiness. If Aristotle rejects tragedies that show good people falling into misfortune, however, then there is a fundamental way in which he—along with Plato—is involved in a "denial" of tragedy since this is the subject-matter of much tragedy.[12]

Aristotle's solution to this problem in Chapter 13 is to introduce the idea of the tragic character's *hamartia* or error as a way of explaining the tragic character's fall to misfortune.[13] If the tragic character is not exceptional in virtue, but is merely a good and decent person who errs but is not wicked, then her misfortune, which is out of proportion to her failings, evokes the audience's pity and fear but is nonetheless understandable in light of her error. In this context Aristotle also emphasizes that the ideal tragic protagonist is someone "intermediate in virtue," suggesting that an aspect in the tragic protagonist's character (albeit no wickedness or vice) leads to her misfortune. Aristotle says that Sophocles' *Oedipus the King* is the best tragedy according to Chapter 13, and Oedipus is listed twice (1453a23, 1453a25–26) as among the subjects of the best tragedies.

But Aristotle also wants to emphasize that "first and foremost the characters should be good" (54a15–20) and he says that tragedy represents those "better than most" (48a3). Aristotle, therefore, wants to keep the character requirements for the ideal tragic protagonist *high*.[14] Thus, Chapter 14 places requirements on the tragic character's state of awareness and intentions, requiring that the best tragedies show harm occurring (or about to occur) to kin or loved ones (*philia*) due to the tragic character's ignorance of what she is doing. Chapter 14 suggests, therefore, an "ignorance of fact" reading of *hamartia*, not an understanding of it as "character flaw." The best plot-patterns show harm that threatened to occur but is in the end averted, with *Iphigenia in Tauris* listed as an example of finest tragedy, while *Oedipus the King* now comes in second best with a plot that shows such harm actually occurring.

One way to resolve the tension between the two chapters would be to make use of Nancy Sherman's recent proposal that *hamartia* includes a range of different kinds of mistakes, including mistake of fact as well as moral failure.[15] Though the Greek tragedies themselves exhibit a range of tragic error, Aristotle's remarks in Chapter 13 and 14 indicate that his notion of tragic error is not that broad, nor is Aristotle's goal to provide an account of tragedy that is merely descriptive. In the *Poetics*, as elsewhere (e.g., the biological works), Aristotle employs what can be called a "norm-defect" methodology for explaining his subject matter.[16] Aristotle's normative account of tragedy selects one kind of error or *hamartia* as the norm; tragedies with other kinds of error count as inferior, or perhaps fail even to count as genuine tragedies at all. I suggest that the tension between the two chapters can be resolved so that the two chapters work together as a unit, but what we see is that tragic error, on Aristotle's view, is a narrow notion, one that fits only a small number of plays, and may not even fit Aristotle's own choice of best tragedies.[17]

Chapter 13 emphasizes that the *hamartia* or error that leads to the change of misfortune is distinguished from vice and true wickedness. According to this standard, the tragic character is implicated in his own misfortune, due to an error connected to his character and choices, but one that is not a serious character defect. Chapter 14 follows this up by stipulating that the best *hamartia* involves harm to kin done in ignorance. The tragic character's responsibility for the misfortune is therefore excusable in that his *hamartia* provides a causal link between his actions and the subsequent misfortune, but it does not *explain* the misfortune in terms of the character's evil intent or motives. The ideal tragic character is not a mere victim of circumstances beyond his control, therefore, but is causally implicated in the tragic misfortune, in such a way that his error is excusable and he retains his good character. Chapter 13 opens with Aristotle rejecting from his list of best tragic plots ones that show the fall of good people. By the end of Chapter 14 he continues to support this, saying his preference is for a tragedy such as *Iphigenia in Tauris* that provides a kind of sobering relief of pity and fear, showing misfortune that threatens to occur to a basically good person, but is in the end averted.

Evaluating Aristotle's View

On Aristotle's view, therefore, the best tragedy shows the ideal tragic character as a basically good person who brings about her own misfortune but who acts in ignorance of what she does. Her actions, therefore, are excusable and she maintains her good character. In fact, no matter how *hamartia* is interpreted, we can see that Aristotle is saying that individual error (be it error of judgment, mistake of fact, or character flaw) is at the heart of misfortune in the best tragedies. Aristotle's view, therefore, eliminates from his list of best tragedy plays whose plots point to external circumstances (be it divine fate, bad luck, or social role) as the source of tragic misfortune. This means that there are a number of type of tragedies that Aristotle's theory fails to fit.[18]

In particular, what concerns us here is tragedies with women protagonists and whether or not these tragedies are included among Aristotle's list of preferred ones. Cynthia Freeland notes that there are at least two categories of "women's plots" that Aristotle's theory downgrades.[19] First, she notes that Aristotle prefers plots that center around agent-centered "moral luck."[20] In these plots it is the tragic protagonist's own mistake or frailty that brings about the tragedy. This means that a play such as Euripides' *The Trojan Women*, which shows women protagonists who suffer, not due to their own actions, but because of the actions of men who have control over their lives as women, could not be ranked as best tragedy on Aristotle's view. Freeland also discusses plays with plots in which women are represented as voluntary sacrificial victims. Drawing on work by Nicole Loraux[21] that suggests that women more often than men are cast in this role, Freeland notes that Aristotle's plot-preferences imply that tragedies with plots that feature women protagonists as voluntary sacrificial victims (e.g., *Iphigenia in Aulis*) do not make it onto Aristotle's list for best tragedy, for in these plays the women protagonists do not experience the appropriate kind of agent-caused misfortune.

In addition, it would seem that women tragic protagonists more often than men are represented as suffering the effects of misfortunate on good character and judgment. In *Hecuba*, for example, the heroine says to her daughter, "The worthless person stays forever base while the man of nobility *is* noble, and no disaster drives him to deplete that inborn nature—he is good forever" (630). But the plot of *Hecuba* raises a challenge to Hecuba's own statement, showing the former queen blinding Polymestor and killing his children to avenge the death of her own children. Hecuba, Clytemnestra, and Electra are tragic protagonists who experience an erosion of character due to the strains of misfortune. Tragedies with these women characters, therefore, also do not count as best tragedy on Aristotle's view, since he requires that a tragic character must be a basically good person whose actions and character are admirable and worthy of emulation, but who meets misfortune due to some error, not on account of a real character flaw or frailty.[22]

Central to Aristotle's critical rejection of these women's tragedies from his list of best tragedies is his view that it is the error of a good and decent protagonist that brings about tragic misfortune. Given that Aristotle's theory fails to fit these women's tragedies, we need to ask what views about tragedy and its proper purpose prevent Aristotle from including them as best tragedy and whether or not feminists should find these views acceptable.

We can begin to answer this question by considering Brecht's view that for Aristotle, tragedy is not a "theatre for instruction" but is instead a "theatre for pleasure."[23] What Brecht means is that Aristotle holds that tragedy's narratives should please, but not instruct or provide real learning about the source of human suffering. Brecht attacks Aristotelian catharsis as a kind of "opium of the masses" in which the pleasure provided by a catharsis of pity and fear gives a kind of emotional closure, preventing the viewer from critically reflecting on the ways in which oppressive social structures make for needless suffering and misfortune. Tragedy, on Brecht's reading of Aristotle, dissipates the viewer's capacity for thought and political action by presenting narratives that provide pleasurable emotional involvement without educating.

Although Brecht does not mention *Poetics* 13 and 14, we can locate the target of Brecht's criticism in Aristotle's criteria for best tragedy. The best kind of plots represent misfortune brought about by individual error that was in some significant sense involuntary and beyond the tragic character's control because he was not aware of the particular circumstances of action (*NE* 3.1). The sufferings of Oedipus, for instance, are what Brecht would call "inevitable" in that there is a significant sense in which Oedipus's misfortune is not explained by his character or any error he makes.[24] Given this, one might wonder, if Aristotle does think that tragedy instructs, rather than just providing pleasure, what kind of instruction does Aristotle think it should provide?

Recent interpretations of Aristotle's view of tragedy by Martha Nussbaum and Stephen Halliwell offer answers to this question.[25] Brecht's interpretation and criticism of Aristotle is all the more striking, in fact, in light of these interpretations. Nussbaum develops an Aristotelian account of the emotions of pity and fear to argue that Aristotelian catharsis involves genuine learning and understanding. It is in the nature of the emotions of pity and fear, as Aristotle understands them, that they require some kind of identification and involvement with the individual from whom pity and fear are felt. Tragic characters who evoke pity and fear in us, the audience, must be like the audience in some way in that one pities another for things, "which one could expect to suffer oneself," (*Rhetoric* 1385b14–15), and one feels fear for someone "like [ourselves]" (*Poetics* 53a50). When we feel pity and fear for another, in other words, that person models what we take to be the relevant possibilities for our-selves.

Using Aristotle's account of these emotions, Nussbaum suggests that Aristotelian catharsis does not mean either moral purification or medical purgation through a release of built-up emotion. Rather, she suggests, pity and fear "can be genuine sources of understanding, showing the spec-tator the possibilities there are for good people,"[26] and so Aristotelian catharsis involves, "through pity and fear, a clarification (or illumination) concerning experiences of the pitiable and fearful kind."[27]

Stephen Halliwell present a rich and interesting account of the con-nection among pleasure, understanding, and emotion in Aristotle's ac-count of what it is to respond to a tragedy, developing Aristotle's remarks in *Poetics* 4 1448b4–19 that mimetic representation provides pleasurable learning. Interpreting this section together with *Rhetoric* 1.11, Halliwell agrees with Nussbaum that, on Aristotle's view, we experience the emo-tions of pity and fear in response to a tragic representation, "because we recognize, in the represented actions and sufferings, human possibilities which call for them."[28] Furthermore, *Poetics* 4 tells us that, "tragedy does not just confirm us in pre-existing comprehension of the world: it pro-vides us with imaginative opportunities to test, refine, extend and per-haps even question ideas and values on which such comprehension rests."[29]

Thus, on both Nussbaum's and Halliwell's interpretation of Aristotle, tragedy engages both the understanding the emotions, providing repre-sentations that call for genuine, independent critical reflection on the possibilities for a good person. Moreover, if Nussbaum and Halliwell in-terpret Aristotle correctly, we would have in Aristotle's aesthetics of trag-edy an account that appeals to feminists for some of the same reasons that feminists have found Aristotle's theory of virtue appealing. Aristot-le's *Ethics* gives an important place to the emotions in the development and maintenance of good character, and this is one reason that some feminists have found a significant point of connection between Aristotle's ethics and feminist discussions of the ethics of care.[30]

In addition, Aristotle's own theory of the emotions is a cognitive one, according to which emotions like pity and fear are constituted by certain beliefs and judgments.[31] Aristotle's account of the emotions appeals to feminists in that it would seem to go a considerable way to breaking down the dichotomies of reason versus emotion, or of judgment versus feeling, upon which much of the history of philosophy is based.[32] If we can indeed interpret Aristotle's view of tragedy as Nussbaum and Halliwell suggest, the emotions aid the viewer in reflecting on the possibilities for human life that tragedy represents; therefore, the experience of tragedy involves both reason and emotion, judgment and feeling. Aristotle's aesthetics might, therefore, appeal to feminists because it offers a rich and complex view of aesthetic response. This complex view of aesthetics would be preferable from a feminist point of view—in fact, to Brecht's own aesthetics, insofar as Brecht often writes as if feeling empathy as part of a response to a dramatic representation is incompatible with also engaging in critical reflection on the play's social messages.[33]

Nussbaum and Halliwell seem to be right in suggesting that best tragedy for Aristotle engages both the understanding and the emotions.[34] Moreover, Nussbaum's interpretation of Aristotle is valuable insofar as her view shows us how our emotional responses to tragedy, on Aristotle's view, are an important source of reflection on who we are and what we value. In this way Aristotle presents an aesthetic framework for responding to tragedy that is useful for feminists, and my own proposed feminist framework for reading tragedy (see below) suggests that both empathy and reflection can be part of a feminist aesthetics of tragedy. But Aristotle's discussion of best tragic plots in Chapters 13 and 14 and his discussion in Chapter 15 of appropriate characters shows that he does not value tragedy that either elicits from the viewer her own critical response to the social messages presented in the play, or gets her to question and perhaps revise the values and ideas upon which her understanding of the world rests.

If anything, Aristotle's remarks in these chapters suggest he has a very limited and selective view about who are the appropriate role models and just what are the relevant possibilities of living a good life that the audience should be considering. In Chapter 15, Aristotle draws on the class and gender hierarchies argued for in the *Politics* in stating his requirements for a tragic character: the goodness of a woman is inferior, he says, while the goodness of a slave is wholly worthless (54a20). Here women are described as potential subjects for tragedy, but "it is not appropriate for a woman to be so manly or clever"—while, as Elizabeth Spelman recently notes, slaves and the sufferings that slaves goes through could not even be considered as possible subject matter for tragedy, on Aristotle's view.[35]

Furthermore, Aristotle's description of the ideal tragic protagonist as a person who "is one of those people with a great reputation and good fortune, e.g. Oedipus, Thyestes, and distinguished men from similar families," suggests his norm for the best tragic protagonist is a wealthy powerful man, someone with room for significant action and choice. Certainly the women in the Greek tragedies we have all are wealthy members of the aristocracy, yet because they are women in a patriarchal society, their class privileges do not provide them with the significant scope for action and unimpeded choice that a male aristocrat such as Oedipus enjoys. This raises a doubt, at least, as to whether most women, including the aristocratic women that Greek tragedies represent, could fit Aristotle's ideal tragic protagonist, For Aristotle has very specific views about just what kind of person (i.e., from what kind of class, gender, and social role) it is appropriate for the audience to pity and feel fear for, to take as possibilities for their own lives. Certainly these views are not ones that feminists would agree with since the gender and class hierarchies presented in the *Ethics*, *Politics*, and his biological works have been the subject of much criticism by feminists.

Aristotle's recommendations in Chapter 13 and 14 also show that he has a limited view not only of who and what it is that we, the audience, should learn from in tragedy, but also a narrow view of just what we should learn. Consider Aristotle's requirement that the best plots show virtuous people who regret the harm they unintentionally brought about, rather than characters who deliberately do base or hateful things. With this requirement, Aristotle rules out as appropriate objects for our sympathy and fear: (1) a basically good character, such as Hecuba, who undergoes an erosion of character due to misfortune, and because of this, deliberately harms others, and (2) a character such as Medea, whose character is morally ambiguous and whose actions are morally repugnant but nonetheless still engages the audience's sympathies. *Hecuba* offers the possibilities for critical reflection on the conditions that permit and sustain good character. *Medea* forces us to revise our views about what kind of character deserves our pity: we learn from this play that it is possible to pity, if not excuse, someone whose actions are morally repugnant to us. These plays both help us examine what the relevant possibilities are for a good person, and also help us to challenge and rethink received opinion, including Aristotle's own views, on the relationships among happiness, character, and misfortune.[36] The fact that Aristotle eliminates these kinds of tragedies from his preferred tragedies makes it doubtful he

thinks that tragedy should clarify, test, help to revise, extend, and challenge the preexisting conceptions the viewer brings to her experience of
tragedy.

Aristotle's elimination of these kinds of plays, and his requirements on
appropriate character and action, therefore, suggest there is no room in
Aristotle's view of best tragedy for the viewer to raise her own critical
questions about preexisting conceptions of morality, gender, and social
hierarchies, and also that there is no room given to the playwright to
write a tragedy that presents this kind of a critique. Feminists can learn
from Aristotle's view of tragedy how best tragedy can engage us in a
complex emotional and intellectual response, while rejecting his view
that tragedy should not help the viewer to critically examine, and perhaps revise, the political and moral viewpoints discussed or presented in
the tragedy and accepted by society at large. Once we reject the *Poetics'*
requirements on appropriate plot and character, the way is then open to
see how the women's tragedies Aristotle rejects as examples of best tragedy can be best tragedies from which there is much to learn.

Brecht and Aristotle on Tragedy and Political Learning

At a more fundamental level, then, there is a problem, not just with
Aristotle's choice of plot-patterns and subject matter, but also with the
larger view of the experience of art that emerges from his discussion of
best tragedy. This conclusion may be somewhat surprising for feminists.
Feminists want to find in art visions that disrupt social and political
norms and expectations.[37] We have gotten accustomed, I think, to turning to Aristotle's *Poetics* with some relief and gratitude after Plato's blis-
tering attack on mimetic arts in *Republic* X; Aristotle's *Poetics* would seem
to contain a defense of the importance of an art form like tragedy in the
life of a good person and an account of aesthetic response that is richly
complex, bringing together, as Stephen Halliwell suggested, pleasure,
emotion, and understanding. But our discussion of Aristotle's view brings
out that Aristotle's *Politics* and *Ethics* are important subtexts for reading
his aesthetic theory, and that the views expressed in these other works
influence and direct him to value tragedy that is not politically or socially
disruptive but is in keeping with his political and ethical theories. This
raises the question whether feminists who want to turn to art for a critical

examination of the status quo should ultimately accept Aristotle's vision of art and his view of its proper purpose.

Further, we might have thought that Aristotle's account of tragedy as *mimesis* or imitation seems to be a richer and more interesting one than Plato's view that poetry is just a "copy" of reality. Aristotle shows how tragedy and art more generally can instruct by not simply "copying" reality, but by presenting for our contemplation possibilities for how life can be for people "like us." But rather than providing narratives and characters that set in motion the spectators' own critical reflections on the possibilities for their own lives, Aristotle's view of best tragedy's representations suggest he may think of them as closer to a structure of positive images that select the kinds of situations and characters that it is appropriate for the audience to reflect on and identify with. This role for the mimetic arts is suggested in *Politics* VIII 6, where Aristotle uses the example of music, as an imitative art, to discuss how such an imitative art is not only pleasurable and relaxing, but can also help incline youth and people of all ages toward virtue by setting before them representations of admirable character and action.[38] The audience is presented with the right kind of examples of virtuous character and action, and they acquire the habit of forming, "right judgments on, and feeling delight in, fine characters and good actions" (1340a17, cf. *NE* II 1106b20, and V 1125b32–34). In this way Aristotle's views on tragedy and his vision of art more generally may come closer to Plato's than one might have thought, with an important difference between the two being that Aristotle recognized in tragedy, when it is written and performed correctly, an important tool for the transmission of the "correct" moral and political values.

We can now return to assess Brecht's original criticism of Aristotelian "dramatic" theater—that its plots focus on the inevitability of human error and failure—in such a way that the viewer's attention is taken away from critically examining how oppressive social structures cause human misery. We can ask, with Brecht, what reason Aristotle could give for holding that best tragedy should be limited to examining the misfortunes brought about by individual error, rather than "errors" in the social and political structures that make for human suffering and misfortune? Surely Aristotle's point cannot be that the plots that engage us the most are the ones that focus on individual error, and not flawed social structures, for we can feel pity and fear for someone who suffers because she is deprived of the political power to control her life, as much as we can for someone who has significant freedom but through her actions unintentionally brings harm to herself and those dear to her.

Aristotle's prescriptions for tragic plot-patterns show his concern is not with tragedy that provides critical reflection on the social and political hierarchies his own *Politics* presents. Neither is he interested in tragedy that examines how flawed social structures make for misfortune for the individuals who are constrained by them—a theme presented, for example, in *The Trojan Women*. Rather, Aristotle's preferred narrative structures indicate he is most concerned that tragic plots should engage the viewer in such a way that she learns about how we can encounter misfortune despite, and perhaps because of, our best individual efforts to the contrary.[39] There might be some satisfaction in learning, through Oedipus's example, that even when we have unintentionally done the most horrible and morally offensive things, we can still have a "noble" response to this misfortune.[40] But learning this, and whatever else we can from best tragedy, as Aristotle sees it, is not politically empowering, nor would it seem that Aristotle intended it to be.[41]

I suggest, then, that Brecht is correct in criticizing Aristotle for recommending tragedy that is not socially and politically disruptive, that takes the focus away from oppressive social structures of gender and class, and that does not critically challenge the viewer to reflect on how social structures create misfortune for oppressed groups and how we might change these structures. I shall suggest below, in fact, that certain Greek tragedies about women provide us with plots and subject matter that allow us to reflect on these very issues. This means that feminists need to reevaluate whether Aristotle's theory is ultimately acceptable, providing a view of art and its place in society that is a clear alternative to Plato's view that art is socially disruptive and therefore needs to be censored. With his normative account of plot and character, Aristotle in effect rules out much of what Plato found to be worrisome about tragedy. Feminists can therefore learn from Brecht's criticisms of Aristotle, and learn from Brecht's own "epic theatre" how the viewer can produce readings of drama that highlight social context over individual error as the source of suffering in our society. At the same time, feminists can learn from an Aristotelian theory of the emotions, in contrast to a Brechtian one, that the engagement of the emotions is compatible with and even requires cognition and reflection, and that art can engage both our emotions and our cognitive capacities in a complex aesthetic response. In the next part of the paper, I turn to present a feminist alternative framework for reading

Greek tragedy that uses these different aspects of both Aristotle's and Brecht's aesthetic frameworks.

A Feminist "Re-Reading" of Greek Tragedies About Women

My proposal is a method for re-reading ancient Greek tragedy that borrows elements from both Brechtian and Aristotelian aesthetics to produce readings of Greek tragedy whose focus is social context as the source of tragic misfortune for women protagonists. Although I present this as a proposal for reading Greek tragedy, it also can be adapted to apply to other art forms such as film, and I shall suggest some difference between my proposed framework and other feminist aesthetic frameworks, such as feminist film theory. To begin, let me review the aspects of Brecht and Aristotle that feminist re-reading uses and also discuss how this proposal differs from these two frameworks.

First, feminist re-reading is Brechtian insofar as it reverses the Aristotelian view that the best tragedies involve the *hamartia* of a morally admirable individual, and focuses on how the plays call attention to the ways in which the social context of Greek patriarchy makes women special victims of tragedy. Thus a guiding methodological principle for a feminist re-reading of tragedy is to examine the text to see whether it suggests that it is the social context, rather than the error of an individual, that brings about misfortune for the women protagonists.

Second, this approach to interpreting Greek tragedy is like Brecht's own "epic theatre" in that the goal of producing a reading of Greek tragedy is to produce social change by showing how the texts of the tragedies themselves raise possibilities for critical social commentary on the structure of patriarchy and the ways in which this structure undermines the lives of women living in it. By focusing on the social structure as the source of misfortune for women in these plays—and not individual error, as Aristotle's approach urges us to—we can reflect on how the misery that these women characters experience is not natural or inevitable, but is the product of an oppressive system of social relations. We are then in a better position as feminists to see what changes need to take place in this social structure.

Next, my feminist re-reading uses Aristotle's theory of the emotions to correct Brecht's view that emotional engagement with the characters in the play is incompatible with reflection on the social messages contained in the play. Rather, on Aristotle's view, the emotions themselves are constituted by certain attitudes and judgments; for example, feeling pity for someone requires the judgment that the suffering this person experiences is "undeserved," and fear is felt for someone "like us" (*Poetics* 53a50). Rather than emotion deadening reasoning, therefore, Aristotle suggests how experiencing emotions requires judgment and cognition. Rather than taking our emotional responses to tragedy at face value, as feelings that are to be "discharged," we can learn to attend to these responses, for they reveal whom and what we find deserving of pity and fear. For the same reason, our lack of sympathy for characters in tragedy can be revealing as well. When we combine these two aspects of Brecht's and Aristotle's aesthetics, we can see how it is possible both to feel compassion for the women characters who suffer in the plays, while at the same time analyzing how it is the social context of patriarchy, with its limited gender roles for women, that makes them special victims of tragedy.

My proposed method for reading Greek tragedy also differs from both Brecht and Aristotle in key respects. It disagrees with Brecht's view that the narrative structure of Greek tragedy entails that it cannot, in virtue of its narrative structure, contain critical social commentary,[42] and it also departs from his view that a narrative art form such as Greek tragedy imposes the dominant ideology on the viewer, with no possibility presented by the text for the viewer to respond with her own critique of this ideology. Feminist re-reading is a strategy for producing critical readings by looking beyond the surface appearance of gender stereotyping, misogyny, and gender hierarchy in these plays to examine the possibilities within the text that undermine its surface appearance of sexism. Rather than precluding critical social commentary, as Brecht thought, I claim the plot, narrative, and representational strategies in these plays allow for a reading that points to a critique of the gender hierarchies and stereotyping of Greek patriarchy. Therefore, feminist re-reading attempts to take the goals and practices of Brecht's "epic" theater to see how even a "dramatic" form such as Greek tragedy contains critical social commentary and permits critical spectatorship.

Feminist re-reading also departs from a key element of Aristotle's aesthetics: his view that emotional engagement—compassion, pity and fear—is limited to protagonists with virtuous characters who are "like us." Some feminist critical responses to Greek tragedy implicitly accept this assumption, rejecting plays such as *Hecuba* and *Medea* because the women protagonists are portrayed as evil monsters who do not merit our sympathy.[43] We can accept a basic tenet of Aristotle's view—that it is important to have characters in tragedy that elicit our sympathy and emotional response—but disagree with him that only virtuous characters are the ones who merit such a response. By focusing on how the plays suggest that patriarchy, with its limited gender roles for women, creates special circumstances for tragic misfortune, we can produce readings of Greek tragedy that allows us to see why women protagonists such as Medea and Hecuba, who perform morally questionable actions, still merit our sympathy. While Aristotle's approach limits what we can learn from tragedy by requiring that tragedy must provide examples of admirable character and action for us to emulate, feminist re-reading enables us to see how tragedies with women protagonists present characters who model the relevant possibilities for our own lives as women living in patriarchy without requiring that these characters be presented as positive characters whose actions and characters we would like to imitate.

Methodological Principles

Now I present certain methodological principles of feminist re-reading. What is it to give a feminist reading or interpretation of a Greek tragedy? Is fidelity to the original text and conditions of performance the most important thing? And would fidelity involve an accurate rendering of the original text, a well as visual elements in production? Or does giving a reading of tragedy involve a "rewriting" of the original text and context of performance, adapted to the modern purposes and interests we bring to our examination of the play, so that what we produce with a reading is a "new" work that is inspired by the old one? Or does giving a reading of Greek tragedy involve some kind of "middle position," where the goal is to produce an interpretation in a context, and examine what the text has to say when we use our own feminist interests and purposes to understand the play's action and significance?[44]

I would argue that the first view of interpretation, authenticity to the original text and performance, is not viable, because it ignores the importance of performative features of tragedy. That is, plays invariably will have a different context when they are performed and will therefore take on a different meaning for different audiences; so fidelity to the original production is just not possible. Tragedies cannot be performed as part of civic festivals with select audiences and in certain outdoor theaters, and so forth.

The second view of interpretation—producing new works inspired by the old, by changing the text, lines, the playwright's stage directions, and so forth—is an interesting one, and is something that is worthwhile for feminists to pursue.[45] But I am interested in analyzing elements in the text of tragedy—including narrative and representational strategies—in order to examine critically the views of gender roles and hierarchies presented in the texts. Rather than revising or rewriting the text of tragedy for the purposes of a feminist "revisioning" of the women characters, I suggest we look for elements in the texts themselves that suggest a critical view of Greek patriarchal society. By re-reading these texts to focus on social context, and not individual error, as the source of tragedy for women in patriarchy, we can see new possibilities that the texts themselves present for undermining the surface aspects of Greek tragedy that feminists have found to be troubling—including the sexual stereotyping of women as either helpless victim or avenging monster.

Thus, my proposal adopts the "middle position," suggesting that a feminist reading of tragedy should both (1) attend to the possibilities in the text—including plot, narrative and representational strategies—that suggest it is the social context of patriarchy, rather than individual error, that is the source of tragedy for women protagonists, and (2) aim to produce a reading in a context, by asking questions about the text and highlighting elements in the plot and representation of characters that take on a new importance within the context of a feminist agenda. To give a feminist re-reading of a tragedy is to bring our own interests as feminists to bear on how the texts of tragedy raise possibilities for critical social commentary on Greek patriarchal practices and institutions such as marriage, the confinement of women to the home, the pride of place given to public honor and glory in war versus family ties, and so forth. Feminist re-reading, then, is an interpretation of the original text, but one that shows how the text raises new possibilities for feminist critical commentary when interpretation focuses on social context rather than individual error on human frailty, as the source of tragedy for women in patriarchy.

There are a number of different features in ancient tragedy that feminist re-reading can focus on so as to highlight the play's representation of social context. Among these aspects, the following two are central.

Narrative. Feminist re-reading asks numerous questions about narrative. Does the narrative reach a firm closure in favor of affirming the patriarchal order, or is the ending unresolved and/or ambiguous? If the narrative reaches closure in favor of affirming the social order, does this seem unbelievable given what has happened earlier in the narrative? Does the action of the play suggest that women's limited gender role lead her to make choices that she would not make were she to have a greater scope for freedom of action? Does the action call attention to the ways in which women's social role makes them especially vulnerable to strains on character that leads to misfortune?

Representational strategy. Here feminist re-reading also asks key questions: How are women represented in the play? What is the social role that women characters occupy? Are they the standard ones of dutiful wives and daughters, or do they depart from type? What happens to these characters when they do deviate? Are they punished or vindicated? If they are punished, does the play suggest they deserve what they get, or does their suffering seem tragic and undeserved? If women are presented as victims, does the action of the play simply reinforce the image of women as helpless victim, or does it call critical attention to the way that patriarchy limits women's freedom to determine their own lives?

In analyzing a tragedy's narrative and representational strategies in this way, we bring out elements of the play that take on a new significance within the context of feminist re-reading. In this way feminist re-reading is "contextual" in that it provides a reading of the narrative and representational strategies within a feminist focus on social context as the source of tragedy for women living in patriarchy. Performances of plays may also provide the context for a feminist re-reading of tragedy. The lines in the play, for example, may take on different significance depending on the performance. Jules Dassin's film *A Dream of Passion* (1978) provides a good example of how performance can alter the meaning of a tragedy's text.[46] The film in fact is about the relevance of a contemporary context of interpretation for a modern production of Euripides' *Medea*.

A Dream of Passion tells the story of Maya (Melina Mercouri), a famous actress who returns to Athens to star in a revival of *Medea*. The director, Kostas, and Maya argue about how to interpret the play. Kostas sees it as a play about the fall of the mighty, showing a heroic character who is brought down by the passionate side of her nature. While the director thinks the play has the same meaning for a modern audience as it did for an ancient Greek one, Maya looks for the contemporary relevance of the play, acting the role of Medea more as a modern-day feminist than a woman brought to misfortune because of her over passionate nature. Maya's performance of Medea changes when she becomes involved with a woman who is a modern-day Medea, having killed her two children as punishment for her husband's battering and threatening to leave her for another woman. The audience sees a different side of Medea's character as a result of this change of performance.

Visual elements in the production can also provide opportunities for a re-reading of a play. Medea could be played by a male character in drag, for example, for certain lines of the play in which she expresses male-associated themes of public honor and reputation, but then played by a female character for the other part of the play, giving expression to the idea that medea is torn between the male and female values of honor and concern for family and children.[47] Feminist re-reading, therefore, looks at both the play's plot and representational content, as well as the conditions of performance, to produce a reading that locates the source of misfortune for women protagonists in the Greek patriarchal social structure.

Illustrations

I now turn to illustrate feminist re-reading of tragedy with some examples of readings of ancient tragedies about women. These illustrations are not intended to be complete readings of these plays, but will serve to illustrate the use and interest in the feminist re-reading strategy. There are at least three distinctive plot structures that are typical of tragic representations of women. Women are represented as mere victims; as "voluntary" victims; and as avenging monsters. The plays I discuss will be examples from the categories of women as "voluntary" victim and as avenging monster. Cynthia Freeland's reading of Euripides' *Trojan Women*, a play that falls in the first category of women's plays, women as mere victim, suggests that the women in the play suffer "in a way appropriate to women whose fates are decided as a consequence of powerful men's deeds," and therefore provides an example of how feminist re-reading would apply to this play as well.[48]

First, we can consider a tragedy in which the woman protagonist is represented as a "voluntary victim," Euripides' *Alcestis*. In these types of plays, a female protagonist willingly sacrifices herself to preserve family, city or honor, winning praise not normally given a woman. Since the women characters voluntarily sacrifice themselves, they are not straight-forward "victims" in the way that the Trojan women are. In *Alcestis* the time has come for a man, Admetus, to die, but he is granted continued life by the gods if he can find someone to die in his place. His wife, Alcestis, dies in his place after Admetus's elderly parents refuse to die for their son. The story ends with the return of Alcestis to her home when she is rescued from the underworld by Admetus's friend, Heracles.

A feminist concern with this play is that Alcestis simply confirms the stereotype of the good Greek wife, offering to die in place of her husband so that he can live. Nancy Sorkin Rabinowitz, for example, subjects the play to a feminist "ideology" critique,[49] saying the play's project is to encourage women to take self-sacrifice for their families as a goal.[50] Her reading of the play stresses that Alcestis is represented as a "liminal" figure, bordering between life and death, outsider to Admetus's family versus committed insider; her strength, which is emphasized in describing Alcestis as having chosen to die for her husband, is a threat to male power that needs to be contained. By the end of the play, Alcestis is literally an object of exchange between Admetus and Heracles when Her-acles prevails upon Admetus to accept Alcestis, veiled, silent and her true identity unknown to her husband, after Admetus had promised to take no woman in her place after her death.

By shifting our critical attention to highlight the play's representation of social context, we can give another reading of the play's representa-tional strategy, one that shows how the character of Alcestis is used to comment critically on the limitations imposed on women by the institu-tion of marriage, the devaluing of the family in favor of social reputation, and the ways in which male friendships are given pride of place over a husband's relationship to his wife.

First, consider the representation of Alcestis and the contrast between her and her husband. Alcestis does not simply confirm the stereotype of acceptable behavior for women; she revises it by displaying a courage normally found only in representations of men in Greek culture.[51] ("Thereby, daring this generous action, she has made the life of all women become a thing of better repute than it was," Admetus' father tells him [622]). Further, she is not represented as the image of the silently suffering women, but instead makes demands on her husband, se-curing his promise that, after her death, he will not remarry, which she supposes will be harmful to the children, especially to the daughter, who is left without her real mother to care for her (312). Alcestis can be seen, therefore, to be a sympathetic character to feminists, for we can see her struggle to assert her importance as wife and mother while also coming to terms with the limited options that the institution of marriage in a patriarchal culture gives her.

In contrast, Alcestis's husband, Admetus, is represented as weak and short-sighted, when, for example, he beseeches Alcestis not to leave him even though he was willing to let her die in his place: "Before the gods, do not be so harsh as to leave me, leave your children forlorn. No, up, and fight it. There would be nothing left of me if you died" (275).[52] One commentator, Richmond Lattimore, suggests that Admetus is ordinary in every way, but has one significant virtue, his hospitality to strangers, which makes him a friend to Heracles, and moves Heracles to wrench Alcestis from the jaws of Death.[53] But Admetus is represented as valuing hospitality in the excess, taking in Heracles as a guest when his house is mourning the loss of Alcestis: "there would be one more misfortune added to those I have, if my house is called unfriendly to its friends" (555). Here the social virtue of hospitality is valued over showing respect for family and wife. Further, Admetus is shown to be blind to the sacrifice that his wife has made for him, and as not recognizing the love of family that motivated her choice. Commenting that he would be better off dead now that Alcestis is gone, he says of her, "She has her glory and is free from much distress" (937), while he laments that his reputation is now ruined, with people thinking he is a coward for allowing his wife to die in his place and blaming his parents for not doing so (950–60).

The action of the play does not simply reinforce Greek patriarchal values of concern for glory and courage in death. Alcestis does not simply win glory in death by "acting like a man." The action of the play focuses on Alcestis's courage in helping her family, rather than courage in battle or war, suggesting that were women given the opportunity for significant action, they would create an alternative to the male-associated one of glory in death at war. Furthermore, the play is an extended examination of the family and the importance of the wife and mother for its well-being and survival. Even while the play underscores that Admetus cannot really recognize and appreciate the kind of sacrifice his wife has made for him (not once do we see him thank her for this act of kindness though other characters in the play express their appreciation for her), the dialogue and action show that other members of the household, such as the servants and the children, recognize her true worth. In one long speech, a servant speaks of how Alcestis "gentled her husband's rages" and thereby "saved us all from trouble after trouble" (770). After his mother's death, the son tells his father, "She died too soon. Mother, with you gone away, the whole house is ruined," (415), placing the mother at the center of the household. Alcestis herself calls attention to the importance of the mother, in contrast to the father, in the lives of children, when she tells Admetus that with her death, "you must be our children's mother, too, instead of me" (377), and she gets his agreement to this.

Besides focusing on the family, the action of the play thematizes the institution of marriage, in effect equating marriage with death for women. The plotline may emphasize that Alcestis dies willingly in place of her husband, but the text of the play is equally clear in implicating marriage, and the obligations and restrictions it places on women, as bringing about Alcestis's death. In a key scene in her bedroom chamber, Alcestis addresses her bed as the symbol of her marriage, saying "O marriage bed, it was here that I undressed my maidenhood and gave myself up to this husband for whose sake I die. Good-bye, I hold no grudge. But you have been my death and mine alone. I could not bear to play him false" (175ff.). Here we see that Alcestis may "choose" to die for her husband, but that the Greek view of marriage, which determines that the good wife must value her husband's life over her own, leaves Alcestis with no option but to die in his place. Rather than being an "exceptional" woman, bringing credit to her gender by her self-sacrifice, Alcestis' speech makes clear she is simply fulfilling the obligations to her husband that come with her marriage. The play takes the idea that a good wife must be self-sacrificing and exaggerates this, showing that marriage in Greek patriarchal culture literally equates to death for women, for she must now regard her own well-being as secondary to that of her husband and children. This point is not undermined or obscured because she receives praise for her action of self-sacrifice. If anything, the praise she receives only underscores that a woman's act of self-sacrifice for her family must be taken to the extreme before she can be praised for being a "good wife."

Finally, the ending needs to be considered in relation to the feminist commentary found in the rest of the play. Nancy Rabinowitz would seem to be correct that in the final scene between Admetus and Heracles,

Alcestis is literally reduced to an object of exchange between men. Alcestis is veiled, silent, and mysterious, and remains that way through the end of the play, when she is ushered back into her home by Admetus. Rabinowitz suggests this is evidence that the play reaches narrative closure by maintaining that the earlier threat that Alcestis presented as a courageous and active woman should be contained.

I would suggest instead that the ending needs to be read in context with the feminist themes highlighted earlier in the play. Earlier scenes suggest that at least prior to her death, Admetus did not recognize and appreciate the sacrifice his wife was willing to make for him, while other members of the household, most notably the servants and children, did appreciate this and recognized its significance. Admetus made Alcestis a promise that he would not take another woman in her place, yet Admetus allows Heracles to prevail upon him and take the mysterious veiled women, aka Alcestis, into his home. This scene recalls the earlier one in which Admetus valued hospitality to a male friend over honoring the memory of his wife. The ending shows that despite his loss, Admetus still has not learned to honor his wife, and still values the esteem of a male associate more than he does his promise to his wife. Alcestis' identity is then revealed to Admetus, and she reenters her home and enters again into married life with Admetus, this time as a silent and mysterious woman, not as the active agent of earlier scenes.

Rather than suggesting that the threat of an active, strong woman has been contained, therefore, the ending suggests that marriage for a woman such as Alcestis will continue to be like her death so long as her husband values his male associates and reputation over her. She is silent and unknown, the play suggests, because marriage affords her no other options, leaving her desires and value unrecognized and unappreciated by her husband. The play, therefore, provides a critique of the culturally imposed limitations on women in the Greek institution of marriage as well as highlighting the importance of the wife for the Greek family and life.

My second example is Sophocles' Antigone, which also represents a young woman as a voluntary victim, sacrificing herself for the sake of paying proper respect to her dead brother. This play concerns the conflict between Kreon, the king of Thebes and a young woman, Antigone, who defies him. When Kreon declares that the body of Antigone's brother, Polyneices, shall lie unburied, Antigone defies him by giving her brother's corpse a token burial. Kreon condemns her to be buried alive, and ignores the counsel of Tiresias. Kreon regrets his action too late, and

Antigone and her son, Antigone's fiancee, kill themselves, along with Kreon's wife, Eurydice. Readings of this play often focus on character traits in the two main characters that lead to misfortune for both[54]—a certain kind of inflexibility in reasoning or adherence to a unified ideal—or trace the source of the tragedy to an irrational world with conflicting standards of right action.[55] My feminist re-reading of this play focuses on its representation of a flawed male-dominated political structure as the source of tragedy for the people in this society, the important role that women, who fall outside the system of political representation, can play as critics of this society, and the price that women who attempt to challenge male authority must pay.

Near the end of the play Tiresias warns Kreon to reconsider his decision to have Antigone killed and her brother's body remain without a proper burial saying, "The state is sick. You and your principle are to blame" (1170). But the play makes clear that Kreon's fault is not just that of a tyrant unwilling to reconsider a poorly made decision concerning what is in the state's best interests. We don't have to look far beneath the surface action and dialogue of the play to see that it suggests that Kreon is interested in maintaining a specific kind of political structure, one in which the hierarchies of male-female, elder-youth, master-servant are maintained and political power is controlled by aristocratic, older males. The play suggests that it is not just Kreon as an individual, who is flawed, but so is the social structure, with its sexual, age, and class hierarchies, which Kreon defends. The character of Antigone, a young woman who has no real power in this society despite her aristocratic background, is used to examine critically a political structure that fails to balance civic and family interests, and a family social structure that is organized around the hierarchies of male-female, elder-youth, master-servant.

From the beginning of the play, Antigone's position of powerlessness as a young woman in a male-dominated society is highlighted, and when she challenges Kreon's decision in spite of this position, Antigone's action is taken by Kreon as a direct threat not just to his personal control, but to the male-dominated order. The play opens with Antigone's attempt to get her sister, Ismene, to help her in a scheme to bury their brother. Ismene reminds Antigone that they are just women, "born unfit to battle men, and we are subjects while Kreon is king" (72).[56] Kreon is incredulous when informed that Antigone is the culprit who dared to defy him ("This girl?" he exclaims [485]), and he vows not to be defied by a woman: "I'm no man—she is a man, she's the king—if she gets away with this" (590). In defending his decision to his son, Haimon, he says, "when men are ruled right their obedience to authority saves their lives. That's why we have to defend orderly people, and never let women get the better of us. If we must fall, better to fall to a real man and not be called worse than women" (820), again suggesting that his son as a male should join with him in suppressing the threat Antigone poses to the male-dominated order. When Haimon continues to try to talk his father out of his decision, Kreon replies, "Don't 'father' me. You're no man. You're a slave. Property of a woman" (915). Antigone is represented as threatening to Kreon, therefore, not just because she is a subject who dares to defy the order of a ruler. She is willing to defy Kreon in spite of her social role as a young woman, and she is perceived as threatening not just as a courageous, rebellious subject but as a woman willing to go against male control.

Further, the Chorus, the elderly male courtiers who surround Kreon, are shown to be weak in supporting Kreon's decision until the very end, when Kreon relinquishes his authority and asks them for counsel (1277).[57] Kreon in fact explicitly tells them that it was their decision, as well as his, that has determined that Antigone will die (713), indicating that Antigone poses a threat not just to himself personally, but to the entire male-controlled society that he rules over. In an inversion of the hierarchies of class upon which Thebes is based, the servant is more willing than Kreon's cronies to express his disagreement with him, telling him, "Sir, it's terrible; you make your mind up when even what's wrong looks right" (405).

In another reversal of received wisdom on family hierarchies, Kreon's son, Haimon tells him that he needs to reconsider his decision to have Antigone die, and that he should deliberate in a more democratic fashion, saying that "the whole nation denies" that Antigone did wrong (880), and that "no country belongs to one man" (885). Kreon rebuffs Haimon's advice, saying to his male courtier, "Men our age, learn from him?" (875), suggesting again that his concern is with upholding the hierarchies upon which his state and his family are based.

Much commentary, including commentary by feminists, has analyzed the character of Antigone and looked to the common flaws of inflexibility and adherence to a narrow vision as the cause of the misfortune that ensues for the members of Kreon's and Antigone's families.[58] From the perspective of my methodology of feminist re-reading this interpretation of the play is flawed. It focuses on the character of Antigone and her flaws to the exclusion of the numerous reference to the social context of Greek patriarchy that is highlighted in the scenes noted above.

Antigone may be faulted, for example, for the cold way in which she responds to her sister Ismene when she refuses to help bury their brother, appearing to value the dead below and adherence to the family in the abstract. Ismene, by contrast, may be submissive to male authority, but she is warm and caring about her sister, volunteering to die with Antigone after Kreon had condemned her to death for her rebellion. But only an Aristotelian who thought that the virtues could not conflict but cooperate with one another under the guidance of practical wisdom (*Magna Moralia* 1199b36–1200a11) would be able to point to a failure in Antigone's ability to deliberate well as the cause of misfortune in the story. Shifting our focus to the representation of the social context in the play, we can give another reading of the conflict between Antigone and Kreon and the tragedy that ensues, one that finds in the play a critical commentary on a patriarchal society that values the interests and preservation of the male-dominated polis and family over the interests and well-being of all its members. Antigone may choose family (*philia*) over marriage and *Eros*, honoring dead family members over a loving relation with living ones, and she may be criticized for these choices by those with different priorities and attachments. But the play suggests that it is the flawed society she lives in that mandates she must choose between respect for family or obedience to the state, and the play ends with the suggestion is that it is Kreon, not Antigone, who should regret what has happened.

The play presents a stark contrast between the two main female characters, Antigone and Ismene, and it seems that the only character who is able to combine the virtues that both display, adherence to principle, as well as love and concern for immediate family, is a male character, Haimon. A feminist concern with the representation of the female characters could then be that each sister in her own way invokes a female stereotype: Antigone that of the hard-bitten crusader, who displays a male-associated adherence to principle and family in the abstract, while Ismene is acquiescent and subordinate to male authority, but loving and concerned for her sister. But Antigone's own speech before she is taken away to her death reveals that her character is more complicated than this characterization of her suggests. When the Chorus suggests that she will be remembered as going to her death with "fame and glory," "of your own accord," you alone of mortal women," (970), she rejects this characterization of her as the noble warrior for a cause, accusing them of laughing at her with this remark and suggesting instead that "I have been unlucky." Her speech reveals that she is a vulnerable human being, a woman who regrets that she will not have had the attachments of marriage and motherhood, and that the decision she has made to give up these things in favor of honoring the memory of her dead brother was not a welcome one, rather a "burden." We can see that the characters of Antigone and Ismene are used to show that women under patriarchy have two main options: they can be like Antigone and challenge the decision of powerful males, but this entails alienation from their family and forgoing of the traditional roles of wife and mother; or they can be like Ismene and remain obedient to and suffer under male authority, but thereby alienate themselves from their more rebellious sisters. Feminists may fault the play for not presenting a female character that shows how it is possible to embody the virtues that both sisters display, but *Antigone* remains a realistic critical commentary on the limited options available for women under patriarchy.

Third, and finally, let us consider how feminist re-reading applies to Euripides' *Medea*, an example from another subgenre of women's tragedies, those in which the women protagonists depart from the feminine norm and take on traits typically associated with men, as do Clytemnestra and Medea, and then suffer for doing so. These women characters are represented as a menacing force to be reckoned with, "avenging monsters," yet they are criticized by the male (and sometimes female) characters in the play for departing from the female norm. Some may question whether *Medea* is a good example of this type of plot-pattern insofar as Medea escapes at the end and appears to "get away" with her crimes.[59] But it is difficult, I think, to read *Medea* as a play which shows that "crime pays" in that the play represents the devastating consequences for Medea of deciding to preserve her honor by killing her own children.

With its choice of subject matter—a woman who is wronged by her husband—and speeches like no other in Greek tragedy denouncing the lot of women in Greek patriarchal culture, *Medea* would seem to be ripe material for producing a critical social commentary on the institution of marriage in ancient Greek patriarchy. Some feminists have suggested, however, that the play is about "male concerns" such as honor and possession, and that it has structures of address that are aimed at a male audience who could identify with Medea's desire for revenge.[60] But Medea's defiance of her husband's authority would challenge the same male

audience's views concerning women's proper social role. Medea's character, is in fact, hard to "gender-type." In her desire to avenge her honor,
she embodies typical Greek male values; but she also is identified with
Greek female concerns. In her famous speech (214–66) she gives a scath-
ing attack on the institution of marriage in Greek society, saying, "I
would very much rather stand three times in front of battle than bear one
child." Because of the way in which marriage favors male interests, she
exclaims, "Of all things which are living and can form a judgment we
women are the most unfortunate creatures."[61] Rather than fitting a male
or a female stereotype, therefore, Medea's character shows a woman who
embodies characteristics associated with both male and female interests
in Greek society. The play suggests that the conflict that takes place
within her about how best to address her husband's infidelity reflects a
larger conflict between male- versus female-associated values in Greek
patriarchy.

Further, rather than simply identifying the character of Medea with
male-associated values of public reputation over family, the play suggests
a critique of those values by presenting a character who goes to extreme
lengths to avenge her reputation, to the point where she could kill her
own children. If we shift our focus away from criticizing the character of
Medea, and focus on the play's representation of social context, we can
see that the play provides a critical social commentary on the way in
which systems of oppression make its female victims suffer by internaliz-
ing the values of the oppressor, to the point where they have values that
are not in their own self-interest. When Medea says, "of all things that
are living and can form a judgment, we women are the most unfortunate
creatures," her statement carries a double meaning. She is on the one
hand, bemoaning the oppression of women, but it is clear that women's
inferior social status is also a reason that she herself looks down on
women and wishes to dissociate herself from them.

Medea's use of her own children to get back at her husband raises the
issue of whether she can be a sympathetic figure in spite of these actions,
or whether in the end Euripides leaves the audience, not with a critique
of the institution of marriage, but instead provides, as Nancy Rabinowitz
suggests, a powerful image of a "castrating female" who provokes male
anxiety at what a strong woman can do when given the opportunity.[62] In
response to this, I would note that Medea is introduced as a sympathetic
figure from the start of the play, with a speech by her Nurse which highlights the suffering she has endured ("She lies without food and gives

herself up to suffering, Wasting away every moment of the day in tears"
[22–25]), followed by the introduction of Medea herself, crying offstage,
and then her own famous speech bemoaning the lot of women. Even
when she kills her own children, the Chorus of women is horrified but
does not denounce her, suggesting instead that it would have been better
for her not to have been a mother at all, rather than now experience the
terrible grief she will feel at their loss (1115). At the same time, through
Medea's relation to the Chorus, the play suggests that women need the
support of other women to help them make the right choices, and it
criticizes patriarchy for setting up a social structure in which this support
is not forthcoming. By attending to the way that social context is represented as an important influence on Medea's decision to take revenge, we
can read this play not as a critique of the figure of the fury of an avenging
monster, but as a commentary on the social circumstances that lead
Medea to enact her revenge. We can see how the play suggests that rather
than being an unsympathetic monster, Medea deserves our sympathy in
spite of her actions.

The conclusion of the play, in which Medea appears as a goddess,
escaping by superhuman means to take revenge with King Aegeus, is
criticized by Aristotle (*Poetics* 1461b), because it appears to disrupt the
narrative with an unnatural and unbelievable ending. Along the same
lines, Nancy Rabinowitz suggests that the sympathy that has been built
up for Medea gets dissipated because she is now represented as the
"Other," something superhuman, not "like us" and so no longer capable
of evoking our sympathy. In response I would suggest that the audience
can surely still sympathize with characters who are not exactly "like
them," and there has been much presented in the play to suggest that
Medea *is* worthy of our sympathy. Some feminists might fault Euripides
for an ending that is open to several different interpretations. When
Medea leaves earth for the realm of the gods, this suggests that there is
no room on earth for a woman who defends her right to honor and self-
esteem and questions traditional ideas about women's role as dutiful wife
and mother.[63] This ending could be understood as either critical of patriarchy or critical of Medea's attempt to challenge patriarchy. Here I suggest we need to read the ending in the context of what has gone before
it in the play. The critical focus has not been on Medea's character but
instead on the institution of marriage and the limitations it places on
women. This ending is consistent with this idea, suggesting that patriarchy cannot make room for a powerful woman who challenges male au-

thority. When we highlight the play's representation of the social context of patriarchy, therefore, we find that there is much in this play that provides a useful critique of the institution of marriage and the harm it brings to women.

Using the feminist re-reading strategy I have shown how we can produce readings of three plays, *Alcestis*, *Antigone*, and *Medea*, that are quite different from readings that have an Aristotelian focus on individual error as the source of misfortune in them. By focusing on social context rather than individual error, we can look beyond the surface representations of women that feminists have found to be objectionable and can show that these plays actually contain critical feminist social commentary. Using the methodology of feminist re-reading, therefore, we are able to reveal what Greek tragedy can offer for feminism. Feminist re-reading can be applied in principle to any Greek tragedy; it can also be useful in highlighting parts of a play that would be useful for feminist commentary, even if the play as a whole does not contain a fully developed critique of patriarchy. For example, although I lack space to show this here, I am skeptical that feminist re-reading can be applied to Aeschylus's *Oresteia* to show it presents a critique of patriarchal hierarchies and women's traditional place within that structure. Still, it may contain elements that are useful for feminist commentary, and feminist re-reading suggests a strategy for uncovering these parts of the trilogy.

To conclude, I note some relations between Aristotle's aesthetics and recent feminist aesthetics. We have seen that Brechtian aesthetics presents some useful criticisms of Aristotelian aesthetics and stands opposed to it. My feminist re-reading proposal uses elements from both Brecht's and Aristotle's aesthetics. Along with Brecht, I reject Aristotle's focus on individual error as the source of misfortune in best tragedy; I also, however, criticize Brecht's view, because he does not allow enough of a role for the emotions in a response to tragedy. I thus present a feminist aesthetics of ancient tragedy that goes back to Aristotle on this issue, at least in some respects.

After having examined Aristotle's aesthetics of tragedy, we can in fact see there are other important connections between the aesthetic tradition that Aristotle's *Poetics* gave birth to and recent feminist aesthetic theories. My remarks will focus in particular on feminist film aesthetics because of the similarities between theater and film. Many feminist film critics reflect an Aristotelian tradition in their search for characters with which to identify. Feminist film critics such as Claire Johnston and Laura Mulvey argue for a critical rejection of classical Hollywood cinema because women are absent on screen as well as assumed to be absent in the audience.[64] Johnston finds that the images of women in film, such as Marilyn Monroe or Grace Kelly, represent the absent phallus, rather than the representation of women as active subjects. Mulvey argues that the voyeuristic aspect of cinema and the nature of the camera look or gaze show that Hollywood cinema conventions construct a male viewing position by aligning the male "gaze" to that of the fictional hero, inviting him to identify with the male hero and to objectify the women in the film. Both Johnston and Mulvey thus reflect an Aristotelian concern with the importance of having characters in cinema with whom women can identify and they fault Hollywood cinema because its narrative structures do not, in their view, provide women with such characters. Recently feminist classics scholar Nancy Sorkin Rabinowitz adapts the psychoanalytic film framework to give an analysis of Greek tragedy that is critical of Greek tragedy for much the same reasons that Johnston and Mulvey are critical of Hollywood cinema.[65]

Other alternative approaches to feminist film aesthetics, such as the "image of women" in film approach most recently defended by Noël Carroll, similarly reflect an Aristotelian concern with the analysis of film images in terms of their positive or negative influence on an audience's way of thinking.[66] This approach analyzes the image of women in film to see the messages the film contains about women and to identify negative patterns of representation of women that may influence the emotional response of men to women and vice versa.

Yet another type of feminist film aesthetics takes the form of an "ideology critique," analyzing Hollywood film, literature, and art to see how the representation of women in these media serves to make the subordination and oppression of women seem natural and inevitable. This approach to feminist film aesthetics is advocated by Teresa de Lauretis,[67] for example. She presents a proposal to analyze the gender ideology in Hollywood cinema and "read against the grain" by resisting the messages of sexual inferiority and stereotyping presented in the film texts.

Although there are significant differences between these three approaches, each is connected to Aristotle by a common concern with how the narrative structures in conventional film influence audience response. Both the feminist psychoanalytic framework and feminist ideology critique assume that the narrative structures in Hollywood cinema "construct" a viewing position that leaves women out, both in the audience and on the screen. Even the feminist strategy of "reading against the grain" to produce subversive "counterreadings" concedes that the narrative structures in Hollywood film typically impose on the viewer a gender ideology, but then give the feminist viewer the role of "resisting" this ideology by analyzing and viewing in opposition to these messages.

These approaches to feminist film aesthetics share with an Aristotelian aesthetics an emphasis on narrative structures and on the role played by narrative in structuring an audience response. It is also true that even much feminist theater theory, which stands in stark contrast to much feminist film aesthetics in its assumption that spectators can be critical, assumes the narrative structures of tragedy, for example, impose an oppressive gender ideology on the viewer and so must be supplemented with Brechtian performance techniques that make the gender attitudes encoded in the play's text visible to the spectator.[68] Much feminist aesthetics, therefore, shares an Aristotelian focus on narrative structures as the key determinate of a text's meaning. I would fault all these approaches for failing to consider the possibilities that the narratives of these popular art forms present for feminist re-readings, and for neglecting the role that the viewer herself can play in uncovering these subversive readings in the texts themselves.

Recent developments in feminist aesthetics suggest new alternatives to Aristotelian-influenced feminist aesthetics.[69] Ruby Rich, for example, calls for feminist film criticism that takes into account the Brechtian view of the role that the viewer can play in constructing an interpretation when she says, "It is crucial to emphasize here the possibility for texts to be transformed at the level of reception and not to fall into a trap of condescension toward our own developed powers as active producers of meaning."[70] This is promising. Yet I would caution at the same time that feminists influenced by Brecht who reject identification as a response to characters in film or literature *do* have things to learn from an Aristotelian framework. The important lesson Aristotle teaches us is that emotional engagement and critical reflection can go together as part of a response to these art forms. By examining and borrowing from both Aristotelian and Brechtian aesthetics, feminists will be in a better position to develop new alternative aesthetic frameworks. My account of the strategy of feminist-re-reading of ancient tragedy is an example of these new possibilities.

Notes

1. An earlier version of this essay was read at the University of Massachusetts—Amherst and Mount Holyoke College. I am grateful to the audiences at these presentations for helpful discussion and comments, especially to Lisa Tessman, for her excellent commentary on the presentation at the University of Massachusetts. Thanks to Awam Ampka, Eugene Hill, Al Mele, Mecke Nagel, Barbara Simerka, and Charlotte Witt for their valuable comments on an early draft of the essay, and thanks also to an anonymous referee for the volume for critical comments that helped me clarify my argument. Special thanks to Tom Wartenberg for his comments on the penultimate draft that helped me to make substantial improvements in the form and content of the essay. Very special thanks to Cynthia Freeland for her enormously helpful comments and editorial suggestions, for inviting me to contribute to this volume, and for encouraging me through her teaching and work to care about Aristotle and feminist philosophy.

2. *The Medea*, translated by Rex Warner in *Euripides I*, ed. David Grene and Richmond Lattimore (Chicago, 1955), line 230.

3. For a discussion of this point see Sally Humphreys, *The Family, Women and Death: Comparative Studies* (London, 1983), especially chap. 1, "*Oikos* and *Polis*"; Helene Foley, "Attitudes To Women in Greece," in *The Civilization of the Ancient Mediterranean*, ed. M. Grant and R. Kitzinger (New York, 1988): 1301–17, and Bernard Knox, *The Oldest Dead White European Males* (New York, 1993): 49–60.

4. Helene Foley, "Medea's Divided Self," *Classical Antiquity* 8, no. 1 (April 1989): 78.

5. Froma Zeitlin, "Playing The Other: Theatre, Theatricality, and the Feminine in Greek Drama," *Representations* 11 (1985): 67.

6. Knox, *Oldest Dead*, 55.

7. See his essays in Bertolt Brecht, *Brecht on Theatre*, ed. and trans. John Willett (New York, 1964), especially his essay, "Epic Theatre and Dramatic Theatre" and also his "Notes to *Mahogonny*." Also see the criticism of what Augusto Boal calls Aristotle's "coercive system of tragedy" in his *Theatre of the Oppressed*, trans. Charles A. and Maria-Odilia Leal McBride (New York, 1985).

8. "Theatre For Pleasure or Theatre For Instruction," in *Brecht on Theatre*, 71.

9. I call this a "feminist" revision of Brecht, because it emphasizes that emotional engagement is not incompatible with critical reflection. For a recent feminist discussion deconstructing this emotion-reason dichotomy in the history of philosophy, see Ann Ferguson, "Does Reason Have A Gender?" in *Radical Philosophy: Tradition, Counter-Tradition, Politics*, ed. Roger S. Gottlieb (Philadelphia, 1993). For Brechtian-feminist drama criticism that accepts Brecht's view that critical drama is "distanced" drama, see Elin Diamond, "Brechtian Theory/Feminist Theory: Toward a Gestic Feminist Criticism," *TDR* 32, no. 1 (Spring 1988): 82–94, and "Mimesis, Mimicry, and the True-Real," *Modern Drama* 32 (1989): 58–72; and Jill Dolan, *The Feminist Spectator As Critic* (Ann Arbor, 1988).

10. For discussions of *hamartia* that take it to include a range from character flaw to mistake of fact, see T. C. W. Stinson, "*Hamartia* in Aristotle and Greek Tragedy," *Classical Quarterly* 25 (1975): 221–54, and Nancy Sherman, "*Hamartia* and Virtue," in *Essays in Aristotle' Poetics*, ed. Amélie Oksenberg Rorty (Princeton, 1992), 177–96. For a reading of *hamartia* as character flaw, see E. R. Dodds, "On Misunderstanding the *Oedipus Rex*," in *The Ancient Concept of Progress and Other Essays on Greek Literature and Belief* (Oxford, 1973). For a discussion of the problems in interpreting *hamartia* see Cynthia Freeland, "Aristotle's *Poetics* in Relation to the Ethical Treatises," in *Aristotle's Philosophical Development: Problems and Prospects*, ed. William Wians (Totowa, N.J., 1995): 327–45.

11. Aristotle uses the term *epieikes* to describe the exceptionally virtuous person. The literal

translation of this is "good" or "decent." A bit further in the text (53a5–10) he says that when the three plotlines he discusses are eliminated there remains the plot that shows a tragic character who is intermediate in virtue between the person "superior to us in virtue and justice" and the wicked person. As commentators have pointed out (e.g., Richard Janko, trans. *Aristotle's Poetics I* [Indianapolis: Hackett, 1987], 100), this makes the translation of Aristotle's use of "*epieikes*" as "person of exceptional virtue," rather than merely "good or decent person," the most reasonable one.

12. For this argument see Stephen Halliwell, "Plato and Aristotle on the Denial of Tragedy," *Proceedings of the Cambridge Philological Society* 30 (1984): 49–71.

13. For a different account of this section, see Martha Nussbaum, *The Fragility of Goodness* (Cambridge, 1986), 388, who argues that the tragic character's *hamartia* does not explain her fall to misfortune, but is instead a means to enhance identification with the tragic protagonist. Aristotle does say here that pity and fear are felt for "one like ourselves," and so it is plausible to think that giving the tragic character a "*hamartia*" aids the average viewer in identifying with the tragic protagonist, but Aristotle also would seem to be saying that the *hamartia* helps to explain the character's fall. For helpful commentary on this section, see Janko, *Aristotle Poetics I*: 100.

14. See Stephen White, "Aristotle's Favorite Tragedies," in *Essays on Aristotle's Poetics*, ed. Rorty 221–41, for the argument that admirable action is at the heart of Aristotle's favorite tragedies, and that the protagonist's regret at the harm she performs (or is about to perform) is crucial for her to be worthy of admiration. White's argument that admirable action is key to the best tragedy would seem to work better for *Oedipus* (with his "noble" response when he learns of the harm he has unintentionally brought about) than for *Iphigenia in Tauris*, which presents the character of Iphigenia in a more ambiguous and questionable light.

15. See Nancy Sherman, "*Hamartia* and Virtue," in *Essays on Aristotle's Poetics*, ed. Rorty. Sherman does not, however, present this view as a way of resolving the tension between the two chapters.

16. The term "norm-defect" theory is borrowed from Gareth Matthews. For a discussion of how the biological works employs a "norm-defect" theory of gender differences, see his "Gender and Essence in Aristotle," *Australasian Journal of Philosophy* 64 (supplement): 16–25.

17. For this argument see my unpublished paper, "Aristotle on Learning From Tragedy." My thanks to Charlotte Witt for stressing in her comments on an earlier version of this essay that Aristotle in the *Poetics* has a narrow view of tragic error, and also for allowing me to read her unpublished paper, "Tragic Error and Agent Responsibility."

18. As other commentators have noted (e.g., H. D. F. Kitto, *Greek Tragedy*, [London, 1950]), Aristotle's theory more generally favors Sophocles' tragedies, but misdescribes Aeschylus's and Euripides' plays.

19. See the final section of her "Plot Imitates Action," in *Essays on Aristotle's Poetics*, ed. Rorty.

20. Ibid., 119. Freeland borrows the term "agent-centered moral luck" from Bernard Williams and Thomas Nagel. See Bernard Williams, "Moral Luck," *Proceedings of the Aristotelian Society*, suppl. vol. 50 (1976): 115–35, and Thomas Nagel, "Moral Luck," in *Mortal Questions* (Cambridge, 1979), 24–38.

21. *Tragic Ways of Killing A Women* (Cambridge, 1987). Loraux suggests that in Greek tragedy men and women have their own distinctive ways of meeting misfortune. She analyzes the implicit rules governing the proper ways for women to act in Greek tragedy, and suggests there are specific plot-structures and language implicitly associated with the representation of female tragic characters.

22. Another famous play with a woman protagonist, Sophocles' *Antigone*, has a plot that fails to fit into Aristotle's preferred narrative structures. Here there are at least several different

ways to interpret the plot-pattern of *Antigone*. Martha Nussbaum argues that there is a flaw in the two main characters, Antigone and Kreon—an inflexibility that makes them deliberate poorly—that leads to misfortune for both (see *Fragility of Goodness*, chap. 3). Or we can read this play as Hegel does (G. W. F. Hegel, *Phenomenology of Spirit*, trans. A. V. Miller [Oxford, 1977], para. 469, p. 283), who suggests that the error or failure that brings about misfortune in the story is not located in any individual, but is located in a world in which individual virtue comes up against a social structure with conflicting standards of the right. If *hamartia* is an aspect of character that leads, in certain special circumstances, to misfortune, rather than a "character flaw," then *Antigone* does not fit into Aristotle's category of best tragedy, no matter which of these two lines of interpretation one adopts. I shall present below a feminist "re-reading" of the play that is different from either of these two interpretations.

23. See his essay "A Short Organum for Theatre," in *Brecht on Theatre*, 181.

24. I am not persuaded by attempts to show that there is some kind of error or limitation in Oedipus's character that leads to his misfortune.

25. Martha C. Nussbaum, *The Fragility of Goodness*, esp. 378–90, and "Tragedy and Self-Sufficiency: Plato and Aristotle on Pity and Fear," in *Essays on Aristotle's Poetics*, ed. Rorty, 280–83; and Stephen Halliwell, "Pleasure, Understanding, and Emotion in Aristotle's Poetics," *Essays in Aristotle's Poetics*, ed. Rorty 241–60.

26. Nussbaum, "Tragedy and Self-Sufficiency," 281.

27. Nussbaum, *The Fragility of Goodness*, 391.

28. Halliwell, "Pleasure, Understanding," 246.

29. Ibid., 253.

30. For the connection between feminist discussions of the ethics of care and Aristotle's ethics, see the article by Ruth Groenhout in this volume (Chapter 7), as well as Marcia Homiak, "Feminism and Aristotle's Rational Ideal," in *A Mind of One's Own*, ed. Charlotte Witt and Louise Anthony (Boulder, Colo.: 1993): 1–18.

31. See Nussbaum, "Tragedy and Self-Sufficiency."

32. For a feminist deconstruction of this dichotomy, see Ferguson, "Does Reason Have a Gender." For the appeal in Aristotle's theory of virtue and account of the emotions for feminism, see Homiak, "Feminism and Aristotle's Rational Ideal."

33. For example: "Nowadays the play's meaning is usually blurred by the fact that the actor plays to the audience's hearts. The figures portrayed are foisted on the audience and are falsified in the process. Contrary to present custom they ought to be presented quite coldly, classically, objectively. For they are not matter for empathy; they are there to be understood. Feelings are private and limited. Against that the reason is fairly comprehensive and to be relied on." *Brecht on Theatre*, 15. See also 136–37, *Brecht on Theatre*, where Brecht suggests that empathy may have a part to play in aesthetic response.

34. A central feature of Nussbaum's and Halliwell's interpretation is that the pleasure of tragedy is the pleasure of learning, and that tragedy educates, on Aristotle's view. This interpretation of tragedy and tragic catharsis has been called into question by commentators such as Jonathan Lear in "Katharsis," in *Essays on Aristotle's Poetics*, ed. Rorty, 315–40, and by Andrew Ford, "Katharsis: The Ancient Problem," in *Performativity and Performance*, ed. Andrew Parker and Eve Kosofsky Sedgwick (New York, 1995), 109–32. One text these commentators cite as a problem for the "education" view of catharsis is *Politics* VIII 6, where Aristotle distinguishes the use of music for catharsis from its use in ethical training. Even if Lear and Parker are right in their interpretation of Aristotle, they are still committed to saying that tragic catharsis involves an intellectual and emotional response, though on their view it does not "educate" by involving the audience in drawing moral conclusions.

35. Elizabeth V. Spelman, "Slavery and Tragedy," in *Radical Philosophy: Tradition, Counter-Tradition, Politics*, ed. Roger S. Gottlieb (Philadelphia, 1993), 221–44.

36. Freeland, "Plot Imitates Action," esp. 119–22, for an argument that Aristotle's view of tragedy rules out plots that go against his own views on the relationship between character, happiness, and fortune.

37. For a discussion of some recent efforts along these lines in feminist theatre, see Peggy Phelan and Lynda Hart, ed., *Acting Out: Feminist Performances* (Ann Arbor Mich., 1993).

38. One problem for using *Politics* VIII 6 to support this reading of the *Poetics* is the one previously mentioned, namely, that in this chapter Aristotle distinguishes between the use of music to produce catharsis versus the use of music to educate or instruct in virtue (6 1341a15ff.). I would argue that this text presents a problem not just for my view of catharsis as political learning, and for Nussbaum's view of catharsis as moral education, but also for Lear's view that catharsis involves a kind of emotional reinforcement of basic truths concerning the rationality and order of the world (see Jonathan Lear, "Katharsis," 334–35). Andrew Ford argues ("Katharsis: The Ancient Problem") that "Aristotle offers no Platonic demand that tragic stories be true or morally improving. The role of structure is simply to drive us more surely into involvement with the experience" (113). In contrast, I have argued that Aristotle recommends tragedies with plots and characters that we *could* and *should* engage and identify with.

39. For this point see Amélie Rorty, "The Psychology of Aristotelian Tragedy," in *Essays on Aristotle's Poetics*, ed. Rorty, 16–18.

40. See Stephen White, "Aristotle's Favorite Tragedies," in *Essays on Aristotle's Poetics*, ed. Rorty 236–237.

41. For an argument that Aristotle thought of tragedy as a form of democratic education, see Stephen G. Salkever, "Tragedy and the Education of the *Demos*: Aristotle's Response to Plato," in *Greek Tragedy and Political Theory*, ed. J. Peter Euben (Berkeley and Los Angeles, University of California Press, 1986), 274–304. He says, "If we use the key Aristotelian terms *form* and *matter* metaphorically, as Aristotle himself often does, we can say that the function of tragedy is the unobtrusive imposition of a certain form upon a certain kind of matter (the democratic audience) by encouraging the acceptance of a certain opinion about what is truly fearful; not the weakness of the powerless, but the mistakes of the especially powerful" (300). This picture of political education by tragedy does not suggest that Aristotle thought of the audience as capable of reacting to the social and political messages in tragedy with their own critical responses; if anything, Salkever's image of the *demos* as "matter" that is subtly shaped by the "form" of tragedy's text indicates just the opposite.

42. For a critical examination of this aspect of Brecht's aesthetics, see Noël Carroll, *Mystifying Movies: Fads and Fallacies in Contemporary Film Theory* (New York, 1988), 90–105.

43. Nancy Sorkin Rabinowitz, *Anxiety Veiled* (Ithaca, N.Y., 1993), is one example of this type of approach. Her view will be discussed in greater detail below.

44. For an interesting discussion of how these problems of interpretation arise in the adaptation of Greek tragedies to films, see Kenneth MacKinnon, *Greek Tragedy Into Film* (London, 1986), 4–21.

45. For a discussion of new feminist "revisionings" of the character of Electra, see "Envisioning Electra Anew, as a Heroic Figure," *New York Times*, 22 September 1996, sect. H, p. 4.

46. Thanks to Cynthia Freeland for suggesting the relevance of this film for my discussion.

47. For an excellent discussion of how Medea can be seen as having a "divided" male and female self, see Helene Foley, "Medea's Divided Self," in *Classical Antiquity* 8 (1989): 60–85, and Bernard Knox, "The *Medea* of Euripides," in his *Word and Action* (Baltimore, 1979), 295–322.

48. Cynthia Freeland, "Plot Imitates Action," 127.

49. By "ideology" I mean, following Marx, a system of representation by means of which relations of power and oppression are made to seem natural and inevitable. See Karl Marx,

"Introduction to the Critique of Political Economy," in *Dramatic Theory and Criticism: Greeks to Grotowski*, ed. Bernard F. Dukore (New York, 1974).

50. Rabinowitz, *Anxiety Veiled*, 84.

51. For this point see Nicole Loraux, *Tragic Ways of Killing A Woman*, especially 28 and 46.

52. *Alcestis*, in *Euripides* I, trans. Richmond Lattimore (Chicago, 1955).

53. Lattimore, *Euripides* I: 4.

54. For example, see Martha Nussbaum, *Fragility of Goodness*, chap. 3, and Arlene W. Saxonhouse, *Fear of Diversity: The Birth of Political Science in Ancient Greek Thought* (Chicago, 1992), 63–76.

55. See Hegel's *Phenomenology of Spirit*.

56. Sophocles' *Antigone*, trans. Richard Emil Braun (New York, 1973).

57. For a discussion of the role of the Chorus in the play, see Braun, *Antigone*, 16–18.

58. For a feminist analysis of Antigone as a character who denies her "difference" as a woman who is different than men and dependent on the city, see Saxonhouse, *Fear of Diversity*. She says that by attachment to, "the uncreated, uncreating, eternal, and unmoving dead, as well as to the unmoving, ungenerated laws of Zeus, Antigone neuters herself; she is neither male nor female" (69).

59. For the suggestion that *Medea* fits the plot-pattern of the wicked person changing from bad to good fortune, see Elizabeth Belfiore, *Tragic Pleasures* (Ann Arbor, Mich., 1992), 161.

60. For this point, see Sue Ellen Case, *Feminism and Theatre* (London, 1987), 17.

61. For an excellent discussion of how Medea can be seen as having a "divided" male and female self, see Foley, "Medea's Divided Self," and Knox, "The *Medea* of Euripides," in his *Word and Action*.

62. See Rabinowitz, *Anxiety Veiled*, 125–54.

63. See Froma Zeitlin, "Playing the Other," in her *Playing the Other: Gender and Society in Classical Greek Literature* (Chicago, 1996), 348.

64. See Claire Johnston, "Women's Cinema as Counter Cinema," in *Notes on Women's Cinema*, ed. Claire Johnston (London, 1973), and Laura Mulvey, "Visual Pleasure and Narrative Cinema," *Screen* 16 (Autumn 1975): 6–18.

65. Rabinowitz, *Anxiety Veiled*. See especially her introductory chapter where she links her own work with that of feminist film critics Laura Mulvey and Teresa de Lauretis.

66. Noël Carroll, "The Image of Women in Film: A Defense of a Paradigm," *Journal of Aesthetics and Art Criticism* 48, no. 4 (Fall 1990): 349–60.

67. Teresa de Lauretis, *Technologies of Gender* (Bloomington, 1987).

68. For interesting discussion of Brechtian feminist theater theory see Diamond, "Brechtian Theory/Feminist Theory" and "Mimesis, Mimicry and the True-Real"; and Dolan, *The Feminist Spectator as Critic*.

69. See for example, Cynthia Freeland, "Realist Horror," in *Philosophy and Film*, ed. Cynthia A. Freeland and Thomas E. Wartenberg (New York, 1995), 126–42, and "Feminist Frameworks for Horror Films," in *Post-Theory: Reconstructing Film Studies*, ed. David Bordwell and Noël Carroll (Madison, Wis., 1996), 195–218; bell hooks, "The Oppositional Gaze: Black Female Spectators," in *Black American Cinema*, ed. Manthia Diawara (New York, 1993), 288–302; B. Ruby Rich, "In The Name of Feminist Film Criticism," in ed. *Multiple Voices in Feminist Film Criticism*, ed. Diane Carson, Linda Dittmar, and Janice R. Welsch (Minneapolis, Minn., 1994), 27–47; Laurie Shrage, "Feminist Film Aesthetics: A Contextual Approach," in *Aesthetics in Feminist Perspective*, ed. Hilde Hein and Carolyn Korsmeyer (Bloomington, 1993), 139–49.

70. Rich, "In the Name of Feminist Film Criticism," 35.

12

(Re)positioning Pedagogy
A Feminist Historiography of Aristotle's *Rhetorica*

Carol Poster

To discuss Aristotle's *Rhetorica* as it has been received in the twentieth century is to discuss what appear to be two separate books. The version of the *Rhetorica* that appears in discussions by philosophers is a minor work, peripheral to Aristotle's central projects, and elaborating on trivial points investigated to greater philosophic depth in the *Organon* and *Ethics*.[1] Professional rhetoricians, located in English and speech departments, read a different version of the *Rhetorica*: a work of overwhelming importance, central to classical thought and the classical tradition, and forming the foundation of their own discipline.

Feminist philosophers need to interrogate both models of the *Rhetorica* from two perspectives, that of historical accuracy and that of feminist theory. Although it could be argued that the notion of "historical accuracy" per se is antithetical to the subjectivist epistemologies favoured by many feminist theorists, close historical examination of the reception history of Aristotle's *Rhetorica* reveals a pattern of systematic overestimation of the importance of the philosophical tradition in rhetorical scholarship and a concomitant marginalization of the (feminized) pedagogical tradition in philosophical scholarship.

Both the marginalization of Aristotle's *Rhetorica* in philosophical historiography and the centrality of the *Rhetorica* in rhetorical historiography exemplify the way in which prestige hierarchies construct intellectual history. Rhetoric, in the past two centuries, has been associated with the (feminized) low prestige task of introductory writing instruction. Women tend to predominate in the poorly paid and minimally respected positions of governess, schoolteacher, or adjunct composition instructor, while men tend to dominate the upper ranks of the university professoriate. The way in which Aristotle's *Rhetorica* has (or has not) functioned as an authorizing text has depended on the class and gender hierarchies within which its reception has been situated.

Philosophers, on the one hand, working in a higher prestige discipline of *Geisteswissenschaft,* unproblematically treat Aristotle's rhetorical treatises as minor footnotes to his major philosophical tasks.[2] Rhetoricians, on the other hand, working in the lower prestige discipline of writing pedagogy, attempt to authorize their own projects by making Aristotle central to their own discipline, trying to use the *auctoritas* of Aristotle as a means to increase the prestige of composition studies.

From the point of view of feminist historiography, however, what ought to be the case is precisely the reverse of what is the case: we need to reposition rhetoric, with its acceptance of subjectivist epistemology and emotional discourse and its traditionally feminine connection with pedagogy closer to the center of philosophy, and reconstitute rhetoric by displacing Aristotle's philosophical treatise to the margins of the discipline and reasserting the value of (feminine) pedagogical rhetoric against the agonistic and dialectical Aristotelian model.

Richard Rorty's is one of the most useful models for understanding the historiography of rhetoric and the marginalization of pedagogy within it. Rorty categorizes philosophical historiography into four genres: historical reconstruction, rational reconstruction, *Geistesgeschichte*, and doxography.[3] While he considers the first three types of historiography as in themselves useful and contributing to his larger project of intellectual history, he dismisses the fourth category, doxography, as a "calamity."[4]

Some feminist historiographies can fit quite easily under the first three of Rorty's rubrics. The feminist recovery movement as exemplified by Mary Ellen Waithe's *A History of Women Philosophers* or Madeleine Henry's *Prisoner of History: Aspasia of Miletus and Her Biographical Tradition,* can be classified as forms of historical reconstruction. Elizabeth Spelman's "Hairy Cobblers and Philosopher-Queens" and many of the other essays in Bat-Ami Bar On's recent collection, *Engendering Origins: Critical Feminist Readings In Plato and Aristotle* that look at the problem of gender in ancient philosophy could be read as rational reconstructions.[5] Works of many such French theoretical feminists as Cixous, Irigaray, and Kristeva redefine the boundaries of philosophy in a manner typical of what Rorty terms *Geistesgeschichte.* If there is one genre of historiography occupying the excluded feminine space of pedagogy, it is the "calamity" of doxography.

While speaking from the privileged position of a professor at the summit of the prestige hierarchy of the American academy, Rorty can casually dismiss doxographies as "books which start from Thales or Descartes and wind up with . . . some contemporary, . . . ticking off what various figures traditionally called 'philosophers' had to say about problems traditionally called 'philosophical.' "[6] These books, however, serve a purpose Rorty ignores.

For those who teach introductory survey courses that fulfill distribution requirements in general humanities or philosophy at public undergraduate or comprehensive institutions, ones drawing their students from the lower part (in grades and standardized tests) of the college-bound population, doxographies are far more effective pedagogical tools than Rorty's recommendation of, say, examining the intricacies of Kant's three *Critiques* or how they might inform Schleiermacher's theology,[7] which would indeed be the true calamity in the classroom. These doxographies, while marginalized within elite academic institutions, are more influential in terms of sheer numbers of readers than the more rarefied and prestigious works valorized by Rorty. In any given year, far more students are enrolled in general introductory courses at second- or third-tier institutions than are enrolled in graduate seminars at elite institutions. The press runs of elementary textbooks outnumber those of scholarly books by at least an order of magnitude. Despite their numerical influence, however, pedagogical texts receive little respect in the academic community, often not even counting in the tenure and promotion process at Ph.D.-granting institutions.

The privileging of "pure" scholarship over the pedagogical/doxographical tradition reflects a gendering of academic prestige and economic hierarchies. In the specific field of rhetoric, women are a statistical majority at the lowest ranks of the professional hierarchy (part-time and community college teaching), but become progressively smaller minorities at higher ranks and higher prestige institutions. The gender distribution of published articles is similarly skewed. A survey by Theresa Enos[8] examined articles published from 1982 to 1987 in rhetoric journals. Men dominate the theoretical journals, authoring 76 percent of the articles in *Pre/text* and 81 percent of the articles in *Rhetoric Society Quarterly*. Women are the majority of the authors in only two rhetoric journals, *The Journal of Basic Writing* (58 percent), a journal focusing on remedial writing pedagogy, and *The Writing Instructor* (62 percent), a pedagogy-centered graduate student-edited journal.

The way in which contemporary scholars have (re)constructed histories of rhetoric very much reflects the gendered anti-pedagogical bias of the discipline. Majorie Curry Woods has pointed out:

> We can see their suppression of the pedagogical focus of classical rhetoric in the choice of rhetoric texts from earlier eras that traditional historians elevate to authoritative status. At one extreme is the modern canonization of Aristotle's *Rhetoric,* a text that was never popular as a pedagogical treatise in the ancient world, and at the other the rejection of Cicero's *De inventione* and the Pseudo-Ciceronian *Rhetorica ad Herennium,* two rhetorical handbooks widely used in schools for hundreds of years.[9]

Another factor contributing to the eclipse of the pedagogical tradition in rhetoric is its tendency to anonymous or plural authorship. As Foucault[10] has argued, texts derive *auctoritas* from the naming of individual authors, itself a patriarchal concept that is susceptible to feminist critique. Much of the pedagogical tradition in rhetoric, however, lacks this *auctoritas*. Classroom texts and practices often are handed down in the form of scholia or commentaries on popular school texts, such as the commentaries on Vinsauf's *Poetria Nova* that have been edited and translated by Woods.[11] Anonymous scholia on Homer or Cicero, however, are not names that conjure with the same efficaciousness as Aristotle, no matter how many students they had influenced, and so often take a marginal place in contemporary histories of rhetoric and philosophy. The

unique editorial problems of handbooks, commentaries, and scholia further exacerbate this problem.

The modern tradition of textual editing is based on the notion of a
recovery of an archetype authorizing the text by its closeness to a unique
original. While McGann[12] has challenged the validity of the notion of a
unique originary text as the telos of the editorial project for modern texts,
editorial theory in classical studies, outside the limited discipline or oral-
ity-literacy theory, tends to privilege stemmatic theories. Pedagogical
texts, however, rarely possess a unique archetype, but instead have tended
to go through several versions or revisions as knowledge or fashion had
changed. If time machines existed, we could imagine retrieving the
"best" text of a Platonic dialogue in the form of an autograph papyrus,
but such is not the case with collections of *progymnasmata*, which like
the classroom exercises and handbooks of today varied from teacher to
teacher and decade to decade, and even could be revised multiple times
by a single author in response to changing pedagogical environments or
theoretical fashions (e.g., the short and long versions of Vinsauf's *Docu-
mentum*). As Reynolds and Wilson mention,[13] manuscripts of textbooks,
commentaries, and scholia exhibit variations consistent with deliberate
as well as accidental scribal alterations. The handbooks of rhetoric that
competed with Aristotle's *Rhetorica* thus tend not to have been preserved
as individually authored texts, but instead incorporated into a constantly
changing collaborative and anonymous tradition of handbook rhetoric
lacking in the *auctoritas* that has caused Aristotle's work to dominate our
historical narratives of ancient rhetoric.

While the *Rhetorica*, a treatise located in the context of philosophical
study of rhetoric in the advanced and elite educational settings of the
Academy and Lyceum, has been preserved in the esoteric Aristotelian
corpus, the more elementary treatises or those not associated with the
prestige of an important author have vanished. Even the preservation of
the *Rhetorica ad Alexandrum*,[14] the only other extant handbook from the
period, depended on its ancient misattribution to Aristotle.

The contrast between the *Rhetorica* and the *Rhetorica ad Alexandrum*
illustrates the major differences between philosophical and handbook
rhetoric. Aristotle's *Rhetorica* outlines a theory of rhetoric firmly
grounded in dialectic and assumes a mastery of philosophical logic on the
part of the student. Of the three types of proof (from *êthos*, *logos*, and
pathos) Aristotle clearly privileges the logical mode, and sees the enthymeme, which he defines as a rhetorical syllogism, as the most impor-

tant form of argument. Aristotle firmly distinguishes between the *entechnai* (intrinsic) and *atechnai* (extrinsic) *pisteis* (proofs) and focuses almost exclusively on the *entechnai pisteis* due to their being the matters proper to the discipline of rhetoric. The *Rhetorica ad Alexandrum*, on the other hand, rather than theorizing rhetoric in relation to dialectic and ethics or being concerned with ideal abstract disciplinary divisions simply describes how to compose speeches for various occasions and recommends whichever practical techniques will work best, including manipulating the emotions of the audience and behaving morally in one's private and public life to obtain the sort of good reputation that will appeal to a jury.

The Reception of Aristotle's *Rhetorica*

To understand how Aristotle's *Rhetorica* achieved its status in current scholarship, it is necessary to examine both its textual and critical reception from antiquity through the present. In addressing the question of the centrality or marginality of the *Rhetorica* in Aristotle's corpus from a strictly historical perspective, at least during the period from classical antiquity through the nineteenth century, the philosophers are right concerning its insignificance. Generally, rhetoricians either have ignored the *Rhetorica* or appropriated only small sections of it: Hellenistic rhetoricians didn't know it; Neoplatonic commentators overlooked it; the Byzantines didn't understand it; the early Middle Ages didn't have it; the late Middle Ages and Renaissance scholars were puzzled by it; and not until the prejudice against Aristotle due to his association with Scholasticism died away was the *Rhetorica* revived alongside Ciceronian rhetoric in the eighteenth and nineteenth centuries. Some of the explanation for the marginal position of the *Rhetorica* in the rhetorical tradition can be traced to the dual problems of the textual tradition of the work and to the apparently self-contradictory nature of Aristotle's opinions concerning rhetoric.

What we know as the Aristotelian corpus is not a group of polished essays written for publication, but rather a miscellaneous collection of school papers: lecture notes from which Aristotle spoke, students' notes, memoranda, and drafts.[15] The textual tradition of the *Rhetorica* and the other treatises that compose what we know as the Aristotelian corpus between the death of Theophrastus (288 B.C.E.) and the editorial work of Andronicus of Rhodes (c. 40 B.C.E.) is somewhat unclear. Both Strabo and Plutarch provide accounts of the loss of Aristotle's treatises after the death of Theophrastus and their rediscovery by Sulla and subsequent arrangement by the grammarian Tyrannio (c. 80 B.C.E.) and publication by Andronicus,[16] but it is difficult to determine precisely the degree to which these accounts are reliable with respect to details. In terms of the reception of the *Rhetorica,* however, the tradition of the unavailability of the Aristotelian corpus does accord well with the apparent lack of influence of the *Rhetorica* on Hellenistic rhetoric.[17]

Unfortunately, much of the scholarship on the Aristotelian influence on Hellenistic rhetoric suffers by assuming that any idea found in the *Rhetorica* is unique to Aristotle, and therefore a later treatment of an idea found in the *Rhetorica* is prima facie evidence for Aristotelian influence.[18] This assumption is based on marginalizing or discounting the possibility of an independent handbook tradition in rhetoric, grounded in professional oratory and pedagogy, with an importance at least equal to, if not greater than, the philosophical tradition. There is, however, solid evidence of such a handbook tradition in ancient sources. Unfortunately, since such a handbook tradition is located within the low prestige (feminine) discipline of elementary writing pedagogy, it has not received the same scholarly attention as recovery of higher prestige philosophical texts. While, for example, pre-Socratic philosophers for whom few or, in the case of Pherecydes, no fragments are extant have been the subject of innumerable books and articles, the bibliography on even such relatively significant figures in ancient composition pedagogy as Alcidamas is comparatively meager.

Dionysius of Halicarnassus (fl. C. 30 B.C.E.) addresses precisely this point of a tradition of rhetorical theory independent of Aristotle when, in his "First Letter to Ammaeus," he rebuts the claim of an anonymous peripatetic that Demonsthenes had read Aristotle's *Rhetorica.*[19] Instead, Dionysius suggests that many other orators and writers of handbooks made equally important contributions to rhetorical theory, including Theodorus, Thrasymachus, Antiphon, Anaximenes, Alcidamas, Theodectes, Philiscus, Isaeus, Cephidorus, Hyperides, Lycurgus, Aeschines, and Isocrates ("First Letter To Ammaeus," 2). Quintilian (c. 30–100 C.E.) also suggests that the Isocratean school was quite as important as the Aristotelian, and that later rhetoric was greatly influenced by the highly original work of Hermagoras (fl. c. 150 B.C.E.) whose system of stasis

theory dominated Roman forensic oratory (*Institutio Oratoria* III.i.14–
19).[20] [Demetrius's] *On Style*, whose dates unfortunately are quite uncer-
tain, perhaps shows the strongest peripatetic influence of the extant
Hellenistic rhetorical treatises, but still differs with Aristotle concerning
the four types of style, the value of lucidity, the use of wit, and definition
of the enthymeme.[21] Hermogenes (born c. 161 c.e.), whose work was
extremely important to Latin and Greek rhetoric from late antiquity
through the Renaissance, shows no particular indebtedness to Aristotle,
but rather combines Hermagorean stasis theory with a platonizing model
of the ideas of style.[22]

Even Cicero, who certainly displayed a greater interest in Greek rhetoric and philosophy than most of his Roman contemporaries, probably was
acquainted with the *Rhetorica* only through florilegia or later handbooks.
William Fortenbaugh argues convincingly that even in *De oratore* "in
regard to Aristotle and Theophrastus, Cicero does not seem to have advanced much beyond handbook knowledge" and that "no passage speaks
strongly in favour of direct acquaintance with either Aristotle's *Rhetoric*
or any comparable Theophrastean work."[23] Similarly, as George Kennedy
mentions, Quintilian does not consider Aristotle's *Rhetorica* especially
important.[24] Late antique Greek works, such as Menander Rhetor's *On
the Divisions of the Epideictic*[25] or the letter-writing treatises attributed to
Libanius and Proclus[26] are indebted to Hermogenes rather than Aristotle,
and Cicero is naturally the *fons et origo* of the Latin rhetorical tradition.
The figure of Hermogenes dominates Byzantine rhetoric. As Thomas
Conley points out, "Aristotle's *Rhetoric* was at most a rather shadowy
presence in Byzantium and exerted little, if any, influence."[27]

In the Latin west, the *Rhetorica* was, if anything, even less accessible
than in Byzantium. Boethius was the last major rhetorical theorist of the
Latin west able to read Greek fluently until the twelfth century, and
Boethius, despite writing extensively about and translating Aristotle's
treatises on dialectical and rhetorical subjects, almost entirely ignored
the *Rhetorica*. The major rhetorical innovations of the medieval period
were in the areas of grammatical instruction, especially teaching techniques of amplification and modification of existing material rather than
the more philosophically based study of invention, and *dictamen*, professional training in letter-writing. While many specialized studies of medieval rhetoric have been published in the past century,[28] precisely because
of the low prestige of the pedagogical innovations of the Middle Ages,
these advances often are overlooked in the main traditions of rhetorical

historiography in favor of the more philosophical rhetoric of the Aristotelian tradition.[29]

The *Rhetorica* was not available in Latin until it received two translations in the thirteenth century, the relatively unpopular *translatio vetus* (c. 1250) possibly by Bartholomew of Messina and the better-known translation done by William of Moerbeke (1270) under the sponsorship of Thomas Aquinas,[30] as well as the commentary and paraphrase by Hermannus Alemannus. There is only a single major medieval commentary on the *Rhetorica*, that by Aquinas's disciple, Giles of Rome (c. 1285), which was not actually printed until 1523. When the *Rhetorica* was included in the medieval school curriculum, it was not studied as a rhetorical treatise but as a minor political or ethical work and had little or no influence on the primarily Ciceronian rhetorics of the period.[31]

The Renaissance tradition of the *Rhetorica* is similar to the medieval. As a rhetorical treatise, it is not particularly influential, but rather continues to be read as a minor ethical treatise. Vives (1531), for example, sees it as a work concerning political prudence, and Barbaro (1544) reads it as a treatise on the passions and faculties.[32] While Ramus's attacks on Aristotle (*Aristotelicae animadversiones*, 1543) show knowledge of Aristotle's *Rhetorica*, for Ramus, Aristotle, though the authority to be attacked on questions of logic, is less important a rhetorical *auctor* than either Quintilian or Cicero.[33] John Rainolde's lectures at Oxford during the 1570 were "the earliest critical study of Aristotle's *Rhetoric* in England."[34] A familiarity with Aristotle's rhetorical as well as logical works is assumed by Antonio Riccobono in his 1579 translation and commentary on the *Rhetorica*, but Ludovico Carbone's 1597 *Introductio in logicam* firmly subordinates rhetoric to dialectic.[35] While the *Rhetorica* becomes steadily better known each succeeding century, its influence continues to be slight.

Vossius's rhetorical treatises (1606–26) are unusual in their reliance on Aristotle.[36] The *Rhetorica* did not even receive an English translation until Thomas Hobbes's 1637 *A Briefe of the Art of Rhetorique* and Bernard Lamy (1640–1715), Dominique Bouhours (1628–1702), and Charles Rollin (1661–1741) still use Quintilian and Cicero as classical models rather than referring back to Aristotle.[37] The elocutionary movement, as exemplified by John Bulwer's *Chirologia* (1644), Michel la Faucheur's *Traité de l'action de l'orateur, ou de la Prononciation et de geste* (1st ed., 1657; 2d ed., 1686), and Thomas Sheridan's *A Course of Lectures on Elocution* (1762), relies on psychological theories of gesture rather than

Aristotelian notions of *entechnê pistis*.[38] Considerably more scholarly attention, however, has been devoted to Aristotle's influence on early modern rhetoric than to study of the methods of the grammar books that
were actually used to instruct the majority of the educated population,
including women and the middle classes.[39]

Of the major rhetorical theorists of the late eighteenth century and
early nineteenth century who were to influence the development of rhetorical theory and writing instruction in America, only Richard Whately
demonstrates a strong interest in Aristotle, but even his model of argumentation is primarily the syllogistic of the *Analytics* rather than the
enthymeme of the *Rhetorica*.[40] The more important faculty-psychology
grounded rhetoric of George Campbell and the bellelettristic rhetoric of
Hugh Blair show little Aristotelian influence.[41] Alexander Bain's tremen-
dously popular *English Composition and Rhetoric: A Manual* (1866), which
became the dominant text of the new discipline of English composition
(contemporary first-year composition), was primarily grammatical and
bellelettristic in orientation.[42] While the *Rhetorica* continued to be of
specialized interest to classicists, its sphere of influence did not expand
beyond the narrow compass of classics and university pedagogy. The Aristotelian model of rhetoric did not strongly influence vernacular rhetorics
or grammar books used for instruction in the Dissenting academies and
other non-elite pedagogical institutions.[43]

While Aristotle's *Rhetorica* was studied in America in the early and
mid-twentieth century as a theoretical text, especially at the University
of Chicago,[44] its pedagogical circulation continued to be limited. Perhaps
a convenient landmark for the introduction of Aristotle into the university first-year and advanced composition curricula was the publication of
Edward Corbett's *Classical Rhetoric for the Modern Student* in 1965.[45] Over
the past thirty years, the *Rhetorica* has become a central authoritative
text in composition studies, and both Aristotle's treatise and composition
textbooks closely modeled on it have proliferated throughout both first-
year and advanced composition courses.[46]

The valorization of Aristotle's *Rhetorica* in composition studies as the
central authoritative text in the tradition of rhetoric has little merit on
strictly historical or philological grounds; it does, however, have an important polemical and rhetorical purpose. Composition as a field has traditionally been at the bottom of the prestige hierarchy in English
departments, and, as Thomas Miller suggests, "[c]omposition specialists
have used the prestige of a classical heritage to make the teaching of

writing respectable in English departments."[47] Kathleen Welch also accounts for the current prestige of Aristotle's *Rhetorica* as resulting from a nostalgic criticism that (1) depends on faith to suppress thought and (2) creates an unchangeable hierarchy of privileged texts depending on argument from questionable authority.[48] She suggests: "One modern reception of Aristotle's *Rhetoric* acts as a useful example of both these problems: when the *Rhetoric* is treated as an Arnoldian touchstone. . . . In . . . the creation of a hierarchy of texts, the *Rhetoric* is placed at the top of the hierarchy. This placement goes so far as to make the *Rhetoric* the beginning of classical rhetoric, rather than a product of and response to at least a century and a half of intense rhetorical inquiry, pedagogy, and writing."[49]

The Place of the *Rhetorica* in Aristotle's Philosophical System

Three distinct issues could be addressed by a specifically feminist reading of the text, rather than the reception, of Aristotle's *Rhetorica*: (1) the use of the theories propounded by Aristotle as models for feminist rhetoric; (2) whether Aristotle was himself advocating the theories sympathetic to feminist goals he sets forth in the *Rhetorica* or whether he merely collates and summarizes opinions of others; (3) Aristotle's specific treatment of women within the *Rhetorica*.

At first reading, Aristotle's account of rhetoric, while not specifically advocating anything even remotely resembling contemporary feminism(s), does seem to leave open a space for a discourse of the type advocated by many feminists.[50] As many feminist rhetoricians have argued, public discourse generally has been a space from which the woman rhetor has been excluded. Any general rhetoric that theorizes public speaking as the sole legitimate subject of rhetorical theory tends to silence or marginalize women. The practical project of recovering historical women's rhetoric has depended on the theoretical foundation of deconstructing the public/private opposition, and thus revaluing the (feminist) historiography of private speech, including letters, diaries, and autobiography.[51] Perhaps because Aristotle was writing within a relatively small democratic community, the *Rhetorica* does portray the private sphere as a legitimate object of rhetoric, and like contemporary feminist rhetorical historiography does not sharply demarcate the public from the private spaces within which oratory is practiced:

ἔστι δ' ἐάν τε πρὸς ἕνα τις τῷ λόγῳ χρώμενος προτρέπῃ ἢ ἀποτρέπῃ, οἷον οἱ νουθετοῦντες ποιοῦσιν ἢ πείθοντες (οὐδὲν γὰρ ἧττον κριτὴς ὁ εἷς: ὃν γὰρ δεῖ πεῖσαι, οὗτός ἐστιν ὡς εἰπεῖν ἁπλῶς κριτής), ἐάν τε πρὸς ἀμφισβητοῦντας, ἐάν τε πρὸς ὑπόθεσιν λέγῃ τις, ὁμοίως (τῷ γὰρ λόγῳ ἀνάγκη χρῆσθαι καὶ ἀναιρεῖν τὰ ἐναντία, πρὸς ἃ ὥσπερ ἀμφισβητοῦντα τὸν λόγον ποιεῖται),

(And there is judgement whether the speaker addresses a single individual and makes use of the speech to exhort or dissuade, as do those who give advice or try to persuade, for this single individual is equally a judge, since, speaking generally, he who has to be persuaded is a judge; if the speaker is arguing against an opponent or against some theory, it is just the same, for it is necessary to make use of speech to destroy the opposing arguments.) (*Rhet.* II.xviii.1)

If persuading an individual is indeed a legitimate function of rhetoric, then Antigone is, in fact, functioning as a rhetorician, albeit an unscientific one, when she attempts to convince Creon of the legitimacy of her action in burying her brother and Aristotle does in fact use one of Antigone's arguments as an example of the type of supporting reason that can be used in construction of *êthos* in the narrative section of a speech (*Rhet.* III.xvi.9). Even given their extremely restricted roles within Athenian society, women certainly had occasions on which they found it necessary to engage in private persuasion of other individuals, even in such quotidien domestic matters as a housewife bargaining with a fishwife over the price of a fresh mullet. Aristotle's theories would allow such private activities to be rhetorical, even if, as I shall discuss below, he might consider the unphilosophical female rhetor's speech distinctly inferior to that of more scientific or technical rhetoricians.

Aristotle states that "the orator persuades by *êthos* when his speech is delivered in such a manner as to render him worthy of confidence" (*Rhet.* I.ii.4). This persuasion by character is certainly accessible to women. Even if most women did not have the rhetorical education necessary for scientific techniques of constructing *entechnos êthos*, the *atechnai* feminine virtues such as chastity, thriftiness, and other appropriate womanly behaviors they displayed in private life could certainly be used to support their cases in legal proceedings. Although Aristotle nowhere advocates giving women the sort of rhetorical education that would enable them to produce the enthymematic reasoning characteristic of the best type of oratory, he does insist that the orator, to speak well, must be acquainted with the nature of true happiness (*Rhet.* I.iv.2) and the virtues and vices (*Rhet.* I.ix.1), things of which women would need at least some knowledge in order to lead virtuous lives. From the extensive treatment of emotions in Book II, it is apparent that the emotions are important to Aristotle's model of oratory, a position again congruent with many current feminist rhetorical and philosophical theories, such as Martha Nussbaum's treatment of the role of emotion in philosophy.

Even the opening of the *Rhetorica* appears to open a universal space for discourse, not limited to any one class or gender:

> Ἡ ῥητορική ἐστιν ἀντίστροφος τῇ διαλεκτικῇ: ἀμφότεραι γὰρ περὶ τοιούτων τινῶν εἰσιν ἃ κοινὰ τρόπον τινὰ ἁπάντων ἐστὶ γνωρίζειν καὶ οὐδεμιᾶς ἐπιστήμης ἀφωρισμένης: διὸ καὶ πάντες τρόπον τινὰ μετέχουσιν ἀμφοῖν: πάντες γὰρ μέχρι τινὸς καὶ ἐξετάζειν καὶ ὑπέχειν λόγον καὶ ἀπολογεῖσθαι καὶ κατηγορεῖν ἐγχειροῦσιν.

> Rhetoric is the counterpart of dialectic; for both have to do with matters that are in a manner in the cognizance of all people and not confined to any special science. Hence all people have a share of both; for all, up to a certain point, endeavour to criticize or uphold an argument, to defend themselves, or to accuse. (*Rhet.* I.i.1)

The apparent inclusiveness of Aristotle's model for rhetoric is, however, immediately undercut by his insistence on two hierarchies: a hierarchy of types of knowledge (in which rhetoric occupies a relatively low position) and a hierarchy of types of argument within rhetoric in which the logical means of persuasion, especially the enthymeme, which resemble dialectic, are presented as superior to the less properly technical emotional and ethical appeals.

In the Aristotelian hierarchy, the more noble and serious sciences (αἱ ἐπιστῆμαι καλλίους ἢ σπουδαιότεραι) have more noble and serious subjects (*Rhet.* I.vii.20), and rhetoric, being a means to an end is less noble than the ends (politics) to which it is a means.[52] Even though Aristotle treats rhetorical technique at length, there is considerable evidence, both in the text of the *Rhetorica* itself, and in *testimonia*, that he considered rhetoric an art considerably inferior to dialectic,[53] and only necessary due to the lamentable ignorance of audiences. The private, unscientific, emotive rhetoric most congenial to feminist theory that Aristotle describes, is, in fact, also a type of rhetoric he specifically considers inferior. He states:

δια γὰρ τοῦτο τῆς αὐτῆς οὔσης μεθόδου περὶ τὰ δημηγορικὰ καὶ δικανικά, καὶ καλλίονος καὶ πολιτικωτέρας τῆς δημηγορικῆς πραγματείας οὔσης ἢ τῆς περὶ τὰ συναλλάγματα . . .

The method of deliberative and forensic rhetoric is the same and although the pursuit of the former is nobler and more worthy of a statesman than that of the latter, which is limited to transactions between private citizens . . . (*Rhet.* I.i.10)

Like the other *endoxai* that Aristotle collates at the beginnings of his works, the theories of earlier rhetoricians concerning emotional appeals are included primarily to be dismissed.[54] Aristotle even condemns rhetorical techniques in the same passages in which he explains how best to use them, for example, in his treatments of how to praise undeservedly (*Rhet.* I.ix.28–32) and how to manipulate judges' emotions (*Rhet.* II.1.1–7).[55] Aristotle apparently considers ignoble emotional appeals necessary because of the generally inferior quality of the audiences to which rhetoric is addressed; he says, for example:[56]

ἔστι δὲ τὸ ἔργον αὐτῆς περί τε τοιούτων περὶ ὧν βουλευόμεθα καὶ τέχνας μὴ ἔχομεν, καὶ ἐν τοῖς τοιούτοις ἀκροαταῖς οἳ οὐ δύνανται διὰ πολλῶν συνορᾶν οὐδὲ λογίζεσθαι πόρρωθεν.

The function of rhetoric, then, is to deal with things about which we deliberate but for which we have no systematic rules; and in the presence of such hearers as are unable to take a general view of many stages, or to follow a lengthy chain of argument. (*Rhet.* I.ii.12)

This necessity for unscientific speaking in order to persuade the crowd can explain why Aristotle found it necessary to give lectures on rhetoric even if, within the course of his lectures, he seemed to disapprove strongly of the entire art. As he says, "it would be absurd if it were considered disgraceful not to be able to defend oneself with the help of the body, but not disgraceful as far as speech is concerned" (*Rhet.* I.i.12–13), a statement that accords well with the account that he originally started teaching rhetoric because it would be shameful to remain silent and allow Isocrates to speak (Diogenes Laertius V.3).

Not only does Aristotle marginalize the forms of discourse most accessible to women, but his statements about women are far from congruent with feminist ideals. He speaks of the Mytileneans honouring Sappho "although she was a woman" (*Rhet.* II.xxiii.11), and suggests that the best way to praise a woman is by listing her distinguished male relatives (*Rhet.* I.ix.31). As an example of the *topos* of greater and lesser, Aristotle says:

οἷον εἰ ὁ μέγιστος ἀνὴρ γυναικὸς τῆς μεγίστης μείζων, καὶ ὅλως οἱ ἄνδρες τῶν γυναικῶν μείζους, καὶ εἰ οἱ ἄνδρες ὅλως τῶν γυναικῶν μείζους, καὶ ἀνὴρ ὁ μέγιστος τῆς μεγίστης γυναικὸς μείζων· ἀνάλογον γὰρ ἔχουσιν αἱ ὑπεροχαὶ τῶν γενῶν καὶ τῶν μεγίστων ἐν αὐτοῖς.

If the biggest man is greater than the biggest woman, men in general will be bigger than women; and if men in general are bigger than women, the biggest man will be bigger than the biggest woman; for the superiority of classes and the greatest things contained in them are proportionate. (*Rhet.* I.vii.5)

It would be possible to read this comparison of the size of men and women as purely physical, but when read against, for example, G.A. II.i, it is hard not to read this as yet another example of woman's inferiority.[57] Especially in light of the absence of women students from the Lyceum, it is quite difficult to read Aristotle as an advocate of women's rights. Instead, the evidence of the *Rhetorica* is that he was equally dismissive of both women and rhetoric.

Of the two accounts of the *Rhetorica* found in contemporary scholarship—the philosophical one that dismisses it as a minor work concerning an unimportant topic, and the rhetorical one, valorizing it as foundational of a discipline and historically seminal—the philosophical historiography is clearly the more historically accurate. The question that still remains, however, is whether it is possible to divorce the ideas expressed in Aristotle's *Rhetorica* from their historical, textual, and authorial contexts and recuperate them for feminist rhetoric.

Aristotle, Feminism, and the Historiography of Ancient Rhetoric

The fruitfulness or barrenness of Aristotle's *Rhetorica* for the project of feminist rhetoric is a topic located in a larger context of reappropriations of ancient rhetoric for feminism(s). Of the many efforts to reclaim ancient rhetoric for feminist discourse few have proven beneficial either to feminism or to the study of ancient rhetoric.[58] While Susan Jarratt, for example, has tried to argue that the Older Sophists were antifoundationalists, and that antifoundationalism, ipso facto, makes their work congruent with the goals of feminism,[59] her theories are born out neither by the preponderance of textual evidence nor by testimonia. For example, Gorgias's "Encomium on Helen," as Isocrates points out, could hardly be construed as genuine praise of Helen ("Helen," 14).[60] The extant writings of Gorgias and Protagoras nowhere explicitly adumbrate feminist agenda, and our accounts of the Sophistic schools scarcely show a plethora of female students.

Superficially more promising might appear the efforts to write Aspasia and Diotima into rhetorical history, but two women who could, with some degree of legitimacy, be described as a courtesan best know for her sexual involvement with a famous politician and a male fantasy are hardly desirable prototypes for feminist behavior or discourse. Rather than Plato's creation, Diotima, Plato himself, who did admit women to his Academy and allowed them the roles of Guardians in his *Republic*, might be a more fruitful source for protofeminist rhetoric, as C. Jan Swearingen has argued quite compellingly.[61] Because of his overt hostility to rhetoric, however, Plato has generally not proved particularly popular among feminist rhetoricians, and most of the efforts to recuperate Plato for (nonfeminist) rhetoric have relied on rather egregious misreading of his work.[62]

Like Plato, Aristotle has generally proven uncongenial to feminist rhetoricians. This might, at first sight, appear an error in feminist rhetorical historiography in need of rectification, for Aristotle does discuss pathetic appeals, probabilistic reasoning, and private as well as public persuasion—all areas that might seem quite fruitful for feminist theory. There are, however, several reasons why Aristotle has not, and in my opinion, should not, be appropriated for feminist rhetoric. First, as discussed earlier in this chapter, Aristotle only discusses the aspects of rhetoric most useful for feminist thought in a strongly negative fashion; they are included tentatively in order to be rejected decisively. Second, the elements of rhetoric most congenial to feminists that are discussed in Aristotle's *Rhetorica* are not his original contributions to the field, but part of a broader pedagogical/handbook tradition of rhetoric, one of which Aristotle himself strongly disapproved. Reassigning credit for the achievements of a collaborative anonymous pedagogical tradition to a male *auctor* would undermine the work of women's recovery, which has tended to move in precisely the opposite direction of valuing anonymous, marginalized, and feminized traditions. Third, Aristotle's firm conviction of the natural inferiority of women makes him quite an undesirable originary figure for feminist theory. Most important, however, is that the central reason for recovering Aristotle for rhetoric would be to use his prestige to authorize the marginalized discipline of pedagogy. The notion that rhetoric needs some canonical patriarch as an originary figure in order to legitimize itself within the academy is utterly antithetical to feminist ideals. For feminist rhetoric to reclaim Aristotle as some sort of male mother would be, ipso facto, for rhetoric to accede to the traditional patriarchal judgment of its (feminine) inferiority, and to rely on the reflected prestige of Aristotle to associate itself with the higher prestige, traditionally masculine discipline of philosophy rather than asserting the (perhaps separate but) equal validity of the traditionally feminine discipline of pedagogy. Relying on Aristotle to authorize feminist rhetoric would be to participate in a cultural logic that denies the legitimacy of areas of cultural and economic production traditionally associated with women.

Pedagogy, in the broad context of Western culture of the past century, has many parallels with the even more strongly feminized activity of housework. Both are women's work, and thus not "real work." The housewife's contribution to the functioning of our culture is rarely reported in standard instruments that measure national economic productivity. Pedagogy also often stands partially outside the narratives of economic production—especially the substantial amount of pedagogical activity that occurs in the home either as home schooling or as supplementary to formal education. Just as housework is erased from economic narratives because it is not "real work," so pedagogy too is often not considered "real scholarship," and is excluded from the historical narratives of such disciplines as philosophy—even though the majority of people writing histories of philosophy in our century have earned their livings as teachers.[63]

To write a specifically feminist history of rhetoric is to domesticate rhetoric, to emphasize its connections with the pedagogical, the feminine, and the private. Rather than trying to appropriate Aristotle's *Rhetorica* for feminism, we should concentrate on reconstructing the traditions of ancient handbook rhetoric, and applying to them the same degree of meticulous philological care that we have heretofore reserved primarily for the higher prestige works of philosophical authors. We do not need to justify feminist rhetoric by adumbrating its extremely tenuous lines of filiation with Aristotle. Feminist rhetoric can stand on its own as a legitimate project without authoritative male antecedents and to do so must bring into the light histories of the pedagogical traditions rather than leaving pedagogy obscured in the shadows of Aristotle's *Rhetorica*.[64]

Notes

1. I use, with some modifications, the translations of the *Rhetorica* found in Aristotle, *The "Art" of Rhetoric*, trans. John Henry Freese, Loeb Classical Library. (Cambridge: Harvard University Press, 1982). The Greek text is: Aristotle, *Aristotelis ars rhetorica*, ed. W. D. Ross (Oxford: Clarendon Press, 1959). All quotations from Greek are pasted directly from the *Thesaurus Linguae Graecae* CD ROM Version D.

2. Two recent attempts to rectify the philosophical neglect of Aristotle's *Rhetorica* are: *Aristotle's* Rhetoric: *Philosophical Essays*, ed. David J. Furley and Alexander Nehamas (Princeton: Princeton University Press, 1994) and *Essays on Aristotle's* Rhetoric, ed. Amélie Rorty (Berkeley and Los Angeles: University of California Press, 1996). The Furley and Nehamas volume, however, tends to marginalize rhetorical scholarship despite its effort to include the *Rhetorica* in the conversation of Aristotelian philosophical scholarship, as discussed in Carol Poster, "Review of *Aristotle's* Rhetoric: *Philosophical Essays*," *Philosophy and Literature* 19, no. 2 (October 1995): 361–62.

3. Richard Rorty, "The Historiography of Philosophy: Four Genres," in *Philosophy in History*, ed. Richard Rorty, J. B. Schneewind, and Quentin Skinner (Cambridge: Cambridge University Press, 1984), 49–75.

4. Ibid., 62.

5. See *A History of Women Philosophers*, vol. 1, 600 B.C.–500 A.D., ed. Mary Ellen Waithe (Boston: Martinus Nijhoff, 1987); Madeleine Henry, *Prisoner of History: Aspasia of Miletus and Her Biographical Tradition* (Oxford: Oxford University Press, 1995); and *Engendering Origins: Critical Feminist Readings in Plato and Aristotle*, ed. Bat-Ami Bar On (Albany: State University of New York Press, 1994).

6. Rorty, "Historiography of Philosophy," 56.

7. Ibid., 57.

8. Theresa Enos, "Gender and Journals, Conservers or Innovators," *Pre/text* 9, nos. 3–4 (Fall–Winter 1988): 211–12.

9. Marjorie Curry Woods, "Among Men—Not Boys: Histories of Rhetoric and the Exclusion of Pedagogy," *Rhetoric Society Quarterly* 22, no. 1 (1992): 18.

10. Michel Foucault, "What Is An Author?" in *Language. CounterMemory. Practice: Selected Essays and Interviews by Michel Foucault* (Ithaca: Cornell University Press, 1977).

11. *An Early Commentary on the* Poetria Nova *of Geoffrey of Vinsauf*, ed. and trans. Majorie Curry Woods (New York: Garland, 1985).

12. Jerome McGann, *A Critique of Modern Textual Criticism* (Charlottesville: University Press of Virginia, 1992), 37–50.

13. L. D. Reynolds and N. G. Wilson, *Scribes and Scholars: A Guide to the Transmission of Greek and Latin Literature*, 3d ed. (Oxford: Clarendon Press, 1991), 234.

14. *Anaximenis ars rhetorica*, ed. M. Fuhrmann (Leipzig: Teubner, 1966).

15. W. K. C. Guthrie, *A History of Greek Philosophy VI: Aristotle: An Encounter* (Cambridge: Cambridge University Press, 1981), 40–52.

16. *Aristotle: A Theory of Civic Discourse*, trans. and intro. George Kennedy, (Oxford: Oxford University Press, 1991), 305–6. Carnes Lord, "On The Early History of the Aristotelian Corpus," *American Journal of Philology* 107 (1986): 137–61, discusses the problems of tracing the early textual history of Aristotle's rhetoric in detail. Felix Grayeff, *Aristotle And His School: An Inquiry in the History of the* Peripatos (New York: Harper and Row, 1974) provides cogent albeit somewhat speculative arguments for reconsidering our concept of authorship and textuality with respect to the Aristotelian corpus.

17. Fredrich Solmsen traces how certain specific components of rhetorical theory found in the *Rhetorica* affected later rhetoricians, but does not specifically concentrate on the reception of the text of the *Rhetorica* itself in "The Aristotelian Tradition in Ancient Rhetoric," in *Aristotle: The Classical Heritage of Rhetoric*, ed. Keith Erickson (Metuchen NJ: Scarecrow, 1974), 278–310.

18. See, for example, Doreen C. Innes, "Period and Colon: Theory and Example in Demetrius and Longinus," in *Peripatetic Rhetoric after Aristotle*, ed. William W. Fortenbaugh and David C. Mirhady (New Brunswick, N.J.: Transaction, 1994), 36–53.

19. Dionysius of Halicarnassus, *Critical Essays II*, trans. Stephen Usher, Loeb Classical Library (Cambridge: Harvard University Press, 1985).

20. Quintilian, *The* Institutio Oratoria *of Quintilian I*, Books I–III, trans. H. E. Butler, Loeb Classical Library (Cambridge: Harvard University Press, 1989).

21. [Demetrius], "On Style," in *Aristotle XXIII*, trans. W. Rhys Roberts, Loeb Classical Library (Cambridge: Harvard University Press, 1982). For a discussion of the dating of Demetrius and the Aristotelian influence on his work, see G. M. A. Grube, *A Greek Critic: Demetrius On Style*, Phoenix, supp. Vol. 4 (Toronto: University of Toronto Press, 1961) and Carol Poster, "Demetrius," in *The Encyclopedia of Rhetoric*, ed. Theresa Enos (New York: Garland, 1996), 174–75.

22. Cecil Wooten describes Hermogenes' theory of the forms of style as belonging to a tradition beginning with Theophrastus and present in Dionysius of Halicarnassus and [Aristides] in *Hermogenes' On Types of Style*, trans. Cecil Wooten (Chapel Hill: University of North Carolina Press, 1987), xvii.

23. William W. Fortenbaugh, "Cicero's Knowledge of the Rhetorical Treatises of Aristotle and Theophrastus," in *Cicero's Knowledge of the Peripatos*, ed. William W. Fortenbaugh and Peter Steinmetz (New Brunswick, N.J.: Transaction, 1989), 43.

24. George Kennedy in *Peripatetic Rhetoric*, ed. Fortenbaugh and Mirhady, 179.

25. Menander Rhetor, *On the Divisions of the Epideictic*, ed. and trans. D. A. Reynolds and N. G. Wilson (Oxford: Clarendon Press, 1981).

26. See Abraham Malherbe, *Ancient Epistolary Theorists* (Atlanta, Ga.: Scholars Press, 1988) for ancient letter-writing treatises.

27. Thomas M. Conley, "Aristotle's *Rhetoric* in Byzantium," *Rhetorica* 8, no. 1 (Winter 1990): 29.

28. See James J. Murphy and Martin Camargo, "The Middle Ages," in *The Present State of Scholarship in Historical and Contemporary Rhetoric*, ed. Winifred Bryan Horner, rev. ed. (Columbia: University of Missouri Press, 1990).

29. Marjorie Curry Woods, "The Teaching of Writing in Medieval Europe," in *A Short History of Writing Instruction: From Ancient Greece to Twentieth-Century America*, ed. James J. Murphy (Davis, Calif.: Hermagoras, 1990), 77–94.

30. James J. Murphy, *Rhetoric in the Middle Ages: A History of Rhetorical Theory from Saint Augustine to the Renaissance* (Berkeley and Los Angeles: University of California Press, 1974), 93–94.

31. For a discussion of the manuscript tradition of the *Rhetorica* and its position in the medieval school curriculum, see John Ward, "Renaissance Commentators on Ciceronian Rhetoric," in *Renaissance Eloquence: Studies in the Theory and Practice of Renaissance Rhetoric*, ed. James J. Murphy (Berkeley and Los Angeles: University of California Press, 1983), 157–67 and *John Rainolde's Oxford Lectures on Aristotle's* Rhetoric, ed., trans., and commentary by Lawrence Green (Newark: University of Delaware Press, 1986), 18–19.

32. Lawrence D. Green summarizes the medieval and Renaissance reception of the *Rhetorica* as follows:

> Aristotle's *Rhetoric* was not a major treatise for scholars during the Latin middle ages, who considered it largely an adjunct to Aristotelian ethics and politics. It was not a major treatise for the early Italian humanists, who knew about the treatise, but who found their principal inspiration for rhetoric in the rediscovered works of Cicero and Quintilian. Nor was it a major treatise for the Greeks of Renaissance Byzantium, who viewed Aristotle primarily as a precursor to the principal writers of their own rhetorical tradition. ("Aristotle's *Rhetoric* and the Renaissance Views of the Emotions," in *Renaissance Rhetoric*, ed. Peter Mack [New York: St. Martin's Press, 1994], 1).

See also Lawrence D. Green, "Aristotle's *Rhetoric* in the Renaissance," in *Peripatetic Rhetoric*, ed. Fortenbaugh and Mirhady, 320–48. George Kennedy gives a similar assessment of the Renaissance influence of Aristotle's *Rhetorica*:

> [I]n the Renaissance . . . [n]ew translations of the *Rhetoric* into Latin and the vernacular languages were repeatedly made; university professors sometimes lectured on the text and occasionally published commentaries, and parts of the *Rhetoric* influenced theories of poetics or politics or moral philosophy, but no true Aristotelian rhetoric was composed in the Renaissance (*Classical Rhetoric and its Christian and Secular Tradition from Ancient to Modern Times* [Chapel Hill, University of North Carolina Press, 1980], 204).

33. *Peter Ramus's Attack on Cicero; Text and Translation of Ramus's* Brutinae Quaestiones, ed. and intro. James J. Murphy, trans. Carole Newlands (Davis, Calif.: Hemagoras, 1992), 79, for example, includes several unflattering *obiter dicta* concerning Aristotle's *Rhetorica*. See also *Arguments in Rhetoric Against Quintilian: Translation and Text of Peter Ramus's* Rhetoricae Distinctiones in Quintilianum, intro. James J. Murphy, trans. Carole Newlands (DeKalb: Northern Illinois University Press, 1986). For a description of Ramus's attacks on Aristotle, see Walter Ong, *Ramus, Method, and the Decay of Dialogue: from the Art of Discourse to the Art of Reason*, (Cambridge: Harvard University Press, 1983), 172–75.

34. *John Rainolde's Oxford Lectures on Aristotle's Rhetoric*, ed., trans., and commentary by Lawrence Green (Newark: University of Delaware Press, 1986), 9.

35. See Jean Dietz Moss, "The Rhetoric Course at the Collegio Romano in the Latter Half of the Sixteenth Century," *Rhetorica* 4, no. 2 (1986): 137–51, and "Dialectics and Rhetoric in Renaissance Pedagogy," in *Learning from the Histories of Rhetoric: Essays in Honor of Winifred Bryan Horner*, ed. Theresa Enos (Carbondale: Southern Illinois University Press, 1993), 114–32. Although somewhat dated, quite comprehensive treatments of early modern English rhetoric can be found in W. S. Howell, *Logic and Rhetoric in England, 1500–1700* (Princeton: Princeton University Press, 1956) and *Eighteenth-Century British Logic and Rhetoric* (Princeton: Princeton University Press, 1971).

36. See Thomas M. Conley, *Rhetoric in the European Tradition* (New York: Longman, 1990).

37. See ibid., 199–203, and *The Rhetorics of Thomas Hobbes and Bernard Lamy*, ed. and intro. John T. Harwood, Landmarks in Public Address, (Carbondale: Southern Illinois University Press, 1986), 131–64.

38. *Rhetoric*, Conley, 213–16. See also John Bulwer, *Chirologia: or the Natural Language of the Hand (and) Chironomia: or the Art of Manual Rhetoric*, ed. James W. Cleary (Carbondale: Southern Illinois University Press, 1974 [1644]) and Thomas Sheridan, *A Course of Lectures on Elocution Together with Two Dissertations on Language* (London, 1762).

39. Linda Mitchell, "Letter Writing in Seventeenth-Century Grammar Books," paper presented at meeting of Rocky Mountain Modern Languages Association, Spokane, Wash., October 1995.

40. Richard Whately, *Elements of Rhetoric*, ed. Douglas Ehninger (Carbondale: Southern Illinois University Press, 1963 [1846]).

41. See Hugh Blair, *Lectures on Rhetoric and Belles Letters*, ed. Harold F. Harding, 2 vols. (Carbondale: Southern Illinois University Press, 1965 [1783]), and George Campbell, *The Philosophy of Rhetoric*, ed. Lloyd Bitzer (Carbondale: Southern Illinois University Press, 1988 [1776]).

42. Alexander Bain, *English Composition and Rhetoric: A Manual* (London: Longmans, Green, 1866).

43. The continued scholarly interest among classicists in Aristotle's *Rhetorica* is evidenced by two major publications. Theodore Buckley's new translations of the *Rhetorica* and *Poetica*, bound with a reprint of Thomas Hobbes *A Brief of the Art of Rhetoric* and a set of "analytic questions for self study" appeared in 1847—*Aristotle's Treatise on Rhetoric with an Analysis by Thomas Hobbes, and a Series of Questions. Also the Poetics of Aristotle*, trans. Theodore Buckley (London: Henry H. Bohn, 1847). Cope's 1867 *Introduction to Aristotle's Rhetoric* was followed by a major posthumous commentary edited by John Edwin Sandys in 1877—Edward Merideth Cope, *The* Rhetoric *of Aristotle with a Commentary*, ed. John Edwin Sandys (Cambridge: Cambridge University Press, 1877; reprint, Hindesheim: Georg Olms, 1970). The grouping of the *Rhetorica* with the *Nicomachean Ethics* and *Politics* as a statutory examination text for the *Litterae Humaniores* at Oxford in the early part of the nineteenth century suggests that it continued to be read primarily as an ethical treatise.

The major rhetoricians of the period, such as Cambell, Blair, Jardine, and Bain, however, were interested primarily in new theories of faculty psychology and taste, and when influenced by classical rhetoric at all, followed the traditions of Cicero and Quintilian. For a solid bibliography of the major primary texts and scholarship on nineteenth-century rhetoric, see Donald Stewart, "The Nineteenth Century," in *The Present State of Scholarship in Historical and Contemporary Rhetoric*, ed. Winifred Bryan Horner. (Columbia: University of Missouri Press, 1990), 151–85. For a summary of the main trends in nineteenth-century rhetoric, see Winifred Horner, "Writing Instruction in Great Britain: Eighteenth and Nineteenth Centuries," in *A Short History of Writing Instruction: From Ancient Greece to Twentieth-Century America*, ed.

James J. Murphy (Davis, Calif.: Hermagoras, 1990), 121–50. For the influence of nineteenth-century British rhetoric on American composition studies, see Winifred Horner, *Nineteenth-Century Scottish Rhetoric: The American Connection* (Carbondale: Southern Illinois University Press, 1993). For the "demise of the classical tradition" in nineteenth-century American writing instruction see the first chapter of James A. Berlin, *Writing Instruction in Nineteenth-Century American Colleges* (Carbondale: Southern Illinois University Press, 1984). He points out that John Quincy Adams's *Lecture on Rhetoric and Oratory* (1810), the only major American rhetorical treatise strongly influence by Aristotle's *Rhetorica*, "had little impact even in [its] own time" (17).

44. *Essays on Classical Rhetoric and Modern Discourse*, ed. Robert J. Connors, Lisa S. Ede, and Andrea Lunsford (Carbondale: Southern Illinois University Press, 1984), 9.

45. Edward P. J. Corbett, *Classical Rhetoric for the Modern Student* (New York: Oxford University Press, 1965).

46. For a summary of the history of classical rhetoric in the twentieth-century composition classroom, see James A. Berlin, *Rhetoric and Reality: Writing Instruction in American Colleges, 1900–1985* (Carbondale: Southern Illinois University Press, 1987), esp. 155–59 and 185. Several essay collections have been devoted to the application of classical rhetoric to composition theory, including *The Rhetorical Tradition and Modern Writing*, ed. James J. Murphy (New York: Modern Language Association, 1982); *Essays on Classical Rhetoric*, ed. Connors et al.; *Rhetoric and Praxis: The Contribution of Classical Rhetoric to Practical Reasoning*, ed. Jean Dietz Moss (Washington, D.C.: Catholic University Press, 1986); and *Learning from the Histories of Rhetoric: Essays in Honor of Winifred Bryan Horner*, ed. Theresa Enos (Carbondale: Southern Illinois University Press, 1995). Kathleen Welch's *Contemporary Reception of Classical Rhetoric* (Hillsdale, N.J.: Lawrence Erlbaum Associates, 1990) serves as a polemic supporting the appropriation of classical rhetoric by postmodern composition theorists against what she terms the "Heritage School" of classical philosophers and philologists. Several current first-year composition textbooks rely heavily on Aristotle's *Rhetorica*, including Sharon Crowley, *Ancient Rhetorics for Contemporary Students* (New York: Macmillan, 1994); John Gage, *The Shape of Reason: Argumentative Writing in College*, 2d ed. (New York: Macmillan, 1991); and Winifred Horner, *Rhetoric in the Classical Tradition* (New York: St. Martin's, 1988).

47. Thomas Miller, "Reinventing Rhetorical Traditions," in *Learning from the Histories of Rhetoric: Essays in Honor of Winifred Bryan Horner*, ed. Theresa Enos (Carbondale: Southern Illinois University Press, 1993), 26.

48. Welch, *Contemporary Reception*, 31.

49. Ibid., 32.

50. Martha Nussbaum does address how Aristotle's treatment of the emotions can be useful for feminist philosophy, but does not specifically discuss rhetoric. See especially *Love's Knowledge* (Oxford: Oxford University Press, 1990).

51. Karlyn Kohrs Campbell, *Man Cannot Speak for Her: A Critical Study of Early Women's Rhetoric*, vol. 1 (New York: Greenwood, 1989), argues cogently for the necessity of inclusion of "private" discourse in the project of recovering women's rhetoric. For comments on and critiques of much of the scholarship on this subject, see Barbara Biesecker, "Coming to Terms with Recent Attempts to Write Women into the History of Rhetoric," *Philosophy and Rhetoric* 25, no. 2 (1992): 140–61, and Janet Carey Eldred and Peter Mortensen, "Monitoring Columbia's Daughters: Writing as Gendered Conduct," *Rhetoric Society Quarterly* 23, nos. 3–4 (1993): 46–69. Patricia Bizzell and Bruce Herzberg, *The Rhetorical Tradition: Reading from Classical Times to the Present* (Boston: Bedford Books, 1990), esp. 483–88 defend incorporating noncanonical genres of discourse in their historical rhetoric anthology specifically in order to include the voices of marginalized groups, including women.

52. Glenn W. Most, "The Uses of *Endoxa*: Philosophy and Rhetoric in the *Rhetoric*," in

Aristotle's Rhetoric Furley and Nehemas, 167–90, argues for a hierarchy of argumentative precision in Aristotle, with dialectic superior to rhetoric. Barbara Warnick, "Judgment, Probability, and Aristotle's *Rhetoric*," *Quarterly Journal of Speech* 9 (1989): 299–311, also attempts to situate Aristotle's *Rhetorica* within a hierarchy of argumentative precision and an analogous hierarchy of the sciences pertaining to argumentation. See also Carol Poster, "Aristotle's *Rhetoric* Against Rhetoric," *American Journal of Philology*, 118 (1997): 219–49.

53. Aristotle (*Rhet.* I.i.3) claims "αἱ γὰρ πίστεις ἔντεχνόν εἰσι μόνον, τὰ δ' ἄλλα προσθῆκαι" ("for proofs are the only things in it [the art of rhetoric] within the province of the art; everything else is merely an accessory.")

54. Aristotle specifically criticizes previous arts for primarily addressing issues of how to arouse "prejudice, compassion, anger, and other emotions" that have no intrinsic connection to the case. For "it is wrong to warp the dicast's feelings, to arouse him to anger, jealousy or compassion, which would be like making a rule crooked which one intended to use". To this sweeping condemnation, Aristotle adds that in a well-administered state there would be nothing left for such rhetoricians to say (*Rhet.* I.i.4–6).

55. Cf. "For the only thing to which their [writers of rhetorical handbooks] attention is devoted is how to put the judge in the right frame of mind" (*Rhet.* I.i.9–10) in which he condemns earlier writers for treating precisely the same topics he covers at the opening of Book II.

56. Several passages in the *Rhetorica* insist on the inferiority of rhetorical audiences including I.1.12, which describes rhetoric as for those for whom "instruction is impossible" and III.xiv.6 which describes pathetic appeals as addressed to "a hearer whose judgment is poor". In fact, given the illogical nature of the mob, Aristotle claims, the ignorant will often be more persuasive than the educated (II.xxii.3).

57. I thank Dr. Cheryl Glenn for calling my attention to the reference in G.A.

58. Recent essay collections that focus on reclaiming women's histories of rhetoric are *Reclaiming Rhetorica*, ed. Andrea Lunsford (Pittsburgh: University of Pittsburgh Press, 1995) and Molly Wertheimer's forthcoming collection from the University of South Carolina Press. Neither discusses Aristotle. I should note that, as other contributors in this volume discuss, there might well be areas other than rhetoric in which study of Aristotle might be useful for feminism, and I do consider Aristotle's *Rhetorica* important in the history of philosophical rhetoric and its relation to dialectic, but I think that feminist approaches have little to contribute to our understanding of Aristotle's *Rhetorica* and that Aristotle's *Rhetorica* has little to contribute to feminist rhetoric.

59. Susan Jarratt, *Rereading the Sophists: Classical Rhetoric Refigured* (Carbondale: Southern Illinois University Press, 1991). For a critique of her book, see John Poulakos, "John Poulakos on *Rereading the Sophists*," *Rhetoric Society Quarterly* 22, no. 2 (1992): 66–68.

60. Isocrates, *Isocrates II*, trans. George Norlan (Cambridge: Harvard University Press, 1982).

61. Jan Swearingen, "Plato's Feminine: Appropriation, Impersonation, and Metaphorical Polemic," *Rhetoric Society Quarterly* 22, no. 1 (1992): 109–23. For recent feminist readings of Plato, see Nancy Tuana, ed. *Feminist Interpretations of Plato* (University Park: Pennsylvania University Press, 1994).

62. For a discussion of some of the problems in attempts to reinterpret Plato's *Phaedrus* as advocating a reformed rhetoric, see Carol Poster, "Plato's Unwritten Doctrines: A Hermeneutic Problem in Rhetorical Historiography," *Pre/text* 14, nos. 1–2 (1993): 127–38.

63. It is worth noting in this context that Plato, who allowed women some degree of equality with men in both his writing and in his Academy, is one of the ancient philosophers most explicitly concerned with pedagogy.

64. I thank Dr. John T. Kirby and Dr. Jameela Lares for many extremely valuable comments on drafts of this chapter.

Selected Bibliography

Achtenberg, Deborah. "Aristotelian Resources for Feminist Thinking." In *Feminism and Ancient Philosophy*, edited by Julie K. Ward, 95–117. New York: Routledge, 1996.

Addelson, Kathryn Pyne. "The Man of Professional Wisdom." In *Discovering Reality: Feminist Perspectives on Epistemology, Metaphysics, Methodology and Philosophy of Science*, edited by Sandra Harding and Merrill B. Hintikka, 165–86. Dordrecht, Holland: D. Reidel, 1983.

Allen, Prudence. "Aristotelian and Cartesian Revolution in the Philosophy of Man and Woman." *Dialogue* 26 (1987): 263–70.

———. *The Concept of Woman: The Aristotelian Revolution, 750 B.C.–1250 A.D.* Montreal: Eden, 1985.

Annas, Julia. *The Morality of Happiness.* New York: Oxford University Press, 1993.

———. "Women and the Quality of Life: Two Norms or One?" In *The Quality of Life*, edited by M. Nussbaum and A. Sen, 279–96. Oxford: Clarendon Press, 1993.

Baier, Annette. *Moral Prejudices.* Cambridge: Harvard University Press, 1994.

Bar On, Bat-Ami, ed. *Engendering Origins: Critical Feminist Readings in Plato and Aristotle.* Albany: State University of New York Press, 1994.

Beisecker, Barbara. "Coming to Terms with Recent Attempts to Write Women into the History of Rhetoric." *Philosophy and Rhetoric* 25, no. 2 (1992): 140–61.

Blundell, Sue. *Women in Ancient Greece.* Cambridge: Harvard University Press, 1995.

Cantarella, Eva. *Pandora's Daughters: The Role and Status of Women in Greek and Roman Antiquity.* Baltimore: Johns Hopkins University Press, 1987.

Carson, Anne. "Putting Her in Her Place: Woman, Dirt, and Desire." In *Before Sexuality: The Construction of Erotic Experience in the Ancient Greek World*, edited by David M. Halperin, John J. Winkler, and Froma I. Zeitlin, 135–69. Princeton: Princeton University Press, 1990.

Case, Sue Ellen. *Feminism and Theatre.* New York: Routledge, 1988.

Chanter, Tina. *Ethics of Eros: Irigaray's Rewriting of the Philosophers.* New York: Routledge, 1995.

Clark, Lorenne M. G., and Lydia Lange, eds. *The Sexism of Social and Political Theory: Women and Reproduction from Plato to Nietzsche.* Toronto: University of Toronto Press, 1979.

Clark, Stephen R. "Aristotle's Woman." *History of Political Thought* 3 (1982): 177–92.

Code, Lorraine. *What Can She Know? Feminist Theory and the Construction of Knowledge.* Ithaca: Cornell University Press, 1991.

Cohen, David. *Law, Sexuality and Society: The Enforcement of Morals in Classical Athens.* Cambridge: Cambridge University Press, 1991.

Cole, Eva Browning. "Women, Slaves, and 'Love of Toil' in Aristotle's Moral Philosophy." In *Engendering Origins: Critical Feminist Readings in Plato and Aristotle,* edited by Bat-Ami Bar On, 127–44. Albany: State University of New York Press, 1994.

Coles, Andrew. "Biomedical Models of Reproduction in the Fifth Century B.C. and Aristotle's *Generation of Animals.*" *Phronesis* 40, no. 1 (1995): 48–88.

Coole, Diana H. *Women in Political Theory: From Ancient Misogny to Contemporary Feminism.* Sussex, England: Wheatsheaf Books, 1988.

Cooper, John. "Aristotle on Friendship." In *Essays on Aristotle's Ethics,* edited by A. Rorty, 301–40. Berkeley and Los Angeles: University of California Press, 1980.

———. "Political Animals and Civic Friendship." In *Friendship: A Philosophical Reader,* edited by N. Badhwar, 303–26. Ithaca: Cornell University Press, 1993.

Daly, Mary. *Gyn/Ecology: The Metaethics of Radical Feminism.* Boston: Beacon, 1978.

Dean-Jones, Lesley Ann. *Women's Bodies in Classical Greek Science.* Oxford: Clarendon Press, 1994.

Deslauriers, Marguerite. "Aristotle's Conception of Authority." In *Law, Politics and Society in the Ancient Mediterranean World,* edited by Baruch Halpern and Deborah W. Hobson, 122–36. Sheffield: Sheffield Academic Press, 1993.

Dover, Kenneth. *Greek Homosexuality.* Cambridge: Harvard University Press, 1978.

———. *Greek Popular Morality in the Time of Plato and Aristotle.* Berkeley and Los Angeles: University of California Press, 1974.

du Bois, Page. *Centaurs and Amazons: Women and the Prehistory of the Great Chain of Being.* Ann Arbor: University of Michigan Press, 1982/1991.

Elshtain, Jean Bethke. *Public Man, Private Woman: Women in Social and Political Thought.* 2d ed. Princeton: Princeton University Press, 1981.

———. ed. *The Family in Political Thought.* Amherst: University of Massachusetts Press, 1982.

Femenías, María Luisa. "Women and Natural Hierarchy in Aristotle." *Hypatia* 9, no. 1 (1994): 164–72.

Foley, Helene. "Attitudes To Women in Greece." In *The Civilization of the Ancient Mediterranean: Greece and Rome,* edited by Michael Grant and Rachel Kitzinger, 1301–17. New York: Scribner, 1988.

Foot, Philippa. *Virtues and Vices and Other Essays in Moral Philosophy.* Berkeley and Los Angeles: University of California Press, 1978.

Fortenbaugh, W. W. *Aristotle on Emotion: A Contribution to Philosophical Psychology, Rhetoric, Poetics, Politics, and Ethics.* London: Duckworth, 1975.

———. "Aristotle on Slaves and Women." In *Articles on Aristotle,* vol. 2, *Ethics & Politics,* edited by J. Barnes, M. Schofield, and R. Sorabji, 135–39. London: St. Martin's, 1977.

Frazer, Elizabeth, and Nicola Lacey. *The Politics of Community: A Feminist Critique of the Liberal-Communitarian Debate.* Toronto: University of Toronto Press, 1993.

Freeland, Cynthia A. "Aristotle's *Poetics* in Relation to the Ethical Treatises." In *Aristotle's Philosophical Development: Problems and Prospects,* edited by William Wians, 327–45. Totowa, N.J.: Rowman and Littlefield, 1996.

———. "Nourishing Speculation: A Feminist Reading of Aristotelian Science." In *Engendering Origins: Critical Feminist Readings in Plato and Aristotle,* edited by Bat-Ami Bar On, 145–87. Albany: State University of New York Press, 1994.

———. "Plot Imitates Action: Aesthetic Evaluation and Moral Realism in Aristotle's *Poetics.*" In *Essays on Aristotle's Poetics,* edited by Amelie Rorty, 111–32. Princeton: Princeton University Press, 1992.

Garside, Christine. "Can A Woman Be Good in the Same Way as A Man?" *Dialogue* 10 (1971): 534–44.

Green, Judith. "Aristotle on Necessary Verticality, Body Heat, and Gendered Proper Places in the Polis." *Hypatia* 7, no. 1 (Winter 1992): 70–96.

Grimshaw, Jean. *Philosophy and Feminist Thinking*. Minneapolis: University of Minnesota Press, 1986.

Harding, Sandra. *The Science Question in Feminism*. Ithaca: Cornell University Press, 1986.

Harding, Sandra, and Merrill B. Hintikka, eds. *Discovering Reality: Feminist Perspectives on Epistemology, Metaphysics, Methodology and Philosophy of Science*. Dordrecht, Holland: D. Reidel, 1983.

Hawkesworth, Mary E. "Re/Vision: Feminist Theory Confronts the Polis." *Social Theory and Practice* 13 (1987): 155–85.

Homiak, Marcia. "Feminism and Aristotle's Rational Ideal." In *A Mind of One's Own: Feminist Essays on Reason and Objectivity*, edited by Louise Antony and Charlotte Witt, 1–17. Boulder: Westview, 1993.

Horowitz, Maryanne Cline. "Aristotle and Woman." *Journal of the History of Biology* 9 (1976): 183–213.

Hursthouse, Rosalind. "Virtue Theory and Abortion." *Philosophy and Public Affairs* 20 (1991): 223–46.

Irigaray, Luce. "Is the Subject of Science Sexed?" Translated by Carol Mastrangelo Bové. In *Feminism and Science*, edited by Nancy Tuana, 58–68. Bloomington: Indiana University Press, 1989.

———. "Place, Interval: A Reading of Aristotle, *Physics IV*." In *An Ethics of Sexual Difference*, translated by Carolyn Burke and Gillian C. Gill, 34–55. Ithaca: Cornell University Press, 1993; reprint, this volume (Chapter 2).

———. *Speculum of the Other Woman*. Translated by Gillian C. Gill. Ithaca: Cornell University Press, 1985.

———. *This Sex Which Is Not One*. Translated by Catherine Porter, with Carolyn Burke. Ithaca: Cornell University Press, 1985.

Jaggar, Alison M. *Feminist Politics and Human Nature*. Totowa, N.J.: Rowman and Allenheld, 1983.

Joint Association of Classical Teachers. *The World of Athens: An Introduction to Classical Athenian Culture*. Cambridge: Cambridge University Press, 1984.

Kaplan, Laura Duhan. "Woman as Caretaker: An Archetype that Supports Patriarchal Militarism." *Hypatia* 9, no. 2 (Spring 1994): 123–33.

Keuls, Eva. *The Reign of the Phallus: Sexual Politics in Ancient Athens*. New York: Harper & Row, 1985.

Knox, Bernard. *The Oldest Dead White European Males and Other Reflections on the Classics*. New York: Norton, 1993.

Kotzin, Rhoda H. "Aristotle's View on Women." American Philosophical Association *Newsletter on Feminism and Philosophy* (June 1989): 21–25.

Lange, Lynda. "Woman is Not a Rational Animal: On Aristotle's Biology of Reproduction." In *Discovering Reality*, edited by Sandra Harding and Merrill B. Hintikka, 1–15. Dordrecht, Holland: D. Reidel, 1983.

Laqueur, Thomas. *Making Sex: Body and Gender From the Greeks to Freud*. Cambridge: Harvard University Press, 1990.

Lefkowitz, Mary R., and Maureen B. Fant. *Women's Life in Greece and Rome: A Source Book in Translations*. Baltimore: Johns Hopkins University Press, 1982; 2d ed. 1992.

Lloyd, Genevieve. *The Man of Reason: "Male" and "Female" in Western Philosophy*. Minneapolis: University of Minnesota Press, 1984.

Lloyd, G. E. R. *Science, Folklore and Ideology: Studies in the Life Sciences in Ancient Greece*. Cambridge: Cambridge University Press, 1983.

Loraux, Nicole. *The Children of Athena: Athenian Ideas About Citizenship and the Division Between the Sexes*. Translated by Caroline Lenne. Princeton: Princeton University Press, 1993.

———. *Tragic Ways of Killing A Woman*. Translated by Anthony Forster. Cambridge: Harvard University Press, 1987.

Lord, Carnes. *Education and Culture in the Political Thought of Aristotle*. Ithaca: Cornell University Press, 1982.

Matthews, Gareth B. "Gender and Essence in Aristotle." *Australasian Journal of Philosophy*, supplement to vol. 64 (June 1986): 16–25.

Modrak, Deborah. "Aristotle's Epistemology: One or Many Theories?" In *Aristotle's Philosophical Development: Problems and Prospects*, edited by W. Wians, 161–70. Lanham, Md.: Rowman and Littlefield, 1996.

———. "Aristotle: Woman, Deliberation, and Nature." In *Engendering Origins: Critical Feminist Readings in Plato and Aristotle*, edited by Bat-Ami Bar On, 207–22. Albany: State University of New York, 1994.

———. "Political Hierarchies and Family Structure." In *Aristotle's Political Philosophy: Proceedings of the Sixth International Conference on Greek Philosophy*. Ierissos, 1995.

Mulgan, Richard. "Aristotle and the Political Role of Women." *History of Political Thought* 15, no. 2 (1994): 179–202.

Nussbaum, Martha C. "Aristotelian Social Democracy." In *Liberalism and the Good*, edited by R. B. Douglass et al., 203–52. New York: Routledge, 1990.

———. "Emotions and Women's Capabilities. In *Women, Culture and Development: A Study in Human Capabilities*, edited by Martha C. Nussbaum and Jonathan Glover, 360–95. Oxford: Clarendon Press, 1995.

———. *The Fragility of Goodness*. Cambridge: Cambridge University Press, 1987.

———. "Human Functioning and Social Justice: In Defence of Aristotelian Essentialism." *Political Theory* 20 (1992): 202–46.

———. *Love's Knowledge*. Oxford: Oxford University Press, 1990.

———. "Nature, Function, and Capability: Aristotle on Political Distribution." *Oxford Studies in Ancient Philosophy* supplementary vol. 1 (1988): 145–84.

———. *The Therapy of Desire*. Princeton: Princeton University Press, 1994.

———. "Tragedy and Self-Sufficiency." In *Essays on Aristotle's Poetics*, edited by Amelie Oskenberg Rorty, 261–91. Princeton: Princeton University Press, 1992.

Nussbaum, Martha C., and Amartya Sen. "Internal Criticism and Indian Rationalist Traditions." In *Relativism: Interpretation and Confrontation*, edited by Michael Krausz, 299–325. Notre Dame: University of Notre Dame Press, 1989.

Nussbaum, Martha C., and Amartya Sen, eds. *The Quality of Life*. Oxford: Clarendon Press, 1993.

Nye, Andrea. *Words of Power: A Feminist Reading of the History of Logic*. New York: Routledge, 1990.

Okin, Susan Moller. *Women in Western Political Thought*. Princeton: Princeton University Press, 1979.

Pomeroy, Sarah B. *Goddesses, Whores, Wives and Slaves: Women in Classical Antiquity*. New York: Schocken Books, 1975.

Poster, Carol. "Review of *Aristotle's Rhetoric: Philosophical Essays*." *Philosophy and Literature* 19, no. 2 (October 1995): 361–62.

Rorty, Amelie, ed. *Essays on Aristotle's Ethics.* Berkeley and Los Angeles: University of California Press, 1980.

———. *Essays on Aristotle's Poetics.* Princeton: Princeton University Press, 1992.

———. *Essays on Aristotle's Rhetoric.* Berkeley and Los Angeles: University of California Press, 1996.

Rorty, Amelie, and Martha C. Nussbaum, eds. *Essays on Aristotle's De Anima.* Oxford: Clarendon Press, 1992.

Ruddick, Sara. "Maternal Thinking." In *Mothering: Essays in Feminist Theory,* edited by Joyce Treblicot, 213–30. Totowa, N.J.: Rowman and Allanheld, 1983.

Salkever, Steven G. *Finding the Mean: Theory and Practice in Aristotelian Political Philosophy.* Princeton: Princeton University Press, 1990.

———. "Tragedy and the Education of the Demos." In *Political Theory and Greek Tragedy,* edited by J. Peter Euben, 274–303. Berkeley and Los Angeles: University of California Press, 1986.

———. "Women, Soldiers, Citizens: Plato and Aristotle on the Politics of Virility." *Polity* 19, no. 2 (1986): 232–53.

Saxonhouse, Arlene W. "Aristotle: Defective Males, Hierarchy and the Limits of Politics." In *Feminist Interpretations and Political Theory,* edited by Mary L. Shanley and Carole Pateman, 32–52. University Park: Pennsylvania State University Press, 1991.

———. *Fear of Diversity: The Birth of Political Science in Ancient Greek Thought.* Chicago: University of Chicago Press, 1992.

———. *Women in the History of Political Thought: Ancient Greece to Machiavelli.* New York: Praeger, 1985.

Scaltsas, Patricia Ward. "Do Feminist Ethics Counter Feminist Aims?" In *Explorations in Feminist Ethics: Theory and Practice,* edited by Eve Browning Cole and Susan Coultrap-McQuin, 5–26. Bloomington: Indiana University Press, 1992.

Scheman, Naomi. "Though This Be Method, Yet There is Madness in It: Paranoia and Liberal Epistemology." In *A Mind of One's Own: Feminist Essays on Reason and Objectivity,* edited by Louise Antony and Charlotte Witt, 145–70. Boulder: Westview, 1993.

Senack, Christine M. "Aristotle on the Woman's Soul." In *Engendering Origins: Critical Feminist Readings in Plato and Aristotle,* edited by Bat-Ami Bar On, 223–36. Albany: State University of New York Press, 1994.

Sherman, Nancy. *The Fabric of Character: Aristotle's Theory of Virtue.* Oxford: Oxford University Press, 1988.

Smith, Nicholas D. "Plato and Aristotle on the Nature of Women." *Journal of the History of Philosophy* 21 (1983): 467–78.

Sparshott, F. "Aristotle on Women." *Philosophical Inquiry,* 7, nos. 3–4 (1985): 183.

Spelman, Elizabeth V. "Aristotle and the Politicization of the Soul." In *Discovering Reality: Feminist Perspectives on Epistemology, Metaphysics, Methodology, and Philosophy of Science,* edited by Sandra Harding and Merrill B. Hintikka, 17–30. Dordrecht, Holland: D. Reidel, 1983.

———. *Inessential Woman: Problems of Exclusion in Feminist Thought.* Boston: Beacon, 1988.

———. "Who's Who in the Polis." In *Engendering Origins: Critical Feminist Readings in Plato and Aristotle,* edited by Bat-Ami Bar On, 97–125. Albany: State University of New York Press, 1994.

Stoljar, Natalie. "Essence, Identity and the Concept of Woman." In *Philosophical Topics* 23 (1995): 261–93.

Swanson, Judith A. *The Public and Private in Aristotle's Political Philosophy*. Ithaca: Cornell University Press, 1992.

Thom, Paul. "Stiff Cheese for Women." *Philosophical Forum* 8 (1976): 94–107.

Tong, Rosemarie. *Feminine and Feminist Ethics*. Belmont, Calif.: Wadsworth, 1993.

———. "Feminist Justice: A Study in Difference." *Journal of Social Philosophy* 22, no. 3 (1991): 81–91.

Tress, Daryl McGowan. "The Metaphysical Science of Aristotle's *Generation of Animals* and its Feminist Critics." *Review of Metaphysics* 46, no. 2 (December 1992): 307–41.

Tuana, Nancy. "Aristotle and the Politics of Reproduction." In *Engendering Origins: Critical Feminist Readings in Plato and Aristotle*, edited by Bat-Ami Bar On, 189–206. Albany: State University of New York Press, 1994.

———. "The Weaker Seed: The Sexist Bias of Reproductive Theory." In *Feminism and Science*, edited by Nancy Tuana, 147–71. Bloomington: Indiana University Press, 1989.

———. *Woman and the History of Philosophy*. New York: Paragon House, 1992.

Tumulty, Peter. "Aristotle, Feminism and Natural Law Theory." *New Scholastic* 55 (1981): 450–64.

Whitford, Margaret. *Luce Irigaray: Philosophy in the Feminine*. London: Routledge, 1991.

Witt, Charlotte. "Teleology in Aristotelian Science and Metaphysics." Forthcoming in *Methodos in Ancient Philosophy*, edited by Jyl Gentzler. Oxford: Oxford University Press.

Woods, Marjorie Curry. "Among Men—Not Boys: Histories of Rhetoric and the Exclusion of Pedagogy." *Rhetoric Society Quarterly* 22, no. 1 (1992): 18–26.

Xu, Ping. "Irigaray's Mimicry and the Problem of Essentialism." *Hypatia* 10 (1995): 76–89.

Contributors

ANGELA CURRAN teaches at Bucknell University in Pennsylvania. Her dissertation (University of Massachusetts, Amherst, 1992) was on topics in Aristotle's essentialism. Her current research is on Aristotle's metaphysics and biology, philosophy of film, and feminist aesthetics.

MARGUERITE DESLAURIERS is associate professor of philosophy at McGill University, and a member of the Centre for Research and Teaching on Women there. She has published on Aristotle's moral philosophy and his logic, and is at work on a book about his theory of definition. She was educated at McGill and the University of Toronto.

CYNTHIA A. FREELAND is professor of philosophy and associate dean of the College of Humanities, Fine Arts, and Communication at the University of Houston. Her philosophical interests include ancient philosophy, feminist theory, and aesthetics. She is co-editor of *Philosophy and Film* (1995), and her articles on Aristotle have appeared in various journals and collections.

RUTH GROENHOUT is assistant professor of philosophy at Calvin College, and the author of "Theoretical Approaches to Medical Ethics: Virtue and Its Critics" (Ph.D. diss., University of Notre Dame, 1993).

MARJORIE HASS is assistant professor of philosophy at Muhlenberg College in Allentown, Pennsylvania. Her teaching and research focus on issues in philosophy of logic and feminist philosophy. She received her Ph.D. in 1993 from the University of Illinois at Urbana-Champaign; her dissertation was entitled "Interpreting Negation: A Semantic Theory of Negation for Standard and Non-Standard Logics."

LINDA REDLICK HIRSHMAN will be the Allen/Berenson Distinguished Visiting Professor of Philosophy and Women's Studies at Brandeis University beginning September 1998. She is the author of *Hard*

Bargains: The Politics of Sex and *A Woman's Guide to Law School* (both forthcoming 1998). Dr. Hirshman holds both a J.D. (University of Chicago) and a Ph.D. in philosophy (University of Illinois at Chicago).

LUCE IRIGARAY is director of research in philosophy at the Centre National de la Recherche Scientifique, Paris. She is the author of numerous books, including *Speculum of the Other Woman*, *This Sex Which Is Not One*, and *Je Te Nous*.

BARBARA KOZIAK is assistant professor of political science at American University. She received her Ph.D. from Yale University in 1994; her book entitled *Retrieving Political Emotion* is forthcoming from Pennsylvania State University Press.

DEBORAH K. W. MODRAK is professor of philosophy at the University of Rochester. Her areas of interest include ancient Greek philosophy, philosophy of mind, and feminist philosophy. She is the author of *Aristotle: The Power of Perception* (1987). She has published numerous articles on Aristotle's philosophy of mind, metaphysics and epistemology, and political theory in journals and collections. She is currently at work on a book entitled *Aristotle: Language, Truth and Reality*.

MARTHA C. NUSSBAUM is professor of law, philosophy, and divinity at the University of Chicago. She is the author of *The Fragility of Goodness* (1986), *Love's Knowledge* (1990), *The Therapy of Desire* (1994), and *Poetic Justice* (1996), and the editor of several collections, including *Women, Culture, and Development: A Study of Human Capabilities* (with Jonathan Glover, 1996). In 1996 she was an Amnesty Lecturer in Oxford in the series "Women's Voices, Women's Lives." From 1994 to 1997, she was chair of the Committee on the Status of Women in the American Philosophical Association.

CAROL POSTER is associate professor of English at Montana State University. Her articles on philosophy, rhetoric, and literature have appeared in numerous journals, including *American Journal of Philology*, *Phoenix*, *Philosophy and Rhetoric*, *Rhetoric Society Quarterly*, *College English*, *Victorian Newsletter*, and *Pre/text*. Her verse translations include Plautus' *Stichus* (in *Plautus IV*, 1995) and Aristophanes' *Clouds* (forthcoming in Penn Complete Greek Drama). She co-edits *Disputatio: An International Transdisciplinary Journal of the Late Middle Ages*, and is currently editing an essay collection, *Letter-Writing Manuals from Antiquity to the Present*.

CHARLOTTE WITT is professor of philosophy at the University of New Hampshire, where she teaches in the Women's Studies Program. She is the author of *Substance and Essence in Aristotle* (1989) and co-editor of *A Mind of One's Own: Feminist Essays on Reason and Objectivity* (1992).

Index

abstraction, in logic and feminist theory, 6, 26–30, 99–100, 103–4

admirable action, Aristotelian tragedy and, 323n.14

Aeschylus, 21, 289, 323n.18

aesthetics, Aristotle's vs. feminist, 6–7, 319–21

Agamemnon, 289

Ajax legend, 265, 286n.21

Alcestis, 309–12, 319

Alcibiades, 264

Alemannus, Hermannus, 335

anagnorisis, 263, 271–75

Andronicus, 333

angels, Irigaray's metaphor of mucous and, 72–75, 79–80, 82–86, 91n.44

anger, Aristotle on, 182

animal species: Aristotle's biology and, 149–54, 165n.35; sexual difference and, 11, 12, 139, 141–42, 162n.7, 163n.13

Anna Karenina, 254

Antigone, 265, 289, 312–16, 319, 323n.22, 326n.58, 338

Antony, Louise M., 19, 116n.21

Aquinas, Thomas, 2, 176, 335

Arendt, Hannah, 230, 240n.100

Aristoleicae animadversiones, 335

Aristophanes, images of lovers in Plato's *Symposium*, 57–58, 71

Aristotle: demonstrative knowledge and, 95–101; ethics of, 174–81, 187–94, 209–10; feminist critique of, 1–2; feminist jurisprudence and, 205–11; Hass on Aristotelian logic, 25–30; Irigaray on, 41–58, 60–61, 67–69; on language and logic, 29–30, 38n.25; logic of feminist evaluation of, 20–37; medieval and Renaissance reliance on, 335–36, 346nn.31–32; negation in logic of, 34–37; place, concept of, 87–88; politics and feminism and, 9–10, 211–12, 239n.88; on reproduction, 18, 136n.16; on sexual difference, 139–61, 161nn.5–6; on women and the feminine, 3–5

Ascher, Marcia, 38n.15

auctoritas concept, 328, 330–31

autonomy, of reason, 94–95

Ayer, John, 243n.158

Bain, Alexander, 336, 347n.43

Baltzly, Dirk, 91n.54

Barbaro, 335

Bar On, Bat-Ami, 329

Bartholomew of Messina, 335

Bartlett, Katharine, 203–4, 209, 226, 233nn.17–18, 245nn.193–94

Being and Time, 68

Benhabib, Seyla, 195n.14

Bérubé, Michael, xii

biology: Aristotelian concept of, 99–101, 121, 126, 136n.26; hierarchy of reproduction, 219–26; misogyny in, 248–50, 257nn.3–4; sexual difference and, 38–39, 138–39, 147–54, 161n.5, 165–66nn.29–36

Blair, Hugh, 336, 347n.43

blood imagery, misogyny in Aristotle and, 157–58, 166n.43. *See also* fluid imagery; menses

Bloom, Harold, 201

Boethius, 334
Bouhours, Dominique, 335
Brecht, Bertolt: on Aristotle, 7, 14, 290–91,
    296, 298, 322n.9, 324n.33; tragedy and politi-
    cal learning and, 300–303; women in Greek
    tragedy and, 303–4, 319–21
Briefe of the Art of Rhetorique, A, 335
Broadie, Sarah, 179, 198n.68
Brown v. Board of Education, 213
Buckley, Theodore, 347n.43
Bulwer, John, 335
Burnyeat, M. F., 237n.65

Campbell, George, 336, 347n.43
care. *See* ethics of care
Carroll, Noël, 320
Categories, 20, 28, 30, 63; sex differences in spe-
    cies and, 140, 142–43, 163n.17
catharsis. *See* katharsis
"Celarent," 24
"Chance for Life, A," 79
Chanter, Tina, 64, 68, 78
charity: feminism and, 285n.9; Irigaray's philos-
    ophy and, 85
Chirologia, 335
Christianity, Aristotelian ethics and, 254,
    259n.26
Cicero, 334–35, 347n.43
circularity, Aristotle on, 38n.22
citizenship: Aristotelian political emotion and,
    260–84; egalitarianism and, 215–18, 240–
    41nn.114–15, 242n.131; feminist jurispru-
    dence and, 214, 226–28, 240n.112; heroic
    warrior ethos and, 265–66; surrogacy politics
    and, 220–26, 243n.156; *thumos* and, 262–63
*Civic Virtue and the Feminine Voice in Constitu-
    tional Adjudication,* 226–27
Civil Rights Act of 1964, 222
Cixous, Hélène, 329
classical philosophy: feminist jurisprudence,
    226–31; logic, 32; *Rhetorica* in, 337–42; surro-
    gacy politics and, 224–26
Classical Rhetoric for the Modern Student, 336
classicists, Aristotelian rhetoric and, 336–37,
    347n.43
class structure: Aristotelian logic and, 22–23,
    26; elites as knowers, 105–8, 116n.32; emo-
    tions and rationality and, 262, 285n.9; trag-
    edy and, 279–80
"cluster concepts," 39n.26

Code, Lorraine, 5, 94, 183; on demonstrative
    knowledge, 96–101; on epistemology, 101–2;
    ethics of care and relativism, 198n.75; on ob-
    jectivity, 9, 135n.7
cognition, knowledge and, 103–8
Coles, Andrew, 34, 136n.18, 165nn.29–30
community: feminist jurisprudence and, 226–
    28, 234n.28; feminist theory and, 217–18;
    logic and, 26; separateness and, 251–53,
    258n.11; *xenia* and *polis* concepts, 264–66
composition. *See* writing
Conley, Thomas, 334
consiousness raising, 9, 205–6
container, view of women/place, 43, 47, 54–55,
    56, 76, 79
contingency, ethical relevance of, 253–54
contract ethics, ethics of care and, 186
contrarieties: vs. contradiction, 34–37, 39n.44;
    sex differences in species and, 141–47, 162–
    63nn.11–14, 164n.19
Cooper, John, 136n.18, 225–26
cooperation: classical philosophy and, 263–64;
    polis and, 266
Cope, Edward Merideth, 347n.43
Corbett, Edward, 336
Cornell, Drucilla, 213–14, 226, 233n.17,
    240n.102
courage, Aristotle on, 215–16
Course of Lectures on Elocution, A, 335–36
cultural norms: Aristotle and, 8, 75, 132–34;
    feminization of, 240n.113; scientific theory
    and, 118–34; virtue ethics and, 177–81,
    197n.36
Curran, Angela, 3, 6–7, 289–321

Daly, Mary, 5, 95, 108, 110
Dassin, Jules, 307–8
De Anima, 103
Dean-Jones, Lesley, 161n.5, 167n.51
De Beauvoir, Simone, 95, 108, 110
De Caelo, 64
deconstructionism, feminist jurisprudence and,
    204, 233n.17
De Lauretis, Teresa, 25, 320
democratic education, tragedy as, 325n.41
dēmos concept, 267
Derrida, Jacques, 66, 68
Descartes, René, 60–61, 94, 182
De Sica, Vittorio, 215

Deslauriers, Marguerite, 3–5, 12, 135nn.16–17, 138–61
detachment, male sexuality and, 97
dialectic: Aristotle's use of, 137n.41; vs. rhetoric, 340
difference feminism, 13, 31–34, 35, 66–67, 79–80, 90n.25, 108, 288n.62
Dionysius of Halicarnassus, 333
Dish (logic game), 38n.15
domination, logic in context of, 26–30
doxographies, feminist theory and, 328–29
dramatic theater, Brecht's criticisms of, 290–91, 301
Dream of Passion, A, 307–8
dualism, in surrogacy politics, 222–26
Dworkin, Ronald, 213, 240n.108

ecofeminism, 133; Irigaray's support of, 80
elites: Aristotelian logic reserved for, 22–23, 26; as knowers, 105–8, 116n.32; tragedy and, 279–80
Ellis, John, 29–30
elocutionary movement, Aristotle and, 335–36
Elshtain, Jean B., 216–18, 227–30, 240n.113, 241n.127, 242n.133
emotions: Aristotelian ethics and, 182–83; Aristotle's theory of, 14, 209, 303–4; citizenship and, 260–84; ethics of care and, 282–84; katharsis and, 278–79, 286n.52; pity and tragedy, 266–71; rationality of, 250–51, 257n.10, 262–63, 285n.8; rhetoric and, 339–42, 349nn.54–56
endoxa: Aristotelian rhetoric and, 340; female experts and, 79, 91n.54, 117n.34; theory of knowledge and, 104, 107–8
Engendering Origins: Critical Feminist Readings in Plato and Aristotle, 329
English Composition and Rhetoric: A Manual, 336
Enlightenment, Aristotle and, 220–21, 223–24
Enloe, Cynthia, 241n.129
Enos, Theresa, 330
envelopes, Irigaray on women as, 46, 51, 57, 58n.2, 76, 82
epic theater: Brecht's concept of, 290–91, 302, 303; Greek tragedy and, 303–5
epieikes, Aristotelian tragedy and, 292–93, 322n.11
epistemology: Aristotle's theory of knowledge and, 93–114, 115n.1; demonstrative knowledge and, 96–101; feminist jurisprudence and,

203–11, 233n.18, 238n.81; feminist theory and, 5; ideological and sociological applications of, 100–101, 116n.21
equality, gender and, 212–14, 217–18, 239n.99, 240n.101, 242nn.131–32, 255–56
Equal Rights Amendment, 239n.99, 242n.133
ergon, Aristotle's concept of, 127–30, 136n.29
essence (essentialism) in Aristotle, 12–13; biology and, 149–54, 165n.35, 166n.39; demonstrative knowledge and, 96–101; ethics and, 179–81, 197n.48; ethics of care and, 185–94; Irigaray on place and, 48–58, 81–86; knowledge and, 95; sexual difference and, 108–11, 117n.38, 138–39, 143–47, 159–61, 162n.9
ethics: contingency and, 253–54; emotion and rationality with, 250–53, 258n.19
ethics of care: Aristotelian ethics and, 8–9, 14, 171–73, 183–94; feminist theory and, 171–74, 195n.12; political theory and, 282–84; revisionist view of Aristotle and, 187–94; tragedy and, 297–98, 324n.30
Ethics of Eros, 64
Ethics of Sexual Difference, An, 60, 68, 81–83, 85–86, 91n.61
êthos, Aristotelian rhetoric and, 338–39
Euclid, 98–99
Euripides, 10, 268, 289, 295, 308–9, 316–19, 323n.18
experience, knowledge and, 105–8, 116nn.27–28

Falmagne, Rachel Joffe, 39n.26
family, Greek tragedy and, 311–12
Farber, Daniel A., 235n.41
fear, Aristotelian tragedy and, 279–80
femininity: Aristotle on, 3–5; biology and, 38–39, 147–54, 165–66nn.29–36; ethics of care and, 185–94; Irigaray's philosophy of difference and, 66–67; as matter, 122–26; place in context of, 42–58; sex differences in species and, 22, 141–47, 162–63nn.11–14, 164nn.19
Feminist Opposition to the Draft, A, 241n.129
feminist theory: Aristotelian ethics and, 174–81; Aristotle in context of, 7–10, 59–60, 181–83, 249–57, 257n.8; class, race and ethnicity and, 288n.62; classical philosophy and, 226–31; components of, 2–3; emotions and rationality in, 261–84, 285n.8; epistemology and Aristotle's theory of knowledge, 93–114, 115n.1; essences and sexual difference and,

110–11; ethics of care and, 171–74, 195n.12; feminist separatists, 217–18, 242n.133; feminist vs. classical politics, 211–12; functionalism and, 254–56; games of logic and, 27, 38n.16; generality and logic and, 30, 39n.26; historiography of ancient rhetoric and, 342–44, 349n.58; hylomorphism and gender and, 122–26; of Irigaray, appraisal of, 61–86; jurisprudence and classical philosophy, 202–11, 232n.6; logic and, 6, 19–37; narrative structure of tragedy and, 289–321; objectivity and, 118–34, 135n.7; philosophical canon and, xi–xiii; politics and tragedy and, 300–303; recovery movement, 329; *Rhetorica* and, 327–28, 337–44, 349n.58; rights issues and, 254–56, 259n.32; tragedy and, 280–84, 298–300, 303–21

Ferejohn, 164n.26

fetus: Irigaray on place and, 50–58, 71–72, 80; rights of, 239n.99; surrogacy politics and, 221–26

Field, Martha, 243n.151

film, Greek tragedy and, 307–8, 319–21, 325n.44

Fletcher, Joseph, 186, 199n.85

fluid imagery: Aristotle's biology and, 147–54, 219–26; Irigaray's use of, 55–58, 72–75, 79–80, 82–86, 91n.44

Fogelman, Brian, 166n.38

Foley, Helene, 290

form: biology and, 149–54, 165nn.34–35; essence and, 110, 117n.40; hylomorphism and, 122–26, 136n.21; normativity and gender and, 118, 126–30; place and, 52–53, 62–63, 73–74; sexual difference and, 139, 142–43, 156–58, 162n.6, 163n.17

Fortenbaugh, William, 334

Foucault, Michel, 243n.150, 330

Frazer, Elizabeth, 176

Freeland, Cynthia, 1–15, 30, 37n.1, 135n.17; on Aristotelian theory of tragedy, 295, 308–9; on Irigaray's critique of Aristotle, 59–88

Frege, Gottlob, 33, 39n.32

Freud, Sigmund, 66–67

Friedan, Betty, 232n.6

friendship: Aristotelian ethics and, 178, 193–94; community and, 251–53, 258nn.12–15; gender and, 230; pity and, 267–71; political theory and, 224–26, 244n.184; *xenia* and *polis* concepts, 264–66

functionalism: Aristotelian ethics and, 254–56; form and, 127–30, 136n.28; sexism and, 130–34

Furley, David J., 344n.2

Fuss, Diane, 39n.26, 91n.61

games of logic, 27, 38n.15

Garden of the Finzi-Contini, The, 215–18, 240n.113

Geistesgeschichte, 328–29

Geisteswissenschaft, 328

gender: Aristotle and, 8; epistemology and Aristotle's theory of knowledge, 93–101, 115n.10; essentialism and sexual difference, 109–11; ethics and, 180–81; feminist jurisprudence and, 207–14, 238n.74; form and normativity and, 118, 126–30; Greek tragedy and, 303–21; hylomorphism and, 122–26; Irigaray on place and, 61–62, 64–69; of knower, knowledge and, 32, 103–8, 113–14, 116n.27; negation of logic and, 34–37; pedagogy and, 329–44; political theory and, 225–26, 261–84; rhetoric and, 337–42; science and, 31–32, 78–79, 91n.52

gendered concepts, 61, 65–66, 90n.15, 94, 110, 118, 122–23, 129

generality, feminist theory and, 30, 39n.26

Generation and Corruption, 64, 71, 81

Generation of Animals, 68, 81, 100–101, 103, 116n.19; biology in, 147–54, 165n.29; Laqueur on, 242n.142; sexual difference in, 17, 108–11, 140, 158–59, 162n.9, 163nn.13–14, 164n.19, 196n.21; surrogacy politics and, 222–26

geometry, Aristotle on, 98–100

Giles of Rome, 335

Gilligan, Carol, 172, 183–84, 211, 238n.83, 246n.229

Ginzberg, Lori, 285n.9

God, Irigaray on women and, 42, 53–54, 67, 75, 82–83

Goldhill, Simon, 265

Green, Lawrence D., 346n.32

Griffiths, Morwenna, 183

Groenhout, Ruth, 3, 7–9, 13–14, 171–94

Halliwell, Stephen, 275–76, 287n.42, 296–98, 300, 324n.34

hamartia concept, 232n.13, 290, 292–94, 303, 322n.10

happiness (*eudaimonia*), Aristotelian tragedy and, 292
Haraway, Donna, 2, 197n.48
Harding, Sandra, 78, 91n.54, 119, 134n.4, 135n.8
Hass, Marjorie, 3, 6, 13, 19–37
Hecuba, 295
Hegel, G. F. W., 60
Heidegger, Martin, 4, 66, 68, 78, 90n.33
Held, Virginia, 183, 188, 282–84
Henry, Madeleine, 329
Heraclitus, 66
Hermagoras, 333–34
Herman, Gabriel, 264, 266
Hermogenes, 334, 345n.22
hierarchy: Aristotelian ethics and, 177–81; feminist vs. classical philosophy, 229–31; in reproduction, Aristotle on, 219–26; revisionist view of Aristotle and, 189–94; rhetoric and, 339–40, 348n.52; sexual difference in Aristotle and, 156–58, 171–72; surrogacy politics and, 221–22
Hirshman, Linda, 3, 7, 9, 13–14, 161n.5, 201–31, 248–49; Nussbaum's critique of, 248–57
historiography: of philosophy, 10–12, 84–86, 92n.69; *Rhetorica* and, 327–29, 342–44
History of Animals: biology in, 153–54; Laqueur on, 242n.142; misogyny in, 154–55
History of Women Philosophers, A, 329
Hobbes, Thomas, 261, 267, 335, 347n.43
Homer, 263
Homiak, Marcia, 172, 181
human functioning, 9, 206, 254–57
humility, Aristotle on, 181, 188–89
Hussey, Edward, 63
hylomorphism, of Aristotle, 8, 78; dialectic and, 137n.41; gender and, 122–26, 137n.33, 167n.53; normativity and, 120–21, 128–30, 135n.11; sexism and, 132–34

ideas, place and, 45
"imaginary" concept in Irigrary, 31, 33
immigration policy, Aristotelian political emotion and, 260–84
impartiality, male sexuality and, 97
In a Different Voice, 183–84
In re Baby M., 221–22
Institutio Oratoria, 334
intended interpretation, Aristotelian logic and, 28

intercourse (sexual), Irigaray on Aristotelian place and, 48–58, 50, 69–79, 82–86, 91n.44
Introductio in logicam, 335
Iphigenia in Aulis, 295
Iphigenia in Tauris, 10, 268–75, 281, 293–94
Irigaray, Luce: on Aristotle's theory of place, 41–58, 60–61; critique of Aristotle, 3–5; Freeland's critique of, 59–88; on knowledge, 95; logic critiqued by, 6, 20; on negation of logic, 30–37; overview of philosophy of, 64–69, 329; poetic style of, 60, 69–70, 90n.23; science critiqued by, 78–86; on sexual difference and essentialism, 110–11; translation methodology in work of, 58n.2; on Western canon, 10–12, 108; on women and matter, 136n.22
Irwin, Terence, 115n.5
Isocratean school, 333–34
Isocrates, 342
"Is the Subject of Science Sexed?," 31–32

James, William, 204, 254
Jarratt, Susan, 342
Jerome (Saint), 175
Johnston, Claire, 320
jouissance, Irigaray on place and, 55–58, 73
Journal of Basic Writing, 330
judgment, emotions and, 250–51; particular vs. general in, 253
jurisprudence: feminist ethics and, 9; feminist jurisprudence, 202–31; feminist vs. classical methods, 203–11, 232n.6
justice, ethics of care and, 191, 200n.105

Kant, Immanuel, 60, 255, 329; ethics of care and, 186; Irigaray on, 90n.34; political theory and, 261
Karst, Kenneth, 119, 215–16, 240–41nn.114–15, 242n.134
katharsis: classical philosophy and, 263; pity and, 267–68; recognition and, 271–72; tragedy and, 51–52, 275–79, 287n.42, 299–300, 324n.34, 325n.38
Keller, Evelyn Fox, 134nn.3–4, 135n.9
Kelly, Grace, 320
Kennedy, George, 334
Kenny, Anthony, 179
kinship relations, logic of, 26; *xenia* and *polis* concepts, 264–66
knowledge: Aristotle's theory of, 93–114, 115n.5; conditions for, 102, 116n.24; demon-

strative knowledge, 95–101, 111–14; knowers and, 101–8; objectivity and, 13
Knox, Bernard, 290
Kohlberg, Lawrence, 212, 238n.83
Korsmeyer, Carolyn, 65
Koziak, Barbara, 3, 7, 10, 13, 260–84
Kraut, Richard, 175
Kristeva, Julia, 329

Lacan, Jacques, 66–67, 233n.17
Lacey, Nicola, 176
la Faucheur, Michel, 335
Lamy, Bernard, 335
Lange, Lynda, 2, 161n.5
language, Irigaray on, 66; logic and, 29–30, 38–39nn.25–26
Laqueur, Thomas: feminist jurisprudence and, 207–9, 218–20, 223–26, 227–28, 237n.61, 238n.85, 242n.142, 243n.150, 244n.172, 246n.209; Aristotelian political theory and, 161n.5, 166n.46
Lattimore, Richmond, 310
Law's Empire, 213, 240n.108
Lear, Jonathan, 324n.34, 325n.38
leisure, knowledge and, 104–5
Levinás, Emmanuel, 60
Libanius, 334
liberalism: feminist theory and, 236n.51, 237n.72, 243n.157, 248–49; functionalism and, 255–56; surrogacy politics and, 224–26
limoralism, 212–15
Literary Imagination in Public Life, The, 205–6, 235n.43
Locke, John, 39n.26, 261
locomotion, place and, 45–46, 52–58
logic: feminist critique of Aristotelian logic, 6, 19–37; form and content in, 27–28, 38n.22; "games" of logic, 27, 38n.15; negation operator of, 30–34; Nye on Aristotelian logic, 21–25
Longino, Helen E., 113–14
Loraux, Nicole, 295, 323n.21
Lord, Carnes, 263, 267–71, 276–77, 279–80
Lutz, Catherine A., 257–58n.10, 286n.52

Macey, Jonathan R., 239n.91
MacIntyre, Alasdair, 14, 176
MacKinnon, Catharine, 161n.1, 203, 212–13, 226, 238n.85, 240n.102, 241n.129, 246n.229

Magna Moralia, 315
Making Sex, 207–8, 237n.61
Manning, Rita, 200n.103
Marx, Karl, 254–55, 325n.49
masculinity: Aristotle on sex differences in species and, 24, 141–47, 162–63nn.11–14, 164n.19; biology and, 38–39, 147–54, 165–66nn.29–36; thumos and, 263; war culture and politics and, 280–81
maternity: ethics of care and, 184–85, 187–94, 198n.76; surrogacy politics and, 220–26
mathematics: cultural contexts for, 26–27, 38n.15; sex differences in species and, 25, 164n.21
matter: feminine as, 122–26, 129–30, 156–57; form and, 128–30; sex differences in species and, 144–47, 164n.22
Matthews, Gareth, 162n.8, 163n.13, 167n.51, 323n.16
McClintock, Barbara, 134n.3
McGann, Jerome, 331
Medea, 289, 299, 307–8, 316–19
medicine, art of, knowledge and, 106–7
Mendell, Henry, 63
menses imagery, Aristotle's biology and, 148–54, 157–58, 165nn.30–35, 219–26
Merleau-Ponty, 60
metaphysical paradigms of Aristotle: normativity and, 118, 128–30; sex differences and, 141–47; sexism and norms of, 130–34
Metaphysics: Aristotle's theory of knowledge and, 94–95, 102, 104–8; biology in, 153–54; Deslaurier on, 4–5; form and matter in, 124–25; misogyny in, 156–58; sexual difference in, 108–11, 138–47, 158–61, 162nn.11–12, 163n.16, 164n.23
military service: egalitarianism and, 215–18, 240n.114, 241n.129, 242n.133; feminist theory and, 214
Miller, Thomas, 336–37
mimesis concept, 292
Minow-Michelman school, 213, 240n.109
mirror imagery, Irigaray's philosophy and, 86
misogyny of Aristotle, 2, 138–39, 154–61, 161nn.5–6, 202, 209n.246, 220–26, 229–31
Modrak, Deborah, 3–5, 12–13, 93–114
Monroe, Marilyn, 320
moral reasoning: Aristotle on, 13–14; ethics of care and, 186–87; virtue ethics and, 176–81

mothering, as key practice for ethics and care, 187–88, 198n.76

mucous, Irigaray's metaphor of angels and, 72–75, 79–80, 82–86, 91n.44

Mulvey, Laura, 320

Murnaghan, Sheila, 273

mystical discourse, Irigaray on, 66

narrative structure: Aristotelian tragedy and, 292–94; feminist theory and *Poetics* and, 289, 307

National Organization for Women (NOW), 242n.133

natural language, Aristotelian logic and, 28–29

Natural Law theory, virtue ethics and, 196n.26

nature: Aristotle and, 8; feminist vs. classical philosophy, 229–31; misogny of Aristotle and, 166n.46, 246n.228; normative descriptions, 134n.3; science and, 120, 135n.9

necessary connections, demonstrative knowledge and, 98–101, 112–14, 116n.17

negation operator, Aristotelian logic and, 34–37; logic and, 32–34

Nehamas, Alexander, 344n.2

Nicomachean Ethics, 105, 111–12; *ergon* concept in, 127–30; feminist perspective on, 174–75; *katharsis* in, 278–79; philosophical method in, 235n.39; political activity in, 181–82, 239n.91; *Rhetorica* and, 347n.43; surrogacy politics and, 244n.184

Nietzsche, Friedrich: Irigaray on, 58, 66; sexism of, 59

Noddings, Nel, 172, 183–86, 190

normativity: form and gender and, 126–30; misogny and, 130–34, 230–31; scientific theory and, 118; sexual difference in Aristotle and, 140–61

norm-defect theory of gender difference, 162n.8, 293–94, 323n.16

numbers, place and, 45

Nussbaum, Martha, 3, 7, 9–10, 13–14, 161n.5; on Aristotelian ethics, 180–82; emotions in Aristotle, 339, 348n.50; feminist jurisprudence and, 43, 205–7, 209–10, 213–14, 218, 230, 235nn.39, 237nn.70–71; functioning and feminism, 248–57; on *katharsis*, 286n.51; "non-scientific deliberation," 206; surrogacy politics and, 225–26; on tragedy, 34, 296–98, 323n.13, 324n.22, 325n.38

Nye, Andrea, 6, 13, 25–30; on Aristotelian logic, 21–25; on classical logic, 39nn.32–33; Hass's critique of, 20

objectivity: Aristotelian hylomorphism and, 124–26; demonstrative knowledge and, 97–101, 115n.13; feminist theories of science and metaphysics and, 8–9, 13, 114, 117n.51; feminist theory and, 118–34, 134nn.3–4; Irigaray's philosophy and, 85–86

object relations theory, 134n.4

Oedipus the King, 268, 272–75, 293, 296, 298–99, 324n.24

Okin, Susan Moller, 122, 130–34, 137n.41, 209, 229, 237n.61

Oliver, Kelly, 91n.44

On Interpretation, 20, 28, 35

On Style, 334

On the Divisions of Epideictic, 334

Oresteia, The, 21–24, 27–28, 37n.6, 265, 319

Organon, 327

Ousia and Grammē, 68

Owen, G. E. L., 63

paradox of vulgar relativism, 177, 197n.36

Parker, Andrew, 324n.34

particularism, 210, 238n.76

paternity, surrogacy politics and, 221–22

patriarchy, Greek tragedy and, 306–7

pedagogy, Aristotelian rhetoric and, 11–12, 327–44

penis imagery: Aristotle's biology and, 148–54, 165nn.30–35; Irigaray's use of, 55–58, 72–75, 91n.44

perception, knowledge and, 102–8

per se predication, demonstrative knowledge and, 97–101, 116n.16

Phillips, Anne, 288n.62

phronesis, 279–80

Physics IV, 4, 59–60; gendered concepts in, 65–69, 78–86; Irigaray on, 41–58, 77–78; overview of, 62–64, 87–88

pity, as tragic emotion, 266–71

place, Aristotelian theory of: Freeland's critique of Irigaray on, 59–88; Irigaray's critique of, 4, 41–58, 78–86; overview of, 62–64, 87–88; teleology of, 75–78

Plato, 60, 63, 65, 67, 71; on courage, 241n.117; emotions critiqued by, 267; essentialism and,

109; feminist critique of, 1–2; friendship and community and, 252, 258nn.13–14; political theory of, 261; property and, 286n.25; proto-feminist rhetoric and, 342, 349nn.62–63; on role of women, 166n.46; theory-building, 235n.46; theory of knowledge in, 103–4; on *thumos*, 263; tragedy and, 293, 300–303

Plumwood, Val, 6, 20, 25–26, 30; on negation of logic, 33–37

Plutarch, 333

"pneuma," Aristotle's biology and, 148–54, 165n.30

Poetics: Curran on, 7; emotions in, 304; *hamartia* concept and, 292–94; *katharsis* in, 277–79; narrative structure and, 289; politics and tragedy in, 300–303; recognition and, 271–75; *Rhetorica* and, 347n.43; tragedy in, 263–64, 267–68, 280–81, 296–97, 318–21

Poetria Nova, 330

polis, Hellenic concept of, 264–66, 281

political theory: *Antigone* and, 313–16; classical philosophy and, 216–18; ethics of care and, 186–94; feminist view of Aristotle and, 9–10, 181–84; feminist vs. classical politics and, 211–12, 230–31, 282–84; form and matter and, 124–26, 129–30; functionalism and, 131–34; Irigaray's philosophy and, 83–86, 92nn.66–67; masculinity and, 280–81; misogny of Aristotle and, 156–58, 166n.46; sexual difference and, 5, 138–39, 161n.2; tragedy and, 260–62, 300–303, 325n.41; virtue ethics and, 177; *xenia* and *polis* concepts, 264–66

Politics: ethics in, 181–84, 191–92; gender and form in, 123; ideal state in, 210; misogyny in, 155–56, 166n.44; *thumos* in, 262–63; tragedy and, 298–303, 325n.38

Pomeroy, Sarah, 166n.46

pornography, opposition to repression of, 241n.115

positionality, 204, 233n.18

Posner, Richard, 240n.113

possessions/privations, Aristotle on sex differences in species and, 164n.19

Poster, Carol, 3, 11–13, 327–44

Posterior Analytics, 5, 20, 336; sex differences in species, 143–47; theory of knowledge in, 94–102, 104–8, 112–14, 115n.5, 116n.28

postmodernism: epistemology and, 204; ethical relativism in, 253; ethics of care and, 186, 199n.84; scientific theory and, 134n.6

power, in *Antigone*, 313–16; sexual difference and, 138–39, 155–58, 166n.46

pragmatism, feminist jurisprudence and, 204–5, 234n.28

pregnancy: feminist jurisprudence and, 236n.55; Irigaray on Aristotelian place and, 47–58, 69–72; surrogacy politics and, 220–26, 243n.151, 243n.167

Pre/text, 330

pride, Aristotle on, 188–89

Prior Analytics, 20–21, 25

Prisoner of History: Aspasia of Miletus and Her Biographical Tradition, 329

Proclus, 334

progymnasmata, 331

property, vs. equality, 240n.100, 241n.127

proxenos concept, 265

psychoanalysis, Irigaray's philosophy and, 85–86

Pythagoras, 164n.21

Quintilian, 334–35, 347n.43

Rabinowitz, Nancy, 311–12, 317–18, 320

Radin, Margaret, 204–5, 209, 213, 224–26, 234n.28, 240n.104

Rainolde, John, 335

Ramus, Peter, 335, 346n.33

rational empiricism, feminist jurisprudence and, 203–4

rationality: Aristotle and, 10, 116n.19; emotions and, 250–51, 257n.10, 261–84, 285n.8; ethics and, 182–84; ethics of care and, 186; pragmatism and, 204–5; virtue and, 239n.91

Rawls, John, 235n.46, 255–56

reason: Code on autonomy of, 94–95; feminist jurisprudence and, 206–7; hylomorphism and, 129–30; leisure as prerequisite for, 105; male dominance of realm of, xi–xii, xiiin.1

Reclaiming Rhetorica, 349n.58

recognition, Aristotelian concept of, 271–75

Reeve, C. D., 196n.21

relationships, ethics of care and, 183–84, 187–94

relativism: ethics of care and, 184–85, 198n.75; feminist jurisprudence and, 209–10, 237n.70

religion, Irigaray's philosophy and, 83–86, 92n.66

repression, of feminine, in Aristotle, 4

reproduction: Aristotle on, 18, 135n.16, 137n.40, 147–54, 165nn.29–35, 218–26; surrogacy politics and, 221–26

Republic, 1, 67, 166n.46, 300–301
Reynolds, L. D., 331
Rhetor, Menander, 334
Rhetorica, 11–12, 250–51, 278, 296–97, 325–44; feminist appraisal of, 337–42; Latin translations of, 335; in modern composition studies, 336–37, 348n.46; in nineteenth-century curriculum, 335–36, 347n.43
Rhetorica ad Alexandrum, 331–32
Rhetoric Society Quarterly, 330
Rhode, Deborah, 204
Riccobono, Antonio, 335
Rich, Ruby, 321
rights issues, gender and, 256, 259n.32
Rollin, Charles, 335
Rorty, Amélie, 344n.2
Rorty, Richard, 12, 92n.69, 328–29
Ruddick, Sarah, 188–89

Salkever, Stephen, 191, 226, 230, 263, 267–71, 276–81, 325n.41
Sandel, Michael, 14, 176
Sandys, John Edwin, 347n.43
Sappho, Aristotle on, 341
Saxonhouse, Arlene, 230, 326n.58
Schauer, Frederick, 210, 238n.76
Schleiermacher, 320
Schopenhauer, Arthur, misogyny of, 59, 175
science: Aristotle on biology and subordination of women, 138–39, 161n.5, 248–50; Aristotle's *Physics* and, 63–64, 78–86; demonstrative knowledge and, 96–101, 111–14, 116n.17, 117n.44; essences and sexual difference and, 108–11; feminist theory and, 118–19, 134n.3; form, normativity and gender in, 126–30; gender and, 31–32; hierarchy of reproduction in Aristotle and, 220–26; Irigaray's critique of, 78–86; nature and, 120, 133–34, 135n.9
Scottish Moral Sense theory, 176
semantic definitions, Aristotelian logic and, 28–29
semen imagery: Aristotle's biology and, 148–54, 157–58, 165nn.30–35, 219–26
Sen, Amartya, 213, 255
separatist feminism, military service and, 217–18, 242n.133
sexism, Aristotle in context of, 14–15, 59; norms and, 130–34
sexual difference: biology and, 38–39, 147–54, 165nn.29–35, 166n.36; essence and, 100,

108–11, 123, 138–61, 161nn.5–6; Irigaray on, 66–67, 79–86; misogny in Aristotle and, 154–58; negation of logic and, 32–34; subordination of women and, 138–39, 159–61, 161nn.1–2; surrogacy politics and, 223–26
sexuality: Aristotle's biology and, 148–54, 165nn.30–35; feminist jurisprudence and, 233n.17; hierarchy of reproduction and, 220–26, 243n.150; Irigaray on Aristotelian place and, 48–58, 50, 60, 69–79, 82–86, 91n.44; in *Metaphysics*, 4–5
sexual organs, Aristotle's biology and, 148–54, 165nn.30–35, 218–26
Sheridan, Thomas, 335
Sherman, Nancy, 257n.8, 258n.17, 293–94
Sherry, Suzanna, 226–27, 235n.41
single-sex draft law, feminism and, 217–18, 242n.129
situation ethics, 186, 199n.85
slavery: Aristotle on, 129–30, 137n.34, 172, 189–90, 230; tragedy and, 298–99
Smith, Robin, 20–21
social conditions: Greek tragedy and, 302; normativity and, 124–25, 135n.10; sexual difference and, 138–39, 161n.2
Socrates, 235n.46, 254
Solmsen, Fredrich, 345n.17
Sophocles, 268, 289, 293, 312–16, 323n.18
species and sex differences, Aristotle on, 141–47, 162–63nn.11–13, 164nn.22–23
spectatorship: Aristotelian recognition and, 273–75; *katharsis* and, 278–79
Speculum of the Other Woman, 60–61, 67–68, 85
Spelman, Elizabeth, 156, 166n.44, 298, 329
sperm banks, surrogacy politics and, 222–23, 244n.171
Spinoza, 60–61
Stack, Carol B., 26
stasis theory, 334
Stein, Edith, 183
Stoicism, 251, 254, 259n.26
Stoljar, Natalie, 39n.26, 90n.25, 197n.51
Strabo, 333
strangers imagery: in classical philosophy, 261–64; *xenia* and *polis* concepts, 264–66
Strauss, Leo, 207, 230, 236n.52, 246n.225
subjectivity: Irigaray on, 85–86, 90n.34; in Western culture, 31, 39n.28
surrogacy politics: dualism of, 222–26, 243n.166; hierarchy of, 220–22, 243n.151

Swearingen, C. Jan, 342
syllogism, Aristotle's theory of: feminist critique, 8, 21–25, 37n.6; demonstrative knowledge and, 96–101; rhetoric and, 331–32, 336
symbolic logic, 39n.32
Symposium, 57, 71

teleology of Aristotle: feminist jurisprudence and, 229–31, 245n.208; form and normativity in, 122–26, 128–30, 136–37nn.30–31; Irigaray's critique of, 75; sexism and, 132–34
temperance, as Aristotelian virtue, 188
Texas Law Review, 9
Theophrastus, 333, 345n.22
theoria, Aristotelian ethics and, 178–79
Theory of Justice, A, 235n.46, 255
"This Sex Which Is Not One," 4, 61, 76, 81
thumos, 262–63, 266–68, 277–79, 282–84, 287n.51
Thus Spoke Zarathustra, 58
Timaeus, 1, 67
time, Irigaray on place and, 52–53
tolerance, virtue ethics and, 177, 197n.36
Tolstoy, Leo, 254
Tong, Rosemarie, 195n.12
Topics, 20, 144, 164n.24
tradition, virtue ethics and, 176–77
tragedy: Aristotelian theory of, 292–300; feminist theory and, 7; heroic warrior ethos and, 265; *katharsis* and, 275–79; lessons and configuration, 279–84; pity and, 266–71; political emotion and, 260–84; recognition and, 271–75; women in, 289–90; women's plots in, 295–99, 308–19, 323nn.21–22
Traité de l'action de l'orateur, ou de la Prononciation et de geste, 335
Tress, Daryl McGowan, 162n.9
Trojan Women, The, 295, 302, 308–11
Tronto, Joan, 282
Tuana, Nancy, 18, 135n.16
Tyrannio, 333

uncertainty, pragmatism and, 205, 234n.28
United Automobile Workers v. Johnson Controls, 239n.99
universal instrumental relations, sexism and, 131–34
universality: demonstrative knowledge and, 96–101, 116n.22; experience and knowledge and, 105–8; perception and, 103; sciences and, 112–14, 117n.48

University of Chicago, 336
utilitarianism, ethics of care and, 186

value-neutrality, scientific theory and, 119–20, 135n.7
Vernant, Jean-Pierre, 265
vessel, woman as, 47–48, 56–58, 73–78, 81–86
Vinsauf, 330–31
virtue ethics: Aristotelian ethics and, 174–81; Aristotle and, 172; feminist theory and, 221, 243n.156; feminist vs. classical politics and, 212, 239n.91; Natural Law theory and, 196n.26; revisionist view of Aristotle and, 187–94
Vives, 335
Vossius, 335

Waithe, Mary Ellen, 329
war culture: classical philosophy and, 215–18, 241n.122, 242n.139; feminist theory and, 240n.113; masculinity and, 280–81; *xenia* and *polis* concepts, 265–66
Welch, Kathleen, 337, 348n.46
welfare debate, Aristotelian political emotion and, 260–84
Wertheimer, Molly, 349n.58
West, Robin, 210–11, 234n.38, 238n.79
Western canon: Aristotle's role in, 6, 10–12; feminist jurisprudence and, 202–11, 227–28, 232n.6; Irigaray on omission of feminine in, 60–61, 66–69, 80–86
Western culture: maternity and ethics of care in, 198n.76; symbolic structure in, 31
Whately, Richard, 336
Whitbeck, Caroline, 117n.40
White, Stephen, 179, 323n.14
Whitford, Margaret, 39n.29, 80
William of Moerbeke, 335
Williams, Bernard, 137n.34, 177, 197n.36
Williams, Wendy, 217
Wilson, N. G., 331
Witt, Charlotte, 3, 7–8, 13, 19, 115n.10; hylomorphism of Aristotle and, 167n.53, 188–34; on tragedy, 323n.17
Wittgenstein, Ludwig, 66
women: Aristotelian rhetoric and, 339–42; Aristotle on, 3–5, 123–26, 135n.18, 136n.21; ethics of Aristotle and, 174–81, 183, 198n.67; exclusion of, as knowers in Aristotelian theory of knowledge, 107–8, 116n.32; in Greek tragedy, 289–300, 303–21,

323nn.21–22; underrepresentation, in philosophical canon, xi–xii
Woods, Majorie Curry, 330
Words of Power: A Feminist Reading of the History of Logic, 6, 20–21
writing: modern composition studies, Aristotelian rhetoric and, 336–37, 348n.46; *Rhetorica* and theories of, 327–44

Writing Instructor, The, 330

xenia, Hellenic concept of, 264–66
Xu, Ping, 91n.50

Zeitlin, Froma, 290
Zeno's puzzles, 41, 62, 76, 79